The Last Ditch

Issued by the Ministry of Information in co-operation with the War Office and the Ministry of Home Security.

If the
INVADER
comes

WHAT TO DO — AND HOW TO DO IT

THE German "threaten to invade Great Britain. If they do so they will be driven out by our Navy, our Army and our Air Force. Yet the ordinary men and women of the civilian population will also have their part to play. Hitler's invasions of Poland, Holland and Belgium were greatly helped by the fact that the civilian population was taken by surprise. They did not know what to do when the moment came. You must not be taken by surprise. This leaflet tells you what to do if the danger comes nearer. Meanwhile, read these instructions carefully and be prepared to carry them out.

I

When Holland and Belgium were invaded, the civilian population fled from their homes. They crowded on the roads, in cars, in carts, on bicycles and on foot, and so helped the enemy by preventing their own armies from advancing against the invaders. You must not allow that to happen here. Your first rule, therefore, is —

(1) IF THE GERMANS COME, BY PARACHUTE, AEROPLANE OR SHIP, YOU MUST REMAIN WHERE YOU ARE. THE ORDER IS "STAY PUT".

If the Commander in Chief decides that the place where you live must be evacuated, he will tell you when and how to leave. Until you receive such orders you must remain where you are. If you run away, you will be exposed to far greater danger because you will be machine-gunned from the air as were civilians in Holland and Belgium, and you will also block the roads by which our own armies will advance to turn the Germans out.

II

There is another method which the Germans adopt in their invasion. They make use, of the civilian population in order to create confusion and panic. They spread false rumours and issue false instructions. In order to prevent this, you should obey the second rule, which is as follows :—

(2) DO NOT BELIEVE RUMOURS AND DO NOT SPREAD THEM. WHEN YOU RECEIVE AN ORDER, MAKE QUITE SURE THAT IT IS A TRUE ORDER AND NOT A FAKED ORDER. MOST OF YOU KNOW YOUR POLICEMEN AND YOUR A.R.P. WARDENS BY SIGHT, YOU CAN TRUST THEM. IF YOU KEEP YOUR HEADS, YOU CAN ALSO TELL WHETHER A MILITARY OFFICER IS REALLY BRITISH OR ONLY PRETENDING TO BE SO. IF IN DOUBT ASK THE POLICE-MAN OR THE A.R.P. WARDEN. USE YOUR COMMON SENSE.

The Last Ditch

Britain's Secret Resistance and the Nazi Invasion Plans

David Lampe
Foreword by Gary Sheffield

Frontline Books, London / Skyhorse Publishing, New York

The Last Ditch: Britain's Resistance Plans Against the Nazis
Published in 2007 by Greenhill Books, Lionel Leventhal Limited
www.greenhillbooks.com

This paperback edition published in 2013 by Frontline Books,
an imprint of Pen & Sword Books Ltd.,
47 Church Street, Barnsley, S. Yorkshire, S70 2AS
www.frontline-books.com
and
Published and distributed in the United States of America and Canada
by Skyhorse Publishing, 307 West 36th Street, 11th Floor, New York, NY 10018
www.skyhorsepublishing.com

Skyhorse Publishing books may be purchased in bulk at special discounts for sales
promotion, corporate gifts, fund raising, or educational purposes. Special editions
can also be created to specifications. For details, contact
Special Sales Department, Skyhorse Publishing,
307 West 36th Street, 11th Floor, New York, NY 10018 or email info@skyhorsepublishing.com

Copyright © David Lampe, 1968
Foreword © Gary Sheffield, 2007

UK edition: ISBN 978-1-84832-719-1
US edition: ISBN 978-1-62087-808-8

CIP data records for this title are available from the British Library.

Library of Congress Cataloging-in-Publication Data is available on file.

For more information on our books, please visit
www.frontline-books.com, email info@frontline-books.com
or write to us at the above address.

Printed and bound by CPI Group (UK) Ltd, Croydon, CR0 4YY

CONTENTS

ILLUSTRATIONS

FOREWORD

W hen David Lampe wrote *The Last Ditch* in the late 1960s, in one sense he was following a fairly well trodden path. Imaginary invasions of England were favourite topics for nineteenth and early twentieth century writers such as Sir George Chesney, whose short story of 1871 *The Battle of Dorking*, and Erskine Childers, whose *The Riddle of the Sands* (1903) were both intended to alert the nation to the state of Britain's defences. Edwardian newspapers used serialisations of invasion stories to increase sales in towns in the invader's path, while Guy du Maurier's play *An Englishman's Home* (1909) gave, in the short term, a timely boost to recruiting for the fledgling Territorial Force. The Victorians and Edwardians, were, of course, writing fantasy, the stuff of strategic nightmares, David Lampe's perspective was rather different. Unlike his predecessors, he was not writing fiction but history.

To a large extent, public fears of invasion had dwindled between the wars, to be replaced by anxieties expressed in books such as L. E. O. Charlton's *War Over England* (1936) that focussed on future air raids and gas bombs. The events of May–June 1940 changed all that. The defeat of the Allied armies in France and Flanders; the hasty evacuation of the remains of the British Expeditionary Force from Dunkirk and other ports, leaving much of their equipment behind; the French surrender and the German occupation of the western European seaboard from Norway to the Spanish frontier; all this seemed to presage a sea and airborne invasion of the United Kingdom. Lampe's subject is the preparations that were made by both sides for Operation Sea Lion the invasion that never happened.

A number of books relevant to Operation Sea Lion, some of them very good, have appeared in the four decades since the publication of *The Last Ditch*.[1] However, I would suggest that it retains its value for three reasons.

---

[1] e.g. Norman Longmate, *If Britain Had Fallen* (Greenhill, 2004 edn.); Egbert Kieser, *Operation Sea Lion* (Arms & Armour 1997); S.P. Mackenzie, *The Home Guard* (Oxford University Press, 1965).

Firstly, David Lampe (1923-2003) was well equipped to write on this subject. Lampe had a military background—an American who settled in Britain, he had served in the USAF for some years—and he had an instinctive 'feel' for his material. He had already published on other Second World War subjects, including the Danish Resistance, and seems to have been indefatigable in tracking down and interviewing witnesses. Writing only 25 years after the event, Lampe was able to talk to many of the participants including former members of the Auxiliary Units, the nascent British resistance. Lampe himself wrote that early in his research 'he stumbled on the right people', and so he was able to give a much fuller picture of this shadowy organisation than had been possible hitherto. His contacts included Major General Colin Gubbins, who as a major was one of the key figures in the creation of the Auxiliary Units, and Eleanor Norman-Butler, a radio operator with the resistance. The book includes two particularly evocative photographs of Auxiliary Unit members a quarter of a century on. One shows Gubbins, the archetypical city gent looking out of place in the swinging London of 1967; the other, Paddy O'Mara, is selling newspapers outside Colchester Railway station, wearing his 203 Battalion badge. This is in spite of the fact that, rather like workers at Bletchley Park, in the 1960s a number of former members of Auxiliary Units still regarded themselves as bound by a vow of silence. 'A well-known Master of Foxhounds in East Suffolk', Lampe recorded, 'one of the first in his county to be taken into the Resistance', refused to say anything except "All I did was go out at night to help train members of the Home Guard"'.

In 2006, the clandestine army of the Auxiliary Units is no longer so secret. A number of other writers have tackled the subject,[2] and official papers unavailable to Lampe can now be consulted at the National Archives.[3] Websites are devoted to the subject, and a 'Museum of the British Resistance Organisation' was set up at Parham airfield in Suffolk in 1997.[4] Although we know a great deal

---

[2] E.g. Arthur Ward, *Resisting the Nazi Invader* (Constable, 1997); John War-wicker, *With Britain in Mortal Danger* (Cerberus Books, 2002).

[3] E.g. WO 199/3265.

[4] http://www.parhamairfieldmuseum.co.uk;
http://www.wartimememories.co.uk/secret/auxiliaryunits.html

more about the British Resistance than we did when Lampe's book appeared, it remains essential reading as a pioneering work.

The second reason why I welcome republication of *The Last Ditch* is that Lampe gives a valuable snapshot of attitudes to the threatened invasion at a time when 1940 was still regarded almost as 'current affairs' rather than history. To take one amusing example, Lampe, referring to the existence of food stockpiled by the Auxiliary Units, commented that 'Speculation about "food stores" still continues in some areas of Britain today, and there are dark rumours about how "They" were going to look after themselves all right'. Similarly, Lampe describes how in the 1960s some Britons, in a display of Gestapo chic, boasted about how high they were on the notorious '*Sonderfahndungsliste G.B.* ('Arrest List Great Britain'). The left-wing publisher Sir Victor Gollancz liked to claim that he was 'number seven' on 'Hitler's list'. Lampe spoiled their fun by printing a facsimile of the list that clearly showed that the names were arranged in alphabetical order.

Finally, *The Last Ditch* is an extremely good read. I was enthralled by the book as an undergraduate and twenty-five years later I reread it with much pleasure—it is good to see it back in print.

Gary Sheffield
Professor of War Studies
University of Birmingham, 2007

PREFACE

THIS book was written in an attempt to satisfy my own curiosity. I wanted to know what would have happened if the Wehrmacht had followed close on the heels of the battered British Expeditionary Force when it retreated across the English Channel in 1940. I wanted to know what the Nazi occupation of Britain would have been like. I knew that at best I would be able to present evidence, that I would be able to draw no conclusions, for few things in life go according to plan, and we can never predict with any certainty how, in life-or-death situations, individuals and groups will react to the actions of other individuals or groups. Therefore I set out to find as many facts as possible, remembering all the time the futility of drawing conclusions.

I believed before I began to write this book—and nothing that I subsequently learned has given me reason to alter my belief—that if Hitler's Army had occupied Britain, Western civilization as we knew it in 1940 and as we still know it today would have been at the last ditch.

I had assumed that the most interesting material was going to come from German sources, for after all, the initiative had been the Germans'. My assumption was, of course, naïve, and I soon learned that the overwhelming majority of Germans who might have contributed useful information prefer to believe that no occupation of Britain was ever contemplated or that they themselves had no part in making the plans. The only German who admitted that he was personally going to participate in the occupation was the one who would have headed the Gestapo in Britain.

I thought that only a chapter or two would be concerned with whatever official attempts had been made to create a British Resistance organization in anticipation of occupation—not because the subject is an unimportant one (it is very important), but because the departments that create secret organizations all too often keep their secrets long after the need for secrecy has passed. However, I have been able to write in the greatest detail about the British Resistance organization. Perhaps this is because early on I stumbled on the right people. And perhaps it is because those people agree with me that this story should be told. A knowledge of what might have happened to the Nazis who occupied Britain could make some future aggressor think twice before attempting another 'Operation Sea Lion'. I am sure that none of my revelations in any way endangers British security. Much that the men and women who formed the nucleus of the Resistance had been prepared to do could be done again, but in slightly different ways and by different people. The existence of new weapons and of new means of communication would of course have to be taken into account. I think that it is very important that the overall pattern for British resistance to an occupation should be on the record. This is the first detailed account to have been published.

DAVID LAMPE

MAPS

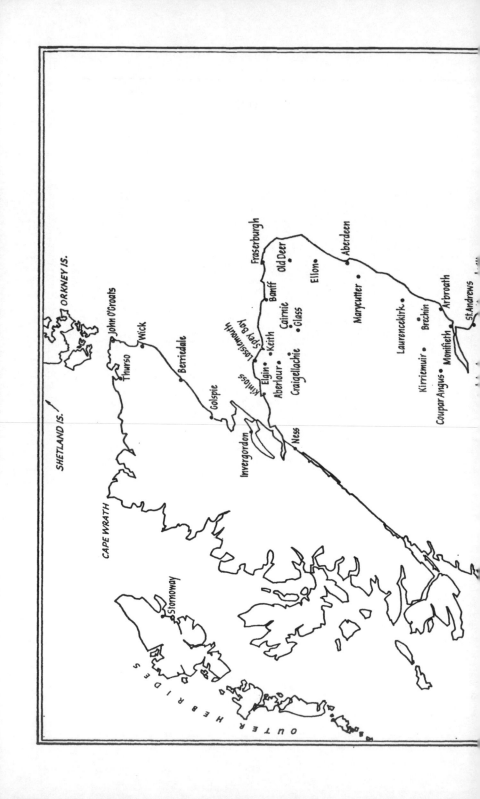

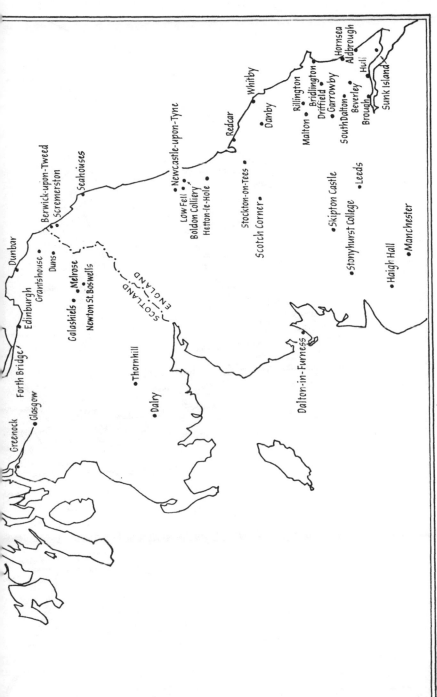

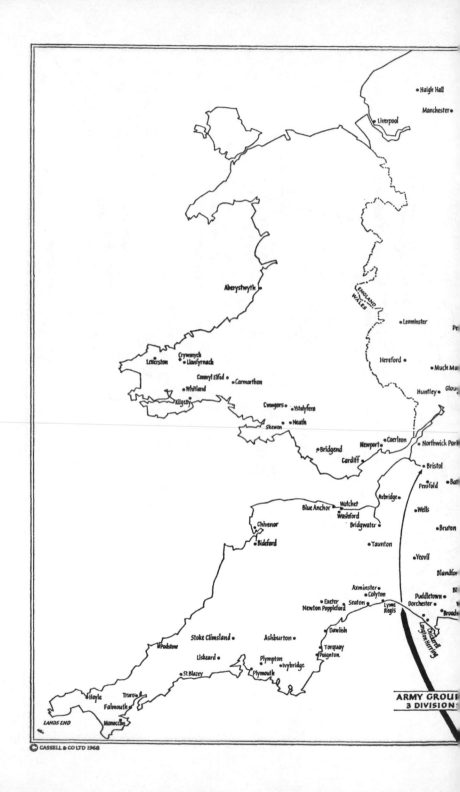

Haigh Hall
Manchester
Liverpool

Aberystwyth

ENGLAND/
WALES

Leominster
Pe

Hereford
Much Mai
Huntley Glou

Leiterston
Crymmych
Llanfyrnach

Conwyl Elfed Carmarthen
Whitland
Kilgetty
Cwmgors Ystalyfera
Skewen Neath

Bridgend
Newport Caerleon
Cardiff Northwick Park

Bristol
Pensfold Bat

Axbridge

Blue Anchor Watchet Wells
Washford
Chivenor Bridgwater Bruton
Bideford
Taunton Yeovil

Blandfor

Axminster
Colyton Puddletown Bl
Exeter Seaton Dorchester W
Newton Poppleford Lyme Broad
Regis

Dawlish Chideck
Stoke Climsland Ashburton Longton Herring
Torquay Burton
Paignton
Liskeard Plympton
Plymouth Ivybridge
Padstow
St.Blazey

Truro
Hayle
Falmouth
LANDS END
Manaccan

ARMY GROUP
3 DIVISION

© CASSELL & CO LTD 1968

The outline German invasion plan, presented by the
Army General Staff on 13 July 1940

INITIAL BRIDGEHEAD
FIRST OBJECTIVE
SECOND OBJECTIVE

ARMY GROUP A
4 DIVISIONS

ARMY GROUP A
6 DIVISIONS

The reader of these pages in future years should realise how dense and baffling is the veil of the Unknown. Now in the full light of the after-time it is easy to see where we were ignorant or too much alarmed, where we were careless or clumsy. Twice in two months we had been taken completely by surprise. The over-running of Norway and the break-through at Sedan, with all that followed from these, proved the deadly power of the German initiative. What else had they got ready—prepared and organised to the last inch? Would they suddenly pounce out of the blue with new weapons, perfect planning, and overwhelming force upon our almost totally unequipped and disarmed Island at any one of a dozen or score of possible landing-places? Or would they go to Ireland? He would have been a very foolish man who allowed his reasoning, however clean-cut and seemingly sure, to blot out any possibility against which provision could be made.

Their Finest Hour
by Winston S. Churchill

1

'THE VEIL OF THE UNKNOWN'

IN the spring of 1940, soon after General Andrew Thorne had
brought 48 Division home from Dunkirk, he was directed
by the War Office to take command of XII Corps—in order
to defend against German invasion a front that extended from
Greenwich, on the Thames in south-east London, around the
Channel coast as far as Hayling Island in Hampshire. If the Germans
had tried to invade, their main landings would almost certainly
have been on the beaches in the XII Corps area, yet when the
General went down to Kent to what was supposed to be his new
headquarters at Tunbridge Wells he had trouble finding any army
people who had even heard of the corps. And when at last he did
come across someone who knew about it and he asked what it
comprised, he was told simply, 'You.'

Thorne did not throw up his hands in defeat, for even in those
bleak days he had good reason to be sceptical about the Wehrmacht's ability to move enough men across the Channel to
establish a beachhead in Kent, Sussex, Hampshire or, for that
matter, anywhere else in Britain. Early in the 'thirties Andrew
Thorne had been Military Attaché in Berlin and had had a number
of conversations with Hitler (they had reminisced about the days
when they were young soldiers on opposing sides in the same
First World War battle), and he had noticed that despite the
Führer's interest in all things military, Hitler had never taken
the trouble to learn anything about the complexities of amphibious
operations, perhaps because he himself dreaded seasickness and
took every precaution to avoid it. General Thorne believed—and
all the Intelligence reports that were shown to him in England in
the summer of 1940 strengthened his belief—that Hitler hoped to
cross the English Channel as if it were merely a wide river. The
Germans might manage a few large-scale hit-and-run raids,
Thorne felt, but he was sure that they would never be able to
establish a beachhead—provided that the coasts of Britain were
reasonably defended.

The only unit of any size that Thorne could put in the field was
a Territorial division armed with rifles and with not much else.

So he took all the officers who could be spared from the Musketry School at Hythe, Kent, and assigned to each of them a Martello tower. These fortresses, which had been built to repel a Napoleonic invasion, now became training centres where small bands of stevedores, contracted to the Government at the Channel ports but with no work to do, were taught to be infantrymen. The stevedores drilled with the only weapons that Thorne could find for them—pickaxe handles.

General Thorne was uncomfortably aware that however cunningly he deployed XII Corps, it would be no match for even the smallest German invasion force. And then he remembered something that he had seen in East Prussia six years earlier. The principal of the Charlottenburg High School, a military training college in Berlin, had shown him around his family's estates in East Prussia. The land had been given to an ancestor by Frederick the Great on condition that a private army be provided to protect it against invasion from the east. When Thorne visited the estates in 1934 some of the descendants of the original peasant soldiers were digging new defences on the crests of hills, and these were being stocked with arms, ammunition and food. The peasants would not be able to stop a modern invading army, Thorne's friend explained, but when it had passed over they would be able to play hell with its supply and other supporting units. Why not, General Thorne asked himself in Kent that summer in 1940, prepare the same sort of civilian 'stay-behind' troops in XII Corps' coastal areas?

He got in touch with General Ismay at the War Office and was told that an officer would be sent along to raise and to train just such a body of civilians who would be known as the XII Corps Observation Unit. Thorne was delighted when the officer sent down to him from London turned out to be Captain Peter Fleming, a young Guards officer for whose father he had fagged at Eton. Thorne believed at the time—and continued to believe for many years afterwards—that he was responsible for an idea that was very soon to spread right around the country.

✳

The state of the defences in the south-east of England was bad that summer—but no worse than the defences anywhere else in the country. When the last of the 368,000 men who had escaped from France had returned from leave, Britain could muster a mere twenty-seven divisions to defend the entire country against invasion. Some 840 anti-tank guns had been left behind in France, so that now only 167 of these weapons were available for home defence. So few anti-tank shells remained in the arsenals that the firing of even a single round for practice purposes was sternly forbidden. Half again as many field-guns had been left behind in France as there were now in all the arsenals in Britain. The twenty-seven home defence divisions were so badly off for weapons that even the Crimean War field pieces of French manufacture that had recently been sent to the Finns, in a moment of what had not then seemed unbridled generosity, would now have been very useful. Museums all over Britain were being ransacked for serviceable weapons, and among those ordered back into service were 300-year-old howitzers.

So few military vehicles had been brought home from France that the few mobile defence units that could be raised in the summer of 1940 had to rely almost entirely on hired civilian motor coaches for their mobility. Eight hours' notice was needed just to get these units on the road—more time than the first wave of Hitler's invasion armada would have taken to cross the English Channel and unload its troops. These defence units would then have crept across the country very slowly, impeded by the absence of signposts which Field-Marshal Ironside, at that time the Commander-in-Chief Home Forces, had ordered to be taken down, and by the blackout. Any military convoys not well supplied with maps would almost certainly have got hopelessly lost, for the public were sternly cautioned that summer to give directions to no one. Ingenious military drivers who had to get around the country did manage to find their way, by reading the local authorities' names on manhole covers or the addresses which were still posted up in most telephone kiosks.

In coastal areas all round Britain gangs of civilian labourers were kept busy building and camouflaging pillboxes. All these fortifications were sited by local commanders, some of whom thought that the invasion force would come from the air and not from the sea. Many of the pillboxes were placed so near to houses and to other buildings that it now seems ridiculous that, instead

[3]

of wasting so many millions of bricks, so many tons of mortar and so many irretrievable man hours, the buildings themselves which probably would have been smashed by German artillery and tanks, anyway, were not simply sand-bagged and made ready to be converted into gun emplacements the moment that enemy landings were reported.

Several hundred vulnerable miles of the East Anglian coast were shielded by an ingenious—and costly—network of explosive-laced steel scaffolding set on the beaches, just below the low-water mark. On the morning of 15 December 1940, months after the first invasion scare had passed, senior officers of the three Services and civilian technicians gathered at Felixstowe to watch as a self-propelled wooden barge smashed head-on into the scaffolding, sliced right through it and then rasped aground—without detonating a single booby trap.

During the weeks immediately following Dunkirk Churchill knew perfectly well that the huffing, puffing, albeit grimly determined members of the Local Defence Volunteers, soon to be re-named by him the Home Guard,* numbered half a million and not a million, as Anthony Eden told the newspapers. Churchill knew that this as-yet-untrained force did not consist entirely of skilled marksmen, as the newspapers were boasting, and that, in any case, its principal weapons were sporting guns, First World

---

* On 14 May 1940 Anthony Eden broadcast to the nation for volunteers for this new force to go on duty against airborne invasion, asking for 'British subjects, between the ages of seventeen and sixty-five . . . [to be] entrusted with certain vital duties for which reasonable fitness and a knowledge of firearms [would] be necessary.' Before he had even finished speaking men all over the country were already queueing outside police stations to join what newspapers called the 'Parashots'. The Home Guard, although it performed many useful functions, was to become a wartime joke, and not entirely without reason. As Liddell Hart pointed out in a series of memoranda written early in 1942, the Home Guard was prepared to fight only along conventional lines and not as a guerrilla force, its members spent too much time on the parade ground and on picket duty, and not enough learning to fight off an invader. He therefore proposed a sort of Home Guard organization which, as we shall see, had been formed secretly almost two years before he wrote his critique.

[4]

War souvenirs, farm tools, pickhelves and oddities like boarding pikes taken from, among other places, Nelson's flagship *Victory*. Yet the Prime Minister somehow managed to convince everyone around him that if the Germans were foolish enough to invade, they would at once be hurled back into the sea. He once remarked defiantly to Lord Boothby, 'If the worst comes to the worst, you can always take one with you!' Lord Avon and Lord Boothby say that the people who worked at Churchill's elbow at that time were so sure themselves that the Germans would not invade that they made no private plans either for escaping or lying low.

However optimistic the politicians in Whitehall may have been—or may have managed to appear—Military Intelligence officers were gloomy. As they studied each new report of enemy activity across the Channel, as they examined each new RAF reconnaissance photo, those officers wondered how soon the codeword 'Cromwell' would have to be given to signal that formations of German troops were wading ashore or were dropping from the skies. That summer a committee set up by Field-Marshal Ironside to co-ordinate all civilian and military defence activity was asked to consider massing a convoy of buses in Hyde Park when the Germans landed, so that key civil servants could be sped to the countryside where they would be hidden. Ironside refused, explaining that if the Germans did land, he would be much too busy to evacuate the white-collar warriors and, in any case, such a convoy would be an obvious target for low-flying Luftwaffe fighters.

Just how edgy were ordinary Britons that summer? A few popular newspapers and magazines published grisly articles revealing the secrets of unarmed combat, and many employers made plans for their assembly-line workers to man the factory ramparts in the event of an invasion, but the average person did not take such preparations very seriously.

Nevertheless, when the Local Defence Volunteers refused to admit women into their ranks—despite the fact that in some places in the country women were to teach the men in the LDV how to fire rifles—fifty indignant female patriots, including Marjorie Foster, who had won the King's Prize on the rifle range at Bisley in 1930, met at 106 Great Russell Street in London to form the Amazon Defence Corps. The Amazons, who would each pay a shilling a year for membership, intended to campaign for their admission into the LDV, for women in the Services to receive the same training in the use of small arms as men, for general weapons instruction for all civilian women, and 'to encourage in all women the spirit to resist the invader by all means available'. Soon groups of Amazons were training all over the country, not only on back-yard rifle ranges but also on improvised grenade ranges—lobbing half bricks at bucket targets at twenty yards. In the summer of 1940 fifty Lambeth Amazons were reported in the Press to have 'armed themselves with broomsticks'.

That summer, in the Herefordshire village of Much Marcle, Lady Helena Gleichen, a cousin of Queen Mary, formed the employees on her estate, Hellens, into a private army, the 'Much Marcle Watchers', arming them and teaching them how to shoot. Groups of women in various places set up teams to watch for Fifth Column parachutists, and militant members of the clergy joined the Home Guard.

As soon as Hitler had recovered from his surprise that Britain did not beg for peace after Dunkirk, he had formally accepted France's surrender and had then given the orders that set into motion the preparations for 'Operation Sea Lion', his plan for the invasion of Britain. At his command the Luftwaffe had begun its systematic destruction of the Royal Air Force's Fighter Command—to clear the skies over what were to be his invasion beaches in Kent and Sussex. At the same time every serviceable river barge in France, Belgium and Holland was 'requisitioned' and ordered to sail to one or another of the ports between Rotterdam and Le Havre. To assemble an armada adequate to transport his three invasion armies across the English Channel, Hitler found that he had to divert a third of Germany's entire merchant fleet. He moved entire armies westward, and soon large-scale amphibious troop manœuvres commenced along those stretches of the French coast which his Intelligence officers had decided most nearly resembled the proposed landing places in Britain. Preparations on this scale could not be camouflaged, and British bombers tried to smash the barge formations. But little damage was done, and the Nazi invasion build-up continued according to plan.

During the first three days of 'Sea Lion' Hitler intended to land more than a quarter of a million troops in the counties of Kent and Sussex. Secure a bridgehead, he believed, and the British would be finished. His men were to take with them more than 60,000 horses, and between 30,000 and 40,000 motor vehicles—including 650 tanks. This at a time when only four British home defence divisions were fully equipped, when fifteen had little equipment worth talking about, and when, despite the fact that the manufacture of arms was being given priority in every factory capable of making any contribution to the nation's arsenals, only 348 serviceable tanks of all types existed in Britain. Hitler, we now know, planned to concentrate the main force of his invasion armies on a relatively small front, but although the British guessed this and guessed correctly which beaches he had chosen for his landings, they had to play safe and deploy their forces widely. Suppose the Germans decided to land in East Anglia? Despite the even greater distance across the water, suppose they landed west of Southampton and moved northward in a column to slice Britain in half on roughly a north-south line? Lacking the armour and vehicles necessary for a strong, mobile counter-attacking force, the British had to spread their meagre butter very thin.

After concentrating virtually his entire war machine on preparations for 'Sea Lion' throughout the summer of 1940, when the British Isles were more vulnerable than they had ever been in the past or were likely to be in the future, why did Hitler decide at the last minute to call off his invasion until the spring of 1941?

This is a question that can never be finally answered. Certainly a number of factors weighed heavily against a successful invasion in 1940. Hitler's admirals had assured him that by a planned deployment of ships and mines they would be able to seal off the English Channel long enough to keep the Royal Navy from interfering with the barges, tugboats, freighters and fishing vessels that were to comprise the invasion task force. But with the ships and mines that Germany possessed in 1940 this could never have been done, and the German admirals must have known it. Hermann Göring either had lied or had been optimistic—or perhaps both—when he had assured Hitler after Dunkirk that by the end of the summer the Luftwaffe would have destroyed Fighter Command and would also have crushed British morale. We also know from

[7]

captured German records that Hitler received Intelligence reports stating that although many senior British officers were so set in their antiquated ways of warfare that they were incapable of ordering an effective defence against a Blitzkrieg, they nevertheless commanded men who were better fighters in every way than the troops of the Wehrmacht. Hitler may also have been put off by German meteorologists' forecasts for the middle of September 1940, when 'Sea Lion' was supposed to be mounted, for these suggested that the Channel weather would be exceptionally rough.

Peered through from either side of that thin strip of water in 1940, what Churchill called the 'veil of the Unknown' was indeed dense and baffling. During the preparatory phase of 'Sea Lion' German monitors had been able to decipher all coded radio messages used for troop communication in Britain and had thus been able to chart with some accuracy the deployment of the main body of the British defence forces. An examination of Wehrmacht military maps prepared at the time suggests that the British military radio networks made the German monitors think that there were some defence formations in Britain which in fact did not exist. But this deception, although probably successful, was on too small a scale to have affected the 'Sea Lion' plans very much. Nevertheless, radio monitoring was the Germans' principal source of information for the development of the final plans for 'Sea Lion', but just when they had steeled themselves to accepting the realities of an invasion, Whitehall ordered the changing of all British radio codes. Was this done as a matter of routine, or had the effect that it would have on the Germans been anticipated and planned? At any rate, for months afterwards, Hitler, with no way of knowing the precise deployment of British home defence forces, dared not risk an attack. And so on 17 September he ordered the postponement of 'Sea Lion' until the following spring.

If he had not made this decision, the corpses of young Germans would no doubt have littered the beaches of Kent and Sussex. Many of those young men would have been burned to death as they stepped out of the water, for preparations had been made to set the beaches alight with barrels of pitch. Others, if rumours still current among British high-ranking officers have any basis in fact, would have been gassed—although even today nobody will say just how this was going to be accomplished.

But who can guess how many tens of thousands of Germans would have survived to get past the beaches and through those miles of winding, unmarked roads, straight to the heart of Britain? Little wonder that the Island's defenders planned against invasion—and also against occupation.

2

HOW TO BEHAVE IN ENGLAND

PERHAPS only as an academic exercise, in 1923 the Wehrmacht produced a detailed blueprint for the conquest of the world. Academic exercise or statement of intentions, the plan was carefully filed away. And as early as 28 February 1934 Hitler was confiding to the heads of the SA and the Reichswehr that a war between Germany and England was an inevitability. In 1938, when General Franz Halder became Germany's Chief of the General Staff, one of the first things he did was to get out the plan for world conquest. His Director of Operations, Max von Viebahn, pointed out to him that the plan was one for aggression. Why did he want to see it? The Chief of Staff supposedly blushed and replied that really he thought that he should be familiar with all plans.

All the more strange, therefore, that until the spring of 1940 no Wehrmacht plans for the occupation of the British Isles seem to have been committed to paper. Stranger still that only when the final details of 'Sea Lion' were being decided did Hitler at last ask his generals to tell him how they thought that the occupation of Britain should be administered—and what they thought that its purpose should be.

In September 1940 a series of Most Secret draft orders and decrees were distributed to senior officers by the German Army's Quartermaster-General. A dozen documents which fell into British hands after the war present an interesting, but incomplete, picture of the Wehrmacht's intentions.

Were there more than these? If there were, none of the official German archives contains them—or so all the archivists claim. Officials in the British Government department which keeps a set of translations, and also will show researchers Photostats of the originals, say that they know of no others. It will be best first of all to list them under their approximate titles, and then to examine each of them separately:

1. Orders Concerning Organization and Function of Military Government in England.
2. Directive for Military Government in England.

3. Chief Supply Officer for England.
4. Guide on How Troops are to Behave in England.
5. Proclamation to the People of England.
6. Announcement Regarding Occupied Territory.
7. Order Concerning the Introduction of German Criminal Law and Penal Regulations in Occupied English Territory.
8. Order Concerning the Summary Police Jurisdiction of Local Commandants in Occupied English Territory.
9. Order Concerning the Possession of Arms in Occupied English Territory.
10. Order Concerning Surrender of Wireless Transmitter Apparatus in Occupied English Territory.
11. Blackout Regulations.
12. Announcement [regarding compulsory requisitions].

The Orders Concerning Organization and Function of Military Government in England was signed by Generaloberst Franz Halder. He was still at that time Chief of the General Staff but was soon to fall out of favour and eventually to end up in the VIP section of a concentration camp because he was believed to have been somewhere on the fringe of the 1944 attempt on Hitler's life. Halder, like many of the Wehrmacht leaders who survived the war and then successfully weathered 'denazification', worked out his days as an adviser to the American forces in Germany. He was living in quiet retirement south of Munich when this book was being written, but he declined flatly to discuss his role in either the invasion or the occupation of Britain. In conversations with Captain Sir Basil Liddell Hart some years earlier, when it had been fashionable for leaders of the conquered Wehrmacht to make such statements, Halder had insisted that the German occupation of Britain would have been moderate—if, of course, the British offered no resistance. Unfortunately, Liddell Hart was unable at that time to confront him with the order he had signed, or the other eleven.

Halder's order for the occupation of Britain gave the general commanding each of the three German invasion armies complete control over his own area of captured territory. Each general was authorized to set up four administrative sub-area headquarters, twelve local headquarters, one section of secret field police, and one local defence battalion which for its mobility would depend on bicycles. Halder's order also stated that there would be a separate 'Defence Economic Staff for England'* which would receive all its instructions directly from the War Office in Berlin. In the field the Defence Economic Staff's offices were each to have its own local 'Defence Economic Command' which at first would be based in one of the captured British ports but would later move inland to set up permanent offices in major industrial areas. These offices were in practice, no matter what the theory, to be the official plunderers, operating under orders to 'seize, secure and remove raw materials, semi-finished products and machinery of military importance', and in special circumstances to take over repair shops 'for unit purposes'. German food and agricultural specialists would be on hand to help and advise the Economic Officers.

Halder's order went on to grant each German Army Commander in Britain 'supreme judiciary power over the civilian population throughout the area under his administration except where an administrative sub-area commandant is competent', and then explained in some detail how the military administrative system in occupied Britain would deal with paper work.

The second order in the folder must be quoted in full:

Most Secret
Directive for Military Government in England
1. The main task of military government is to make full use of the country's resources for the needs of fighting troops and requirements of the German war economy.

2. An essential condition for securing the labour of the country is that law and order should prevail. Law and order will therefore be established. Administrative measures will not violate international law unless the enemy has given cause for reprisals.

3. Armed insurgents of either sex will be dealt with with the utmost severity. If the population initiates active operations *after* the completed conquest of a locality, or in places *behind* the fighting front, the inhabi-

---

* For 'England', of course, the Nazis always meant 'Great Britain'.

tants involved in the fighting will be regarded as armed insurgents. When taking hostages, those persons should if possible be selected in whom the *active* enemy elements have an interest.

4. The able-bodied male population between the ages of 17 and 45 will, unless the local situation calls for an exceptional ruling, be interned and dispatched to the Continent with a minimum of delay.*

5. Local headquarters and unit commanders are forbidden to raise levies or other monetary taxes. The authority for such measures is retained by the Army Commander and the offices expressly empowered by him.

6. Laws of the country operative prior to the occupation will be upheld unless they are contradictory to the purposes of the occupation. English authorities may continue to function if they maintain a correct attitude.

7. Special attention is to be paid to public health affairs.

8. In the interests of the country's national economy, this being the concern of the Defence Economic Staff and its headquarters, the welfare of the inhabitants of the country will be considered in so far as they contribute directly or indirectly toward the maintenance of law and order and the securing of the country's labour for the requirements of the troops and the German war economy.

signed (in draft) C-in-C Army, von Brauchitsch

The next order created a 'Chief Supply Officer for England' who, although he was to draw some troop supplies from the German chief supply officer for Belgium, would 'be responsible for seizing such stocks of food, petrol, motor transport, horse-drawn vehicles, etc., in the country as have not already been taken

---

* During the preparations for 'Sea Lion' camps were actually set up in France for the reception of these British males. No one, however, has discovered a document or found a witness to corroborate the statement made by some British journalists and others at various times that the Germans intended to sterilize these males. Surviving Germans who might be able to shed some light on this—such Germans as Franz Halder—refuse to a man to comment. It seems probable that the British males were to be shipped to the Continent simply to get them out of the way and to supplement Germany's slave labour force. Certainly there would have been very little for these Britons to do at home by the time the 'Defence Economic Staff' had finished plucking the country bare.

over by the armies'. This order ended: 'The Chief Supply Officer for England is in no way concerned with measures of military government in England.'

The *Guide on How Troops are to Behave in England* is particularly interesting:

1. A firm and cautious attitude toward the civilian population is to be adopted; correct soldierly behaviour is a self-evident duty.

2. Strict reticence will be observed when conversing with the local population. *Enemy intelligence* will be particularly active in occupied territory, endeavouring to obtain information on installations and measures of military importance. Any thoughtlessness, boasting, or misplaced confidences may, therefore, have the direst consequences.

3. Acts of violence against orderly members of the population and looting will incur the severest penalties under military law; the death sentence may be imposed.

4. Works of art and historic monuments are to be preserved and protected. Any disparagement of the religious practices of the country will be punished.

5. The soldier will be provided with all essentials by his unit. Unnecessary purchases are to be avoided. Any private purchases by individual soldiers are to be paid for in cash. Any wastefulness is harmful to the unit.

6. Unnecessary interference with the economic life of the country is to be avoided. Factories, workshops, and offices are not to be disturbed; except where operationally necessary, such places may only be entered by soldiers executing orders. The use of stocks of petrol, oil, machinery, tools, etc., found in factories and works is forbidden. In the operational area exceptions may, if necessary, be made on the instructions of unit commanders from battalion commander upward.

7. Goods of all kind and military booty, especially food and fodder and articles of clothing, are to be preserved and secured.

8. Units are forbidden to destroy wireless, telephone and telegraphic installations; if it is necessary to interrupt communications, the task may only be undertaken by specialist personnel, Corps of Signals personnel or unit signallers.

9. Reich credit notes and coins and German small coins to the value of one and two pfennig and one, two, five and ten Reichspfennig or Rentenpfennig are legal tender. Other German money must not be spent. The rate of exchange will be as follows: one English pound

equals 9·60 Reichsmarks. One English shilling equals 48 Reichs-pfennigs.*

Von Brauchitsch's *Proclamation to the People of England* stated:

1. English territory occupied by German troops will be placed under military government.
2. Military commanders will issue decrees necessary for the protection of the troops and the maintenance of general law and order.
3. Troops will respect property and persons if the population behaves according to instructions.
4. English authorities may continue to function if they maintain a correct attitude.
5. All thoughtless actions, sabotage of any kind, and any passive or active opposition to the German armed forces will incur the most severe retaliatory measures.
6. I warn all civilians that if they undertake active operations against the German forces, they will be condemned to death inexorably.
7. The decrees of the German military authorities must be observed; any disobedience will be severely punished.

The *Announcement Regarding Occupied Territory* was unsigned but appears to have been the draft of an order that would have been circulated by lower echelon German commanders. It warned: 'Acts of sabotage are threatened with the most severe punishment. Damage to or removal of crops, of military stores and installations of any kinds, and the tearing down or effacement of official placards will be treated as sabotage. Gas works, water works, power plants, railways, sluice installations, fuel tanks and works of art are specifically under the protection of the armed forces.' The announcement explained that orders for the surrender of firearms would be

---

* During the war there was, of course, no official rate of monetary exchange between Britain and Germany, but if their currencies were both pegged on the Swiss franc, then the exchange rate stated above, which is the same as that stated in Gestapo occupation documents, is fair and not punitive, as was the rate imposed on Germany by the Allies in 1945. The German exchange rate on the Channel Islands was also fair—but the money in circulation there was not backed by the German Government.

issued separately, and it then went on to enumerate those crimes for which Britons might be punished by a German military court:

1. Any assistance given to non-German military personnel in occupied territory.
2. Any help afforded to civilians escaping into unoccupied territory.
3. Any transmission to persons or authorities outside occupied territory of information to the detriment of the German forces of the Reich.
4. Any intercourse with prisoners of war.
5. Any insult to the German armed forces or their commanders.
6. Assembling in the street, circulating of pamphlets or holding of public meetings or processions without previous authorization from a German commander, any demonstration hostile to Germany.
7. Incitement to stop work, stopping work maliciously, strikes and lock-outs.

The order then went on, 'All businesses, trade undertakings and banks are to remain open; if they are closed down without justification, the persons responsible may be punished. Producers and dealers in goods required in everyday life are to continue in their occupations and distribute goods to the consumer.' Wages, the order said, were to remain what they were on the day the Germans arrived—unless specific authorization was given to raise them. The rate of exchange for currency was stated, and Britons were told that individual German soldiers would make their personal purchases in cash but units would issue German credit certificates.

The introduction of German Criminal Law and Penal Regulations in Occupied English Territory was also for von Brauchitsch's signature. It specified that German criminal law was to be applied in any case brought before a German military court. It gave these courts unlimited power, specifying that 'Military courts may also pass judgement on offences committed before the entry of German troops'. And it added the mildest of riders, 'Action in such cases will be discretionary'. It then went on: 'When judging acts of juveniles, German courts may impose the statutory penalty irrespective of the age of the offender if the latter appears to have

[16]

reached the stage of development of a person over eighteen years of age.

'Anyone in occupied territory attempting to commit acts of violence or sabotage of any kind against the German armed forces, its personnel or installations will', the order stated, 'be condemned to death.'

It also warned that anyone

contravening the regulations concerning the surrender of firearms, ammunition, hand grenades, explosives and other war material will be condemned to death or penal servitude or in less serious cases imprisonment. . . . Anyone stopping work with the intention of prejudicing the interests of the German forces of occupation, anyone who locks out employees or who incites others to strike or lock-out will be punished. . . .

. . . Assembling in the street, producing and distributing pamphlets, holding and participating in *public* [von Brauchitsch's italics] meetings and processions is forbidden and will be punished [and so would be those who held] demonstrations of any kind hostile to Germany, [or made] particularly malicious or insulting utterances. . . .

. . . Anyone publishing in newspapers or periodicals information which may be detrimental to the German Reich or information the publication of which has been forbidden by the German Army of Occupation will be punished. . . .

So, of course, would be 'anyone who listens to non-German wireless transmissions publicly or in the company of others or who facilitates such listening'. Announcements might be made, however, by the occupation chiefs, allowing certain non-German broadcasts to be listened to, but the broadcasting of 'information hostile to Germany' would be a punishable offence under this order.

The unsigned order concerning the summary jurisdiction of German police commandants in occupied Britain authorized local German commanders to pass summary sentences on Britons 'not subject to military disciplinary law' if those persons either lived in the areas they commanded, committed offences in them or were arrested in them—whenever 'the facts in the case are evident enough, and if this procedure is adequate in view of the guilt of the offender and the consequences of the offence'. Local commanders were authorized by this order to pass summary sentences of detention of up to six weeks or 'Fines up to 30,000 Reichsmarks [£3,125], or in default of payment, an alternative period of detention of up to six weeks.' Sentences had to be pronounced 'immediately after the accused has been heard. It will be made known to the accused and given effect forthwith.'

Britons who had summary sentences passed on them by the Germans, however, would be allowed to appeal—providing they did so within twenty-four hours of being sentenced—to the next higher German authority, who would then have the right to uphold the sentence, quash it or substitute a new sentence against which there would be no appeal.

The *Possession of Arms in Occupied English Territories* was another proclamation signed by von Brauchitsch. It demanded the surrender of 'All firearms, including sporting guns, ammunition, hand grenades, explosives and other war materials . . . within twenty-four hours at the nearest German administrative sub-area or local headquarters unless instructions are issued locally. The mayors or senior local authorities will be made responsible for the strict observance of this order.' Anyone who contravened this regulation would 'be condemned to death or in less serious cases to penal servitude or imprisonment'.

A separate order signed by von Brauchitsch *Concerning Surrender of Wireless Transmitter Apparatus in Occupied English Territory* called for the handing in of 'All wireless transmitting apparatus, including amateur transmitters and the transportable dynamos, batteries, and accumulators used to operate them.' Anyone who ignored this order might also 'be condemned to death [or] in less serious cases to penal servitude or imprisonment'.

Occupation of the British Isles may not have meant absolute and final domination of the world for Hitler, but certainly for a long time no major offensive could have been mounted against his forces in Western Europe because he would have held the main base from which such an attack would have had to be launched. Nevertheless his generals still drafted a full set of blackout regulations which were to have been issued by their various field commanders in occupied British territory. The German planners decided that there would be a total blackout of buildings from sunset to sunrise, that all unnecessary lighting, including shop signs and illuminated shop windows, would be switched off, and street lights would be dimmed so that they would not be visible 'from the height of five hundred metres . . . either vertically or obliquely'. Vehicle lighting was also to be restricted, and details were given for the masking of vehicle headlamps—details very similar to those already followed in Britain. The German decision that a blackout in Britain was not to be achieved by the cutting of electricity or of gas supplies at the mains duplicated a British blackout order that was already in effect.

The last of the dozen German secret occupation documents was headed simply *Announcement* and was no doubt to have been pasted on walls throughout occupied Britain, and was to have been signed by local army commanders. It stated that the following items were to be 'requisitioned':

Agricultural products, food and fodder of all kinds, ores, crude metals, semi-finished metal products of all kinds including precious metals, asbestos and mica, cut or uncut precious or semi-precious stones, mineral oils and fuels of all kinds, industrial oils and fats, waxes, resins, glues, rubber in all forms, all raw materials for textiles, leather, furs and hides, round timber, sawn timber, timber sleepers and timber masts.

The order then explained that these things were not to be 'alienated, altered or moved to another place. They must be handled with the greatest care and must be protected against deterioration.' The Germans would not take goods 'which are a part of a normal household stock', and 'Farmers and tradesmen, including innkeepers, may retain such stocks of agricultural products, food and fodder as are essential for supplying their clients with absolute necessities. To the same extent local craftsmen and shops may supply goods to customers.'

One witness has claimed to have seen other German occupation orders in addition to these twelve. Captain S. Payne Best, one of the two British intelligence officers who were kidnapped by the Gestapo in neutral Holland in the autumn of 1939 and were incarcerated in concentration camps in Germany, wrote in his book *The Venlo Incident* that in 1940, several days after the order was given postponing 'Operation Sea Lion', his Gestapo warders showed him a file of about fifty documents which appear to have included the dozen discussed above. Best wrote that he was allowed to keep these papers overnight in his cell in the VIP block in Sachsenhausen concentration camp, but that he was unable to transcribe them. It is perfectly possible, of course, that Best, who had been a professional espionage agent for many years and was trained to remember details, may still not have recalled accurately the contents of that file. He claimed that the papers that he saw concerned the take-over of all railways, canals and ports in Britain by the Wehrmacht, and that there was also an order stating that all men in Britain below the age of fifty were to be registered. Several of the orders, he claimed, made it clear that the Germans intended to occupy Southern England only, and he also claimed that one of the documents was a draft regulation concerning the passage of civilians back and forth from occupied to unoccupied British territory.

Why should Payne Best have been shown any Wehrmacht documents at all? Did he perhaps see the captured documents— or hear about them—after the war and, while writing his account of his adventures as a prisoner of the Gestapo, believe that the papers had been shown to him in 1940?

Payne Best's admitted concern while a prisoner of the Germans was to live comfortably, a statement damningly borne out in captured Gestapo documents that describe him as a coldly professional agent, more interested in good living than in anything else.

But whether or not Best was recording accurately what he

read, the Gestapo was certainly preparing to occupy the whole of Britain.

*

Most Britons have never heard of Dr Franz Alfred Six, but had the Germans occupied Britain, his name would undoubtedly have become an English obscenity. For this man—short and narrow-shouldered, completely bald, with bat-wing ears and an angry squint accentuated by pebble spectacles—although only thirty-one years old in 1940, had been chosen to head the Gestapo in Britain.

Nowadays Franz Six discusses his Nazi past no more often than he is compelled to, but in a letter written in English refusing an interview, he admitted that he was

. . . called back to Berlin the first week of September 1940 to take over a group of about 40 officers. This group was supposed to be under the command of the Commander in Chief of the German Air Force, which had to invade England. In the early morning of 15th September the invasion was cancelled by order of Hitler.*

As to me I was going back immediately to my field unit in the West [at this time Six was a member of an SS Einsatzkommando (action group)]. There were questions as to files and other material [about the whereabouts of records and/or orders concerning his 'Sea Lion' assignment]. No files or other stuff was existing, it was no time for it. The general order was: 'Contact the political branch of Scotland Yard and leave all police-measures to it.' The members of the group of the 40 officers should be attached to the different armies and divisions in case of the invasion had been successful. . . .

Who exactly is Franz Alfred Six? Born of working-class parents in Mannheim in 1909, Six did not graduate from Gymnasium until he was twenty-one, because he had to drop out of school from time to time to earn the money to pay for his education. The year that he went on to Heidelberg to study social and political science and history he also joined the Nazi Party. It was either this, he later explained, or the Communist Party, for there were no

---

* In fact Hitler took the final decision to pospone (not cancel) the invasion 'until further notice' on 17 September.

other organizations open to people like him, who wanted so desperately to better the lot of the ordinary German.

Franz Six has said that he found Heidelberg no playground, that the whole time that he was there he lived in a miserable attic and ate in a soup kitchen. He received a doctorate of philosophy in 1934, when he was twenty-five years old, and he then moved on to the University of Leipzig to take up a teaching position. He continued his studies and also found time to act as press and publicity director for a Nazi students' organization. On 20 April 1934 he joined the SS and SD (the Nazi security service) as an officer, later claiming to have done this because it gave him access to the latest newspapers from all over the world.

The following year Six received his higher doctorate at Leipzig, and two years after that was made a professor at that university. By then he was also running the press section of the SD.

In 1939, when Six was thirty years old, he transferred to the University of Berlin to become the first dean of a new faculty of political science—a 'Faculty for Foreign Countries'—that had been created specially to coach members of Hitler's Government on the Nazi attitude toward foreign politics. Then, when the war began, he took over the cultural branch of the German Foreign Office and was given the civil service rank of 'Envoy First Class'. At the same time he joined the Reichssicherheitshauptamt—RSHA, the Nazi Central Security Agency—but he later claimed that his position in that organization was merely an honorary one, as, he says, was the rank of brigadier-general in the SS which he was to receive in 1945.

After he was recalled to participate in 'Sea Lion' and that operation was cancelled, Six returned for a time to his old desk in the RSHA's Amt VII, a department which he headed but which, he said, employed only fifteen people altogether (some Amter had as many as a thousand) and which engaged itself in 'philosophical, scientific and historical research' into such things as Freemasonry and religions. Soon he was reassigned to an SS Einsatzkommando that had Moscow as its eventual destination. Six claimed after the war that his own job on the Russian front had been merely to 'place under protection' the historical archives of Russian churches, universities and other institutions that might otherwise have suffered at the hands of vandals.

[22]

His Einsatzkommando never reached Moscow, of course, but during twenty-five days in Smolensk, according to a statement Six made after the war, he placed an ancient wooden church there under his 'protection'—because it contained valuable archives—and he also 'protected' Smolensk Cathedral because, he said, it had been turned into a museum by the Communists and contained a number of gold crowns and other *objets d'art*. But this was not all that he did in Smolensk. His Einsatzkommando began methodically tracking down local commissars, and during those twenty-five days more than a hundred were shot. Dr Six denied having anything to do with this—but enough SS documents survived the war to establish his guilt. Indeed, when he returned to Berlin from Smolensk, he was promoted because Himmler was so pleased with him.

Six then remained in Berlin where, in 1944, he began to organize a pan-Europe anti-Jewish Congress, but no meetings ever took place. The war ended, and Dr. Six disappeared. Instead of following the route to South America taken by Adolph Eichmann, Six chose to work in Germany as a farm labourer. He knew that he was wanted for questioning by the Allied Occupation forces, but when he was finally arrested in January 1946, he said that he had not surrendered earlier because his wife had not wanted him to.

He was put on trial at Nürnberg in 1948 for his part in the Smolensk massacres. He insisted that he had not had a direct hand in the killings—and no one could prove that he had actually pulled any triggers. All he had done in Russia, he insisted, was protect whatever cultural objects and records lay in his path. He knew nothing of any murders. While he was with his Einsatzkommando its members had also killed several thousand Jews in Russia, but the prosecution was unable to prove that Six was directly implicated in these murders. He denied even being an Anti-Semite but in an involved argument he conceded that if Hitler ordered the killing of Jews, then it was right to kill Jews.

However, captured SS documents alone were enough to condemn Six for his part in the murders of the commissars, and in April 1948 he was sent to prison for twenty years. In 1951 his sentence was reduced to ten years, and in September 1952, like so many other Nazi war criminals, Franz Six was quietly released from prison at the instigation of the US authorities.

The kind of teaching that Franz Alfred Six was capable of doing was no longer fashionable in Germany, but he very soon found alternative employment, as a financial adviser to the manufacturers of the Porsche motor-car.

During the Eichmann trial Six was in a sanatorium in Switzerland, allegedly recovering from a heart attack, but he still offered to testify on Eichmann's behalf. However, when the Jews refused to promise that he would not be put in the glass box alongside his former colleague, Six had second thoughts and decided to remain in Switzerland.

How would Dr Six have behaved in Britain? This the reader must decide for himself. A prominent and reliable anti-Nazi German, Dr Otto John, who had the unpleasant job of interviewing Dr Six along with hundreds of other Nazis describes him simply as 'one of the worst of the lot'.

The order upon which Franz Six was to have acted in England, and to which he referred in his letter, was dated 17 September 1940, and was prepared for Reinhard Heydrich's signature. An unsigned copy was found in the files of Amt II, the Enemy Information Department of the RSHA. It stated that Göring had decided on 1 August 1940 that the SS's Security Police and the SD would

commence their activities simultaneously with the military invasion in order to seize and combat effectively the numerous important organizations and societies in England which are hostile to Germany.
By virtue of Reichsmarschall Göring's authority I appoint you Representative of the Chief of the Security Police and SD in Great Britain. Your task is to combat, with the requisite means, all anti-German organizations, institutions, opposition, and opposition groups which can be seized in England, to prevent the removal of all available material, and to centralize and safeguard it for future exploitation. I designate the capital, London, as the location of your headquarters as Representative of the Chief of the Security Police and SD; and I authorize you to set up small action groups [Einsatzgruppen] in other parts of Great Britain as the situation dictates and the necessity arises.

Other documents found after the war reveal that, as well as London, the Gestapo planned to have headquarters in Birmingham, Bristol, Liverpool and Manchester, and either Edinburgh or, if the Forth Bridge had been destroyed, in Glasgow. According to Ronald Wheatley, the British historian who knows most about the plans for 'Sea Lion', the Gestapo would have systematically created a reign of terror by placing selected British leaders and intellectuals under 'protective custody'. Mr Wheatley found a Gestapo document indicating that only people whose names were on a special 'Search List' were to have been arrested under this order, but other Gestapo orders authorized the arrest of anyone in Britain who might yield information. The residences of the Archbishop of Canterbury and of other British church dignitaries were to have been searched, and the clergymen themselves placed under house arrest. By the time preparations for 'Sea Lion' had been completed, the Gestapo had ready a card file said to contain the names of all British Jews, Freemasons, refugees, socialists, communists and 'liberals' (this meant, among others, *all* Members of Parliament). Each card was marked to indicate whether or not the person whose name was on it was to be taken into custody or for the time being merely to be put under house arrest.

3

WHERE TO GO IN BRITAIN

SEVERAL years before the First World War, when he was still a very junior officer, Andrew Thorne was sent by the War Office to East Anglia to report on the local obstacles that might hinder a German invasion force. Shortly after he began his travels through the back lanes of Suffolk on what he knew was no more than a routine exercise, Thorne advised the War Office that several other men were making a similar study. They were German Army officers and they often shot past him in their big, powerful motor-car. He suggested to the War Office that perhaps he should be provided with something less leisurely than an Army bicycle.

Did those German military intelligence agents of Thorne's day have their counterparts in the years immediately preceding World War II, briskly motoring around Britain to bring the Wehrmacht invasion and occupation handbooks up to date? In October 1944 British soldiers found in a Brussels garage a bundle of green cardboard folders containing what at first looked like faded one-inch Ordnance Survey maps of Great Britain. These maps were prepared for the troops of 'Operation Sea Lion' and were photo-lithographed reproductions of Ordnance Survey maps, overprinted with information that had probably, for the most part, been easy enough to obtain. They indicated the position of every known military installation in the country, harbours and shipyards worth investigation by the German navy, and sundry other places of more than tourist interest. In the margins were various notations printed in German and, on the faces of the maps themselves, symbols indicating the positions of things of interest both to a German invasion army and to an army of occupation. One, a small beer stein, marked the precise location of every brewery, however small, in Britain—probably to show the German troops their most trustworthy sources of drinking water.

The 'Sea Lion' troops were also to be issued with copies of a guide-book that contained maps of all towns of any size in Britain. This impressively comprehensive work was merely a photo-lithographed reproduction of the 1937 Automobile Association *Handbook* for Great Britain, again overprinted with special information for the Wehrmacht. Yet even after the war, when a conscientious security officer learned that one of these curiosities had been presented to the Imperial War Museum, he tried to have it locked away from the public.

Other guides and handbooks were prepared by the Germans for the invasion and occupation of Britain. Various albums of photographs were issued from time to time, some as late as the autumn of 1944, showing important buildings, bridges and other things in Britain that might interest the Wehrmacht. Many of the photographs had been reproduced from *The Times* and *Country Life*, from picture postcards and holiday snapshots, but they were no less useful for that—except when, as in the case of the Germans' photographs of the Ford Motor Company's works at Dagenham, they were so heavily retouched that they were virtually unrecognizable. These photographs were gathered together for the use of Luftwaffe pilots as well as for invading and occupying troops, and many were taken by the Germans from the air. From the absence of certain landmarks it is clear that the compilation of some of these reference works was done at least as early as 1936, even when the dates printed on the photographs are later. Among other things, German Intelligence published sets of large-scale oblique photographs which appear to be the work of Hansa Luftbild, a Lufthansa subsidiary which operated as a completely separate company and specialized in commercial aerial surveys. Hansa Luftbild was formally taken over by the Luftwaffe at the outbreak of the war, but the Abwehr may have employed the company before then. Their photographs, all taken from precisely the same angle and altitude, were reproduced in gravure by the OKW, the German High Command—so superbly that individual panes of glass in windows of houses can be seen when the pictures are examined through a strong magnifying glass. Placed side by side the photographs present an unbroken panorama of the British coastline and the land roughly ten miles behind it. Although primarily for the use of airmen, these photographic surveys would have been extremely valuable to Abwehr or Gestapo agents who wanted to sniff out recently prepared military emplacements in Britain, for freshly taken photographs could be compared with the pre-war ones and changes would be readily apparent.

How were these pictures taken? In the days just before and just after the start of the war, farmers along the coast of Britain sometimes saw German aircraft—whether civilian or military they could not tell—flying low along the coast. This suggests that Britain's coastal defences were less efficient than they were believed to be, for every effort was supposedly being made to prevent photography of the country from the air. When, for example, a Zeppelin flying from Canada to Germany in the mid-'thirties radioed that she was approaching Britain, that she was having some sort of trouble and that she therefore wanted clearance to continue her flight over the land, Schiller, her commander, received a strange reply. His Zeppelin could only pass over land, the British told him, if its actual command was handed over to one of the passengers, Graf von Eckner, the pioneer of Zeppelins, who was known to the British to be so anti-Nazi that he had dared to refuse to name one of his airships *Adolf Hitler*. Schiller agreed to the British request, and von Eckner was allowed for a few minutes to take over the bridge, having given the British his personal assurance that all the passengers had been made to put away their cameras.

Certain employees of Lufthansa itself no doubt made their personal contributions to the collection of information on Britain, although there seems to be no substance to the rumour that during the years before the war every Lufthansa airliner flying to Britain carried one more crew member than similar planes of competing airlines and that, despite this overstaffing, the Lufthansa planes usually took more time to turn around in Britain than the other planes—because the German crews were so busy spying for the Abwehr. Dr Otto John, a wartime Lufthansa executive whose own personal record of opposition to the Nazis is impeccable, says that the airline itself was essentially anti-Nazi. When the Abwehr tried to make wholesale use of it before the war, Dr John says that its head, Baron von Gablenz, whose death in an air crash in April 1942 is believed to have been engineered by the Nazis, convinced the intelligence officers that civilian airline crews spying outside Germany might cause a great deal of embarrassment, and so specific orders were issued to the Lufthansa crews not to spy when abroad. Dr John recalls that once before he left on a trip outside Germany on Lufthansa business he received a postcard inviting him to call on one of the security agencies, but he tore up the card and ignored its invitation, and he heard no more about it.

However, a special questionnaire *was* prepared by the Abwehr for the use of those Lufthansa personnel who were willing to undertake espionage assignments, enabling them to record systematically the details of aerodromes and other places of military interest they saw when flying over Britain or when on the ground.

The Abwehr diligently gathered together a great deal of information that would have helped them to occupy Britain, but inevitably their handbooks contained some howlers. One of the early albums of intelligence photographs illustrated about 150 supposedly primary targets in London—including very minor railway overpasses and the printing works of *The Listener* and *Radio Times*. Another handbook explained that the two aerials on top of Broadcasting House in London had to be destroyed. Some wartime transmissions did actually go out directly from the BBC's headquarters, but not on these two aerials, for they are dummies, placed there by the architect to indicate the purpose for which London's great Portland stone silo had been built.

No evidence has come to light to suggest that Hitler managed to put a large and efficient army of spies into Great Britain, either before or during the Second World War. The few people who were caught in Britain passing or attempting to pass information to the Germans before the war were very small fry and hardly in a position to find out anything very important, while the handful of espionage agents who were turned up during the war were singularly inept, often unable even to speak English. Like most intelligence agencies, the Abwehr appears to have relied for the bulk of its information on the usual humdrum sources available to anybody—encyclopædias, books, newspapers, magazines, trade and other directories—on the reports of military and naval attachés, and occasionally on people sympathetic to the Nazi cause who happened to be travelling in Britain on business or for pleasure.

One full-time German agent whose material is known to have reached Berlin was a match-seller who stood outside St James's Park Underground Station in London before the war. All day long he took snapshots of everyone who emerged from 65 Broadway, a building which housed various intelligence agencies. Officers in the building knew perfectly well who the man was and what he was doing—just as many local school-children knew at that time what went on inside 65 Broadway. But since British agents actually in the field never reported in person to their headquarters—and in almost all cases doubtless had no idea where it was—the match-seller's shapshots could be of no practical use to the Germans. So the British intelligence chiefs let him continue on their doorstep, where they could keep an eye on him, until the war began. They did not know, and it probably would have made no difference to them if they had known, that this agent was not filtering material to the Abwehr but, rather, to that much more sinister organization, the Gestapo.

4

THE GESTAPO HANDBOOK

A MT VI, the section of the RSHA which among other things
supported Nazi groups outside Germany and which also
ran its own international espionage network in competition
with the Abwehr, employed from three to five hundred people at
one time or another in its Berlin headquarters. It was better known
as the 'Gestapo'. A former major in the SS, Walter zu Christian,
was appointed to the British Section of Amt VI in 1936. He claims
that as a boy he had spent a year at 'Seeford College, near Brighton'
where he says that he perfected his English (his name does not
appear in the records of Seaford College, which has since moved
across Sussex to Petworth, but then there were—and still are—a
number of other preparatory schools at Seaford, and zu Christian
may have attended any one of them). He further claims that he
worked as a salesman in Madrid in 1933 in order to spy on the
British in Gibraltar, and that he later visited England several times
to get information. He also claims that he prepared a 600-page
report for Hitler that eventually became the 100-page *Informationsheft G.B.*, the Gestapo's printed handbook on Great Britain, and
that he was also the author of the 'Black List', the *Sonderfahndungsliste G.B.*, the Gestapo Arrest List for Great Britain. Colonel
Walter Schellenberg, chief of Amt VI from the beginning of 1941
until the end of the Nazi regime and an autobiographer in the
Münchhausen tradition, also claimed to be the author of these two
works of reference. Probably both officers worked on them—and
so probably did a lot of others.

Informationsheft G.B. begins with a brief survey of the geography
and climate of Great Britain. Then, with the aid of what appear to
be textbook maps, it examines the country's roads, railways and
canals, its population distribution and even its languages.

However, it never seemed to have occurred to the handbook's
compilers that the British would take action to protect anything
from destruction by invaders or would try to keep anything from
being of use to them. After reading Intelligence reports on the
manner in which the French had scuttled their railway system,
often by leaving rolling stock in stations where a single Luftwaffe

[31]

bomb could destroy the train, the station and points system, the British had made elaborate and sensible plans for saving their railways from complete destruction while at the same time rendering them temporarily unusable.

Plans were issued for the dispersal of rolling stock in the event of invasion, and in every railway station and yard in the country blobs of red paint marked vulnerable spots. If the Germans had landed, trains were to be moved away to designated sidings, while certain railway employees would have gone around with hammers, smashing at the red markings—doing effective, but not irreparable, damage. This system would undoubtedly have worked. Indeed, once it was almost put into operation.

On Saturday night, 7 September 1940, owing to a misunderstanding, the signal 'Cromwell' was given on the south coast. Very quickly the alarm was relayed to other counties and, before it could be countermanded, in various places actions began to be taken. In Lincolnshire, possibly owing to faulty communications, the local defence forces believed that the signal had been given because an unidentified boat had been seen off the coast, and a motor-cycle dispatch rider raced from church to church in the city of Lincoln. While the bells of five of the churches began to ring out across Lincolnshire, warning the outlying villages that the Germans were coming, two Royal Engineer officers arrived at Lincoln Railway Station, reported to Mr L. J. Stephens, the District Superintendent, and told him that the Germans had landed and therefore they had brought along explosives with which to destroy his railway yard. Stephens, a cautious man, insisted on telephoning the London and North Eastern Railway's Southern Area Central Control. He found out the true situation, and so Lincoln's railway station was saved. But before the 'Cromwell' order was countermanded, several small bridges in Lincolnshire were destroyed by zealous sapper officers.

Informationsheft G.B. also lists Britain's largest towns, and her principal imports and exports. There is a brief survey on the uses of the land, on forestry and fishing, and then a brief explanation of the system of government and the relationship between the monarch and the people. There is no suggestion, however, either in this or any other section of the handbook, that the Gestapo intended to kidnap the Royal Family, as a former SS captain, Otto Begus, has claimed. Begus has stated that with twenty-three officers and about a hundred men, he was to parachute into the grounds of Buckingham Palace and formally arrest the King and Queen and their suite, who would then be held hostage to dissuade individual Britons from actively resisting German occupation.

Assuming that there is any truth in his claim, Begus and his men would first have had to get past the special guard who protected the Royal Family, hand-picked men from the Brigade of Guards and the Household Cavalry. This guard supposedly had orders to get their charges out of the country the moment that a German landing was reported, and during the early years of the war armoured-cars were always kept ready wherever the Royal Family went. King George VI is known to have said that in the event of occupation he wanted to lead Britain's Resistance, but he could have contributed little positive to the sort of resistance organization that was awaiting the Germans.

Informationsheft G.B. includes a list of the members of the Cabinet. After each entry a note explains something of the Minister's background, usually a statement of what the Gestapo thought had been his most important job before attaining Cabinet rank. Somehow the Gestapo overlooked the Regional Commissioners who, although not actually in the Government when *Informationsheft G.B.* was being compiled, would, when the Germans arrived in Britain, have been doing work which would have interested the Gestapo.

In 1939 Britain had been divided into twelve regions, each headed by a Regional Commissioner.* If for any reason the central government had been unable to govern, the Regional Commissioners were to have tried to co-ordinate governmental activity in their areas. These twelve men would have become Britain's twelve regional dictators. Their appointment in 1939 was reported in the Press, and it apparently never occurred to anyone at the time to keep any facts about them secret.

---

* A list of the Regional Commissioners, their regions and head-quarters, is printed as Appendix A, page 156.

The Amt VI researchers saw the public schools of Britain as an essential part of the national power structure, and *Informationsheft G.B.* states that every British public school boy receives exactly the same schooling as his father—providing, of course, that his father went to the same public school. The Gestapo carefully noted which public school produced which political leaders, but expressed some bewilderment that while Eton and Harrow seemed to be the pre-eminent public schools, Neville Chamberlain was a product of Rugby. The public schools, *Informationsheft G.B.* notes,

bring up the future English gentleman who never worries about philosophical problems, who does not worry about foreign culture and, as far as Germany is concerned, thinks of it as the Devil himself, and who thinks that England's position can be touched by no one. The whole system is geared to produce men of very hard will but without scruples. They do not worry about spiritual problems. . . . They are educated to accept their own importance. . . . The public schools do not educate personalities but assume that the upper classes keep the country going and teach their boys to grow up accepting this.

If they had heard the phrase 'old boy network' mentioned in connection with the public schools, the Gestapo researchers did not mention it in *Informationsheft G.B.* Yet this network was to be a vital factor in the formation of the British Resistance.

The Boy Scout movement had been outlawed in Germany at the beginning of Nazi rule, and the Gestapo handbook for Great Britain makes it clear why this was done and tries to justify the ban. The Boy Scout organization in Britain was described as a 'government propaganda agency' that spread to the Dominions 'at the insistence of the British Government'. The handbook stated that the Boy Scouts' leader until recently had been 'a half Jew, Mr Martin', who was also the head of the Passport Office, and that Martin's successor, a 'Mr Wilson', also worked in the Passport Office and for eight years had been chief of police in Calcutta.

The handbook then explained that the Boy Scouts headquarters in London directed Boy Scout movements in other countries, and that the Chief Scout received monthly and quarterly reports on the cultural, political and economic situations in each country in which there were scouts. *Informationsheft G.B.* also had the impression that all letters written by Boy Scout pen pals had to be passed through the London headquarters. 'The Boy Scout movement in England,' the handbook revealed, 'is a cover for English cultural propaganda and a very good source of information for the British Secret Service.' Baden-Powell, the handbook explained, had been a spy in Germany before the First World War, and the Gestapo was convinced that his organization of boys was primarily concerned with spying.

Just how wide of the mark was all this? Hubert Martin, never actually the leader of the Boy Scout movement, was its International Commissioner and later was the Honorary Director of the World Scout Bureau until he died in 1938. He was indeed head of the Passport Office. Colonel John Wilson, former chief of police in Calcutta, took over the job of Honorary Director from Martin. A senior intelligence officer in World War II, Wilson was to serve in the Special Operations Executive, at first in charge of that clandestine organization's training programme and, from early 1942, in charge of the Norwegian Section. Wilson's section, among other things, was to drop into Norway the men who successfully put the Rykan Power Station out of action, thus destroying the Germans' source of heavy water and causing them to abandon the experiments which might have led to their creating an atomic bomb.

Certainly the Gestapo had good enough reason to suppose that a connection existed between the Passport Office and British Intelligence—but had they any reason to assume that the Boy Scouts organization itself was an official British intelligence agency? According to the Boy Scouts Public Relations Officer in London, some reports did go back and forth from one country's Boy Scouts organization to another's, but these reports had to do with the business of scouting and were never concerned with political or economic matters.

The assertion that Baden-Powell was a British spy in Germany has some basis in fact, at least according to B-P's own account. In 1886, while on leave from the Army, the founder of the Boy Scout movement did go to Berlin for several days, and entirely on his own initiative visited a military camp at Spandau, making his way to the rifle range in the hope of seeing the testing of a new machine-gun that he had read about. He heard firing behind a high boarded fence and was squinting through a crack, trying to see what was going on, when a sentry approached. Baden-Powell managed to pour the contents of a brandy flask on his clothes, and by pretending to be drunk he talked his way out of arrest. Later, when he returned to his unit, he was able to make a report on the new German weapon, for although he had not actually seen it, he had at least been able to calculate its rate of fire.

Did the Gestapo know about Baden-Powell's escapade? Probably, for he told the story himself many times. Had he been involved in other espionage activity of which they were aware? If he had been, he never mentioned it. The Gestapo cannot have known in 1940, when they were putting the finishing touches to *Informationsheft G.B.,* that certain ex-Boy Scouts in the British Army were being singled out for very special military duty which would have involved them with the Gestapo if Britain had been occupied.

The Gestapo devoted only a single page of the handbook to British museums and libraries, and the most original fact that was stated was that 'the National Gallery has 4,000 pictures, including quite a few of Jews'. Apparently Amt VI had not discovered that in 1933 the museums of Britain had begun to look around for hiding places for their treasures, partly to protect them against possible bombing, partly to hide them from any enemy troops who might land in Britain. The Ministry of Works had persuaded the owners of several country houses in what were judged to be safe areas to allow their homes to become repositories for the nation's treasures, and the British Museum alone was offered five such houses. The museum chose Broughton House and Drayton House in Northamptonshire and also arranged to have some things hidden in the underground vaults of the National Library of Wales at Aberystwyth and in certain disused Underground tunnels in London. Special collapsible plywood packing cases were prepared, and at seven o'clock on Thursday morning, 24 August 1939, the first packed containers began to leave the British Museum for Wales. By the following Saturday the evacuation of the most important things had been completed. Hundreds of tons of prints, drawings, books, and items of antiquarian and ethnological interest followed. None of the possessions of the British Museum is insured, so there was never a question of first moving those things of greatest sales-room value.

In December 1940, the Ministry of Works began to have second thoughts about the Aberystwyth hiding place. If the Germans occupied Eire, would they not then land in Wales? With this in mind a number of the British Museum's most treasured exhibits were transferred to uninhabited Skipton Castle in Yorkshire, to two stately homes, Northwick Park, Gloucestershire, and Haigh Hall, Lancashire, and to a Tudor house in Warwickshire. At the same time caves in a disused quarry near Bristol, which for some years had been used for the growing of mushrooms, were fitted with air-conditioning units and shelves by the Ministry of Works, so that they too could be used as a hiding place, primarily for treasures from the British Museum and the Victoria and Albert Museum. The precise location of the quarry, which provided altogether some 25,000 square feet of floor space, is still a secret because it could, officials say, be used again for the same purpose.*

Informationsheft G.B. attempts to explain the composition of the British Press, and begins by stating incredulously that British editors do not necessarily hold the political views of the papers they edit, and that British journalists frequently move from a

---

* It was also used as a storage place by the following institutions: Aberdeen University; The Society of Antiquaries; The Athenaeum; The British School at Athens; All Hallows Church, Barking; The Bodleian Library, Oxford; The Fitzwilliam Museum, Cambridge; The Colonial Office; Corpus Christi College, Cambridge; The Egypt Exploration Society; Exeter Cathedral; The Free French Government; The Museum of National Antiquities; Glasgow University; Gloucester Museum; Hereford Cathedral; The Imperial War Museum; Lambeth Palace Library; Litchfield Cathedral; The Guildhall, London; Maidstone Public Library; The National Portrait Gallery; Rochester Cathedral; The Royal Academy; Salisbury Cathedral; Somerset House; Stony-hurst College; University College, London; The Wellcome Medical Museum; Westminster Abbey; Winchester Cathedral. In addition, various objects owned by the Ministry of Works also went into the quarry. Many other museums, churches and art galleries had hiding places of their own which they still prefer not to disclose.

publication of one political colour to one of another. The handbook also expresses amazement at how few different papers there were in the country in 1940—according to their calculation, only one daily for every 150,000 people. Germany, of course, did not have the same sort of national popular Press as Britain, but a multiplicity of local city or regional newspapers.

The Gestapo singled out no particular newspapers in Britain for their special attention, although they of course noted which were Communist and which were Jewish, and they also named some of the directors of newspaper and periodical publishing firms in Britain who were known to be Jews. There is nothing in *Informationsheft G.B.* which suggests that in 1940 it even occurred to the Gestapo that British newspapers might go underground in the event of occupation, nor did the Gestapo handbook point out that *The Times,* at least, had made plans for emergency publication outside London, and that another major paper, the *Manchester Guardian,* had arranged, in the event of total occupation, to continue its existence abroad. Shortly before the war the publisher of *The Baltimore Sun,* Paul Patterson, was made a member of the *Manchester Guardian*'s board of directors. There were, however, no plans or provisions made, as some of the paper's employees today believe, actually to continue publishing in Baltimore if the Manchester plant was overrun by the Germans, but at least the paper's corporate existence would have continued.

The editors of *Informationsheft G.B.* stated that the British Broadcasting Corporation operated along the same lines as the German State Radio, but that the BBC was a public corporation and not a state-owned service. At the same time, they wrote, the Postmaster General 'has a power of life and death' over broadcasting and could censor it at will. They did not say—and to give them their due they probably did not know—what would have happened if ever he tried to exercise that power without some very good reason indeed.

The handbook contains a list of the BBC's regional broadcasting studios, but it says little about the location of the transmitters—and nothing about the transmission arrangements which had been prepared in 1938 and which would undoubtedly have had an important bearing on broadcasting in Britain if a part of the country—but not the entire country—had been occupied.

In 1938 the British Government had set up a committee to look into the problems of broadcasting in wartime, and particularly the problems of domestic broadcasting while enemy aircraft were approaching or were overhead. How could they stop those planes from 'homing' on British radio transmitters without shutting down all broadcasting?

By the time of the Munich Crisis in 1938 a plan for emergency broadcasting had been evolved, and by the beginning of September 1939 equipment for implementing the plan was ready. Low-powered transmitters were dotted all over the country and a number of 'portable' transmitters were mounted on lorries. During an air raid alert instructions would go out to the fixed transmitters —the pre-war ones that the Luftwaffe had pinpointed on their maps of Britain—either to switch off altogether or to reduce power, and broadcasting would then continue on various combinations of the new and old transmitters. Reception on the ground would hardly be affected, but aircraft 'homing' would be impossible. Throughout the war this system operated effectively, and the BBC never helped the Luftwaffe home on to their targets.

If the Germans had invaded Britain, radio would have been the only means of immediate mass communication between whatever was left of free Britain and the people in both the free and occupied areas. Even if the Wehrmacht had secured a beachhead in Britain, weeks would probably have passed before London itself was invaded, and before that happened the British Broadcasting Corporation would have been able to do much more than merely pipe continuous organ music played by Sandy Macpherson. The right words spoken on the radio could have sparked off resistance activity and might—if it was possible to do so—have even rallied some support abroad. Indeed, broadcasting facilities existed in the Government's Horseferry Road underground hideout in London, and Regional Commissioners would have had access to the BBC transmitters in their areas. Yet the possibility of broadcasting being used as a propaganda weapon against the German occupation forces in Britain never apparently occurred to the authors of *Informationsheft G.B.*

After noting a few British organizations, such as Chatham House, interested in studying pan-Germanism and its international consequences, and after listing a few professors and a few colleges in Britain which concerned themselves with Central European politics, *Informationsheft G.B.* deals with religion in Britain. This was an easy enough subject to research, and the Gestapo authors were able to fill several pages with facts—without giving any information that could conceivably be of interest or significance to anybody, least of all to Gestapo men operating in Britain. They concluded that the Anglican Church, because it is a State church, was an 'instrument of power for English imperialistic politics', and that the Oxford Movement was important in sustaining British imperialism around the globe and as a means of drawing together all the different Protestant churches under one leadership.

In its study of Communism in Britain, *Informationsheft G.B.* decided that in 1940 the Communist Party had so little direct political influence that its leaders concentrated almost entirely on 'intellectual propaganda'. The Gestapo researchers singled out several dozen British trade unions as Marxist—among them the National Federation of Building Trade Operatives, the National Society of Packing Case Makers, the Amalgamated Society of Journeymen Felt Hatters, and the Transport and General Workers Union.

Under a separate heading, a few paragraphs on the Communist Party of Eire are the only mention of the Irish Republic in the handbook.

After dealing with organizations of immigrants in Britain—of which the Gestapo had been able to compile an impressive list—the authors of the handbook bravely attempted to explain British Freemasonry, attaching to it sinister motives and making great play of its connection with the Royal Family.

The Gestapo researchers had, of course, spent much time examining the position of Jews in the British society, and their handbook lists Jews who were prominent in every sort of activity, from banking and finance to films, radio and the Press. The handbook's list of Jewish organizations in Britain—or with head-quarters in Britain—was not a long one because these were dealt with at length in the Gestapo Arrest List, the notorious 'Black List'.

The Gestapo had a copy of the Metropolitan Police organizational chart for February 1937. Largely from this chart, copies of which hung in full view in every police station in London, and partly from other sources (the most likely was the *Police Almanac,* a privately printed, unofficial annual which anyone can buy) they were able to put into *Informationsheft G.B.* what appears at a glance to be a full analysis of the British police. They understood—as does every foreign resident in Britain—the arrangements for the registration of aliens by the police. The Gestapo researchers were also very interested in the Special Branch as an organization for the protection of the Royal Family, of important visitors, and of state security generally. Amt VI's British section had somewhere come across the fact—if it was a fact—that as early as 1936 many ordinary British constables were expressing an interest in learning to speak German. And with their usual insatiable appetite for trivia the Gestapo researchers had even taken the trouble to pinpoint the precise locations—the floors as well as the buildings—of various police records.

It seems never to have occurred to the Gestapo that the police of Britain would make any plans against invasion and occupation. Except in Ulster the British police are not normally armed, but at the beginning of the war special orders were given to police all over the United Kingdom for the issue and use of arms in the event of a German invasion. The Metropolitan Police, for example, ordered 25,000 revolvers and half a million rounds of ammunition from the United States in 1940, and when four-fifths of the order was received in 1941, the pistols were quietly distributed to the divisions—but not to individual constables. During the first years of the war about thirty special orders were prepared for the Metropolitan Police concerning action they were to take in the event of invasion, and these orders were distributed to all officers above the rank of inspector. These orders remained in force until 1942, when they were superseded by a comprehensive confidential document entitled 'War Duty Hints', again issued only to the higher ranking officers.

Plans were made for the police to fight the Germans, but the Home Office will not say whether or not policemen would have been under the command of Army officers. In 1941 in London forty-eight-hour supplies of emergency rations were issued to the police. At the chief constable level the police were usually aware of Resistance actions prepared by the Army, but there was a great deal of friction, even at the highest level, when the police discovered that some of their Special Constables were being lured away into the Resistance organization.

The final thirteen pages of *Informationsheft G.B.*—the longest chapter in the book—deal with 'der britische Nachtrichtendienst', the Secret Service and the secret security organizations. Whenever those official agencies in Britain which today possess copies of the handbook show it to anyone, they first wrap these final thirteen pages so that the visitor cannot study them—despite the fact that a microfilm copy of the entire book is elsewhere available to anyone inside or outside Britain who is willing to pay for it, and despite the fact that everything stated in the book was committed to paper in the first place by members of the Gestapo. This unnecessary security clamp makes this chapter seem more important than it actually is.

Where did the researchers of Amt VI's British section get the information that they put into this chapter? Library research no doubt provided much of it, and some came from such sources as the match-seller watching 65 Broadway. But the Gestapo also had in their hands two relatively senior British Intelligence agents, Major Richard H. Stevens and Captain S. Payne Best, both of whose names occur frequently in the final chapter of *Informationsheft G.B.*

Major Stevens, an Intelligence Officer in the Indian Army, had been recalled to England for reassignment in 1937. At the War Office in London he was told that he had been picked for a special job in The Hague; posing as the British Legation's Passport Control Officer he was to run a network of spies in Holland and Germany. He had been selected for this, he was told, because he spoke excellent French, German and Russian. The man he was replacing in Holland had for some reason fallen out with his French opposite number, and British Intelligence hoped that

Stevens, a gentle and affable man, would be able to re-establish cordial relations. There ought to be nothing hazardous about the assignment in The Hague, Stevens was told, but he did not have to accept it if he did not want to. If he preferred, he and his wife would be put on the next boat for India, and nothing further would be said about running the spy ring.

Stevens's first impulse was to turn the job down. He had never before been a spy, much less a spy master, and his intelligence work—mainly the evaluation of military reports on the deployment of armed native tribesmen—had been done on the North-West Frontier. He was accustomed to relaxed, unsophisticated dealings with soldiers and with brother officers he knew he could trust. How would he fit into a world in which nothing was ever straightforward? This—and the fact that assignment to The Hague would mean a drop in allowances of several hundred pounds a year—convinced him that he should ask to be sent back to India. But then he told himself that someone in the War Office must have had good reason for bringing him all the way home to London just to offer him a job that he could turn down out of hand. He felt challenged, and so he agreed to go to The Hague— as long as his superiors realized that he thought himself to be lacking in the experience and training for the assignment and was, in his own eyes, altogether the wrong sort of man for such work.

While he was in London Major Stevens went to 65 Broadway several times, not for training in methods but merely to be briefed on the work he would do in Holland when he was not dealing with the holders of British passports. He was told nothing at that time of another British undercover ring, controlled by an organization identified as 'Z', that had agents working in the same territory as his and which was led by Captain S. Payne Best.

The day before Britain declared war on Germany, Major Stevens received a personal cipher telegram from his chief in London advising him of the existence of the 'Z' group and telling him that if war were declared on Germany—and only then—he was to give Best whatever assistance he asked for and was to arrange to absorb the 'Z' organization into his own. Even when he carried out this order Stevens made a point of learning no more about the details of the 'Z' organization than he had to. This was just as well.

On the afternoon of 9 November 1939, exactly six months before Hitler invaded Holland and just one day after a bomb exploded in the Burgerbräukeller in Munich, where Hitler had just attended a meeting, Stevens, Best and a young Dutch intelligence officer went to the German frontier at Venlo to meet some men they believed were members of an anti-Nazi organization in the Wehrmacht. These German 'Resistance' men were in reality agents of the Gestapo led by Alfred Naujocks, and all of them were heavily armed. In the ensuing scuffle the Dutch officer, fatally wounded, was dragged across the border into Germany with Best and Stevens. This was the famous 'Venlo Incident'.

In the Gestapo's headquarters in Berlin Stevens and Best were separated, and each was bound up with leather straps. Before being interrogated for the first time, Stevens was told by Oberführer Heinrich Müller, the thug known as 'Gestapo Müller', that he would soon be joined by his wife. Stevens realized that this might not be a bluff, for it would certainly be easy enough for Gestapo men in Holland to kidnap his wife. He did not know that as soon as the news of his own abduction had reached the British Legation, his wife had been put on a plane for London.

On 21 November, when Georg Elser, a German carpenter, was accused of having set the time-bomb in the Burgerbräukeller, Heinrich Himmler announced that he had been acting on the orders of Stevens and Best, and the two officers' photographs were given to the German Press. Major Stevens was taken from his cell shortly afterwards and for the first time given clean clothes. He was then led into the Gestapo officers' mess where he was welcomed cordially, offered a drink and a cigar, and a woman he had never seen before was brought in. In reply to a question from one of the Germans she pointed accusingly at Stevens, and he listened in amazement as she insisted to the Gestapo men that she had seen him when he had visited her husband at their flat in Brussels and had given him a suitcase full of explosives and 50,000 Belgian francs.

One of the Gestapo officers, Clemens, then began to question the woman about details of the supposed visit and about the arrangement of the flat, and the woman finally admitted that she had never seen Stevens before. She was taken away, and Stevens was returned to his cell.

[44]

Stevens' confrontation with this woman—who may have been Frau Elser but probably was not—was given no publicity, and after it he heard nothing further about the Burgerbräukeller affair. After the war Allied investigators learned that the Gestapo had rigged the time-bomb incident, promising Elser, who had previously been imprisoned in Dachau as a Communist sympathizer, his freedom afterwards.* Hitler's 'miraculous escape', the Gestapo hoped, would strengthen his following in Germany. The linking of the bomb attempt with the two captured British intelligence officers appears to have been an unsuccessful last-minute improvisation. Stevens afterward said that he thought that he was probably not put on trial because the 'evidence' against him would not have withstood scrutiny, even in a Nazi court.

The separate interrogations of Stevens and Best continued for another fourteen months, during which Stevens wrote many letters to his wife but heard nothing at all from her and had no way of knowing whether or not she got his letters or indeed if she was in the Gestapo's hands. In fact, his letters were never sent out of Germany, and the first attempts by the British authorities to find out anything about him through the International Red Cross came to nothing.

Why had Stevens, Best and the Dutch officer been kidnapped at all? Was it because exposure of the collaboration between British and Dutch Intelligence would give the Germans an excuse for invading Holland? A few months before, the Gestapo officers who did the kidnapping had dressed concentration camp inmates in German military uniforms, taken them to the German–Polish frontier and then had shot them—in order to support Germany's reasons for invading Poland. Or were Stevens and Best kidnapped because the Gestapo hoped that they would yield information that would destroy whatever intelligence networks the British operated inside Germany? Or was there some other, less obvious reason? No matter why, the two officers' interrogations were to provide most of the meat—and the dressing—in the final chapter of *Informationsheft G.B.* This chapter, incidentally, confirms Major Stevens's own account of what he said to the

---

* Instead, Elser was kept in Dachau and was executed by the Gestapo late in the war.

Gestapo interrogators during those months when they grilled him steadily from the time he was awakened in the morning until the time when he was chained to the wall at night and allowed to sleep.

In the beginning Major Stevens was very anxious—less at the possibility that he would be tortured than at the possibility that his wife was in the Gestapo's hands. He knew at the outset that he would have to say something, and very soon after his interrogation began he realized that manipulating his questioners was not going to be very difficult.

They began by asking him to account for his stay in The Hague, and he told them that he had been sent there to run the British intelligence network—a fact that they knew already. Before he had spoken many minutes, his interrogators interrupted to explain that they wanted to know precisely when and where Stevens had arrived in Holland and every detail of everything he had done there. And so a Gestapo stenographer took down the time and the date that the boat brought Stevens and his wife to the Hook of Holland, the fact that they had been allowed to sleep on the ship for several hours after its arrival, the fact that when Stevens had alighted from the ship he had gone to the lavatory. And on and on.

The Gestapo interrogators were so anxious for trivial detail that Stevens had time each night to work out what he was going to tell them the next morning. They made no apparent attempt to conceal from him what they already knew about his espionage activities. One day, after Dr Schombacher, one of the Gestapo officers, had been asking Stevens questions for several hours, he got up, put a file of papers on the table, turned, left the room and locked the door behind him. Stevens assumed that the file had been left behind so that he could read it and he did this. It contained a fairly complete list of his German agents' identity numbers and, in a few cases, the nicknames by which Stevens had known them.

When Schombacher returned he said, 'Now perhaps we can talk a little more openly.'

'If you mean,' Stevens said, 'have I looked in your files?—I have. That I suppose is what you intended me to do?'

'You realize, Major, that it is of vital importance for me to identify these men, and that your life may well depend on the answers you give.'

Stevens had long expected such a threat, and he had rehearsed the answer he would give to it. 'Herr Doktor,' he said, 'I think your list is very accurate—far more so than any I could have made without reference to my safe in The Hague. But I had the strictest orders never, in any circumstances, personally to contact any of my agents. At the time I thought it a bit stupid. But, fortunately, I obeyed it, and now I realize how wise it was.' Major Stevens was telling the truth. And Schombacher must have sensed it, for to Stevens' relief he nodded his head and murmured, 'Na ja—das versteht sich.'

When Stevens was shown photographs taken by the match-seller at the St James's Park Underground station and asked to identify the subject—an academic exercise as far as he was concerned because the names were already pencilled on the backs of the photographs—he did so. He also admitted knowing those members of his organization in Holland who, although the Gestapo did not appear to know it, had been sent to England at the time that Britain went to war.

Exactly how Best fared under questioning is not known, although in his book he insisted that he managed always to be well treated. The Gestapo were never sure whether or not the two officers were telling them the truth, whether they were simply reciting prearranged stories or whether they made up things as they went along. 'One thing however is certain,' *Informationsheft G.B.* noted, 'and that is that their statements were partly susceptible to proof and appeared to contain a large measure of truth. One must not forget that they were very small cogs in the machine. . . .'

Stevens and Best were never allowed to meet during those months when they were being interrogated, and so could never compare notes. According to their own accounts, each was told by the Gestapo that Admiral Sinclair was Chief of British Intelligence, and each agreed that he was—although both men knew that Sinclair had recently died. And so *Informationsheft G.B.* lists Sinclair and not Sir Stewart Menzies as the British Intelligence Chief. Both Stevens and Best tried to explain to the Gestapo why there was no such thing as a comprehensive British intelligence service—'no real secret service as we understand the term in

Germany.' Stevens never learned how much of the information with which the Gestapo confronted him came from Best.

The Gestapo had somehow decided what were the main divisions of British Intelligence, and they got the names of the heads of most of the sections right, although the spellings were often wrong, as in the case of Sir Stewart Menzies, whose Christian name they spelled 'Stuart'. The identity of Menzies, supposedly the 'M' in the James Bond stories, was kept secret in Britain for at least twenty years after the publication of *Informationsheft G.B.*

Possibly because Stevens and Best themselves did not know, the Gestapo were never sure whether or not the organization which employed the two officers was the central organ of British Intelligence or merely a satellite. Neither officer knew anything about the sub-sections of British Intelligence, and in *Informationsheft G.B.* there was no mention either of the organization known as 'D', of 'GS(R)' or 'MI(R)', organizations which would have created special problems for the Gestapo in occupied Britain. The Gestapo were confused by the fact that both Stevens and Best worked for a military intelligence organization that did not confine itself to the discovery and transmission of military information, but they were able to work out without help from Stevens, at least, that the head of 'Z', the organization that later became known as MI6, was an Army officer whose name never appeared in the Army Lists, Colonel Sir Claude Dansey. When Major Stevens admitted to his questioners that he knew no more about the members of his network of spies than he absolutely had to, and that he contacted them through 'cut-outs' and 'letter boxes', the Gestapo were mystified and put down this method of operation—which is the great strength of British Intelligence—as its greatest weakness.

The authors of *Informationsheft G.B.* attempted to size up Stevens and Best as men. Best, they pointed out, was not a professional soldier like Stevens, but he had had a lot of Intelligence experience in the First World War 'and looked at things with a far sharper eye'. They described him as a man 'devoid of scruples, a private individual whose main concern was to live well and make good business', and thought that perhaps he was in a better position than Stevens to see the futility of their situation.

Again and again Stevens was asked by his inquisitors to explain

British Intelligence procedures about which he knew nothing. Even though he said this, the Gestapo officers demanded that he state his opinion about these procedures. Whatever he said was then taken down in full, typed, and he was asked to sign the copies. After the war, when he was being 'de-briefed' by British Intelligence and was shown copies of his Gestapo interrogations, he was shown a signed document that contained material about which he had known nothing. He was then able to recall a day when an exceptionally large pile of typescripts had been thrust at him and he was told not to waste time reading them before signing them. What the Gestapo did not know and could not find out they had, in this instance at least, made up.

Stevens and Best remained toys of the Gestapo for some time. Major Stevens was not allowed to listen to the radio or to see a newspaper until the day one of his warders thrust a pile of back copies of *Völkischer Beobachter* into his cell and barked, 'Now you can read how your country lost the war'. The latest editions of the paper contained the story of Dunkirk. And when, some weeks later, France capitulated, Stevens was taken from his cell and allowed to hear Hitler's broadcast, offering peace terms. When the warders asked Stevens what he thought of the speech and he said that he doubted that it would be taken seriously in Britain, he was hurried back to his cell and chained up again.

At the beginning of September 1940, when the Germans were about to launch 'Operation Sea Lion', Dr Schombacher visited Stevens in his cell to tell him that he was going to be taken to England as an adviser as soon as the German Army had established itself in Britain. Stevens later said that he replied 'that while I could not prevent him from taking me with him, he'd find me a broken reed as an adviser'.

Payne Best was kept in Sachsenhausen concentration camp, near Berlin, until very late in the war, but when the Gestapo tired of questioning Major Stevens he was transferred from that camp to Dachau where he spent most of his captivity with Pastor Niemöller and other special prisoners. After the war Stevens held an administrative post with NATO and then worked as a translator of books until his death in February 1967. In both publishing and military circles he was liked and respected. He never acquired that coldness of personality that makes a good spy master.

Informationsheft G.B. does not mention the hoard of gold which was still in Britain at the time that the finishing touches were being put to the handbook. In June 1940, Churchill called a secret session of the Cabinet to discuss what to do with the nation's stores of gold and securities. They not only had to be protected both from possible invasion and occupation but also from destruction by bombing.

Regional collection centres were designated, and in a ten-day period all sizeable stores of gold in the country and virtually all securities were brought together. The first part of what was to be the greatest transatlantic shipment of valuables of all time left Greenock on H.M.S. *Emerald* on 24 June. Six days later, after a rough crossing, the destroyer ploughed into Halifax, Nova Scotia, at a brisk 28 knots, and the cargo was off-loaded on to a special train at the quayside.

During the next three months, sometimes in ships of the Royal Navy, sometimes in chartered fast passenger liners, the export of Britain's tangible wealth continued. The final destination of the gold and share certificates was a 60-foot-square, 11-foot-high vault three storeys underground, beneath the Montreal office block of the Sun Life Assurance Company of Canada. The vault—constructed of two miles of disused railway tracks, the only steel available at short notice—was equipped with microphones so sensitive that they would pick up the sound of the sliding open of any one of the more-than-three-thousand filing cabinet drawers that contained the securities. The vault could only be entered by opening a combination lock, of which half was known by one banker, half by another. The value of the contents of what was officially known as the 'United Kingdom Security Deposit' was pegged at £1,800 million. The bill for their transport from Halifax under special guard, according to a timetable that allowed for unloading and movement across Montreal in the early hours of the morning alone totalled a million dollars.

Throughout the war two dozen members of the Royal Canadian Mounted Police lived, ate, slept and stood guard in the building. The securities were filed away and coupons were clipped by a team of 120 retired Canadian bankers, brokers and investment men who were sworn to secrecy. Not a speck of gold or a single document was lost—although when the first things were put in the building a freak thunderstorm unexpectedly flooded the basement. Fortunately the seepage of water was discovered just before it began to turn to unrecognizable mush the crates of securities which luckily had been put on trestles two feet above floor level.

An account of this movement of valuables which was published in *Reader's Digest* in 1955 is, according to a Bank of England official, 'reasonably accurate'. However, the magazine stated that the gold and securities were being moved to Canada so that if the Germans occupied Britain, a British Government in exile would have had funds available. Yet everyone who was in the Government in 1940 insists that there were no plans for an *en masse* evacuation of the Government to Canada, that a British Government in exile would have served no purpose. The Continental governments in exile in Britain owed their existence to the fact that Britain was still in the war. But the occupation of the British Isles would have meant the end of the war in the West and the withering of the last vestiges of those exiled Continental governments. During the period when invasion and occupation threatened Britain, the United States was simply not in a position to step into the breach, even if President Roosevelt had been able to persuade Americans that it was worth taking the necessary risks.

The British gold and the securities were not moved to Canada just to keep them from being lost in an air raid or from falling into German hands, but because they had to be accessible for the purchase of arms and other war material for Britain in the United States. At the time, American law decreed that all such purchases had to be paid for on the spot. Britain was standing very much alone, and there was not yet a Lease-Lend arrangement to help out.

In taking the decision to risk sending overseas so much of the national wealth, U-boats notwithstanding, the British may well have displayed greater caution than those countries which the Germans occupied. Norway, France and Poland all faced the same problem, but they did not move quickly enough, and the bulk of their gold holdings had to be snatched from under the Germans' noses. The Polish gold was smuggled out by Polish Army officers who returned to occupied Warsaw for that purpose, and the French Navy managed to get France's gold out. The Norwegians sent theirs out by several routes—in one instance getting small children each to load one box containing one gold bar on to a sledge in order to smuggle it past Nazi sentries and on to a small freighter lying at a berth in a northern fjord. Loading the ship in this way is said to have taken six weeks. The gold was eventually landed safely at Baltimore—and it is still kept in an American bank by the Norwegians.

Amt VI researchers also failed to take note of the existence of another British 'gold mine'—Lloyd's of London. The insurance corporation was urged by worried overseas customers to do something about the possibility of invasion and occupation even before the war began.

In the spring of 1939 Lloyd's American customers became edgy; if the company's dollars were seized by the British Government to spend on American arms, they asked, how would Lloyd's meet their American insurance claims? Lloyd's considered making an official approach to the Government, asking for a firm assurance that the company's dollars would under no circumstances be touched, but they decided in the end not to do this because they realized that even this assurance might not satisfy their American customers, especially if the United States did not repeal its 'cash and carry' law governing arms sales. The only alternative was to set up a new Lloyd's office in America to hold all dollar premiums so that this money could then be used to meet American claims. Before the actual outbreak of war 'Lloyd's American Trust' was a going concern.

This did not, however, solve the problem posed by the possibility of occupation. After the outbreak of war Lloyd's went on issuing cover notes and drawing up policies in London, and the American ship owners and indeed the American authorities did not like the idea of their ships, factories—and even the movement of their nation's population—being detailed in documents which, if the Germans occupied Britain, would fall into their hands. By the time that this worry had been expressed—in 1942—even Lloyd's would have given good odds against a German invasion. But to re-assure the Americans—and to hang on to business which once lost might never be regained—Lloyd's took what for them was an unprecedented step. They sent their chairman, Sir Eustace Pulbrook, to Washington to make a deal. This was the first time in 102 years that a chairman of Lloyd's had gone abroad on Lloyd's business.

The Americans were adamant. They simply would not believe that their secrets could be kept safely in a country so near Nazi-occupied territory, nor would they believe that, even at that late date, Britain was unlikely to be invaded. Lloyd's underwriters stood their ground just as stubbornly, for only a fool would insure a ship or building or anything else about which he knew nothing. Sir Eustace persisted, and eventually he hit on a series of compromises that made everybody happy. In effect, Lloyd's of London became for the duration of the war—in everything except name— 'Lloyd's of London and New York'.

From 1942 until the end of the war, whenever an American insurance broker ordered insurance from Lloyd's he sent full details of whatever was to be insured to the firm's New York office, run by men sent over from London for the purpose of screening applications. In conjunction with the American authorities those men would then cable to London any non-classified information to do with the policy, and the rest—and most vital— information would be filed in the New York office. The London broker, unaware of what he was actually insuring but relying impiicitly on Lloyd's New York men, would then issue a cover note which would eventually be matched up with the information in the New York office. If the Germans had occupied Britain and had ransacked Lloyd's files of American business, all they would have found would have been meaningless lists of cover-note numbers. And so Lloyd's still insures the world.

A few days after the start of the war the author Dennis Wheatley was telephoned by one of his closest friends, who was a member of a secret Government Department. 'Dennis, what do you know about a chap called William Joyce?'

'William Joyce? I don't know anything about William Joyce.'

'Oh yes you do,' his friend insisted.

'Oh no, if I knew anything, I'd tell you. I've never heard of him.'

'Well, he came to one of your parties.'

'Honestly, I don't remember the man. He must have been brought by somebody.'

Later, when Wheatley asked his wife if she could remember anybody named Joyce, she reminded him of a conversation at a party they had given for about a hundred people in their house in St John's Wood about six months earlier, on the publication of one of his books. A small man with a scar on his face—a man Wheatley had never seen before—had asked him if he knew Germany. Wheatley had replied that he did, that he had lived there for a year before the First World War, when he was working in his father's wholesale wine business. The stranger, who had had a great deal to drink, had then urged Wheatley to return to Germany where he personally would put him in touch with all the top Nazis. He knew for a fact that Hermann Göring had read all Wheatley's books.

Wheatley telephoned his friend, told him about his brief conversation with the scar-faced man and added that he had never seen him again. 'Well,' his friend explained, 'why I asked you was because we know all about him, and we went to get him immediately the war was declared. But he'd got out. We got all his papers and all his card indexes, and in them you're noted to be proposed as "Gauleiter for North London"—with the qualification that you may not be quite suitable because you're not entirely clean on the Jewish question. You have Jewish friends.'

William Joyce was very soon to attain fame in Britain as 'Lord Haw-Haw'. It would be interesting to look into those files of his—and more interesting still to know if anybody in Berlin was prepared to take his recommendations seriously. No doubt if the Germans had occupied Britain, they would have employed any Quislings who offered their services. But neither German nor British official historians claim knowledge of a formal list of potential British collaborators, and the Gestapo men who would have accompanied the 'Sea Lion' invaders deny that they were provided with such a list. Some of the Gestapo's lesser fry—such dubious characters as Walter zu Christian—have been quoted as saying that they did not have to compile a list of potential British traitors because the British had done their work for them by interning all such people on the Isle of Wight.* If, however, the

---

* He meant the Isle of Man, where on the outbreak of war, under Emergency Regulation 18b, many 'enemy' nationals were arbitrarily taken and detained. Subsequently many were released and joined the Allied military and civil forces.

Gestapo knew anything about British internment camps in 1940, they did not comment on it in *Informationsheft G.B.* And so the existence of a Nazi 'White List' remains an open question.

On the other hand, we do know that there was a 'Black List' because some copies of it have survived the war. Officially titled *Sonderfahndungsliste G.B.* ('Arrest List G.B.'), this document is believed to have been published by the Gestapo in July 1940. Questioned about it at Nürnberg, von Ribbentrop said that the list had been compiled from material collected by German agents between 1937 and 1940. Walter zu Christian has claimed sole authorship of the list, and he may have been the person who brought all the names together.

At least one original copy of the list exists in Britain, and a number of serious reference libraries have photographically reproduced copies. Like *Informationsheft G.B.*, the arrest list is available on microfilm to anyone willing to pay for it. Because the list of individuals' names has never before been published in full, a cloud of mystery hangs over it. The pages listing the names of individuals appear at the end of this volume in Appendix E, page 167.

The entire *Sonderfahndungsliste G.B.* ran to 350 pages, but these included a number of ruled blank pages on which extra names could be written, as well as a list of 171 large and small commercial firms in which the Gestapo were interested, 389 addresses of trade union offices, of political, religious and social organizations which had attracted the Gestapo's notice, and finally a town-by-town cross-index which would have saved Gestapo men in the field the trouble of searching through the entire book to find addresses in their areas. The researchers of Amt VI were shaky on British geography, and as a result the cross-index sometimes places people or organizations in counties instead of precise towns. All sorts of carelessness can also be seen in the list of individuals' names; often Christian names and addresses were omitted, so that it would have been impossible to catch some individuals without interrogating hundreds—and in some cases thousands—of people who were of no interest to the Gestapo. The list of names seems a little less haphazard when a key has been provided, as has been done in the Appendix, explaining which departments of the RSHA wanted to interview which people.

The reader needs no help in forming his own conclusions about the Arrest List, but several things should perhaps be pointed out. First, this is an arrest list and not a liquidation list. Second, a number of people believed to be contacts of Best and Stevens (among them both officers' wives) were included, as well as people the Gestapo believed were members of other British espionage rings.

A number of Britons whose names are on the list have taken the trouble to get photographs of the pages on which their names appear, and to have them framed. Either because they do not realize (or are confident that their friends will not realize) that the list was compiled alphabetically, these people usually assume that the number next to their name indicates just how high on the list they were. Other people who perhaps have never seen the actual list but have been told that they are on it, tend to assign to themselves high places. Countless Britons maintain that they were Hitler's 'seventh most wanted person in the United Kingdom'.

Many of the people named were not even British subjects—such as the scattering of Americans, from John Gunther to Paul Robeson. A few had died long before the document was published, among them Dr Sigmund Freud, whose death in 1939 had received world-wide notice.

None of the listed people could have been sure in 1940 that they had been singled out for special Gestapo attention, but a number of them guessed that they had been, and a few even made plans in anticipation of German occupation. David Low, the cartoonist, wrote sheepishly in his autobiography of the time when he buried a number of his original drawings in his garden and also took the precaution of secreting a sum of money where he could get at it if he was living in hiding from the Germans. He pointed out that his own personal action was not so extreme, that he knew a Member of Parliament who, in anticipation of German occupation, had gone to the trouble of creating a completely new identity for himself in the Midlands. Low did not say how this was done or who the M.P. was. Sir Victor Gollancz, the publisher, was on the Arrest List. His publications before the war included a number of anti-Nazi books and he was active in various left-wing organizations and was one of those who insisted for years afterwards that 'I was very high on Hitler's list for people to be dealt with in

England (I think, as a matter of fact, I was number seven, out of about 2,000)'. During the week in 1940 when invasion seemed most likely, he carried a lethal opium pill which had been provided for him by his physician because 'I didn't think I could stand torture'. He also made arrangements in the event of occupation to have his younger children enrolled in schools outside London under assumed names.

Some years ago the magazine *John Bull* published an article about the Arrest List and suggested to readers that they should go to the Imperial War Museum, where a copy is kept, to see if their names appear on it. For many weeks afterwards the Museum's library received a constant flow of visitors, all demanding to see the Arrest List. So many called that the Museum had to set up a system whereby the caller's name was checked against the list and only those who appeared on it were allowed to inspect the document.

5

'BRING A KNIFE, FORK, SPOON, CUP AND PLATE'

THE Germans' behaviour had they occupied Britain would have been influenced more than anything else by the resistance that they did or did not encounter. In the unlikely event of the civilian population giving in to them without a murmur, then conceivably the Germans might have ruled Britain benevolently—despite the harsh wording of the regulations that they had drafted for the occupation and perhaps even despite the fact that Dr Six and his forty Gestapo officers would have accompanied the fighting troops. But the Germans stated repeatedly and in no uncertain terms in their orders for the occupation of Britain that any resistance was to be countered with the utmost severity.

Would the British as a whole have resisted? In June 1940, notices were posted all over the Isle of Wight which stated succinctly the 'Stand Firm policy' which was to be followed there and on mainland Britain as well:

The . . . policy does not mean that the civil population are expected to adopt a purely passive role. On the contrary, the Government has always expected that the people of these islands will offer a united opposition to an invader and that every citizen will regard it as his duty to hinder and frustrate the enemy and help our own forces by every means that ingenuity can devise and common sense suggest.

Field-Marshal Ironside, the Commander-in-Chief Home Forces, had noticed in Intelligence reports sent over from France in 1940 that ordinary Frenchmen got in the way of their own army when the Germans invaded. Therefore he had decided that the British public must be encouraged to stay indoors as long as fighting went on around them. His *Stand Fast* leaflet which was distributed nationally in June 1940, assured Britons that German troops moving across the country would not stop to attack a single house, but if possible families should make certain precautions beforehand for their safety. Slit trenches in gardens, the leaflet suggested, would be the safest places to hide (the Women's Institutes, which published earnest leaflets urging every housewife to build a field kitchen of old bricks, sheets of tin and an old stovepipe in her back garden, also produced detailed drawings showing how to buttress slit trenches). People who remained calm and clear-headed when the Germans appeared, Ironside's leaflet said, would be able to distinguish between genuine Britons and Germans disguised as British police constables, troops or perhaps as ARP wardens.

Also because of the experience of the French, Ironside's leaflet reminded the British people not to hoard food in anticipation of occupation. It told them that during the actual invasion they should neither believe nor spread rumours; news would somehow be broadcast to them on the wireless and somehow they might even continue to get their newspapers. The most useful thing that ordinary Britons could do, the leaflet explained, was to keep out of the way and at the same time keep an eye on the Germans so that they would be able to report to the British authorities—police or military—everything that the Germans did. The leaflet did not say how this was to be done, but it did suggest how such reports were to have been worded:

At five thirty p.m. tonight I saw 20 cyclists come into Little Squash-borough from the direction of Great Mudtown. They carried some sort of automatic rifle or gun. I did not see anything like artillery. They were in grey uniforms.

The leaflet then went on more strongly—and in capital letters:

DO NOT GIVE ANY GERMAN ANYTHING. DO NOT TELL HIM ANYTHING. HIDE YOUR FOOD AND YOUR BICYCLES. HIDE YOUR MAPS. SEE THAT THE ENEMY GETS NO PETROL. IF YOU HAVE A CAR OR A MOTOR BICYCLE, PUT IT OUT OF ACTION WHEN NOT IN USE. IT IS NOT ENOUGH TO REMOVE THE IGNITION KEY; YOU MUST MAKE IT USELESS TO ANYONE EXCEPT YOUR-SELF. . . .

Subsequent leaflets were to explain how to puncture the petrol tanks of cars and how to immobilize bicycles—by removing all the vital nuts and bolts and hiding them.

The *Stand Fast* leaflets did not encourage foolhardiness:

... Needless to say ... civilians should not set out to make independent attacks on military formations. Such a course of action would be
futile, and, worse still, might actually impede the operation of our own
forces. The civilian must obviously do nothing which would be of the
slightest help to the enemy, but on the contrary hinder and frustrate
him, and if his help is asked by the [British] military, as it may well be,
it is his duty to answer wholeheartedly any call, however exacting,
that may be made upon him.

In fact, once a state of martial law existed in Britain, any soldier
could legally have ordered any civilian to do anything.

Many *Stand Fast* leaflets were issued. The first ones had these
words boldly printed at the end:

THINK BEFORE YOU ACT. BUT ALWAYS THINK OF YOUR COUNTRY BEFORE
YOU THINK OF YOURSELF.

Incredibly, not until May 1941, almost a year after the publication of the leaflet and almost a year after the formation of the
Home Guard, were the Parish Invasion Committees formed in all
rural areas at the instigation of Herbert Morrison's Ministry of
Home Security. Just as incredibly, although each committee was
required to draw up all sorts of secret contingency plans—such as
those for the evacuation of people from areas where fiercest fighting was likely to take place—no attempt was made to keep the
existence of the committees themselves a secret. Their urban
counterparts, invasion committees run by individual urban
councils, were very secret indeed. The parish committees' war
plans contained precise inventories of all things available that were
likely to be of use to the community if invasion and occupation
occurred—inventories of horses, carts, handcarts, trailers, wheel-
barrows, crowbars, spades, shovels, picks, ladders, buckets,
blankets, rugs, sheets, pillows, hot water bottles, mattresses, oil
stoves for cooking, kettles and paraffin lamps.

All over Britain plans were earnestly drawn up for local action
in the event of invasion. These plans were revised many times.
On 30 October 1942 the Invasion Defence Officer of the Waltham
Holy Cross Civil Defence Service, Waltham Abbey, Essex, wrote
to the Nazeing, Essex, Parish Invasion Committee in a letter
headed *Secret*:

... At the meeting of the 10th September we discussed the probability of evacuation of a portion of the Nazeing population owing to their isolation by anti-tank lines, and it was generally agreed (subject always, of course, to military situations) that the best method and route would probably be by walking from Bumbles Green along the Green Lane to the top of Galley Hill Green, thence to Aimes Green and via Galley Hill Road to Waltham Abbey. With this in view I have already provided for a reception post at Aimes Green, where I have erected an emergency cooking stove at the White Cottage (Mrs Maloney) where also I am providing for an iron ration of tea, sugar, and milk for about 300 people for a passing drink whilst resting. Also I am making arrangements for a certain amount of first-aid requisites to be lodged there. I have it in mind to provide from that point, transportation by car if at all possible.

In this connection there is a small point of very considerable importance which I would like you to take up, and that is to make sure arrangements that people to be evacuated should not fail each to bring a knife, fork, spoon, cup and plate. In the present supply position, this is a matter of first importance. ...

The Invasion Committees, parish and urban, were essentially passive, but each one received secret instructions from the Ministry of Home Security to support any organized Resistance activity occurring in its area during the period of German occupation. This, of course, was precisely the sort of activity which would have hardened the conduct of the Germans. How organized would the Resistance have been?

6

THE MEN FROM MI(R)

ALONE among the countries that opposed Germany in the Second World War, Britain had a complete Resistance organization—trained, armed and waiting more or less patiently for German invaders to arrive. This underground movement had grown rapidly in strength and by September 1940, long before the first threat of invasion had passed, it claimed an efficiency unparalleled at any time during the war by Britain's more conventional fighting units. This organization, one of Britain's best-kept secrets, had been conceived in one of those unpublicized military sections about which the Gestapo—if *Informationsheft G.B.* is anything to go by—knew nothing.

In 1938 a major in the Royal Engineers, Laurence Grand, a tall, slender officer whose uniform was usually a well-cut lounge suit with a scarlet carnation in the lapel, set up a secret department in the Foreign Office known as 'Section D'. Its purpose, according to an official paper, was 'To investigate every possibility of attacking potential enemies by means other than the operations of military forces'. Before the war Section D kept in close touch with a small department in the War Office known as 'GS(R)'—General Staff (Research)—which was headed by another major in the Royal Engineers, John Charles Francis Holland, who, among other things, had been a flier in the Near East in the last two years of the First World War and had spent some time in Ireland during the 'Troubles'. Holland is said to have been allowed to develop GS(R) because ill-health made it impossible for him to do any other more active job; he was supposedly told that he could follow whatever lines of research he chose. His experience in Ireland together with his studies of the way in which Boer forces had pinned down British units ten times their own size, and more recent reports that he had read about irregulars fighting in such places as China and Spain, made him decide to look further into problems of the mobility, weapons and tactics of guerrillas.

Like Laurence Grand, Holland was given neither the authority nor the funds before the war with which to produce very much

[62]

more than written reports and suggestions, but he at least managed to start several subsections of GS(R), one of which allowed yet another Royal Engineer major, Millis Rowland Jefferis, to work on the development of special weapons that would be particularly useful to guerrillas, among them the 'sticky bomb', an armour-piercing grenade covered with a tacky substance which was supposed to make it adhere to tanks, and the 'Blacker bombard', a light-weight anti-tank mortar. In the spring of 1939 GS(R) was transferred to the Military Intelligence Directorate, and at the same time was re-named 'MI(R)'—Military Intelligence (Research).

With Holland in MI(R) was Major Colin McVean Gubbins, a small, bristling, 43-year-old Scot. Major Gubbins had served with distinction in the First World War and had observed Russian guerrillas in action around Archangel when he was with the British troops sent there at the end of the war to 'protect' the equipment sent to the Tsarists to use against the Germans. Later he had been in Ireland with Major Holland, and he had also spent some time in the Polish section of the Military Intelligence Directorate (officers there nicknamed him 'Gubbski'). Colin Gubbins's first task for MI(R) was the writing of three booklets, *Partisan Leader's Handbook, The Art of Guerrilla Warfare,* and *How to Use High Explosives,* which were to become the fundamental training manuals for virtually all the free world's clandestine warriors in the Second World War.

During the summer of 1939, before the war started, when MI(R) was still officially no more than a research organization, Gubbins began to hold private classes for a few very carefully selected British civilians—explorers, mountaineers, linguists and international businessmen—whom he had already earmarked as the cadre of some of the fighting units that he and Holland hoped MI(R) would be able to put in the field in the event of war.

Also before the war began, Gubbins made two secret air trips to the Continent for MI(R), the first to the Danube and the second to the Baltic, to look into the possibility of organizing anti-Nazi guerrillas in those areas. He then left London for Warsaw on 25 August 1939, to take up the post of Chief of Staff to the British Military Mission to the Polish Army, a Mission which was headed by that most colourful of officers, General Sir Adrian Carton de

Wiart, V.C.* Gubbins's specific job with the Mission was to get the Poles and Czechs to organize some form of guerrilla warfare if the Germans invaded their countries, but he barely had time to get started, for on 1 September the Germans marched into Poland, and several nights later the members of the British Military Mission were told to escort their embassy's staff out of Warsaw. They eventually reached Romania where Gubbins was singled out and given a false passport which enabled him to get home.

He then headed a Military Mission to those units of the Polish Army that were re-grouping in France. As before, he dealt with all military matters but concentrated on encouraging subversive activity that he hoped would eventually be carried on behind the enemy lines in Poland itself. By then a lieutenant-colonel, he was recalled from France in April 1940 in order to take to Norway five of the ten newly formed 'Independent Companies'. These units, yet more brain children of MI(R), were all composed of volunteers taken from Territorial Army units and given special training to enable them to fight and to exist independently of the rest of the army. Gubbins's five units were intended—though not in the event employed—to move up and down the Norwegian coast in fishing trawlers, making hit-and-run attacks on the Wehrmacht's over-extended communications lines between Oslo and Narvik.

While Gubbins was fighting in Norway, Whitehall, anxious about the possibility of a German invasion of Britain, had decided that a British guerrilla force must be ready to go on fighting the Germans after they had occupied the country. Instead of giving the task of creating such a resistance organization to MI(R), the men of Laurence Grand's Section D were told to do something about it. A full account of what was or was not done will probably never be published, for the few people who were inside the Military Intelligence Directorate and who might be able to tell the story prefer not to. They point out that, in all fairness, Laurence Grand himself had much more to do at this time than he could possibly have been expected to cope with, and that it is therefore hardly his fault that subordinates who had been wished on him produced

* This remarkable officer's adventures have been recounted by him in his autobiography, *Happy Odyssey*.

a very strange and very ineffectual resistance organization indeed.

Grand's men scattered dumps of explosives and other stores willy-nilly around Britain—apparently in the vague hope that they would be used by 'stay behind parties' to destroy the enemy. But they formed no 'stay behind parties'. No one was ever given any training at all in the techniques of sabotage. No one in Section D seems even to have thought of co-ordinating the activities of this embryonic resistance organization with the police or with the armed services—or with anybody else. One Section D emissary in pin-striped trousers and dark coat turned up in a Scottish village and asked the bewildered postmaster, whom he had never seen before, to hold a store of explosives for him. Not surprisingly the man from Section D was immediately arrested by the village constable. In another village in Scotland, Section D explosives were stored in the home of an old woman. Weeks later, when the organization was being disbanded, a Captain Eustace Maxwell who was sent to the old woman's home to collect the explosives was scolded angrily by her: 'Lord —— never was so foolish as to call here in the daytime! People would have noticed! He always turned up at two o'clock in the morning.'

'*And woke up the whole damned village!*' Maxwell exploded.

'Y-e-s,' the old woman reluctantly admitted. 'Yes, he probably did that.'

Some Army officers who came into contact with Section D's abortive resistance organization understood that its individual members were each given cyanide capsules—although no one was ever quite sure whether they were to use them themselves or try to get the Germans to swallow them.

When Colin Gubbins returned to Britain with some of the forces withdrawn from Narvik he was told that his Independent Companies were to be formed into larger units which were to be called 'Commandos'—two Independent Companies to one Commando—but that he was not to take command of them himself. Instead he was to begin work at once on the creation of an underground army that would operate in the United Kingdom in the event of German invasion and occupation of all or of a part of the country.

Colonel Gubbins knew that little direct material help could be given to him in this enterprise by MI(R), for although that organization had been expanding in size very rapidly since the outbreak of war, it had been widening its scope of activities even more rapidly; one new MI(R) section was devising gadgetry such as the R.A.F. trouser buttons that could be turned into compasses to help airmen escaping from prisoner-of-war camps; another was inventing codenames for military operations; yet another was dealing with specialized security problems; and so on. One section, 'Phantom Reconnaissance', had gone to war; during the retreat across France the men of Phantom Reconnaissance had travelled the other way, reporting the precise positions of German units to the commanders of the retreating British forces. MI(R) was too greatly extended to add British Resistance to its other activities.

Since in any case his new organization would have to be created under the aegis of GHQ Home Forces, Gubbins went directly to the Commander-in-Chief, Field-Marshal Ironside, whom he had served as aide-de-camp in Archangel in 1919. 'Tiny' Ironside promised him whatever men and supplies he asked for, but told him that he wanted to see a private and confidential progress report each week. There was to be only one other copy of that report—for Winston Churchill, who had expressed a great personal interest in the setting up of a fighting last-ditch organization in Britain.

In order to exist, every British military unit must have some formal designation, so Colin Gubbins decided that his new secret organization should have an indeterminate name that would 'cover a multitude of possible lines of action and wouldn't create too much suspicion'. The purposely vague name that he chose was 'Auxiliary Units', a name that he knew had been used elsewhere in the Army in the past, but one which had no association of any sort.

Although many people in Britain at that time believed that the Germans might try to invade from the air, Intelligence reports indicated that this was impossible, since Hitler had neither the aircraft nor the trained airborne troops for such an operation. Therefore the Germans would have to come by sea. Gubbins knew that the invaders would be most vulnerable during the first days after they landed, so he planned to concentrate his Resistance units in a coastal strip no more than thirty miles deep. All information being gathered at the time suggested that the Germans would invade somewhere between Yarmouth in Norfolk and Southampton in Hampshire, a coastal stretch—excluding the Thames Estuary—of some 300 miles, but Gubbins decided that his forces would have to cover a much longer strip. His Resistance cells would be set up in coastal districts from Pembrokeshire in southwest Wales, right round the British coast—through Land's End, Dover, John o' Groats—to Dumfriesshire at the western end of the English–Scottish border. Gubbins reasoned that any landing along the Irish Sea coast was beyond the capabilities of the Germans.

From his office, a room in 7 Whitehall Place, a small building near the War Office, Gubbins asked for the help of a dozen officers. Some of them had served with him in Poland and Norway, 'had initiative and understanding and could get on with things', and like himself had had active and unusual careers. To begin with, he decided to divide the coastal area to be covered into a dozen sectors and to assign one officer to each sector. For want of a better designation, these officers would be known as 'Intelligence Officers', although they were not going to have an Intelligence function. Their task was to create Resistance cells in their sectors, each composed of about half a dozen local men.

It was essential that the Resistance be run somewhat along Service lines so that its activities could when necessary be co-ordinated with those of the regular fighting forces, so Gubbins had asked Field-Marshal Ironside for the authority to go into regimental depots around the country to select any junior officers, NCOs and other ranks he wanted as the Auxiliary Units training cadre. Not surprisingly, Colonel Gubbins and his Intelligence Officers very soon began to encounter some hostility from regimental commanders up and down the coasts, for the best soldiers for Auxiliary Units were invariably those men the commanders wanted least to have taken away from them—men who had been keen Boy Scouts and campers, wildfowlers, gamekeepers, men who had done lots of hiking and mountaineering, men who had initiative, who liked working independently, who could find their way around the country. These men were not supposed to lead the British Resistance but would train it. They would be formed into scout patrols, one to be assigned to each Intelligence Officer.

While he was assembling this military cadre Gubbins was also recruiting civilians for the individual Auxiliary Units patrols, and he told his Intelligence Officers to be on the look out for men 'who know the forests, the woods, the mines, the old closed shafts, the hills, the moors, the glens—people who know their local stuff'. For reasons that will become apparent, only men could be brought into the Resistance at this stage. The women were to come into it much later.

Because all the recruiting would have to be done under conditions of absolute secrecy, Gubbins decided that the best and quickest way to pinpoint the most likely men was through the Local Defence Volunteers—soon to be known as the Home Guard —but without letting anyone in the lower echelons of that organization know what he was doing. To make arrangements to take men from the Home Guard he personally called on all Army corps and divisional commanders—but never the commanders of lower headquarters—in the areas where he planned to establish Auxiliary Units patrols. He explained to them only as much of his plans as he absolutely had to, politely told them that he had the authority to take any men he wished, whether the commander objected or not, and he then asked the commanders to suggest which men he should approach. Although he had the authority to get deferments from military service for any civilians he needed, he preferred whenever possible to recruit veterans of active service in the First World War, for such men would need less training.

A few of the men who had been in Section D's resistance set-up were asked to join the Auxiliary Units organization, but most were politely thanked for what they had been prepared to do for the nation and told simply that their organization no longer existed.

The senior Home Guard officers who had been approached were now beginning to put forward the names of likely recruits. Angry local Home Guard leaders found themselves powerless to keep some of their very best men. In a few cases, almost certainly as a result of administrative error, some of the Home Guard commanders were not officially notified that the men Gubbins wanted were being dropped from their rolls, and so a few of the men who

[68]

slipped off into Auxiliary Units patrols were threatened with court martial for not turning out for local Home Guard drills or, in some instances, for refusing to hand in their arms and uniforms when apparently leaving the Home Guard.

Colonel Gubbins and his officers found the men they were looking for—poachers and gamekeepers, fishing and shooting ghillies, stalkers, Verderers in the New Forest, farmers and farm labourers, tin miners and coal miners, market gardeners and fishermen. In some areas they recruited parsons, physicians and local council officials, as well as blacksmiths, hoteliers and publicans. The few informal local records of Auxiliary Units that have survived the war indicate that the new recruits ranged in age from the early 'teens to the seventies. They were all men who had the ability to blend when necessary into the countryside around them, to keep a secret, to live rough and, if necessary, to go on fighting as they would be taught to fight—until they triumphed or were killed.

All the civilians recruited into the Auxiliary Units organization were eventually given Home Guard uniforms and were told that they were enrolled in the Home Guard, and after a time many of them were informed that they had been secretly assigned to one of three special battalions of the Home Guard—the 201st in Scotland, the 202nd in the North of England, and the 203rd in the South. In fact, these men's names were never officially put on paper, and although many of them wore lapel badges with their battalions' numbers on them, the three battalions do not appear on the official Home Guard Lists. Nor, for that matter, do the names of those members of the Auxiliary Units organization who were later told that they had been commissioned in the Home Guard. So no one in the Auxiliary Units patrols was ever formally enrolled in anything and could never have claimed such protection as was afforded all other uniformed fighting men by the Geneva Convention.

Throughout the war all the civilians—and most of the military— who were a part of the Auxiliary Units believed that somewhere within the Home Guard organization there was some formal recognition given to their existence. A few men who were in Auxiliary Units patrols believed during the war—and in many parts of the country still believe—that when they were taken away from their ordinary Home Guard units they were transferred into some sort of Home Guard intelligence network.

This Home Guard label, which had the disadvantage of precluding the recruitment of women into the fighting patrols, provided a working cover for the Auxiliary Units organization itself and kept members of patrols from being arrested as enemy agents during training exercises. Indeed, their Home Guard uniforms gave the men a valid excuse for being out training at all. To a lesser extent the uniforms gave the members of the organization the feeling that they had some sort of formal status, that if they were captured by the German occupation forces, they might not be shot out of hand.

The security of Auxiliary Units was so good that unless specifically and individually authorized by the Ministry of Defence to say otherwise, most of the men who were in the organization have until now denied any knowledge of anything called 'Auxiliary Units' and that they ever participated in anything more irregular than ordinary Home Guard drill during the war.*

Some of the early Auxiliary Units Intelligence Officers were assigned to sectors in which they had lived, and thus were able to begin by recruiting men they had known all their lives. When an officer starting to organize Resistance in an area in which he had not lived approached his first recruit, he would be extremely cautious. Only when he was certain he was on safe ground would he suggest that the man might consider doing a difficult and perhaps dangerous job for the country.

And only when the officer was absolutely sure of his man—as a

---

* In order to get information about their wartime activities from individual members of the British Resistance organization it was necessary in most cases to get individual clearances from the Ministry of Defence. Those former Auxiliary Units members whom I approached without having first taken this precaution either refused to speak to me at all or, in a number of instances, denied knowing what I was talking about. A well-known Master of Foxhounds in East Suffolk, one of the first in his county to be taken into the Resistance, told me, 'All I ever did was go out at night to help train members of the Home Guard.' And that was the only thing he would say.

good security risk, as an individual almost certain to volunteer, and as the right kind of man for the job—would he even hint that he actually had any work to offer that had something to do with action to be taken in the event of German occupation. Many of the men who were recruited as a result of these mysterious conversations, which usually took place in public houses, thought —and in some cases even today still think—that they had been picked at random from a crowd.

Once a man had been selected as a likely recruit for Auxiliary Units he had to be vetted officially. For this purpose the Intelligence Officers had been given letters of introduction from GHQ Home Forces to the Chief Constables in the counties in which they worked, asking that the officers be given whatever co-operation they required. The local police would then make a thorough investigation into the recruit's background, but the police officer who had to do this was never told the purpose of the investigation or its outcome.

After a man had been brought into the organization he was often asked to suggest the names of other men whom he thought should be approached—which is why in many areas the members of Auxiliary Units patrols were related to one another or were men who had worked together for many years. At every level of the Auxiliary Units organization the 'old boy net' was brought into play, for the officers at the top had more confidence in this than in all the positive vetting in the world.

Most of the civilians who were recruited into the patrols were told that although they would be transferred from their Home Guard units, they would have to continue any other voluntary work—such as fire watching—in order not to draw attention to their new clandestine activity. All the recruits signed oaths of secrecy under the Official Secrets Act, and most recruits did not even tell their wives anything about their Resistance activity—or that if the Germans did overrun their sector, they would disappear from home. The wife of one patrol leader at Weeley in Essex, a few miles west of Clacton, had to know about her husband's patrol—because it was given training lectures in her living-room and because its explosives were stacked in crates in the barn behind the house. If the Germans had landed she would have moved inland, away from the patrol's area, because she knew too much. Many other wives of Resistance men had made similar plans.

The less the men's families knew of their activities, the better for the security of both the families and the men. Some of the men kept the secret of their connection with Auxiliary Units from their families so well that, in at least one instance, the wife of a farm worker member of an Auxiliary Units patrol a few miles north of Dover, believed for more than twenty years afterwards that throughout the war her husband had spent several nights a week with a woman friend.

All the MI(R) studies of clandestine warfare in other times and other countries demonstrated that the most vulnerable point in any guerrilla unit is where the individual Resistance fighter's underground activity overlapped his normal life. These studies also suggested that the most effective Resistance group would be one that could emerge apparently from nowhere, strike an unseen blow against the enemy, and then completely disappear again. The guerrilla group that fought in the open usually found that its first battle was also its last. Therefore Colonel Gubbins had decided that each Auxiliary Units patrol must have its own well-camouflaged underground hideout stocked with arms, ammunition and food. If the Germans invaded any part of the country, all Auxiliary Units patrol members in the area would immediately disappear from their homes and move into their hideouts. They would then wait quietly below ground until the Germans had occupied their area or had simply gone past it, before coming out to attack. And after each attack the Resistance fighters would quietly disappear again. At no time during enemy occupation would they ever have returned to their homes or have tried to communicate with their families.

Although it might in some cases have been tactically useful to have had all Auxiliary Units patrols operating under a single central command during the occupation, a tightly knit organization would have been a great deal easier for the Nazis to destroy, so neither Gubbins nor the officers who succeeded him as commanders of Auxiliary Units can be said ever to have been 'the head of the British underground'. However much individual Auxiliary Units patrols sparked off other Resistance activity, however many other unofficial Resistance cells would have sprung up, each one would have remained as independent of the others as possible, for this would have been the greatest strength of British Resistance. The less each individual patrol knew of the activities of its neighbours, the better. As long as a single patrol functioned, the last ditch would not have been crossed.

'c/o GPO HIGHWORTH'

COLONEL Gubbins soon found a larger and more remote base that could also serve as the training centre for men brought from all over the country. Coleshill House, a Palladian manor house built by Inigo Jones and, in 1940, the property of the Pleydell-Bouveries (the family of the Earl of Radnor), was set deep in a fold of the Berkshire hills, about eight miles north-east of Swindon. Surrounded by its own parklands, woods, fields and streams, and overlooked by only one other dwelling, its own lodge, it was an ideal training headquarters, which could be reached relatively easily from most parts of Britain.

Anyone who travelled to Coleshill by train had to be met either at Swindon or Faringdon, and military personnel who were to find their own way there were usually given orders instructing them simply to report to 'GHQ Auxiliary Units, c/o GPO, Highworth, Wilts'. If they complained that it was not usual to be ordered to report to a village post office, they were always told, 'Why not go to the one in Highworth and see what happens ?' When they finally presented their papers to the elderly post-mistress, Mrs M. A. Stranks, she would ask to see proof of their identity and would then leave them. A few minutes later she would return and say simply, 'Somebody's coming to fetch you.' After that she would go on about her business and refuse to answer any questions. Soon either a civilian car or an army vehicle with a red and white plate bearing the GHQ Home Forces identification number '490' would turn up to take the new arrivals to the head-quarters. Even when obviously genuine military convoys arrived at the Highworth Post Office the post-mistress always refused to direct them to Coleshill House, instead telephoning ahead to announce, 'Some more of your lot are down here'.

During the early days of the headquarters some of the officers' wives helped out by cooking in the Auxiliary Units mess—but only after they had signed the Official Secrets Act. The only other civilians inside the headquarters were the Pleydell-Bouverie sisters, who remained in residence throughout the war. Their dogs, nervous animals to begin with, became frantic as the detonation of explosives in the grounds rattled the windows, especially at the weekends when most of the training was done, and the two elderly ladies solicitously fed them on brandy and aspirins.

From Monday until Thursday the headquarters was relatively quiet because Gubbins and his officers and men, including the detachment of Lovat's Scouts who helped with the training, were away, watching individual patrols training on their home ground and helping to set up new patrols. On Thursday nights members of the patrols would arrive at Coleshill from all over the country; some of them were new recruits for intensive basic training; others were men who had been there before, returning for specialized instruction in the use of new weapons and for discussions on tactics.

GHQ Home Forces having agreed that the Auxiliary Units organization must have top priority in all things, many weapons turned up at Coleshill long before the more conventional forces saw them. Even the Commandos queued up behind Auxiliary Units. The explosive generally used for sabotage and demolition by the British forces until 1940 was gelignite—a gelatinous form of dynamite which is so unstable that if it is allowed to 'weep' or to crystallize it may even set itself off, and which exudes fumes which give its handlers headaches. When 'plastic' explosive was introduced, it was in the hands of the Auxiliary Units patrols all over the country before any other troops saw it. Later to be nicknamed 'marzipan' by Continental Resistance saboteurs—because of its consistency and its smell—plastic is a form of cyclonite, is nearly as stable as TNT but is three times as powerful, and is still today the standard military sabotage high explosive. Many of the men of the British Resistance had the inside pockets of their battledress blouses altered so that they could carry as many as a dozen prepared charges, made up with plastic, wherever they went.

Another sabotage weapon issued to Auxiliary Units personnel before it was issued to anyone else was the 'time pencil'. This chemically-activated, delayed-action firing switch for setting off booby traps was based on a device which Colin Gubbins had brought back from Poland in 1939. Unlike other delayed-action booby-trap firing devices, the time pencil was absolutely silent, for it was activated not by a clockwork mechanism, as were German booby-trap delays, but by acid which ate through a fine copper wire to release a spring-loaded striker. Because the speed at which the acid worked was affected by temperature, and because no chemically activated device can be relied upon all the time, the instructions packed with time pencils clearly specified that two of them and two detonators were to be used with every charge. Later in the war, German conspirators got some time pencils from a captured container that had been parachuted into France by Special Operations Executive. They made the mistake of fixing only a single pencil to a bomb which they then placed in an aircraft carrying Hitler. The bomb, which appeared to be a bottle of liqueur wrapped in brown paper, failed to detonate. In 1966 in a BBC television programme, one of the plotters, Fabian von Schla- brendorff, blandly blamed the failure on the inefficiency of the time pencil—and not on the plotters' failure to take note of the instructions packed with it. Altogether some twelve million time pencils were manufactured in Britain during the Second World War.

Because time pencils were regularly used at Coleshill, the British Resistance indirectly played a part in the destruction of the largest dry-dock in German-occupied France—and in the sinking of a U-boat operating in the North Sea.

One Friday evening early in 1942 a Royal Navy Commander, R. E. D. Ryder, arrived at Coleshill. All weekend the officers at the Resistance headquarters showed him how to handle plastic explosive and how to set time pencils. When Ryder left on the Monday morning the staff at Coleshill knew no more about the reason for his visit than they had known before he arrived. But they were soon to hear a great deal, for several weeks later Ryder led the naval force in 'Operation Chariot', the attack on the St Nazaire dry-dock. Under the cover of what appeared merely to be a massive Commando raid, the Royal Navy managed to repeat the Zeebrugge action of the First World War—ramming the dockgates with a ship which was in fact a fuzed time bomb. When the major portion of the British force had withdrawn, the grounded ship, an obsolete American destroyer that had been re-christened *Campbeltown,* blew up. Ryder was awarded the Victoria Cross.

Coleshill was much more directly involved in the strange and mysterious affair of the 'attack on the German submarine'.

[76]

A Shetland Island shepherd, out night after night during the lambing season, heard a strange, distant humming, apparently coming from beneath a cliff overhanging the sea. One night he peered over the edge, and in the darkness he could just make out the silhouette of a submarine. The humming that he had heard was made by its engines, running to charge its batteries.

The shepherd reported this to the local police, and they in turn notified HQ Scottish Command. When it had been established that the submarine was not British, a young Argyll and Sutherlands officer, Tim Iredale, reported to Coleshill.

Broad-shouldered, nearly six and a half feet tall and a strong swimmer, Iredale had no idea why he had been sent there, but during the next week he learned how to set time pencils, how to handle plastic explosive and how to place limpet mines. He was taken out into the surrounding woodland where several derelict tanks and traction engines were used for training the Resistance people in sabotage techniques, and was shown how to blow holes in them with the plastic. Ireland also studied a scale model of a U-boat which one of the staff had collected from 'Station 12', at Aston House, Knebworth, Hertfordshire, the MI(R) sabotage 'college'.

He then went to the Shetlands. When the watchers reported the U-boat back in the cove, Iredale was taken there at night. He stripped off, strapped a heavy limpet mine to his chest, checked a pair of time pencils and fastened them into the mine, squeezed the soft copper ends of the pencils until he heard the acid capsules crush inside them, and then pulled the safety pins. Silently he waded out into the water and, hardly making a ripple, swam across the cove towards the U-boat.

When he was alongside he unharnessed the limpet mine and, treading water, placed the flat side of the mine against the submarine, just below the waterline. When he could feel the circular magnet touch the hull and could tell that the mine was firmly in place, he swam just as silently back towards the shore.

Just before dawn, the U-boat submerged and departed, as it had done many times before. It was never seen or heard in the cove again. German naval historians say that this could not have happened, that a U-boat would not have risked recharging in sight of British shores; but Auxiliary Units officers who were at Coleshill at the time insist that this attack took place.

The members of the Auxiliary Units patrols were the first Britons to be armed with the Thompson sub-machine-guns which were imported from the United States, the first to be issued with sticky bombs, the first to get the Piat anti-tank weapon, the first to have phosphorous hand-grenades and the special tyre-bursting mines disguised as lumps of coal and horse manure. Before anyone else they were given one of MI(R)'s uglier weapons, the stick pencil—or as it was later known to soldiers in the Western Desert, the 'castrator'. This booby-trap device was issued to the Resistance in parts of Scotland, but because of the way it worked it was never actually planted in training. A metal tube painted matt black, about the size of a fountain pen, the stick pencil contained a firing pin and a spring shaped like an umbrella catch. It was plunged vertically into the ground and a cartridge was inserted into it, nose upward, with the bullet protruding slightly out of the earth. The weight of a man's foot on the bullet's tip was enough to cause the spring to release the firing pin.

One sinister weapon which was given to the members of certain Auxiliary Units patrols was a special ·22 rifle—usually manufactured either by BSA, Winchester or Remington. This rifle, which was fitted with a powerful telescopic sight and a silencer, fired high-velocity bullets capable of killing a man a mile away. The Resistance men who received these weapons were told that they were for sniping at German officers and for picking off tracker dogs before they came too near, but several members of the Resistance have admitted that they intended also to use the rifles on Britons in their areas who they thought might collaborate with the Germans. The assassination of collaborators was not a part of Auxiliary Units' official brief, but the men's anxiety about such people is understandable. However, one Intelligence Officer was aghast when he discovered that—for no reason that seemed adequate to him then or now—one of his patrols had put down as a potential collaborator the Chief Constable of Devon.

The snipers' ·22 rifles never became general Auxiliary Units issue because they would not stand up to rough usage; officers sent out from Coleshill noticed that the telescopic sights needed constant realignment. But even without these special weapons many members of the Resistance would have been deadly snipers, for most of them had used weapons all their lives.

All Auxiliary Units' men were issued with pistols—but not, as many of the members of the patrols believed, to use on themselves in a final moment of desperation. Certainly this was not what Mr Churchill had in mind when he pencilled in the margin of one of Colonel Gubbins's weekly reports, 'These men must have revolvers!'

Rubber truncheons were also handed out to all members of patrols, and they were issued with thick rubber-soled agricultural workers' boots, similar to those which were later given to the Commandos. Outwardly however, the members of the Resistance patrols managed to look to the casual observer like ordinary members of the Home Guard—although they sometimes wore their special battalion badges, and many of them had their uniforms slightly altered to give them greater freedom of movement.

Every man in Auxiliary Units was given a Fairbairn Commando dagger. At Coleshill, Major Harston, a former preparatory school-master, held classes in silent killing. He made his new pupils pretend to be German sentries, and he then demonstrated how they could be approached silently and stabbed before they had time to cry out. Once when he was visiting Aston House, he remarked to an officer there that he was not sure how his pupils would react if they were actually called upon to force a dagger between a live man's ribs. 'What I really need', he said casually, 'is a body for them to practise on.'

'I can let you have one, old boy. Genuine German. It's in our freezer. I'll have it put in your car.'

Bill Harston hastily assured his friend that the straw-filled bag which he was already using was perfectly adequate.

There is no more difficult commodity to prize out of a British Army QM store than its rum issue. Regulations control its storage, distribution and consumption at every turn. But because of the exceptional conditions under which the Auxiliary Units patrols might have had to fight, permission was obtained to supply every patrol with its own gallon jar of treacly Army rum—for use in extreme circumstances—and there are no known instances of the patrols violating the trust put in them.

Even if the Auxiliary Units organization had not had such high priorities, its supply situation would still have been good, for in the early days the officer in charge of supply at Coleshill was Edward Beddington-Behrens, a man famous for getting things done without a lot of fuss. He told his fellow officers that he was at that time Britain's highest paid company director, but he did not tell anybody that the reason he drove from Berkshire into London every night during the Blitz was not to keep track of his business affairs, but because he had made a private arrangement to help an ARP rescue team. When he should have been sleeping, he was in the East End, helping to rescue men, women and children from beneath the debris of bombed buildings.

Special weapons, special uniforms, rum rations and extra special officers were not all that the men of Auxiliary Units had to enable them to do their work more efficiently. The training given them at Coleshill, and continual training on their own home ground, soon made every man a super soldier—so much so that those who later enlisted into the uniformed forces or were conscripted could, if they wished, be assigned immediately to such units as the Commandos.

The officer perhaps most responsible for this high standard of training was Colonel G. H. B. 'Billy' Beyts, a deceptively mild-mannered Regular from the 6th Rajputana Rifles, who had won the M.C. during the Burma Rebellion in 1931. Of all the things that he taught the men of the Resistance, the most important and most useful—and what always seemed the most sinister—was the trick of moving absolutely silently and unnoticed through the night. Under his direction the men learned to accept darkness not as a hostile element but as their best friend. Colonel Beyts and his officers worked hard to impress on the men of Auxiliary Units patrols that anybody who remains absolutely still in the dark is invisible, that it is safer at night to move slowly—as slowly as time allows—than to hurry to a target and then to hurry away from it again. 'Time yourselves,' the men were told. 'If you have eight hours of darkness, then use four to reach your objective and four to get away again. Don't hurry and be killed.' Anthony Quayle, for nearly a year the Auxiliary Units Intelligence Officer in Northumberland, remembers how he learned to make a friend of the night:

[80]

On a course at Coleshill they told us to attack a wood in which they had a few old bits of metal and stuff pretending to be tanks in laager. I can remember coming up across a ploughed field in the middle of the night to attack this thing. Where the ploughed bit finished, there was a piece of grass verge at the edge of the wood which the farmer hadn't ploughed up but had left to walk on. They had some staff—some Lovat's Scouts and people—walking around, simulating a perfectly ordinary German patrol. They came round regularly. *And* irregularly.

I'd crawled slowly all the way up the ploughed field in a furrow, I'd got denims on and I was absolutely caked with mud. I was cold and miserable, too, and as brown as the field. 'Well,' I thought, 'now here's where I get up to go across this grass verge before the sentry comes round.'

And—suddenly I heard him coming. He'd cut through the wood! Instead of going round he'd cut right through—and had come round again! I thought, 'Well, here's where I lie still.'

And so I lay still. But my hands were up on the grass, poised to crawl over it. Brown and muddy, but there. And he came so close to me—he must have been within an inch of my fingers—that I felt the muddy ground give slightly under his foot.

He walked off and I lay there for a bit, and then I crawled in and tied the thing on that I'd got to tie on and went away.

He never saw me, and I asked him afterwards, 'Were you kidding that you didn't see me? Or did you *really* not see me?' And this fellow said, 'I didn't see anyone at all.'

8

THE FIRST INTELLIGENCE OFFICERS

ALTHOUGH thousands of civilians, together with more than a hundred army officers and six hundred other ranks, were to train at Coleshill (and many, for one reason or another, returned a dozen times or more), most of the training of the 5,000 men who were eventually to make up the Auxiliary Units patrols was done in the areas where they were supposed to fight, for travelling to Berkshire wasted time that nobody could spare, and Coleshill could accommodate only a few people at one time. The first regional training centre was established in Kent by Captain Peter Fleming, the officer who had been sent in answer to General Andrew Thorne's request for someone to form the XII Corps Observation Unit.*

Fleming, an old Etonian and a Reserve officer in the Grenadier Guards, at that time was the sort of man his brother Ian might have chosen to head a fictional Resistance organization in Britain. He was tall and slender, rich and urbane, and a fashionable author of books about his travels, often on assignments for *The Times*. In those days he would appear on duty in well-cut riding breeches and highly-polished riding boots. The building he chose for his headquarters in Kent was a romantic looking, brick and half-timber farmhouse called The Garth. It stands on a hillside in Bilting, a village between Faversham and Ashford, just north of the Maidstone–Canterbury road, on the edge of King's Woods.

The Garth appears originally to have been a cottage which was enlarged about a century ago. In the older wing the first floor had been removed—floorboards, joists and beams—and the roof rafters exposed; the exceptional height and the two rows of leaded windows gave the room the look of a slightly impoverished and very old chapel. Everyone who entered it felt that the inglenook fireplace might have sheltered an altar, and the wooden packing cases full of explosives that Fleming and his men used as tables and chairs could have been pews.

---

* Throughout the existence of the Resistance in Britain the Auxiliary Units organization in Kent continued to be known locally as XII Corps Observation Unit.

Captain Fleming installed himself and his staff—Captain Michael Calvert and a sergeant who were demolition experts, another sergeant and a private to do the clerical work, several drivers and two batmen. In addition a room at the back of the house was assigned to two Royal Air Force radio operators who had been lent to Fleming by his friend Lawrence Irving, the grandson of the actor, who was at that time the Air Liaison Officer at XII Corps headquarters. The airmen maintained regular radio contact with a distant station to check their equipment—but they did not know where the control station was, nor why they spoke to it. Whenever Fleming or his successor in Kent, Captain Norman Field, staged an Auxiliary Units exercise, the RAF signallers hauled along their cumbersome battery-powered transmitter, strung up aerials in trees and from time to time sent cryptic messages to their mysterious headquarters. Fleming himself never gave them any signals to send and to this day he has no idea what they spoke to their headquarters about. This side activity merely heightened the unreality of a situation which Peter Fleming says he found it difficult to take very seriously. He is sure that if the Germans had managed to invade, such Resistance activity as he had been able to organize in the South-east would have been futile. Nevertheless, given a difficult job to do, he did it remarkably well.

Like the other officers who helped to set up the very earliest Auxiliary Units patrols, Peter Fleming found that he had to rely a great deal on his own personal training and background for inspiration, for there had been time only for brief discussion before he was sent to Kent. In the beginning he was also responsible for starting Resistance activity in Sussex, so he and Mike Calvert filled milk churns with explosives and fitted them with fuses. They then took these improvised bombs around the countryside together with five three-ton lorries loaded with food and a great quantity of medical supplies, small arms and uniforms, arbitrarily distributing them to men they hoped could be trusted. Many of them became members of Auxiliary Units patrols, but most of these early supplies disappeared without trace.

Fleming, Calvert and their civilian recruits surreptitiously mined houses likely to be taken over as headquarters by the Germans, as well as bridges and roads which, if destroyed, would impede the progress of the invaders. If the 'Cromwell' signal which

[83]

was accidentally given in the autumn of 1940 had instead been given during the early summer, many interesting features of south-east England would have been destroyed within minutes. This setting of explosives was done nowhere else in Britain, and the charges in Kent and Sussex were soon taken away again—but not, according to Calvert, before he and his sergeant had blown out the centre sections of the Brighton, Worthing and Eastbourne piers. They also placed booby traps on the far end of the Brighton Pier—with unexpected results. After they had set all the trip wires and were leaving they suddenly heard an explosion. They turned round in time to see another explosion. A seagull had set off one of the booby traps and the splintered planks that had been hurled into the air had come down on some of the other trip wires.

On one training exercise Calvert and Fleming managed to creep into General Montgomery's 3rd Division HQ at Steyning, near Brighton, to put delayed-action charges inside a row of flower pots around a terrace. When they told the General what they had done, he insisted that his security was too good, that nobody could possibly have got past his guards. Then the first time pencils fired.

Peter Fleming's main training area for his Resistance men was a series of sloping fields high on the hillside above The Garth. East Kent was less suburban than it is today, and only essential users were allowed petrol, but many people still passed back and forth along the Maidstone–Canterbury road and some of them must occasionally have noticed unusual activity on the hillside, especially at the weekends.

If the Germans had invaded, most of the work of Resistance fighters would have been done at night, so Fleming's men often wore dark goggles to practise manœuvres in the daytime on the hillside, attacking other goggled patrols who acted as Germans. The rest of the men at these training sessions sat higher on the hillside and could see the things that were being done right—and the things that were going wrong.

Fleming had packed the big barn next to The Garth from end to end and from floor to roof with explosives, ammunition and weapons—including half a dozen longbows for which he had indented through Auxiliary Units supply channels. He hoped to teach his men to use the bows to hurl incendiary charges into German petrol dumps and to pick off sentries silently. Fleming himself could kill a deer at a hundred yards with bow and arrow, but his plan to train Resistance people to use such weapons never got very far. However, after the war he wrote in *The Spectator* about the days when he had tried to teach men whom he described as 'members of the Home Guard' to use bows and arrows against the Germans. The story began to grow, and now whenever a popular newspaper or magazine publishes an article on archery, it mentions the companies of bowmen who wandered the fields and woods of Kent in 1940, hunting Germans.

Some of Peter Fleming's experiments with weapons and explosives went dangerously awry. One Sunday morning he held a class to demonstrate a home-made mortar fashioned from a length of drainpipe. The projectile, also home-made, was a slightly smaller section of steel pipe stuffed with explosive. Fleming's men placed the 'mortar' behind a pile of chestnut poles, dropped the projectile down the barrel, took cover and lit a safety fuse. The charge went off. A flash—a thick black cloud—and then the ominous whirr of shrapnel hurtling in all directions. The men lay flat on the hillside until the smoke had cleared and the shrapnel had stopped falling around them. When they lifted their heads, they saw that the bomb had burst in the barrel. Fleming moved on to the next experiment.

After he left Kent some of his Resistance men went on experimenting with explosives on the hillside. In one exercise in sabotage they set charges under a derelict car. They were over-generous in their estimate of what was needed, for to their horror the car rose slowly, 150 feet into the air, and fell into the next field. Again, miraculously, no one was hurt.

Usually between fifty and eighty men at a time attended demonstrations at The Garth in 1940. This was bad from a security point of view, for it meant that too many of the Resistance in the south-eastern corner of England got to know one another. If the Germans had captured any of them, enough pressure might have elicited the names of some of the others. Of course, it would have been one thing to discover the names—but another thing altogether to find the men.

*

North of the Thames the Resistance organization that was set up at the same time as Peter Fleming's in Kent and Sussex was a shade less flamboyant. But the officer who created it, although not in any way unusual in appearance, was a very colourful figure indeed. The son of the Vicar of Kelvedon, in Essex, Andrew Croft had been the first Head Boy of Stowe, was an Oxford MA and had received the Polar Medal after taking part in the 1933–4 British Trans-Greenland Expedition. He had then been aide-de-camp to the Maharajah of Cooch Behar before returning to Greenland as second-in-command of the Oxford Arctic Expedition. While employed as secretary to the Director of the Fitzwilliam Museum in Cambridge, he had made a third Arctic journey, this time to Lapland with a team of ethnologists. Andrew Croft could fly a plane, was an expert skier, and could make himself understood in ten languages. He held a reserve commission in the Essex Regiment and had been an early recruit to MI(R).

In 1939 he led a Military Mission to the Finnish Army, moving some dozen shiploads of military supplies across then-neutral Norway and Sweden—everything from first-aid kits to crated Lysander aircraft and Crimean War surplus cannon. The supplies were to be used by a British force of 50,000 men who would fight alongside the Finns. Before this force could be raised, however, Russia and Finland came to terms, and Andrew Croft was withdrawn to Norway. He was in Narvik, in uniform, on the day that the German troops landed there, and from his hotel window watched them march up from the harbour. Shortly afterwards he joined up with Colin Gubbins's Independent Companies as Brigade Intelligence Officer, and he was brought back to Britain in June 1940.

Towards the end of that month Gubbins sent him out to organize Auxiliary Units patrols in Essex, Suffolk and Norfolk. Because he was on his own home ground, Andrew Croft needed no help in finding his first recruits. He used his father's home in Kelvedon as his base, and soon the barn behind the vicarage was filled with stores of arms and ammunition, waiting to be distributed to the patrols.

A lieutenant and about a dozen soldiers sent by Colonel Gubbins helped him to organize his patrols, at first only in Essex and the area of Suffolk south of Woodbridge, which seemed to him to be the part of his territory that German invaders would make for first. His patrol leaders were mainly well-to-do farmers and fruit growers. One very competent leader, at Rayleigh in Essex, was a well-known Canvey Island schoolmaster. He was also the leading local smuggler but had reluctantly to give up that lucrative sideline when France fell. Another, in Suffolk, was a distinguished Master of Foxhounds, with, naturally enough, an unparalleled knowledge of the country which he hunted.

Each patrol leader in East Anglia was allowed to nominate his own men, and then Croft screened them. By the beginning of September Auxiliary Units patrols had been set up in all areas of East Anglia that, according to captured German plans, would have been occupied during the first phase of 'Sea Lion'.

Captain Croft held his first training sessions in the homes of his patrol leaders, but when the men had prepared their hideouts he began to hold classes underground.

Most members of the first Auxiliary Units patrols in Kent believed that after a few days or weeks they would have been flushed out by the Germans, but the Resistance men in Essex and Suffolk were more optimistic. They believed that they could have held out indefinitely, replenishing their stores of food and ammunition if necessary from the Germans' own stores.

Andrew Croft so impressed on his men the necessity for keeping everything about Auxiliary Units secret that even today the majority—including the Suffolk Master of Foxhounds—deny that they ever had anything to do with Resistance activity.*

Several weeks after Andrew Croft began setting up Resistance cells in East Anglia, Captain Stuart Edmundson, an Anglo-

---

* Although I wrote this book in Brightlingsea, Essex, the heart of the area in which Andrew Croft organized Auxiliary Units patrols, local enquiries made over a period of a year failed to lead me to any of the people in the neighbourhood who were in the organization. When contact was eventually made, I learned that one of the members of a patrol that had operated from a hideout within easy walking distance of my home was the brother of the mechanic who regularly serviced my car in a Brightlingsea garage.

Irishman who had been in the fertilizer business in Plymouth before the war and had joined a Devon Royal Engineer territorial unit in 1935, was ordered to report to Colin Gubbins at 7 Whitehall Place. The colonel wanted him to spend a few days in Kent, having a look at what Peter Fleming was doing there, and then to return to Plymouth to start organizing Resistance cells around the coasts of Devon and Cornwall.

Before Dunkirk, Captain Edmundson had set up an assembly line in Fort Austin, a disused fort north of Plymouth, on which he had put some of his sappers to work making Molotov cocktails for distribution to members of the newly formed Local Defence Volunteers. As soon as his makeshift ordnance factory was operating smoothly, Edmundson had been sent around Devon and Cornwall to lecture the civilian soldiers on the use of the bombs. Now—through contacts made while doing this, through contacts supplied by Home Guard officers in the two counties, through people he had known in business there before the war and through his wife's family, the Norringtons, who were well known in Devonshire—he began to set up his Resistance organization.

In the beginning all Resistance in the South-west was run by Edmundson and some local sappers but no personnel were sent him by Gubbins. After he had enrolled a large number of civilians, two subalterns were sent to him from Coleshill, and he assigned one to Devon and the other to Cornwall. Shortly afterwards the two counties became separate Resistance areas, and Edmundson passed control of Cornwall to another officer, John Dingley, a local banker, and ran Devonshire himself. Only then were detachments of soldiers sent down from Coleshill to help with the training.

Each of Stuart Edmundson's Resistance patrols in the South-west at first consisted only of a leader and two men. These early recruits were told nothing about being in a special unit of the Home Guard—or indeed about being in any formal organization— and their names were never committed to paper. At first the men were not given uniforms of any sort, nor were any cover stories invented to explain their activity. After each patrol had received rudimentary training in the techniques of sabotage it was issued with a cardboard box which contained as complete a sabotage kit as MI(R) could at that time assemble, and these things were hidden, sometimes in the men's homes or outbuildings, sometimes in specially prepared holes in the ground.

In the event of occupation Edmundson's Resistance men would not leave their homes and go to ground. Instead they would lead normal lives during the day, but at night do whatever damage they could to the Germans, and then if possible return at once to their beds. Edmundson thought that in his part of the country this would arouse less suspicion than the complete disappearance of the men from their homes. Later, however, when the patrols were as big as those in the rest of the country, and when the men were given Home Guard uniforms and were told that they were in the Home Guard, they were taught the same tactics as the Resistance in the rest of the country.

Until Edmundson turned Fort Austin into the South-west's Resistance headquarters, a steady stream of lorries and pantechnicons, each escorted by an Army officer, arrived at his home in Plymouth to dump what he called the 'cases of frightfulness' in his garden. His wife, who had been let in on the secret, rushed frantically around, trying to find new hiding places in the neighbourhood.

In the early weeks of Auxiliary Units in the South-west even the local Army command, VIII Corps, was not told what was going on in the old fortress. But the bangs that the Corps Commander heard coming from behind its walls at night, and the rumours that reached his office made him sure that something very sinister was going on. To be on the safe side he stationed armed infantrymen around the old fort, with instructions to let out no one who looked as if he was going to cause any mischief with explosives.

When General Frederick Morgan, later to become famous as the author of the D-Day plan, took command of VIII Corps, however, he was told precisely what sort of organization was being set up, and he not only thought it a good idea but also decided to assign to it specific tasks that its members were to carry out in the event of German occupation.

It had been decided that if the Germans had managed to land in the South-west the regular troops in Devon and Cornwall should withdraw to the north-east, behind a line of newly built defences that stretched from Bridgwater down to Axminster. This would leave no other armed Britons in the occupied territory except the Resistance cells. And so General Morgan decided that, among other things, the Resistance were to destroy Brunel's great railway bridge across the Tamar at Saltash, and were to set fire to the petrol in the dumps above Falmouth and outside Torquay.

The Auxiliary Units patrols might be able to get together sufficient explosives to blow up the bridge, Edmundson knew, but he doubted that he would be able to teach them enough about demolition to do the job properly, so he assured the general that his men would do what they could, that they might at least be able to run a train on to the bridge and blow that up, making it impossible for the Germans to use the bridge again for some time.

The petrol dumps would be easier to deal with, Edmundson knew. But he worried about what might happen if the one at Falmouth was set alight and a torrent of burning petrol flowed down into the town to do more damage than the Germans could possibly do.

Fleming, Croft and Edmundson created the Resistance organizations in the three coastal areas that seemed at the time likeliest to be hit by the first wave of German invaders. There were also other Auxiliary Units patrols being set up elsewhere in the country—in Dorset by Lord Tony Ashley, the son of the Earl of Shaftesbury, in Lincoln by an officer named Hamilton-Hill, by another named Gwynn in Sussex and Hampshire. Eventually there were Auxiliary Units patrols covering an almost unbroken thirty-mile coastal belt extending from Cape Wrath in the north-west of Scotland around the country clockwise to central Wales, and there were also units formed in some other counties,* but North Wales and the north-west coasts of England and Scotland were left undefended because the Germans would almost certainly have ruled out these areas as landing places. No attempt was ever made by Auxiliary Units to set up an organization in Northern Ireland.

---

* See Appendix C for complete list.

9

THE HIDEOUTS

ONE day early in 1941 two Army officers walked across a pasture on Charing Hill, above the village of Charing in Kent, through a flock of grazing sheep to a weatherbeaten wooden feeding trough on the far side. Ahead of them the hill dropped away sharply, and the broad view to the south, across Ashford to the English Channel, made them both gasp. The younger officer, Captain Norman Field, suggested to the older one, General Montgomery, that they should rest for a few minutes. Why not sit on the feeding trough and enjoy the view? The General nodded and they sat down side by side. After several minutes of silence the general turned to say something, but—Field was gone.

Montgomery looked around. He could see nothing near by to hide behind, and yet Field had certainly not had time to run out of sight. Where was he?

He heard the younger officer's voice. It seemed to rise up from the ground. Montgomery jerked around in time to see Norman Field's head bob up beside him—through a rectangular opening in the bottom of the sheep trough.

The General's sharp features relaxed into a grin. He had been told about the Auxiliary Units organization when he was commanding troops around Brighton, but when he had taken over command of XII Corps from Andrew Thorne, nobody had thought to tell him that there was a Resistance organization in Kent that was at least as elaborate as the one in Sussex. Only now, after ten months in command of the corps, was he making his first inspection of Auxiliary Units installations, and even this inspection would probably never have come about but for a misunderstanding.

When Norman Field had taken over from Peter Fleming as Auxiliary Units Intelligence Officer in Kent, Fleming had told him that when he wanted to go on leave he need only arrange it with Coleshill and then, as a courtesy, should telephone the Corps Commander to explain how long he would be away. However, when Field telephoned the corps to report that he was going on leave he was put on to General Montgomery, and the general was

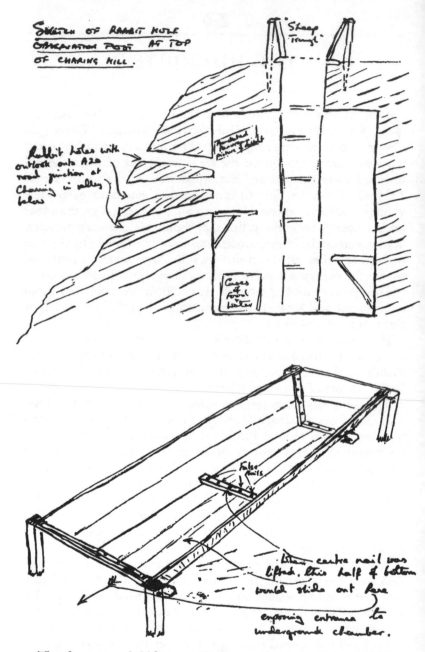

The sheep trough hideout at Charing, a sketch by Colonel Field

at first mystified and then very angry. For no one had told him that XII Corps possessed such a thing as an 'Observation Unit', and he knew nothing at all about Field's existence either.

Field explained what the unit was, and the General became even more angry. Had these people in Kent laid mines and booby traps that could be set off by civilians—perhaps even children? Norman Field hastily assured him that there were no mines, but Montgomery wanted to see for himself what the Resistance organization was doing—hence the visit to the sheep trough.

Captain Field showed the general the secret catch in the bottom of the trough, a nailhead that sprung the trapdoor. He showed him how he wriggled through the small aperture, down into a hiding place carved in the earth beneath them. The room, not much more than six feet long, was a two-man observation post. Its windows were just below the crest of the hill and were a great deal older than the dugout itself. They had originally been rabbit holes, which is what they still looked like from outside, although they had been carefully glazed and were now weatherproof. They gave a clear view across the valley for miles.

This hideout, like so many of the others that astonished General Montgomery that day in Kent, was a monument to the ingenuity of Peter Fleming. New officers brought into the Auxiliary Units organization were usually sent to stay at The Garth for several days so that they could see them, and they became the prototypes for Resistance hideouts all over Britain.

Officially they were known as 'operational bases'. The word 'hideout', the officers who ran the Resistance soon decided, suggested a more passive purpose than that for which these bases had been constructed, and if overheard by the Germans or their friends, would not alert them to their intended use.

Auxiliary Units hideouts were supposed to be merely the places to which the Resistance men could withdraw to eat, sleep and lie low. However, some of the first hideouts in Kent appear to have been built with sieges in mind, for they had their own early-warning outposts several hundred yards away, connected to them by hidden telephone wires. And several of the hideouts in Kent were, like the one entered through the sheep trough, built primarily as lookout points.

By the end of 1940 about 300 hideouts were already in use around the country, and another 61 were ready by the spring of 1941. There were some 534 by the end of that year, and although no later figures are available, upwards of a thousand existed at the time that the Auxiliary Units patrols were disbanded. No two were identical, but most were eventually made large enough to house six or seven men in reasonable comfort, although many at first were little more than fox-holes with log roofs, so badly ventilated that candles sputtered from lack of oxygen and the men who tried sleeping in them all night awoke with headaches. Each hideout was eventually fitted with bunks, cooking stoves, Tilley lamps and other comforts provided by the Army, and each was stocked with food and water—in some cases sufficient to sustain a patrol for as long as a month. Wherever dampness was a problem the tinned foods were frequently replaced so that there was never a chance of besieged Auxiliary Units patrols being finished off by food poisoning. Most hideouts had plenty of room for the patrols' arms, ammunition and sabotage material, but in some areas subsidiary hides were dug near by to hold these and additional stores of food. Many of the hideouts eventually had chemical lavatories, and a few even had running water and some rudimentary form of drainage. The hideouts were so well concealed that anyone walking over them would not notice that the ground beneath their feet had been hollowed out, or that it was unusual in any way. And of course the hideouts had to be made impossible to detect from the air.

Undoubtedly the greatest problem was that of digging the hideouts without anyone noticing—not even the members of neighbouring Resistance patrols. In most of the coastal areas the first hideouts had to be dug by the Resistance men themselves, stumbling around late at night and in total darkness. Incredibly, they usually managed to finish the job unnoticed, but anyone who happened across a half-completed hideout had to be fobbed off with some sort of story that would put an end to questions. The usual cover story was that the hole was being dug for the storage of emergency food supplies for a 'secret government department'— a story that did not make much sense at the time but did stop people asking questions and usually stopped them talking. Speculation about the 'food stores' still continues in some areas of Britain today, and there are dark rumours about how 'They' were going to look after themselves all right.

Another major problem which faced the men who built the hideouts was that of disposing of the subsoil which they had brought up. Carting this away in the dark was no easy task, especially when one remembers that a cubic foot of earth weighs just over a hundred pounds, and the average Resistance hideout in Britain was about twenty feet long, at least ten feet wide, and always high enough for its occupants to stand erect in it.

Many of the methods which were worked out for scattering the spoil in Kent was taken up in other counties, but each new hideout presented new problems. Sometimes the men simply scooped away topsoil in a wood, replaced it with the spoil from their hideout, covered this with the original topsoil and laboriously replanted all the undergrowth. In Devon and Cornwall they sometimes carried out the spoil a bucketful at a time and poured it into streams. At Wickhambreaux in Kent, near the mouth of the River Stour, earth from an Auxiliary Units patrol's hideout was moved across the river on an aerial ropeway and added to a fill that had been begun by the Kent River board as an anti-flood barrier long before Auxiliary Units people appeared on the scene. Not far away, in Stocking Wood, near Baddlesmere, about three miles south of Faversham, the chalky sub-soil was so hard to hide that Norman Field hit on a particularly ingenious solution to the problem. He told his men to put the subsoil in a natural hole in the wood, and he used a camouflet set to mine it. He then placed a line of the sets across the wood and, the next time German bombers flew over, detonated all the charges. What followed looked and sounded like a stick of bombs exploding, and no one questioned the appearance of the chalky craters in the wood.

When Captain Field decided to place an underground observation post on the bare crest of Charing Hill, at a point that could be seen from all directions, he had to solve both the problems of surreptitious digging and soil disposal. After giving the matter a lot of thought he and his men borrowed an anti-aircraft gun, placed it on the spot they had picked for their observation post, and then started filling sandbags to shield it, using for this the earth that they scooped from around the base of the gun. Then, shielded from view by the sandbags, they finished digging the observation post and camouflaging its entrance. For several weeks they manned the gun, and then an Army truck came to tow it away and to cart off the sandbags. This in itself was not unusual, for the guns were often moved from one place to another. All that remained on Charing Hill was a perfectly concealed hideout.

Resistance men for various reasons did not always dig their own hideouts. In several areas they were dug for them by members of Royal Engineer tunnelling companies or simply by ordinary sapper soldiers, and the men in the patrols dug only the entrance tunnels. When the hideouts were dug for the patrols by the soldiers who had been sent from Coleshill to train them, these troops made the entrances, too, and the men who were to use the hideouts were taken into their vicinities and told to find them. This they never did.

In at least one instance civilian labour had to be contracted to produce some hideouts. This happened on the Romney Marsh, where the hideouts were sited below sea-level and only experts could do the sort of concreting that would result in water-tight construction. In those days navvies in provincial areas were rarely transported great distances to their work, but the ones who built the hideouts on the Romney Marsh were brought in from the other side of Kent—and were never given the time to learn their way around the area, so that probably they would not have been able to find their ways back to the hideouts again.

Flooding was a problem in other places as well. On the Essex Marshes, just west of the Blackwater, several patrols each dug and provisioned four successive hideouts, each time hoping that they had at last beaten the problem of flooding, and each time finding that they had not.

Not all the hideouts were fresh excavations. One of Peter Fleming's best was an enlarged badger sett on the edge of a chalk pit at Challock, seven miles south of Faversham, Kent, and another had been the cellars of Evington Manor, at Hastingleigh, near Wye, long before destroyed by fire. The members of one of Reginald Sennitt's patrols on the Essex Marshes who suffered repeated floodings finally recalled that an isolated farmhouse on high ground in the area had a cellar which had been sealed off from the house itself for many years. And so instead of digging themselves yet another hideout, the patrol's members tunnelled from a briar bush several hundred yards from the house into the cellar which, as they had hoped, was completely dry. At no time did the two elderly women who lived in the house have any idea of what was going on down below.

The so-called smugglers' caves along the coasts of Devon and Cornwall were unacceptable as hideouts because they were so well known and were always, even during the war, likely to be visited by tourists. Certainly the Germans would have had no trouble pinpointing them. However, on the Isle of Thanet in Kent the tunnels and underground rooms believed to have been carved in the chalk in the heyday of smuggling are less well known, and the Thanet Resistance group headed by a Manston Grove farmer, Norman Steed, turned several of the excavations into excellent hideouts. When he discovered an old tunnel that reached from the edge of Manston Aerodrome (at that time one of Britain's most important RAF advance fighter stations), right under the runways, he called in his Intelligence Officer to explore it with him. Fifty yards along the tunnel they came to a fall that blocked it completely, and the officer decided to send in a team of sappers to dig it out. Cleared, the tunnel would provide Resistance saboteurs with a perfect way in and out of the aerodrome. However, before the sappers began their work a stray German bomb landed in the middle of the airfield; the only damage it caused was to block the tunnel permanently.

In Wales abandoned coal mines, forgotten even by most of the miners, were turned into excellent hideouts. The Welsh Resistance men, although friendly enough with the English and Scots they met at Coleshill, were reluctant to show their hideouts to Intelligence Officers from the headquarters, and they would not unless flatly ordered to do so. Yet these Welshmen were certainly not all recluses; one had been a rugby international and had been capped for Wales about fifteen times, another had been champion grenade thrower of the BEF in the First World War, and yet another had won the Victoria Cross in that war. But the Welsh,

= original shape of
Airship hole

Colonel Field's sketch of the 'airship hole'

like the Resistance men on the Isle of Wight, hated sharing their deepest secrets with 'foreigners'.

Mine workings were also used as hideouts by patrols in other parts of the country—coal mines in the North-east and, in Cornwall, abandoned tin mines nearly a quarter of a mile deep and in constant danger of caving in because their timbers were rotting, and in which echoed the angry roar of subterranean streams.

In both Cornwall and Scotland, old ice houses and ice pits were taken over and made habitable hideouts, and in the north of Scotland several 2,000-year-old Pictish dwellings were used. Known only to the shepherds, each of these underground dome-shaped rooms had to be entered through a hole in its top which was covered with a weathered stone. All these dwellings needed was a good sweeping, and after the war they were simply abandoned.

One of the most spectacular hideouts built in Kent by Peter Fleming was intended not as a base for a single patrol but was to be a collecting point for stray Resistance men on the run. It contained food, water and sleeping accommodation for about 120 people. Nor was the sheer bulk of this hideout its only unique feature. Fleming had discovered a boat-shaped depression in King's Wood, in a cleft in the hills above The Garth, about sixty feet long, thirty feet wide and thirty deep. Local people told him that this hole had been dug during the First World War as a landing place for an airship. Whether or not this was true, Fleming reasoned that the last place the Germans would look for a secret hole in the earth was underneath a well-known one. He therefore had the bottom scooped out of the airship hole, built a shelter in it, and the earth was replaced.

Any entrance into this hideout through the airship hole itself would have been conspicuous, especially after 120 people on the run had trampled a fresh path down into it. Fortunately an old footpath happened to run alongside the hole, about fifteen yards away from its rim. On the edge of this path Fleming had his men dig a vertical shaft to the depth of the shelter's floor, and a low tunnel was cut between the two. The trapdoor for this entrance was a tree trunk nearly six feet high and weighing about half a ton. It was fixed into place so that when 'unlocked' it could be swung aside at the touch of a finger. The underground counterbalances

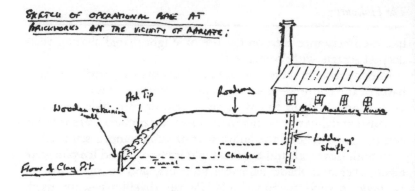

SKETCH OF OPERATIONAL AREA AT
BRICKWORKS AT THE VICINITY OF AYLESGATE:

Wooden retaining wall — Ash Tip — Roadway — Main Machinery House — Ladder up Shaft — Chamber — Tunnel — Floor of Clay Pit

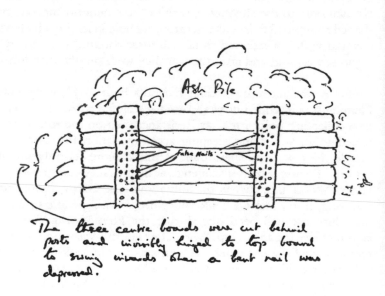

Ash Pile

False Nails

The three centre boards were cut behind posts and invisibly hinged to top board to swing inwards when a bent nail was depressed.

The tunnelling was carried out on this site, and several others in the county, by a detachment of a Tunnelling Coy R.E. which was loaned to us. Its personnel were Welsh Miners who carried out the work at amazing speed and with great enthusiasm even though they had no idea of its purpose.

Colonel Field's sketch of the hideout at Lydden

that supported this lid were later duplicated in several other areas.

Another of Fleming's hideouts on the North Downs in Kent had an even more ingenious method of approach. Anyone wishing to use it had first to find a marble that was hidden in some leaves near by. This then had to be inserted into what appeared to be a mousehole. The marble would roll down a pipe about twelve feet long and plop into a tin can, a signal to the men inside that they should open the trapdoor. The trap itself was concealed in the gnarled, ivy-covered roots at the base of an ancient tree.

Another hideout near Woolton in Kent, just south of the junction of the Dover and Folkestone roads, was built in 1941 by a company of Welsh miners. It was entered through the false bottom of a manger against the side of a hill. Yet another in Kent was under a brickyard at Lydden, about a mile south of Margate, on a site now occupied by an industrialized housing estate. It was entered by moving away a section of what appeared to be a solid wooden wall. But the most common trapdoors on the hideouts were simply oak or elm boxes filled with a foot-thick layer of earth. Most of these trapdoors had to be lifted out, and to make this easier, many of them were mounted on steel springs that, when a hidden catch was pushed, raised the tray enough for a man to get his fingers under its rim. All along the coasts of Britain many hideouts could be entered through what appeared to be cucumber frames, often with the plants actually growing on the trapdoors. One hideout in Scremerston, in Northumberland, just south of Berwick-on-Tweed, was entered through a woodpile; the right twig had simply to be tweaked and an entire section of the pile would slide away. Peter Fleming's badger sett was entered by lifting the rotting remains of what had been a farm cart which long ago had lost its wheels. Because the cart body was so heavy, it was mounted on underground counter-balances.

Several of the trapdoors were inadvertently discovered during the war; one of them in a wood near Great Leighs, Essex, by a courting couple. They suddenly felt the ground begin to move beneath them. When they found out why, in some alarm they notified the police who in turn notified the Army, and that hideout was no longer used.

Certainly everything possible was done to keep the hideouts

inconspicuous. Most were sited in woods, often where the undergrowth looked so dense that even animals could not get through it.
Frequently the trapdoors of the hideouts were at the edges of
footpaths, so that as long as the men who used them were careful,
they could remove and replace the trapdoors without ever actually
stepping off the paths. To reach a hideout in a cave in Scotland,
on the Bowes-Lyons estates in Berwickshire, the Resistance men
had to scale a sheer cliff overhanging a river, then leap into the
cave through a waterfall. Officers from Coleshill who visited this
hideout were given a sumptuous dinner of fresh salmon poached
from a stretch of a river where the fishing rights were owned by
the King's brother-in-law.

At Manston, not far from Margate, an Auxiliary Units patrol
decided to put its hideout in a man-made cave, believed to have
been scooped out of the chalk in the seventeenth century by
members of a religious order. To make sure that this hideout would
not be discovered by the Germans, the Welsh tunnellers who made
it went to the trouble of excavating an entirely new branch off
one of the old passages. They concealed the room with a huge
block of chalk that they mounted on rollers.

The Auxiliary Units hideouts were a major preoccupation of
the men, and one by one they solved all the problems of building
and maintaining the shelters. Paints were found that would resist
condensation, and efficient ventilating systems, often terminating
above ground in tree stumps, were devised. When several senior
officers from Coleshill went to the Lincolnshire fens to inspect
patrols there they were invited to stay for dinner in one of the
hideouts. The officers expected a makeshift meal, probably served
on packing cases full of stores, but when they slipped down
through the trapdoor they were faced with a long dining table
covered with a crisp damask cloth. The candles were in candelabra,
and the cutlery on the table gleamed.

At the end of the war Royal Engineer demolition teams were
sent around the country to destroy all the Auxiliary Units operational bases to keep them from becoming the hideouts of criminals
on the run or play places where small children might easily get
hurt. However, a number of the hideouts were not destroyed and,
although most of them have by now caved in, leaving only rain-

washed dents in the ground to mark their positions, a few still survive, mostly on private land where they are unlikely to become a nuisance. Before it is too late ought not at least one of these be turned into a form of national monument or museum? Historically the operational bases of the British Resistance are at least as interesting as the Martello towers that line parts of the coast.

10

SCOTLAND

AT the beginning of the summer of 1940, a few weeks after he had brought the last British troops off the Channel Islands, Captain Eustace Maxwell was married. While he was still having a sort of honeymoon in a caravan that was parked on the edge of Salisbury Plain, where his unit was stationed, he was told to go to London for an interview at 7 Whitehall Place. He did not take an overnight case with him, but Colonel Gubbins told him that he must not waste time returning to Wiltshire. He was to go straight to Station 12 at Knebworth for a brief course in sabotage techniques, and then he was to go on to Scotland.

On 27 July 1940, still wearing the same things he had worn when he had said good-bye to his wife, Eustace Maxwell made his way by car to Halkirk. Being the second son of the fifth daughter of the seventh Duke of Northumberland made it easier for Captain Maxwell to get Auxiliary Units patrols started in clannish Scotland, as did the fact that he wore the kilt of the Argyll and Sutherlands. Even the vestiges of his boyish charm (in his brother Gavin Maxwell's reminiscences, *The House of Elrig*, Eustace is an exuberant boy who broke things) were a positive asset. So were the facts that Scotland is the area of Britain that is most suitable for resistance activity and the Scots are born clandestine fighters. Their mountains and forests, their hills and moors, their miles of lonely coast all offer places where bands of fighting men could hide away for ever. And the Scots' tradition of independent action, their uncanny ability to survive more or less cheerfully some of the most severe weather and the most rugged isolation forced upon man—even their clannishness—all made them ideal for a guerrilla army. And certainly in 1940 Scotland needed Auxiliary Units patrols or something like them, for although the country was to be used for all sorts of military training throughout the war, few troops could be spared to wait there on the off chance that the Germans would invade. Indeed, the Army was so thin on the ground that much of the task of Scottish home defence fell on the Royal Navy.

In the Highlands Eustace Maxwell found a number of middle-aged men, many of them retired Army officers, who eagerly welcomed the opportunity to serve the country. These men needed little persuading to put aside whatever work they normally did in order to devote full time to setting up Resistance activity, and soon they became so involved in it that many of them kept it their full-time occupation throughout the war. These were the men who were to organize some of the first Scottish Auxiliary Units patrols. Others were raised by a building contractor who later built many hideouts for the patrols, a practising physician and the manager of one of the larger paper mills.

These men in turn enrolled crofters, shepherds, ghillies, stalkers, keepers, poachers and even a few hoteliers and schoolmasters. As in many other areas, in Scotland a great many of the recruits were much younger than the men Colin Gubbins had anticipated would form the main body of the Resistance, but some were in their seventies. In the Highlands, where Captain Maxwell at first concentrated on organizing patrols, townsmen as well as country-men could be brought into the Resistance, for they were all people who knew how to live on the land. Many of the Highland Scots along the coasts were either fishermen or had relatives who were fishermen, and they all knew how to catch rabbits, hares, and even deer. The men always kept traps and snares in their hideouts, and every patrol also had at least one of the snipers' rifles, so food would never have been a problem. And although it may con-ceivably have weakened security, many of the men quietly arranged to have their women leave out food for them—but in secret places away from the hideouts, for the women were never told where these were.

Within three weeks of Eustace Maxwell's arrival in Halkirk more than twenty Resistance patrols were in training, covering the most vulnerable stretches of the northern coast of Caithness and the entire coast of Sutherland. In Scotland the withdrawal of some of the best men from the Home Guard for the Resistance proved less of a problem than in England, for all sorts of special Home Guard units were being organized in Scotland, even a Home Guard Navy.

Captain Maxwell was soon able to hand over leadership in the north-west of Scotland to another officer who in turn eventually passed it on to a Scot sent up from Coleshill, a tall, gaunt captain named A. G. Fiddes-Watt, the son of painters and himself a trained artist, although before the war a practising osteopath. Fiddes-Watt had been an instructor in an Officer Cadet Training Unit and, because he did not take to regimented life, welcomed the opportunity to return to country he knew and liked. Based at first at Aberdeen, he soon became a familiar figure in the Outer Hebrides where he formed at least one Auxiliary Units patrol on every major island from Lewis down to Barra. In his spare time he did a little freelance osteopathy, lectured to Women's Institutes on his favourite subject, reincarnation, and produced a duplicated newsletter, *The Password*. Almost certainly the only publication to spring out of the Resistance movement in Britain, *The Password* provided him with a platform from which to preach the gospel of reincarnation.

Melville House at Ladybank, Fife, the seat of the Earls of Leven, is surrounded by woods and hills and is tucked even more away than was Coleshill House. But like Coleshill it lies within easy reach of a major railway line and is also easy to get to by road. It made an ideal north-of-the-border Coleshill. There was plenty of room for a pistol range complete with spring-up silhouette targets, for demolition practice areas, for training in hand-to-hand combat. The vast tracts surrounding Melville House were ideal for map-reading courses. The Scots in Auxiliary Units did not need maps to find their way around their home territory, but from the beginning the officers who worked out plans for Auxiliary Units patrols believed that counter-intelligence would be an important function of the Resistance in Scotland, and so it would be important for the men in the patrols to know how to use maps when making reports.

In Army depots in Scotland Eustace Maxwell found about forty German specialists whom he was able to add to his staff at Melville House. These soldiers sometimes put on Wehrmacht uniforms obtained for them from costumiers, to add realism to training exercises. They taught Scottish Resistance members how to identify German vehicles and weapons, and they compiled for them long lists of words and phrases which were likely to appear on the Germans' signposts. The Resistance men in Scotland would therefore have known exactly which signs to alter to lead the Wehrmacht up every cart track in Scotland.

Keeping secret the fact that there was a Resistance organization in Scotland was in some ways more difficult than keeping the secret in the rest of the country, for any unusual activity is always most noticeable in those remote, underpopulated areas where life changes so little from day to day. Nevertheless, during the short summer nights of 1940 Captain Maxwell's men dug themselves in and nobody noticed. In the north of Scotland some of their hideouts were in the centres of the smaller towns and villages, and were usually entered through the cellars of houses. Such hideouts always had secondary exits through long tunnels—and in one instance through a disused sewer—that emerged far away from the houses themselves.

Many of the ruined castles that are today classified as national monuments and are visited by tourists were able to provide excellent cover for the Resistance men in Scotland. Usually they dug their hideouts beneath the rock piles at the bases of the crumbling, derelict keeps. Constantly washed by rain, these forlorn stone piles gave no hint of the habitation beneath them, usually entered by moving aside a single large slab of granite resting on underground counterbalances. Auxiliary Units hideouts in Scotland were also sometimes entered through trapdoors hidden beneath hay and peat stacks, and sometimes they were even on bare ground, and not always beside well worn paths, for the Scots knew that the springy heather would not ordinarily show their footprints.

A few of the Scottish hideouts presented problems that could not have been anticipated. Digging near Ness, one of Fiddes-Watt's men dropped into a forgotten Pictish dwelling, and the officer looked on gloomily as hundreds of interesting-looking potsherds were simply tossed aside because this was no time to call in an archaeologist.

Another northern Scottish hideout had to be sited in a wood that was looked after by a gamekeeper for owners who lived away from the area. When the keeper, who was not a member of the local Auxiliary Units patrol, one day saw that someone had been in his woods, had chopped down some trees and was digging a large hole, he anxiously notified the Aberdeen firm of solicitors who represented the landowner's interests. But by the time someone from the solicitor's office had got around to going out with him, the hideout had been finished and he was unable even to find a trace of it. Sure that some sort of enemy espionage activity must be taking place in the wood, the solicitors notified the Army, word eventually reached Eustace Maxwell, and he decided to call on the solicitors. He could not, he told them, say what had been happening in the wood, but he assured them that they need not worry, that it was to do with protecting Scotland and was important. In due course he received a message from the solicitors, telling him that the landowner said that he could do whatever he pleased in the wood, even chopping down all the trees if it was for the good of Scotland.

After the first hideouts were ready the Resistance in Scotland had time to catch its breath, and it then began to become much more sophisticated. Many patrols soon quit their original hideouts for more elaborately constructed ones, and the old hideouts were maintained as emergency bases to be used if the Germans found the newer ones.

When the 'Cromwell' alert was signalled in September 1940, Auxiliary Units men in the rest of Britain only prepared to go to ground, but those in Scotland actually disappeared into their hideouts, where in most places they remained for at least five days. Along the northern coast, however, some of the patrols would not emerge until Eustace Maxwell had been brought up from Fife and had personally gone to each hideout, flushing them all out. This extreme degree of caution may in retrospect seem foolish, but at the time it seemed sensible enough, and afterwards the men in Auxiliary Units in Scotland knew more than the men in the rest of the country about the problems of prolonged existence underground.

The largest, most elaborate Resistance hideout in Scotland was near Eustace Maxwell's headquarters, high on one of the Lomond Hills, just across the Firth of Forth from Edinburgh. When General Thorne moved from Kent to Scotland in 1941 to take over Scottish Command he decided that if the Germans did try to invade Scotland, they would probably land first in Fife because it is so well protected by the Forth and the Tay. He thought that they would then send Panzer columns westward and cut the country in half. So he put some Canadian Army tunnellers stationed in Scotland to work carving the operational base in one of the

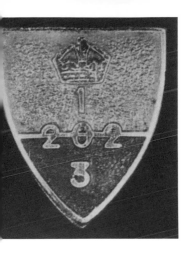

A British Resistance battalion badge. Men in the Resistance were told that they were in one of three Home Guard battalions and were issued with badges such as this (it is $\frac{5}{8}$ in. high). In fact, none of the battalions appears on the official Home Guard lists

A section of an Ordnance Survey map of Kent on which in 1967 Colonel Field marked Auxiliary Units hideouts. The dark squares indicate observation posts, the lighter ones the hideouts, while the bullseye shows the headquarters at The Garth

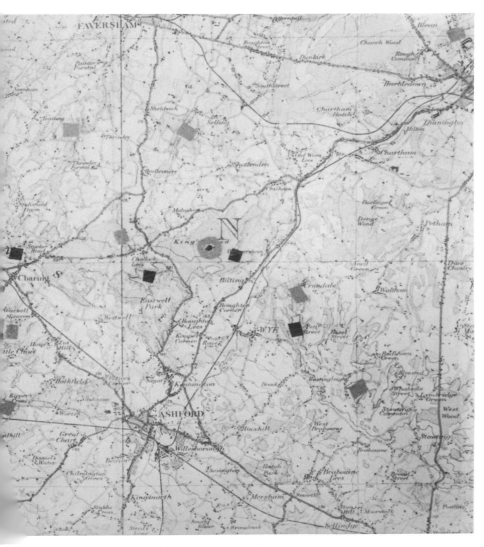

A typical Resistance patrol from Kent, brought together
again in 1967 by the patrol leader in order that this
photograph might be taken. Seated, left to right:
S. Martin, coal merchant; W. Hawkes, farmer; C. J.
Lynes, farmer (the patrol's leader and also a group leader
in the area north of Dover); H. G. Burrows, farmer;
G. Pickard, butcher; Colonel Field (now a mushroom
farmer but once the local Intelligence Officer).
Standing, left to right: W. Roberts, shepherd; G. Marsh,
engineer.

The entrance to one of the
group's wartime hideouts,
dug into the side of an
embankment at Woolton,
just south of the junction
of the Dover and
Folkestone roads.
Another entrance, at the
crest of the bank, has
caved in. The one here
is in fair condition,
although some of the
timbering inside has given
way. Originally this
entrance was reached by
passing through a dummy
manger in a cattle shed,
which effectively
concealed it. Mr Roberts,
the shepherd member of
the group, stands by the
entrance

◁

ss Eleanor Norman-Butler,
ntrol station wireless
rator

Roger Weeley, an Essex
farmer and one-time
patrol leader

RESISTANCE
MEMBERS TODAY

Paddy O'Mara, a
newspaper-seller with a
pitch outside Colchester
Station ; during the war, a
local Resistance member.
He still wears his '203rd
Battalion' badge

R. F. H. Darwall Smith.
headmaster of a Seaford,
Sussex, preparatory
school, and a wartime
Auxiliary Units
Intelligence Officer. His
paperknife was his
Fairbairn dagger

A. G. Fiddes-Watt, a
London picture restorer,
who was an Auxiliary
Units Intelligence Officer
in Northern Scotland

Adrian Monck-Mason, a
retired farmer of Charing,
in Kent, operated an
Auxiliary Units radio
station from a hideout
beneath one of his
chicken houses

Major-General Sir Colin Gubbins, who created the British Resistance Movement. A photograph taken in 1967

A page from *Informationsheft G.B.*, containing snapshots and other photographs of people wanted for interrogation by the Gestapo and whom they believed to be living in Britain

'c/o GPO Highworth'—the old post office in Highworth village, 'gateway' to the British Resistance

Coleshill House, from a nineteenth century engraving. The Inigo Jones building, training centre for the British Resistance, burned down shortly after the war

A photograph of officers serving with Auxiliary Units, taken at Coleshill on 29 January 1942. No record of the names of the people in the photograph was kept, but it has been possible to identify most of them. Where there is any uncertainty, the name is preceded by an asterisk.

1 *Captain Lamb; 2 —— ; 3 —— ; 4 Captain J. W. S. Edmundson; 5 Captain A. G. Fiddes-Watt; 6 Captain Anthony Quayle; 7 Captain G. R. McNicoll; 8 Captain C. Sandford; 9 *Captain J. W. Holberton; 10 Captain R. F. H. Darwall Smith; 11 —— ; 12 Captain J. Dingley; 13 Captain W. D. Clark; 14 Captain R. J. V. Goss; 15 Captain G. Woodward; 16 Captain N. V. Oxenden, MC; 17 —— ; 18 Captain G. C. L. Atkinson, MC; 19 Captain P. Hollis; 20 Captain P. R. A. Forbes; 21 —— ; 22 —— ; 23 —— ; 24 Captain E. R. R. Fingland; 25 Captain E. B. Clive; 26 —— ; 27 Captain O. B. Hall-Hall; 28 Captain K. W. Johnson; 29 —— ; 30 *Major Lord Ashley; 31 Captain Ian Fenwick; 32 Captain C. F. G. Bond; 33 *Captain D. F. B. Stucley; 34 Major W. W. Harston; 35 Captain E. Maxwell; 36 Captain A. R. C. Anderson; 37 Major The Hon. M. T. Henderson; 38 Lieut.-Col. G. H. B. Beyts, MC; 39 Junior Commander Barbara Culleton; 40 Colonel C. R. Major; 41 Major M. Petherick, MP; 42 Senior Commander Beatrice Temple; 43 Major T. H. Winterborn; 44 Captain C. E. Randell; 45 Captain J. S. Collings

Brigadier 'Bill Major in 1967. As a Colonel, he took over command of the Auxiliary Units from Colin Gubbins late in 1940

Miss Beatrice Temple, Lady Mayoress of Lewes, Sussex, in 1967. A niece of an Archbishop of Canterbury, she was the wartime head of the A.T.S. who worked in the British Resistance Movement

RESISTANCE MEMBERS TODAY

Brigadier 'Billy' Beyts

Lieut.-Colonel Norman Field

Colonel Andrew Croft

To the right of the pistol in the photograph above is the German reproduction of the 1937 AA Handbook (see page 26). The strip photograph is part of the pocket-size reproduction of a panoramic view of the entire coast of Britain (see page 27). The other handbooks contain maps, photographs, diagrams, and other information useful to an occupying force. The pistol is an American model, first issued to the Auxiliary Units, and it lies on a map of Kent on which Colonel Field marked, in 1967, various Resistance hideouts. Part of this map is reproduced in greater detail on a later page.

With the exception of the hand grenade (an ordinary Mills bomb) all the weapons shown in the photograph below were issued to the Auxiliary Units before the conventional British forces. They comprise a Thompson sub-machine gun, an American .45 automatic, a sticky bomb and a Fairbairn dagger. Shown with them is the sabotage manual, 'The Countryman's Diary'. pages of which can be seen in greater detail overleaf

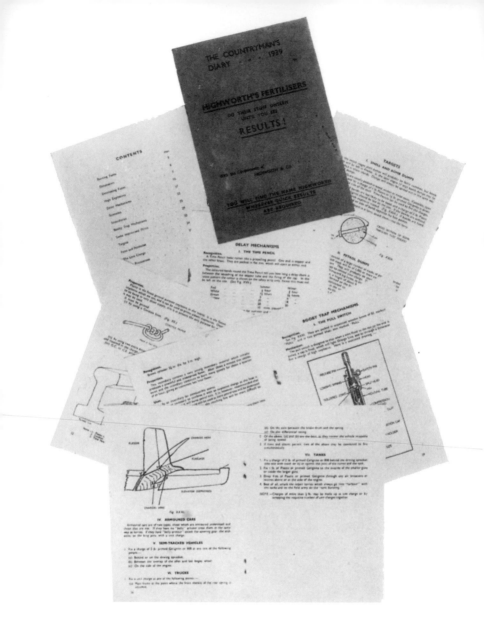

Pages from the Resistance's sabotage
manual, 'The Countryman's Diary'

Lomonds. Detailed plans were worked out for the use of the base if the Germans had landed. Regular troops would have been parachuted on to the base to support the Resistance fighters, and an attempt would then have been made to keep the base supplied by further air drops.

Several very elaborate demonstrations were staged at Melville House for the benefit of senior military commanders in Scotland in an effort to get them to work the Resistance into their local defence arrangements. Before one of these demonstrations began, early in 1941, the officers were seated in the ballroom of Melville House, facing a blank wall, their backs to the only doors into the room. Suddenly they heard a loud bang behind them. Someone had thrown a thunderflash into the room.

The officers all jerked round, stared at the smoke, smiled with relief at what they thought was a practical joke, and turned round again. Miraculously, Captain Maxwell was now standing in front of the blank wall. How had he got there? Why had they not noticed him enter the room? The only time they had looked away from the blank wall was when they had turned towards the doors. No one was more mystified than the senior officer present, Andrew Thorne.

Instead of explaining how he had got into the room, Captain Maxwell began by telling the officers that the Germans could expect the men of the Scottish Auxiliary Units patrols to appear out of nowhere just as mysteriously. And when he had finished his talk—but still had not explained his magic trick—he invited the officers to come outside to watch some Resistance men in action.

He led the way from the house to a large clearing in the park in which was a stack of brushwood. The officers, Maxwell told them, were standing right on top of an Auxiliary Units hideout, and none of them was more than fifteen yards from its entrance. He would give them ten minutes to find the way into it.

For several minutes the officers moved around the clearing, looking for telltale footprints, pulling twigs off the woodpile, prodding the soil with their canes, and scuffling their boots to see if that would reveal anything.

At last Maxwell walked over to the woodpile, firmly pulled one of its hundreds of pieces, and almost majestically the centre of the pile lifted to reveal a trapdoor underneath. When the officers had all peered into it he closed it again and asked them to come with him to a high point from which they could see the hideout and a mock-up of a German wire laager in the wooded parkland.

After a few minutes the rumble of engines and the grinding of gears began to swell, and a military convoy of about a dozen vehicles bearing the black and white Maltese crosses of the Wehrmacht wound through the wood, toward the laager. The drivers all wore square Wehrmacht helmets and grey Wehrmacht uniforms, and their officers and NCOs shouted commands in German. They turned their vehicles into the barbed-wire enclosure, switched off the engines, climbed down and posted sentries.

'Try to imagine,' Captain Maxwell told his guests, 'that it is now night.' He pointed towards the Auxiliary Units' hideout and as the officers raised their binoculars they saw the centre of the woodpile slowly rise. A dozen men—two Auxiliary Units patrols—began to creep out and glide slowly towards the German camp. It was uncanny. The Resistance men moved like night animals, making not a sound. One by one they slithered easily under the barbed-wire concertinas and moved towards the parked vehicles. Surely the 'Germans' would see them. Or would they? The Resistance men really did melt completely into the ground.

Through their glasses the officers watched them begin to fix limpet mines on the vehicles, crimp the ends of the time pencils, and draw back silently towards the barbed wire. Then, without cracking a single twig, they were under it.

Incredibly, the soldiers playing the parts of the Germans had failed to see their attackers.

Slowly, barely visible even in the daylight, the Resistance men worked their way back towards the hideout. One of them lifted the lid and they slid back inside. Maxwell remembers the mounting tension among the spectators as the attack went in and the audible sigh of relief when the last man back had closed the trapdoor behind him.

He glanced at his watch but said nothing. A moment of silence, then a sharp noise. One of the 'German' trucks shuddered. Another explosion. Then a third. And now the officers could hear the angry rattle of small arms being fired by the men dressed as Germans at targets that were no longer there.

The 'total destruction' of the convoy—made up of antiquated

British Army vehicles retrieved from scrap heaps—convinced the officers who witnessed the demonstration that Auxiliary Units had a very important part to play in the defence of Scotland.

Only one thing remained to be explained, and Eustace Maxwell finally admitted to General Thorne that he had got into the ball-room very easily. During the seconds when the officers' attention had been drawn by the thunderflash, he had slipped in through a door set flush in the blank wall—a servant's entrance.

Now commanders all around the coasts of Scotland began to specify places where they thought that Auxiliary Units patrols might strengthen their defences. Two operational bases were even placed inland, in Stirlingshire, because a local commander wanted them to cover Glasgow. As in England, the hideouts in Scotland were nearest one another in the immediate coastal area, more distant from each other farther back, so that the greatest damage could have been done to the Germans during the initial phase of the occupation, before they had a chance to dig in.

No Auxiliary Units patrols were formed immediately around Balmoral, but when the Royal Family were in residence men from Auxiliary Units patrols from other parts of Scotland, and some-times from just over the border in Northumberland, were usually there, moving around in the darkness to strengthen and to test the guard at the castle. Members of the individual patrols were intro-duced to the King and Queen and were photographed with them, and the two princesses watched the patrols during the day, when they were carrying out exercises in the grounds. But the men never learned if the Royal Family knew that they were not a part of the Home Guard organization whose uniforms they wore.

Whenever the King and Queen were in residence at Balmoral armoured-cars were standing ready to hurry them away in the event of a sudden invasion, and so the presence of men from Auxiliary Units patrols was certainly not essential, although they would have helped to make things uncomfortable for any para-chutists who might have landed.

Much more essential to the defence of Scotland as a whole were the attacks which many Auxiliary Units patrols—not those in the extreme north—made on Army and Air Force installations. These raids were the best sort of training the members of the patrols could be given, for the places into which they crept would almost certainly have been occupied by the Germans. And probably the Germans' guards would have had to defend those places in much the same way as the British. Because these raids were usually devastatingly successful, they indicated to the unit commanders the weak points in their defences. The Resistance men in Scotland raided virtually every aerodrome and every Army camp there at least once, proving that none was impregnable.

Once General Thorne asked that Auxiliary Units patrols be sent to test the security of his own headquarters, and in the attack that followed, the raiders penetrated to the very heart of Scottish Command, to place a thunderflash under the seat of the General's private lavatory. The raiders suffered no casualties and indeed were not seen. General Thorne fortunately has a sense of humour, but after this raid his subordinates were urged even more strongly to make use of the Resistance men in their local defences.

During Captain Eustace Maxwell's first year in Scotland he drove more than 70,000 miles in the course of his duties. By the end of that year, well before the final threat of German invasion had passed, the Resistance in Scotland had reached peak efficiency. There were about a hundred fully trained patrols, fully equipped and ready to co-ordinate their activities with the military and, probably more important, to work effectively with no one directing them. As in England and Wales, the men trained every weekend as well as several nights each week, and as they made plans and then tried those plans out, their most fantastic ideas often proved feasible, and Resistance in Scotland became very sophisticated indeed.

Since these men received no pay, and since they produced most of their own operational bases and relied on relatively little support from the uniformed forces, they were undoubtedly the cheapest form of defence that Scotland could have had. And had only a small German force landed in Scotland, it might well have been pushed back into the sea by the Resistance. That or destroyed.

11

SECOND PHASE

B RITISH factories did not, as so many Britons today would like to believe, work at a frantic pace throughout the summer and autumn of 1940 in order to replenish the nation's store of arms. Just as if Dunkirk had never happened, just as if no one in the country was aware that Hitler was massing an invasion armada on the other side of the Channel, just as if there were no war, most people in Britain took advantage of the exceptionally fine weather that summer to loll at the seaside. At the coastal resorts, according to the newspapers, the Bank Holiday crowds were swelled by troops, and many of the non-commissioned officers, although off duty, wore pistols. These reports were no doubt intended for the newspapers' German readers, for the summer of 1940 was the one in which even the weapons normally on display in such places as the Imperial War Museum had to be handed out to the forces, and when even shotguns were being begged from the public so that they could be lent to the Home Guard.

And although the workers did not kill themselves by their exertions, Britain's factories must have produced something that summer, for by early autumn, before the Blitz had jolted the country out of its giddy daydream and before the winter had come to make impossible for another half year a German invasion, Britain's arms situation was noticeably less critical. In November 1940, when Colonel Gubbins was taken away from Auxiliary Units in order to be plunged into yet another MI(R) offshoot, the Special Operations Executive, he was sure in his own mind that as far as the invasion of Britain was concerned, the Germans had lost an initiative which they were unlikely ever to regain. Therefore he did not hesitate to take with him into SOE many of the Auxiliary Units Intelligence Officers who, like himself, were itching for action. SOE, the most special of the Special Forces, had just been set up under the cover of the Ministry of Economic Warfare—but with the same relationship to that Ministry that the Auxiliary Units Organization had to the Home Guard—in order to help create and to support secret groups of men and women in the occupied countries who would do there what the Auxiliary Units patrols would have done in Britain had the Germans invaded. Many more of the Auxiliary Units Intelligence Officers were later to follow Colonel Gubbins into the Special Forces, many into SOE itself, some into the other MI(R)-inspired organizations.

Colin Gubbins's successor at Coleshill was Colonel C. R. 'Bill' Major, a tall, slim Staff Officer who was a descendant of Oliver Cromwell. Although an infantry officer and originally commissioned in the Dorsetshire Regiment, he had spent much of his Service career in the Military Intelligence Directorate, and so he had known Colin Gubbins for some time—and had been aware of Gubbins's special interests. From the time that invasion had become a possibility Colonel Major had been the Intelligence G1 at Eastern Command. But so well had the secret of the very existence of Auxiliary Units been kept that until he was actually put in charge of the organization—and, indeed, until he had actually installed himself at Coleshill House—Bill Major did not even know that Britain possessed such a thing as an official Resistance organization.

He was delighted with his new command in every way, and such changes in the character of Auxiliary Units that occurred after his take-over were largely a result of the organization's normal growth and maturity. By the end of 1940 most of the crudest hideouts had been replaced by more elaborate ones, and individual patrols had developed more specific and realistic tactics. The time had now come to form new patrols in the secondary areas, those where invasion strikes were possible but improbable. Bill Major also set out to make the entire organization a more cohesive one without letting it become less secret, and also without its individual members losing any of their almost fanatical enthusiasm.

When Colonel Gubbins and the officers who helped him to create the Auxiliary Units organization had first set to work they had envisaged cells of 'stay-behind troops' that would have survived only the first weeks—or perhaps only the first days—of a German occupation. The only chance of longer survival, many of the officers had at first thought, would have come about if the patrols had failed to emerge to attack the Germans at all. Indeed, in many of the coastal areas the men in the patrols had been told when they were recruited that their chances of lasting out even the first twenty-four hours of a German occupation were probably slim. But as the Auxiliary Units organization grew, and as its capabilities became more apparent, many of the officers supervising its activities realized that the patrols might well carry on much longer, that indeed the elimination of the British Resistance by the Germans might even mean the destruction of Britain's population. So it was just as well that the new Auxiliary Units Intelligence Officers who were to serve under Bill Major were of a somewhat different cut from their predecessors. True, they were young and sometimes tended toward flamboyant gestures. Lambert Carmichael, a Northumberland patrol leader, recalls that his Intelligence Officer, Anthony Quayle, today the quietest of men, 'never came into our house through a door if a window happened to be open'. But then those were days in which most young Britons in uniform needed occasionally to swagger. Certainly Colonel Major's new Intelligence Officers appear on the whole to have been more serious in their approach than Colonel Gubbins's. They included the same high proportion of men with titles and men from titled families, but fewer were professional soldiers or professionals in Military Intelligence. Public school accents still predominated. Several had been preparatory schoolmasters (one, R. F. Darwall Smith, was a Cambridge cricket blue); S. Sandford had been a book publisher specializing in limited editions, and another was Ian Fenwick, a cartoonist whose name was already well known to the readers of *Punch*. Many were brought in through the 'old boy network' or at least were vetted through it, but many others came into the organization from the regimental depots, often having been sent from hospitals after the wounds which they had suffered either in the retreat across France or in the fighting in Norway had healed. All insist today that they were perfectly ordinary wartime officers, but all were in some way unusual, either in background or in personality—or in both.

Nothing about the Auxiliary Units organization intrigued Colonel Bill Major more than the fact that the individual patrols had been able to exist actively for so long before he had come on to the scene—and were to go on existing actively for so much longer afterwards—without apparently drawing attention to themselves. How, for example, had they managed to train without arousing curiosity locally?

At first, men had received their instruction either in the homes of their patrol leaders or, in a few cases, in the billets of the local Intelligence Officers. Saboteurs must learn a great deal of the theory of explosives and a fair amount about the mechanisms of booby-trapping devices before they can be trusted to handle live charges, and in most areas explosives could be demonstrated out of doors without arousing undue attention, for blasting is often done on farms to remove tree stumps and boulders. In any case, at that time all over Britain there were strange bangs about which it was unpatriotic to ask questions. Usually these demonstrations were staged in fields or in woods well away from roads.

Much more important was to know how to get the explosives to the places where they were to be used—and how to come away unseen—so the greatest amount of time spent on training Auxiliary Units patrols on their home ground was concentrated on practising moving silently through the darkness. If the men were completely successful at this, then no one noticed them. And if they were seen—well, then they were simply members of yet another Home Guard group on yet another exercise. In summer the Auxiliary Units patrols' practices rarely began before midnight, and they then went on until three or four in the morning—several nights each week. In the winter the patrols ignored the weather and went right on training, but they then could begin much earlier in the evening, usually around ten o'clock, and could carry on until perhaps five in the morning, at which time they returned to their homes, slept a few hours and then somehow managed to turn out to do a full day's work. No one remembers an Auxiliary Units training session ever being called off because of rain, fog or snow. Indeed, the men welcomed inclement weather because it afforded better cover, and in the snow they practised entering and leaving their hideouts in a way that would leave no trails for the Germans to follow.

Often two patrols would participate in the same training exercise, completely unknown to each other. Starting from points perhaps five or ten miles apart, each of these patrols would be instructed to make its way across fields and through woods by the straightest possible routes, to the point from which the other patrol had set out. Under no circumstances were they to allow themselves to be noticed by anyone, and they were to report anyone they saw. Diaries kept privately by Auxiliary Units group leaders* contain numerous accounts of these night exercises in which patrols passed within thirty or forty feet of each other, unnoticed.

A variation on this manœuvre consisted of moving two patrols along a road, one patrol starting from one end, one from the other, but on opposite sides of the road. The men were allowed to move no farther back from the roadway than the verges, so that at the point where the patrols passed they were only the road's width apart. Yet entire patrols would pass each other unnoticed.

The Intelligence Officers frequently went into the patrols' areas to set up exercises for them. Anthony Quayle agreed to park his staff car one blustery winter night on a lonely Northumberland road where one of his patrols, composed of miners, operated. His car would represent a parked German tank, and the men would go through the motions of destroying it.

Powdery snow swirled on the roadway and the temperature was almost down to zero when Captain Quayle told his driver to pull over to the side of the road. Then, to give the Resistance men some sort of chance, he told his driver and sergeant to come out with him for a smoke, just as the crew of a German tank might do. They lit their cigarettes and stamped a few yards up and down the road, frequently glancing back towards the car to see if they could detect the patrol.

An hour passed. Then another, and another. Quayle and the two men drew their greatcoats around themselves, stamped their feet and shivered. Finally he glanced at his watch and said, 'I don't think they're coming. They must have had to work an extra shift.'

He and his two men turned back towards the car. It was just

---

* Colonel Major set up the group system, placing about half a dozen patrols under the command of one patrol leader who then continued to have his own patrol as well. Patrol leaders were told that they were sergeants in the Home Guard, and group leaders that they were captains; when they wore Home Guard uniform they wore the appropriate insignia of rank.

as they had left it, the windows still steamed up. They had spent over three hours out in the snow for nothing.

Quayle opened the door of the car and immediately saw two glowing orange dots inside. Two members of the Resistance patrol had somehow got into his car. Quayle heard scuffling, and another member of the patrol crawled out from underneath the car. He had, he explained cheerfully, fitted a limpet mine to the underside.

At the edge of the road Quayle saw the rest of the patrol stand up, their Sten guns ominously pointed at him. The Resistance men had been watching them from a few feet away for two hours.

The Auxiliary Units patrols were so eager to test themselves that they frequently made their own arrangements for exercises with local army units. When, for example, J. F. Montgomery, the leader of the Wickhambreaux patrol in east Kent, got to know the second-in-command of a local coastal artillery regiment's headquarters, he suggested one Sunday that his patrol, which he described to the officer as 'a little Home Guard group', should test the security of the headquarters. The officer smiled patronizingly and explained that his establishment was completely secure, that such a test would be a farce. But the Auxiliary Units patrol leader, a well-to-do farmer, spoke very persuasively, and the officer at last agreed to a test. He would, he said, tell his sentries to go on duty with unloaded rifles for the next week. 'Fine,' the Resistance leader replied, 'and I'll tell my men not to carry live grenades.'

For several days afterwards nothing happened, for the patrol leader had decided to wait until the artillerymen relaxed their vigil. Then, late on the Thursday night, faces blackened, his patrol approached the headquarters. They had already had a good look at it in the daytime, and they knew that the barbed wire concertinas around it were fifteen feet deep. This did not particularly perturb them, however, for they had also noticed exactly where the earth was lowest beneath the wire.

Now in the darkness they slithered under it. Cautiously, slowly, blending into the shadows, they groped their way across the grass. When they touched trip wires they gently ran their fingertips along them to the thunderflashes to which they were fastened.

Making sure that they had not encountered pressure-release booby-trap switches, they then unhooked the wires.

Instead of entering the front door of the headquarters, which afterwards they learned had been booby-trapped, they found a side door. The artillerymen had taken the precaution of propping an old iron bedstead against the inside, but the Resistance men had little trouble moving this away without making a sound.

Down a corridor they could see a crack of light under a door, and they moved silently towards it. From the other side of the door they could hear the soft, even rasp of a man snoring. Slowly, very slowly, they turned the knob, then eased the door open gently and crept into the orderly room. A soldier lay asleep on a cot in the corner.

Pinning a note to the man's tunic that said, '*You're dead*', they then went over to a desk, pocketed several very official looking papers and some rubber stamps, and then moved silently back out into the corridor, gently drawing the door shut behind them.

Making sure that the bedstead was propped back in place, the Resistance men made their way outside through a third door, picked their way past several more tripwires, hooked up the thunderflashes that they had unhooked on the way in, and slid out under the barbed wire. It was time for them to return to their homes.

In the morning Montgomery called at the artillery headquarters, found his friend and asked: 'What did you think of our visit?'

The officer looked puzzled. 'What visit?'

'We got in here last night.'

'You couldn't have done.'

'We were here, I tell you.' And he explained to the officer precisely what he and his patrol had done.

'Impossible. I don't believe you.'

The patrol leader then reached into his pockets, took out the papers and the rubber stamps and dropped them on the desk.

The gunner officer frowned and told his sergeant-major to send some men out to find the break in the barbed wire through which the Home Guard had got into the headquarters the night before.

Montgomery waited, smiling to himself. When at last the sergeant-major returned he reported that there were no breaks in the barbed wire, that all the trip wires were still in place.

The gunner scratched his head. 'Your lot must have got in here last night, but how in the world did you come through the barbed wire?'

Montgomery promised to bring one of his men along to demonstrate, and later that day, while a group of amazed artillery officers watched, the civilian eased his way under their barbed-wire barricade with the speed and confidence of a ferret.

'Easy enough,' one of the officers said, 'for your chap to do it in the daytime. But you say that you came in here at night. You couldn't possibly have got under all that barbed wire in the dark.'

Montgomery smiled. 'Blindfold this chap,' he said, 'and he'll go through your precious wire again.' And he did.

In a similar exercise in Northumberland, when Anthony Quayle and a demolitions training officer from Coleshill invaded a battalion headquarters of 51 Highland Division, they set up thunderflashes in and around the building, attached time pencils to them and then, at the demolitions officer's suggestion, decided to wait and see what would happen.

At two o'clock in the morning Quayle and the other officer sat crouched in a clump of rhododendron bushes in front of the country house that was the battalion headquarters, munching chocolate bars. Suddenly the first thunderflashes detonated. Then the second set. And then the third. The two officers could hear men scuffling about and cursing inside the building. It was all very funny, even when the doors were thrust open and they could make out the silhouettes of some very angry Scottish soldiers. But it stopped being funny altogether when they heard a voice say 'Shoot the ——' followed by the noise of metal against metal as the soldiers drew back and then sent home the bolts of their rifles.

Quayle and his companion could only remain where they were, absolutely silent, praying that the Highlanders would not decide to fire their rifles wildly into the night or prod the rhododendrons with their bayonets. Both of which things, fortunately, they did not do.

By far the most interesting training exercises for the Auxiliary Units patrols on their home grounds were those in which they were part of much bigger manœuvres. Although no official accounts are available of Auxiliary Units' participation in such exercises, mainly because for security reasons all mentions of the patrols had to be omitted from Army reports of exercises, ample evidence exists to prove that even some of the most fantastic stories are not apocryphal. In one major exercise in South-east England, in which a number of Resistance patrols participated, the men fixed limpet mines to the underside of every one of the vehicles used by whole formations of the regular troops. When the umpires were told about the mines in the morning, they ruled that the exercise would have to restart, for had those mines been live, most of the participating units would have been immobilized.

When 77 Division was advancing through Cornwall on a similar exercise some headquarters vehicles were suddenly attacked and captured by Resistance men. The attack, which had been ordered by General Morgan, VIII Corps Commander, was much more effective than even he had anticipated, and in the end he had to call off the Resistance so that 77 Division could continue its training.

The Army was not the only Service to suffer such embarrassments. One winter night fifty men of the Resistance in Devonshire drifted down the River Taw in open boats. When they were abreast of RAF Chivenor they slipped into the icy water, silently swam ashore and set to work. They mined aircraft, vehicles and buildings with thunderflashes and time pencils. Had their charges been real ones, Chivenor would have been put out of action. And had the Resistance men been less careful, they would have been shot, for although the attack was a part of a much larger defence exercise, no one had alerted RAF Chivenor, and the guards were armed with loaded rifles.

Although it had never been intended that Auxiliary Units patrols should ever emerge to fight the Germans openly, and although this was a policy that Colonel Major could never have reversed without altering altogether the entire structure of the British Resistance organization, he introduced hand-to-hand combat training at Coleshill, and a team of instructors from the Army Physical Training Corps turned up every Saturday afternoon to hold classes. Most of the members of most of the patrols were taught at least a few of the tricks of killing with their bare hands as well as with their Commando knives.

Often in training exercises the members of Auxiliary Units patrols had to pretend that they were fighting at close quarters. In one such exercise—one of the comparatively few in which patrols ever worked in London—an attack was made on a railway yard at Bethnal Green. The Railway Police had agreed beforehand that if they felt a slight tap on their heads, they would pretend to have been knocked out. But one Resistance man, a member of a north-east Essex patrol, must have been over-eager, for the Railway Policeman he tapped with his rubber truncheon had to be revived in hospital.

Accounts of such actions never ceased to amaze Colonel Major, just as he never ceased to be amazed by the fact that the miners in Auxiliary Units patrols were better at making up sabotage charges than trained sappers, by the fact that gamekeepers and stalkers were much better scouts that even the most highly trained infantrymen. Most incredible in some ways were the soldiers, all of them volunteers and taken from almost every regiment in the country, who helped to train the Resistance. All of the members of these so-called Scout Sections were enthusiastic almost beyond belief, and one section, to toughen themselves, regularly went on twenty-mile route marches bare-footed.

Colonel Major was impressed by the fact that wealthy farmers would give up so much time voluntarily to his organization, that the van Moppes brothers, industrial diamond merchants who were group leaders in Worcestershire, were more concerned about their hideouts and the way they could prepare sabotage charges than they were about the strong room full of diamonds that they had in their home.

During his fifteen months with the organization Colonel Major drew it together and increased the number of patrols until there were even some on the Shetlands. More than this, he created, entirely unknown to the organization he had already inherited, a second Auxiliary Units organization with an entirely different purpose.

12

THE SECRET SWEETIES

LIKE so many of those very secret wartime organizations that simply vanished when they had achieved their purpose, the Auxiliary Units organization has left behind it many mysteries. Those people who belonged to it were seldom told any more about it than they absolutely had to know, and others who were brought into contact with the organization but were never actually enrolled in it were told even less.

In 1942 and 1943 ninety-three women, many of them in the ATS, were quietly asked to volunteer for an interesting and possibly dangerous assignment. Those who volunteered were told to report for an interview in, of all places, the public lounge on the fourth floor of Harrod's, in Knightsbridge.

At the interviews the women were never told what the work was that they were being considered for, what special qualifications or qualities it demanded—or anything else. Some of them may have discovered in the conversation that their interviewer, Beatrice Temple, a pretty ATS officer who wore the crowns of a major on her shoulder straps, and who on some occasions wore a tartan skirt with her uniform, was the niece of the newly enthroned Archbishop of Canterbury.

Some women heard nothing more about the interviews, but many eventually received formal orders from the War Office to proceed by train to Marks Tey in Essex, to change there to the Cambridge line, and to get off at Haverhill in Suffolk, where they were to cross the road to the Rose and Crown public house. There they were met by an Army car with the number '490' on a white and red formation plaque on its wing, and were taken through narrow, winding lanes to a large farmhouse set back from a lonely lane on the outskirts of a village.

In the house the women were given slips of paper by a Royal Corps of Signals officer who, with no further explanations at all, asked them to read into a microphone. When the women had done this they were given cups of tea and, still no wiser, were driven back to Haverhill, put on the train and told to return to their units.

For some of the women the mystery remained a mystery. The

others were ordered to report to 'G.P.O. Highworth'. But only when they had been collected by another '490' vehicle and had been taken to Hannington Hall, Hannington, in Wiltshire, a house owned by the Fry cocoa family five miles to the west of Coleshill. Only when they had signed the Official Secrets Act at Hannington were the women at last told that they had been enrolled in the most secret part of Britain's most secret wartime organization, Auxiliary Units.

These women would be needed to expand a newly formed side of the organization, one which was to function under the meaningless cover name of 'Special Duties Section'. Most of the members of this new section, apart from the ATS, would be civilians in the coastal areas in which there were already Resistance patrols. With very few exceptions, however, members of the new section would be told nothing about the existing Resistance organization, and the men in the patrols would be told nothing about the new section. At carefully predetermined points in their structure the two completely separate streams of Auxiliary Units would have to cross, but the greatest care was to be taken to keep the crossing points as few and as secure as possible. The organization of thoroughbred cloak-and-dagger ancestry was now going more intensively into the cloak-and-dagger business. In addition to attacking the Germans from inside occupied territory, the British Resistance was perfecting its arrangements to spy on them, too.

At Hannington Hall, Major Maurice Petherick, at the time Member of Parliament for the Penryn and Falmouth Division of Cornwall, began dipping further into the old boy net for suitable Intelligence Officers to send into the field to recruit more spies.

Meanwhile Royal Corps of Signals experts at Coleshill began designing a new short-range wireless set. This would have to be so simple that untrained people would be able to work and maintain it. It would have to be small enough to be concealed easily, able to withstand prolonged exposure to damp, able to work on 6-volt car batteries, able to broadcast voice because there would be no time to teach anybody morse code. And if such a thing was possible, the set would have to be able to broadcast signals difficult for Gestapo locator vans to pinpoint.

No such radio sets were available commercially at the time, yet the experts at Coleshill produced a prototype within weeks. Instead of using a normal military frequency, the Auxiliary Units transmitter-receiver was designed to broadcast on 60 and 65 megacycles, the five-metre band which is today familiar to most Britons because it is used for transmitting BBC-1 television in England, but which in 1941 was so rarely used that the Germans probably did not monitor it.

Because of their relatively high frequency and their low power, under normal conditions the Resistance transmissions would barely be received beyond the horizon. Under freak atmospheric conditions, the stations could be heard on the Continent. However, these conditions would have become apparent to the broadcasters as soon as they went on the air, and they could switch off before they were overheard and properly monitored.

The Auxiliary Units radio set was only about fifteen inches long, five inches wide and six high. It was so straightforward in design that it could be made entirely from components still available at the time on the civilian market. When the prototype had passed every field test that War Office signals experts could devise, Colonel Major was allocated £2,000 for parts, and production was begun. Partly to save time, partly for security reasons, the sets were built by Royal Corps of Signals men working on an assembly line at Coleshill.

When the wireless sets were ready, a few were put into the hands of carefully selected members of operational patrols. But most of the out-stations were to be operated by men completely new to the Resistance organization, men who would not have gone underground had the Germans occupied Britain. No cover story could account for the radios, and so the broadcasters were not provided with one. They all knew that if they were captured by the Germans, they would probably be tortured first and then shot. R. G. Potts, an operator at Braxted, Essex, says that they were told at the time that their radio transmission could not have been pinpointed by the Gestapo's radio locators, but this was untrue.

Sometimes regular British military radio operators intercepted the Resistance signals. One clandestine operator, Adrian Monck-Mason, a chicken farmer who lived on a hilltop outside Charing, Kent, was once going to his radio hideout, under his chicken houses, when he saw a Royal Corps of Signals soldier wandering around near by, a tall fishpole aerial extending from a knapsack radio slung on his back. Monck-Mason asked him what he was doing and the soldier explained that signals from a strange station had been picked up in the area; the Army could not recognize the code, had not been able to break it and had therefore decided that German spies were at work in the area. Monck-Mason assured the soldier that he would report anything strange that he saw, and eventually the soldier went away. Monck-Mason continued to broadcast messages undetected throughout the existence of the Special Duties Section of the Resistance. Generals Montgomery and Alanbrooke were among the many senior officers who were taken into his radio hideout at one time or another to watch him at work.

Wearing civilian clothing and provided with cover stories, the Special Duties Intelligence Officers moved into the coastal areas to recruit spies and to train them. Usually these officers got to know their opposite numbers in Operations, but the two rarely worked together. Neither tried to learn anything about the details of the other's operation, and no plans were made to use the radio network to co-ordinate the operations of the Resistance patrols. Most of the operational Intelligence Officers would not have known how to get in touch with the radio networks themselves, but individual members of certain patrols—men such as R. G. Potts—also served as radio operators, and certain members of patrols knew who their local communications people were. They did not, however, always know that these people had radio sets. On Thanet, for example, a Special Duties radio operator named Lamont, who had allowed an operational hideout to be dug in a corner of his farmyard and who maintained close liaison with the patrol that used it, convinced its members that all he himself ever did was pass on messages he got from holes in the ground to 'other people down the line'. The members of the patrol did not learn until after the war that he had been issued with broadcasting equipment.

Unlike the leaders of the Resistance organizations that were beginning to grow in the occupied countries, the men behind the British Resistance realized from the start that in occupied territory espionage and operational personnel had to be kept separate, both to keep out of each others' way and to keep from compromising each other. Partly because of this, partly because the patrols in occupied territory would have had plenty to do without taking on the additional task of spying, men and women were recruited just to do this work. Theirs was the most secret of organizations—so secret that they had to be trained in their own areas, not at Coleshill or at Hannington Hall. Most of them were never told where their headquarters was or the names of any people in the organization whom they did not actually meet. These spies (about a thousand were found when the Special Duties organization was begun, and there were about three thousand at the end) received some training in night movement, but apart from that they were taught only how to prepare simple Intelligence reports and pass them on. They were never told that they were members of a nationwide body of selected men and women and their names were never committed to a roll. They were all men and women whose jobs allowed them to move about a great deal. Whenever possible the Special Duties Intelligence Officers recruited among such people as doctors and midwives, postmen and parsons, farm workers and bus drivers.

In each area secret 'letter boxes' were designated where reports could be left to be collected later either by the radio operators themselves or, more often, by 'cut-outs' who would then move them on to other letter boxes. Normally the spies did not know who the cut-outs were and the cut-outs did not know who collected the messages from the letter boxes or where they dropped them. This very sensible system was one of the things that made no sense at all to the Gestapo inquisitors who relentlessly badgered Major Richard Stevens for 'facts' about the methods of British Intelligence.

Neither the spies nor the cut-outs knew who the radio operators were or, in a number of areas, that the messages would be sent out by wireless to control stations which, in the event of invasion, were to be taken over by GHQ Home Forces. Some radio operators, among them R. G. Potts, were asked by their Special Duties Intelligence Officers to suggest people who should be their spies and cut-outs. However, the actual recruiting was done by the SDIO, and the members of some teams, although they had known one another all their lives, did not learn until after the war that they had been working together.

The Auxiliary Units' letter boxes were very carefully chosen. Eustace Maxwell remembers one in Scotland, a drain next to a house. Messages were put inside slit tennis balls, which were dropped down the drain and, instead of rolling to the sewer, fell into a trap some distance from the house. The people who dropped these messages did not know where the drain terminated, and the cut-out who collected the messages did not know where the drain emerged above ground.

In other places the letter boxes were tin cans on rubbish heaps, hollows in trees, the abandoned nests of wild animals and sometimes hen houses and dovecotes. The hiding places were usually in the open and were passed frequently by large numbers of people, including those who used them.

In some coastal areas the radio transmitters were concealed by the out-station operators themselves, but usually they were given some help by Auxiliary Units. Moving the out-stations from location to location to foil detector vans, as was done with considerable success by the extremely ingenious and efficient Resistance radio operators in Occupied Denmark, would not have been possible in Britain, for high-frequency broadcasting requires careful tuning, and few of the British Resistance radio operators knew how to tune their own sets. Most knew only how to switch them on and off, how to test and to change the batteries, and where to bang the vibrators with their fists when they stuck.

Ideally the transmitters should all have been sited in unobstructed places on high ground, but this was seldom possible, for the stations were often most useful in positions from which the operators could actually keep an eye on roads and open country while they were on the air. And, of course, the stations had to be in places that the operators could reach quickly without drawing attention to themselves.

The aerials were forty feet long and, except when they could be embedded in the walls of buildings, had to be strung in trees. They were virtually invisible, however, for Royal Corps of Signals men, many of whom had been employed by the Forestry Commission before the war, climbed the trees, carved half-inch-deep channels up their trunks, buried the concentric wires in them, and finally filled in the channels again with plaster of Paris painted to match the bark. From time to time the foresters returned to the out-stations to make sure that the camouflage was still in place, and the officers who inspected the stations all over the country say that, even from a few feet away, the wires could not be seen.

The out-station transmitters themselves were even more cunningly concealed, almost always underground but occasionally in other places; one is said to have been fixed in the top of the Boston 'Stump', the famous Lincolnshire church tower and landmark. One, in a public house near Arundel in Sussex, was approached through the pub's cellar. A knitting needle had to be inserted in a crack in one of the cellar walls and a panel then slid aside to reveal the way into another, smaller room. This chamber, about four by eight feet, would probably not have aroused the Germans' suspicions, for it was stacked high with crates of what appeared to be smuggled spirits. But behind the crates a second hidden trapdoor led into a long gallery that had been carved in the earth and was timbered like a mine shaft. Dug for the publican by Canadian Army engineers stationed in his area, the gallery led under the road to another secret room where a broadcasting set was concealed behind yet another false wall.

A similar out-station, in another public house on a main road about ten miles north of Bournemouth, had to be entered through a shed at the bottom of the garden. The radio operator then went through a succession of rooms, each connected to the other by a hidden trapdoor. In the last the transmitter was hidden behind the wall.

Yet another station, on a farm outside Yeovil, had to be entered through what appeared to be a disused privy behind the house. The transmitter station itself was not so primitive—and even had fitted carpeting on the floor.

No one recalls any of the out-stations having been found inadvertently, although one of the stations in the Charing area of Kent was off the air throughout the three days of a major military exercise because the Colonel commanding one of the Army units taking part had, quite by chance, pitched his tent on the trapdoor of the radio hideout.

Had the Germans landed in Britain the Auxiliary Units radio networks would have been handed over to GHQ Home Forces, but even then the organization would not have been altogether centralized, for there was never a senior control station. Instead 'controls' were dotted around the country, with a telephone link to Hannington Hall which would have been switched to GHQ Home Forces. There were no more 'controls' than necessary but enough to serve the hundreds of out-stations. No one who was in the espionage section of British Resistance can recall precisely how many there were or precisely where they were sited, but Beatrice Temple recalls thirty-two—as far north as Elgin, south and west as Taunton, south and east as Canterbury. Because East Anglia is mainly flat and the control stations could sometimes be sited no higher than their out-stations, in that part of the country the control stations were much closer than anywhere else. In Essex the station at Halstead was only twelve miles from another at Hatfield Peverel.

Control stations were all supposed to be within the perimeters of Army divisional headquarters. Many were in woods, but some were on the edges of towns or even in their centres. The one at Canterbury was right outside the barracks, while the Winchester station was in the garden of a cottage on the edge of the town. The Auxiliary Units signals section which installed and maintained the control stations and the out-stations had its headquarters at Bachelors Hall, Hundon, in Suffolk, five miles south of the control station at Ousden, also in Suffolk, and not much farther away from another in a wood just south of Bury St Edmunds. Some of the other control stations were in Tunbridge Wells and Bilting, Kent; Thornham Parva, Suffolk, just south of Diss; Rackheath Hall, Rackheath, five miles east of Norwich; in Aberdeen; at Scotch Corner; in Dalton-in-Furness; at Ardingly and Heathfield in Sussex; at Garrowby, South Dalton and Whitby in Yorkshire; at Horncastle, twenty miles east of Lincoln. The control stations were all carefully destroyed as soon as they were no longer needed, and the official records concerning them, although said still to exist, are not accessible. Most of the people who actually operated the stations remember them only by their code names; to confuse any German monitor who by chance happened to tune in on them, the stations were given either the names of places that were far away from them and usually inland, or imaginary place names.

Each control station had two transmitters and two receivers, one set that was in use every day during the existence of the radio network, the other for special occasions and for the ultimate occasion, when the Germans arrived in Britain. The 'everyday' broadcasting equipment was usually in a hut in plain view above ground. The only things secret about these stations were the transmitters themselves, and the operators had strict instructions to throw covers over them before allowing anyone not in the Auxiliary Units to enter the huts.

The alternative 'underground' broadcasting stations were always near by, usually within five hundred yards of the 'everyday' stations. These special stations—called 'zero' stations because whenever the operators broadcast from them they followed the station name with the code suffix 'zero'—were concealed in elaborate hideouts built by a special detachment of Royal Engineers. A few of the earliest were crudely carved into the earth, had mud walls and rough timber ceilings, but most were concreted and at least as comfortable as the larger air-raid shelters.

The entrances were elaborately disguised. Beatrice Temple describes one where the operators had to pull loose a panel of bark from a tree to get to a switch. A trapdoor in the ground, thirty feet from the tree, lifted a few inches, and the operators had then to swing it open and descend a ladder into a small room. All the walls were lined with shelves, on most of which were packing cases full of explosives, ammunition and other things that would be found in any of the operational patrols' hideouts or dumps. But when a hidden catch in the room was triggered, one of the shelves would pivot, revealing an opening into a much larger room in which there were bunks, spare clothes and sufficient food to sustain the operators for a month, as well as a cooker, a chemical toilet, a table with the set on it, extra batteries and a generator which would recharge them and would also provide lighting and work the blower that kept the air fresh.

Because every control station would have to be able to keep a round-the-clock vigil, each would need a staff of three people. Soldiers being in short supply, Colonel Major asked Dame Helen Gwynne-Vaughan, at that time the Chief Controller of the ATS, to assign female officers to his organization. Regulations flatly forbade the assignment of fewer than ten ATS personnel to any establishment where there were also men unless a very good reason was given, but Colonel Major refused flatly to give any reason at all. The work the women were to do, he said, was too secret.

However, partly because his request was backed by the CIGS and by the Prime Minister, partly because he could at least say something about the operational work of Auxiliary Units, the colonel was promised all the ATS officers he asked for. The actual singling out of candidates was done for him by Dame Helen Gwynne-Vaughan's successor, Lady Carlisle. At the same time Auxiliary Units was authorized its first ATS other ranks, about twenty young women who would work at Coleshill as cooks, clerks and drivers.

After forty-three women had been selected to work the control stations and the first broadcasting had begun, Colonel Major asked that a slightly more senior ATS officer be assigned to Auxiliary Units to be in charge and to take over the recruiting of new operators. So it was that in November 1941, Beatrice Temple was taken away from other work and posted to 'GPO Highworth'. It was she who decided that all prospective radio operators should be looked over in the genteel setting of Harrod's —'the chairs were far enough apart so that we could carry on a conversation without being overhead. After the interviews, whether the women were acceptable to Auxiliary Units or not, I always rewarded them with a free afternoon in which to shop.'

The women that Beatrice Temple selected to operate the control stations were either ATS officers already, ATS other ranks, members of the VAD or FANY or, in a few cases, civilian women not engaged in war work. On assignment to the organization, which was officially designated 'ATS Auxiliary Units', they were all commissioned as junior subalterns, and were later given a second pip. As soon as the organization began to expand, the 'old girl network' was dipped into, and many friends of the first control station operators followed them into the organization.

As well as having clear voices and accents that would be easily understood in any part of the country, the women had to be intelligent, even-tempered and completely self-reliant. Once at their stations, they were their own bosses. No daily check was ever made to see that they were all right, but the Auxiliary Units signals officer made regular checks to ensure that the equipment was in good order and to deliver revised codes. Once every month

Beatrice Temple visited each station, mainly to see that the domestic arrangements were satisfactory and that the women were getting their pay and allowances on time.

When possible the women lived in local ATS messes or in mixed messes, but sometimes they had to be installed in private billets. One control station's staff camped in Lord Halifax's gazebo on his estate at Garrowby in Yorkshire, and others lived in the statelier parts of stately homes. The ATS officers sometimes wore the insignia of the units with which they lived, including the fighting divisions, sometimes Royal Corps of Signals insignia, sometimes GHQ insignia, and sometimes no particular insignia at all. If anybody asked them what their work was, they merely answered 'Signals'. They were under specific orders to tell no one about their work, and when they lived in divisional messes only the divisional commanders knew what their job was.

The women were very firm about secrecy, and their final reply to persistent questioners greatly superior in rank was, 'I'm not allowed to tell you, but I can give you the name of somebody who can.' The 'somebody' was usually the officer commanding the Resistance's signals headquarters at Hendon.

Male officers who served with the Auxiliary Units organization recall that the women were exceptionally pretty. They ranged in age from nineteen to the mid-forties, and many of them were either already married when they joined the organization or got married while they were with it. In the divisional headquarters mess at Doncaster where the women from one of the Yorkshire stations lived, the other officers always referred to them as 'the secret sweeties'.

Someone in ATS headquarters in the War Office once asked Miss Temple, 'What exactly do your officers do? We hear that they sit in caves all day and knit.'

Miss Temple smiled. 'That's what they do.'

In fact, quite often there was no time at all for knitting. Although most of the out-stations usually came on the air only twice a day, and then only for a few minutes, they did not have broadcasting schedules to which their operators could adhere precisely, so the ATS officers at the control stations had to maintain long listening watches. Sometimes this was done only at night, sometimes only during the day, sometimes for a set number of minutes at thirty or sixty minute intervals. From July 1943 until the stations went off the air, controls were triple-manned and two of the women had to be on duty at each transmitter all the time. They usually slept beside them.

At their headquarters in Wiltshire most of the ATS in the Auxiliary Units Special Duties Section were taught how to fire rifles, Sten guns and Service revolvers, but they were not issued with weapons to keep in the zero stations.

As long as possible after the country had been invaded, even after the stations themselves had been overrun, the women were to try to keep on the air. This would probably have been suicidal, and the women knew it. Nevertheless, their orders were that all three would remain with the zero transmitter until they heard Germans actually breaking into the outer room. Only then would the operator have stopped broadcasting, removed and smashed the transmitter's frequency crystal, and scurried through an emergency escape hatch, say a pipe that ran horizontally about twelve feet before turning upwards towards the surface. The camouflaged escape exits were supposed to be far enough away from the main entrances to give the women at least a slight chance of sneaking away, with luck even before the Germans had found their way into the radio rooms.

To make sure that the zero stations were always ready for use, they were visited at least once a week, and all the equipment in them was checked. When the Auxiliary Units Special Duties Section participated in military manoeuvres—or had exercises of its own—the women actually broadcast from the zero stations, sometimes staying cooped up in them continuously for five days at a stretch.

A civilian friend of Bill Major in the Military Intelligence Directorate had developed the one-time pad code that was being taught to SOE-assisted Resistance groups and would later be adopted by most of the world's espionage organizations. After Colonel Major had prepared a list of five hundred military phrases which were likely to be used by his spies in Britain, his friend produced a list of five hundred words to match the phrases. Next a simple letter code was devised, and a practical way was found to alter this code every twenty-four hours. Simple as it was, it was estimated that the Germans would have had to intercept half a dozen British Resistance radio messages in any one twenty-four-hour period to break it—and within hours or even minutes the Resistance would in any case be using a completely new code.

After 1941, whenever the Auxiliary Units organization was invited to participate in Army exercises, the Special Duties Section practised spying on the uniformed troops, but very discreetly so that the existence of the spy network was kept secret. However, special exercises not involving troops were devised to test the Special Duties Section's efficiency. Messages were given to the spies who then put them into the letter boxes. The cut-outs took them to other letter boxes, the radio operators eventually collected and coded them, then passed them to the control stations. While one ATS officer took down the messages, another decoded them, then telephoned them to the headquarters controlling the exercise. In very little time the messages got through. None was ever lost. Nothing in any German records suggests that their radio monitors ever heard men and women in Britain reciting random combinations of letters of the alphabet to each other. If they did, they certainly attached no significance to it.

The Special Duties Section of Auxiliary Units was beyond doubt the part of the organization that would have collapsed most quickly after the Germans got a foothold in Britain, for underground broadcasting from fixed stations is untenable. The outstation operators would have been in great danger, but not in as great danger as the control station operators who had to remain on the air until their hideouts were penetrated. The secret sweeties accepted this fact. They say now that excitement came only when they got the sub-harmonics of aircraft transmissions overhead. Eleanor Norman-Butler recalls hearing a pilot, his voice pitched high in fear, call, *'Achtung! Spitfiren!'*—then she knew that they were in the war.

13

STAND DOWN

IN February 1942, when Colonel Major was moved on from Auxiliary Units, the battle for Stalingrad had not yet been fought, the British had yet to achieve a significant victory in North Africa or indeed anywhere else, America was only nominally in the war, and so the tide of victory cannot be said to have yet turned inexorably against the Nazis. Nevertheless, throughout 1942 the possibility of an invasion and occupation of the British Isles seemed remote to all but a few Britons. They did not know then that by 1942 the plans for 'Operation Sea Lion' had been put away, even though the Abwehr diligently kept their publications of material for the use of their occupation troops in Britain up to date until the autumn of 1944.

By 1942 there seemed to be no really compelling reason for keeping a Resistance organization at the ready in Britain, and yet a stand down of the Auxiliary Unit patrols or of the espionage network at that time would have been, at the very least, incautious. Hitler, we now know, had not yet discarded the notion of developing a nuclear weapon, he had technologists working hard on the development of flying bombs, and he already possessed or very soon was to possess vast stocks of a nerve gas that would have penetrated any known gas masks. Any of these weapons, or any combination of them, or, for that matter, any weapons that may have existed but about which we still know nothing, might have turned the tide of battle in Hitler's favour. Then a Resistance organization in Britain would have once more been essential. In any case, the Resistance units continued to be useful in two ways: they tested the security of the uniformed troops and thus helped to keep them on their toes, and in some areas of the country they were the main defence force, and so freed conventional units for more aggressive tasks.

In the areas where the Auxiliary Units patrols functioned, and especially in the more out-of-the-way ones, members of the individual patrols still believed that they might yet have a decisive role to play. For whatever they read in their newspapers or heard on the radio, they remained convinced that a clever invader could land in Britain, that he could get a foothold. The men of the British Resistance—and the women, too—were not the only people in the country who still found the 'veil of the Unknown' just as opaque as ever.

Colonel the Lord Glanusk was the third officer to take command at Coleshill. He arrived in his own Rolls-Royce, appointed Lord Delamere his staff captain, and, when he had installed himself in the headquarters, sent to London for his cellar. Very quickly much of the sombre atmosphere of wartime austerity lifted, especially when Glanusk invited the young officers on his staff to share his wine and pay no more for each bottle than he had paid when he laid it down. From then until the disbanding of the Auxiliary Units organization more and more of the staff officers at Coleshill were to be the wealthy, the well-to-do and the titled. The place became like a Guards' Mess in peacetime, public school accents predominated, and there was more talk of shooting animals and less of shooting Germans. J. F. Montgomery found the officers unwilling to talk about anything except horse racing (one of Glanusk's officers owned the largest private racing stud in the country, Colonel Hancock was Clerk of the Course at Lincoln, and yet another was a famous National Hunt Starter).

Around the coasts of Britain at the beginning of 1942 the Auxiliary Units Intelligence Officers still felt that their work had some urgency, but as the months passed they could see that the country's defences were becoming much stronger, that their Resistance organization was becoming pretty much an academic exercise. The soldiers who had helped with the training in the coastal areas were withdrawn, and any special training with uniformed troops had to be done at Coleshill. To maintain a high level of enthusiasm the individual patrols now competed with one another on the rifle range, at throwing grenades, and at night patrolling. In each county there were discreet competitions for the best patrols, and the winners then went on to Coleshill to compete in national championships. A secret organization that had begun with the help of certain former Boy Scouts was now becoming a national secret troop of adult Scouts. Yet somehow the individual patrols' security remained as tight as ever.

As for the Special Duties Section's security—it was absolutely

[137]

muscle-bound. The operators of some of the out-stations, increasingly afraid that their broadcasts were being monitored by the Germans, kept off the air for so long that their batteries ran down and deteriorated. In some areas the actual network of spies and cut-outs became so security conscious that even the Intelligence Officers sent out from Coleshill were unable to make contact with the organization. And yet the network of men and women who were to gather information when the Germans occupied their territory continued to grow. To train these people, security was relaxed, and in the coastal sectors secret night classes were held.

In the early days it would have been unthinkable to put anything to do with Auxiliary Units activity into print, and nothing in the one Resistance newspaper, Captain Fiddes-Watt's *The Password,* even hinted that the Captain had anything to do with Resistance. Even today veterans of the Auxiliary Units patrols are not supposed to show anyone any of the official documents that they may have saved from the war. But in July 1942 the Resistance headquarters at Coleshill decided for reasons of its own to publish its first and only official handbook, intended for distribution to all operational patrol leaders. If the Germans had occupied the country and had happened to see a copy of the handbook lying around, however, they might not have given it a second glance, for printed on its cover were these words:

THE COUNTRYMAN'S
DIARY —— 1939
HIGHWORTH FERTILISERS
DO THEIR STUFF UNSEEN
UNTIL YOU SEE
RESULTS!
With the Compliments of
HIGHWORTH & CO.
YOU WILL FIND THE NAME HIGHWORTH
WHEREVER QUICK RESULTS
ARE REQUIRED

The 42-page diary was in fact a sabotage handbook. Its author, Philip Tallent, a captain in the Royal Engineers, had managed to put into remarkably few words almost everything a Resistance saboteur would have to know about explosives. The booklet explained in some detail, in words and in drawings, how to make the least amount of explosives do the greatest amount of damage, how to blow up railway lines, how to set booby traps, how best to place charges on the petrol tanks of vehicles, how to blow up aeroplanes on the ground, how to set off bomb dumps, how to destroy petrol stores ('In large dumps concentrate on the up-wind end of the dump. The heat and wind will help to spread the fire'), how to blow up armoured-cars and tanks. It explained how all the different anti-personnel mines issued to Auxiliary Units patrols worked, and it went into some detail about improvising mines when ready-made ones were not available, among other things suggesting that a cocoa tin should be filled with gelignite and buried inside a biscuit tin full of scrap metal or flints. 'Another very good method,' it advised, 'is to use an old motorcycle cylinder filled with Gelignite. The fins fly very well.'

Little of this was new to any but the most recent recruits to Auxiliary Units, for all the patrols had spent many weekends inventing and testing their own anti-personnel mines. The Weeley patrol in Essex nearly wiped themselves out with mines which they hung in trees—mines made from unwanted pickling crocks filled with scraps of metal swept from a factory floor. 'With a little imagination dozens of ideas will present themselves,' Captain Tallent wrote in *The Countryman's Diary*, 'and they will probably be better suited to your part of the country. The essential point is that for outdoor booby traps you must aim at killing by splinters—not by blast.'

The book contained only one indication of the organization for which it was intended. On page 13, discussing the wrapping of gelignite, it comments, 'Auxunit packing is O.K. . . .'—which is almost certainly the nearest that the official name of the British Resistance organization ever came to being set up in type and printed on paper until after the official stand down order had been given.

When Lord Glanusk had a heart attack and had to leave Coleshill, the command of Auxiliary Units was passed on to his deputy, Colonel Frank Douglas, a well-known London stockbroker who had been a member of the Military Intelligence Directorate and of the Coleshill staff for some time. Colonel Douglas continued the routine at the headquarters as before, encouraging the individual patrols in their exercises and continuing to build up the Special Duties espionage network. Colonel Beyts had by then gone on to SOE where his talent was most urgently needed to help train Asian guerrillas, many of whom, certainly through no fault of his, were to bide their time until they could turn their newly acquired knowledge against British troops.

The stand down of the Auxiliary Units organization did not take place all at once. During the first months of 1944 a number of the operational sectors were amalgamated so that, for example, East Anglia, which had been opened up by one officer but had then had a separate Intelligence Officer assigned to each county, found itself once again with just one officer and just one Resistance headquarters. At the same time some of the Special Duties control stations went off the air, the zero stations were blown up, and the first of the ATS officers were sent off, in the words of Eleanor Norman-Butler, 'to be trained to be ordinary officers'. However, the men in the operational patrols who had worked so hard and had kept their secrets so well were offered one last chance of glory.

Group leaders in many parts of the country were told that the members of their patrols should be asked to volunteer to be parachuted into France ahead of the Allied landings so that they could use their special skills to impede any possible rush of German reinforcements to the beaches. They would, the British Resistance men were told, enable conventional but less well-trained soldiers to participate in the spearhead across Europe.

In some sectors almost all the Resistance men volunteered, but certainly not in others, for many patrol and group leaders thought that the whole project was irresponsible. Norman Steed, the Resistance group leader on the Isle of Thanet explained, 'We were only useful, we thought, on our own home ground. We weren't even of any use as soldiers. Once we were sent to Coleshill in uniform, and in London only my brother and I, who'd had some Officer Cadet training before the war, knew how to salute. So when we saw an officer approaching the lot of us had to turn away and pretend to stare into a shop window. I remember that we got a rocket about it afterwards. They told us we'd have to learn to *look* like soldiers before we were reported as spies. Imagine how we'd have behaved in France.'

At any rate, not a single member of the British Resistance was ever even to receive parachute training. Nevertheless, in May 1944, less than a month before D-Day, several Auxiliary Units patrol members in Northumberland received secret movement orders, and with them railway warrants. They put on their Home Guard uniforms, shouldered their weapons and reported to a railway station where the RTO eventually put them into reserved compartments on a train. Lambert Carmichael recalls that the train stopped several times on the journey south, and at each stop more men in Home Guard uniform climbed aboard.

At Portsmouth the Resistance men were put on to a ferry which threaded its way through the middle of what looked to the Northumberland men like the entire Allied invasion fleet, lying at anchor in the Solent. The men were put ashore on the Isle of Wight where they were told that the Overlord planners thought that after D-Day the Germans might attempt a counter-landing on the island. If this happened, the Auxiliary Units patrols were to destroy this force from behind its own lines.

Unnoticed, the Resistance men reconnoitred the entire island, selecting the most likely looking landing places and also the best places to set up their own defences. Then they dug in and waited. D-Day came and went, and a fortnight afterwards the men of the Resistance were taken off the island as quietly as they had arrived, and returned to their homes.

Did anyone ever seriously contemplate sending these 'civilian soldiers' to France? Major-General Gubbins points out that if this were going to be done, he would have known about it, for at the time he was in command of SOE and any parachute training of special forces would have had to have been co-ordinated with him. Yet he heard nothing about it. He also points out that the parachuting into France before D-Day of anyone who could not speak French was never even contemplated.

On their own home grounds the civilians of the British Resistance may have been superb, but they could hardly have coped on foreign soil. Some of the military who were connected with Auxiliary Units have suggested that the proposal was merely a sort of left-handed way of patting them on the head and thanking them for the services they had been prepared to give Britain.

Perhaps. But the headquarters at Coleshill was warned in the spring of 1944 that after D-Day the Germans might parachute troops into some of Britain's coastal areas to make nuisance raids on roads, railway lines and bridges. To guard against this, a number of Auxiliary Units patrols in the South-west were put on the alert. Because of the sort of attack that was expected, the men were not to go to ground if a landing was reported, but their tactics would of necessity have been the sort that they had been training for four years to perfect. They would have hit at the enemy without letting him see them.

Auxiliary Units personnel *were* parachuted into France, but not civilian members of patrols. Captain Ian Fenwick, the *Punch* cartoonist who had been the Intelligence officer in Somerset, and Captain G. F. D. Bond, one of the officers in Sussex, received parachute training and shortly before D-Day were transferred to the Special Air Service. Both were dropped into France and both were killed there. Bond, at least, is known to have expected this to happen and was apprehensive about it. Much more is known about Ian Fenwick's fate.

The cartoonist commanded an SAS group, codenamed 'Gain', that was parachuted complete with heavily armed, hotted-up jeeps, just south of Paris, between the Seine and the Loire, on 14 June 1944. Fenwick's men operated like a motorized Auxiliary Units patrol, hiding by day and racing out at night to hit the German supply convoys speeding towards the Normandy front. They would wait in a side road until a convoy passed, then pull out and follow it. Before the Germans had a chance to take evasive action, they accelerated, caught up with the convoy and raced alongside it, blasting it with their machine-guns.

German security police based on Paris managed to sniff out Fenwick's hide. When, early in the hours of 5 July, reinforcements from Britain were parachuted in, the Germans were waiting on the edge of the dropping-zone. Fenwick was killed and a dozen of his men were captured. Interrogated fruitlessly for a month, the SAS men, all of whom had dropped into France in uniform, were made to put on civilian clothing and were then taken back to the area where they had worked. There they were marched in front of a firing-squad. Only one of them escaped execution. He noticed that the Germans were armed with machine pistols, and he knew that machine pistols were not very reliable. So he took a chance, ran for it and kept on running. Fenwick's driver also survived because he was lucky enough to be unconscious when captured at the dropping-zone. In a German military hospital a French nurse found a doctor's uniform for him, and he put it on and limped away.

On 18 November 1944, General Sir Harold Franklyn, the Commander-in-Chief, Home Forces, wrote to Colonel Douglas:

In view of the improved war situation, it has been decided by the War Office that the Operational Branch of Auxiliary Units shall stand down, and the time has now come to put an end to an organization which could have been of inestimable value to this country in the event of invasion.

All ranks under your command are aware of the secret nature of their duties. For that reason it has not been possible for them to receive publicity, nor will it be possible even now. So far from considering this to be a misfortune, I should like all members of Auxiliary Units to regard it as a matter of special pride.

I have been much impressed by the devotion to duty and high standard of training shown by all ranks. The careful preparations, the hard work undertaken on their own time, their readiness to face the inevitable danger of their role, are all matters which reflect the greatest credit on the body of picked men who form the Auxiliary Units.

I should be glad, therefore, if my congratulations and best wishes could be conveyed to all ranks.

Twelve days later copies of this letter were circulated to everyone who had been in the operational patrols, along with a letter from Colonel Douglas:

The War Office has ordered that the operational side of Auxiliary Units shall stand down. This is due to the greatly improved war situation and the strategic requirements of the moment.

I realize what joining Auxiliary Units has meant to you; so do the officers under my command. You were invited to do a job which would require more skill and coolness, more hard work and greater danger

than was demanded of any other voluntary organization. In the event
of 'Action Stations' being ordered you knew well the kind of life you
were in for. But that was in order, you were picked men, and others,
including myself, knew that you would continue to fight whatever the
conditions, with, or if necessary, without orders.

It now falls on me to tell you that your work has been appreciated
and well carried out, and that your contract, for the moment is at an
end. I am grateful to you for the way you have trained in the last four
years. So is the Regular Army. It was due to your reputation for skill
and determination that extra risk was taken—successfully, as it turned
out—in the defence arrangements of this country during that vital
period. I congratulate you on this reputation and thank you for this
voluntary effort.

In view of the fact that your lives depended on secrecy no public
recognition will be possible. But those in the most responsible positions
at General Headquarters, Home Forces, know what was done, and
what would have been done if you had been called upon. They know
it well. It will not be forgotten.

There were, of course, still many things to be done. The last
Special Duties control stations had been shut down in the summer
and their hideouts were now pits full of rubble. Sappers moved
around the country, blowing up all the operational hideouts they
could find. Most of the explosives and weapons that had been
handed out to the Auxiliary Units patrols were collected, but far
from all of them. Hundreds—perhaps thousands—of the men
still retain their rubber truncheons and their Commando knives,
and some of the veterans of the organization have in their possession much stranger souvenirs of their secret war service. One of
the ATS Special Duties officers, for example, keeps a magnetic
limpet mine, its explosive charge removed, under a wardrobe.
She drags it out from time to time, she says, because it is very
useful for finding pins and needles lost in the deep pile of carpets.

Many of the patrol leaders whose stores of explosives were not
collected simply destroyed them themselves or used them to help
local farmers clear boulders or tree stumps. But other hoards
continue to turn up. During the arms amnesty in 1966 two old
ladies in Devonshire turned in one of Stuart Edmundson's boxes
of sabotage equipment, and in 1966 a labourer in Tavistock drove
a pick into a box of squishy explosives buried at the base of a
tree. In April 1966 a cache of explosives—which from the des-

cription of the individual items may possibly have been put there in 1940 by representatives of the short-lived Section D resistance organization—was found in a solicitor's garden in Atwick Road, Hornsea, Yorkshire. Such finds are so common that they seldom rate more than a line or two in the Press, but it was in 1964 that the most complete store of Auxiliary Units' explosives was handed in.

Reginald Sennitt's beautiful old house at the end of a lonely road in Essex on the western end of the Dengie Marshes was, during the early years of the war, both a Home Guard headquarters and a headquarters for one of the Highland Light Infantry units which patrolled the Essex coast during the period when invasion seemed at least a possibility. After he had been recruited into Auxiliary Units in 1941 and had formed the Dengie Group of operational patrols that covered the Essex marshland from Southminster to Bradwell, Sennitt began to receive weapons, ammunition and other stores, always sent down to him late at night from the local Intelligence Officer's headquarters in the Colne Valley. Sennitt's few neighbours probably did not notice the things arrive, and when the soldiers billeted in his fields questioned him about the supplies, he told them that they were for the Home Guard. When the Home Guard asked him about them, Sennitt said that the things were for the Army. And so, arousing no attention at all, he was able to keep his five patrols well supplied.

Because his patrols' hideouts were on low ground and kept flooding, for three years Mr Sennitt had to keep reordering supplies, especially of explosives. To accommodate the patrols, and also to keep from losing to the floods any more of the things than was absolutely unavoidable, he kept the stores at first in his outbuildings and later in the house itself. He and his wife got used to having hand grenades stacked around their bedroom, canisters of plastic explosive behind the settee in the living-room, sticky bombs in the shed behind the house. Had there been an invasion, the Germans would have had to traverse several miles of mudflats to get to the areas covered by the patrols of the Dengie Group, so there would be plenty of time for the patrol leaders to go to Sennitt's house for stores.

Towards the autumn of 1944, like the Resistance patrols all over the country, the men of the Dengie Group cut back on their training. By then the Essex operational Intelligence Officer had departed, and his successor failed to call on Reginald Sennitt. In fact, Sennitt heard nothing more from any Auxiliary Units higher headquarters until he received copies of Colonel Douglas's stand down order to pass on to his men.

Every night Reginald Sennitt's patrol leaders drove up to his house with crates of sabotage equipment for him to return to the Army. Mr Sennitt kept expecting an Army lorry to turn up for the things, but none ever did. And eventually he realized that as far as he was concerned, the Resistance organization to which he had devoted some three years had simply vanished, leaving him stuck with enough explosive ordnance to keep a small army of saboteurs going for years.

Should he, he wondered, notify the Army? No, he could not do that because he had signed the Official Secrets Act and had specifically sworn to tell no one outside the Auxiliary Units organization anything about it. So in the end he decided to move the things to a disused milking shed. Just as he had been taught at Coleshill, he was careful to keep the detonators away from the safety fuses and the safety fuses away from the high explosives. Surely the Army would remember the things some day and would collect them.

But the Army did not remember. Periodically Reginald Sennitt unlocked the milking shed and went in to make sure that everything was all right. He even turned over some of the crates of explosive to minimize 'weeping'. By 1964, however, he was getting a little uneasy. A veteran of the First World War, he knew that he could not live for ever, that somebody else would have to take on the responsibility of the things in the milking shed. So, throwing caution to the winds, he went to the local police and told them about the explosives in the shed. The police, not having the slightest idea what to do, got in touch with East Anglia Command Headquarters in Colchester, and they passed on the problem to the Eastern Command Ammunition Inspectorate at Hounslow.

On 7 April 1964, Staff-Sergeant R. Sibson of the Royal Army Ordnance Corps took a lorry to Mr Sennitt's house and made the following inventory:

14,738 rounds of ammunition for pistols, rifles and sub-machine-guns, including a quantity of incendiary bullets;

1,205 lb of gelignite, of Nobel 808 and of plastic explosive, most of it in a safe enough condition to take away;
3,742 ft delayed action fuse;
930 ft instantaneous safety fuse;
250 ft detonating cord;
1,447 time pencils;
1,207 L-delay switches [a later form of time pencil which, instead of relying on acid, is triggered by induced metal fatigue];
1,271 detonators of various types;
719 push, pull and pressure-release booby-trap switches;
314 paraffin bombs and
340 igniters for these bombs and for the safety fuses;
131 fog signals;
121 smoke bombs;
212 thunderflashes;
571 primers;
36 1-lb slabs of gun-cotton;
4 hand-grenades;
10 phosphorous grenades;
33 time-pencils and booby trap switches attached to made-up charges.

In April 1945, when the war in Europe was drawing to a close, the War Office announced to the Press that a Resistance organization had existed in Britain since 1940, and Sir Harold Franklyn's message of thanks to the men and women who would have been the Auxiliary Units Special Duties Section's spies was published in *The Times* on Saturday, 14 April 1945:

I realize that every member of the organization from the first invasion days beginning in 1940 voluntarily undertook a hazardous role which required both skill and courage well knowing that the very nature of their work would allow of no public recognition. This organization, founded on the keenness and patriotism of selected civilians of all grades, has been in a position, through its constant and thorough training, to furnish accurate information of raids or invasion instantly to military headquarters throughout the country.

The Times pointed out that the organization was so secret that most of the members did not know one another, that it came into being before France, Belgium, Holland, Denmark or Norway had Resistance organizations of their own—and that the whole thing was run by '300 specially picked officers of the Army Special Duties Branch'.

The popular Fleet Street newspapers also carried the story, and their reporters embellished it, among other things claiming that the Resistance was really a skeleton force that was intended to raise little private armies all over the country, and that its weapons even included 3·7-inch anti-aircraft guns.

A week after publishing their first article *The Times* devoted a leader to Auxiliary Units:

In Secret

There is no one but must be stirred by the news that the secret underground movement in this country, a movement of which most of us had never dreamed, has been officially stood down. It evokes as of course certain ordinary, straightforward emotions. One is the unutterable sense of deliverance, of thankfulness that those hidden radio transmitters were never needed. Another is a feeling of admiration for the vaguely named authorities for having conceived the secret band and for its members for undertaking what might have been a desperate duty. But the supreme thrill is given by something more childish, the ineradicable love of secrecy for its own sake. That the members of this body were unknown to the world at large, that we ourselves may all unknowing have sat next to a member in a bus, nay that one of them may be among our intimate friends—that in all conscience is stunning enough. But that many of them did not know one another—ah! there comes the real shiver down the spine; that is the ultimate of piquancy. Did they perchance wear amulets round their happy necks? Had they a grip or password? We do not know, and though curiosity pulls hard one way, love of mystery pulls harder still the other; we are far more blissful for not knowing.

Of all the cards the story-teller can play that of a secret society is the ace of trumps, an unquestioned winner. Consider the gorgeous villain Count Fosco, who wore the mark of the brotherhood on his mighty arm, a mark that was afterwards obliterated by the T for Traditore. The harmless little Professor Pesca did not know Fosco but Fosco knew him and fled instantly at the sight of another branded brother. It is one of the ecstatic moments of the story. There is 'Kim' too. There are greater things in that great book, but there is no instance so quivering with excitement as that in which Kim creeps into the dark garden to seek Mahbub Ali's Englishman to deliver his message, 'The pedigree of the white stallion is fully established.' 'Have you never heard', said Sherlock Holmes to unromantic Watson, 'of the Ku Klux Klan?' And his voice rings for ever in the reader's head, investing the five cryptic orange pips with infernal glory. There is nothing like a secret society all the world over, and poor little weak-minded Sim Tappertit with his Prentice knights had got the gist of the matter in him. But to think there has been one in our very midst and that we had not even a presentiment. The thought is only less beautiful than that the society is now no longer wanted.

Auxiliary Units might have had much more publicity in 1945 but for the fact that the first announcement of its existence had been made to the Press just two days after the death of President Roosevelt, and the newspapers were full of obituary notices. During the following weeks, reports began to come in about the first concentration camps liberated by the Allied troops, about the race towards Berlin, about the ending of the blackout, about VE Day. Without pausing to dig into it very deeply, the newspapers simply forgot all about Britain's Resistance movement.

When the war was finally over, Colin Gubbins, who had been too busy in April 1945 even to notice the brief publicity given to Auxiliary Units, tried to arrange to have the individual members of the operational patrols admitted into the newly formed Special Forces Club, but he was told that this could not be allowed because it would mean giving away too many secrets. Some of the other officers who had been connected with the British Resistance tried to have the Defence Medal (which was awarded to those who served in the Home Guard) given to the members of the Auxiliary Units patrols, but this was not done, either—possibly because of secrecy or possibly because none of the men in the Resistance had ever been enrolled officially in anything.

Colin Gubbins himself was so sure that some higher authority had decided that the full story of the Auxiliary Units Organization must remain secret that he told no one about his own connection with it until the first time he saw the organization mentioned in print, in Peter Fleming's *Invasion 1940*. General Gubbins then had his own entry in *Who's Who* altered to state that he had raised and for a time had commanded the organization.

The Auxiliary Units organization should be remembered for what it did as well as what it might have done. More than providing a force to combat German occupation, to defend parts of the country and to test the security of the established forces, it gave Colin Gubbins his first opportunity to test MI(R) theories about modern guerrilla warfare. Many of the trials and errors of the first Auxiliary Units patrols were to be a guide for him later on when he went into Special Operations Executive. And so the British Resistance organization had through him a direct influence on resistance activity behind the German lines. The British Resistance also tested and proved some of the basic modern weapons of an underground army—time pencils and plastic explosives in particular. Moreover, Auxiliary Units provided and gave invaluable experience to many of the officers who led Resistance forces later in countries which were occupied. Anthony Quayle, for example, applied experience gained in Northumberland in Albania; Peter Fleming was involved in various Eastern SOE activities, and so was Stuart Edmundson, the officer who set up Resistance cells in the West Country. Andrew Croft, the officer who organized Resistance in East Anglia, served with the airborne forces, with the Special Air Service, with the Commandos, with the Long Range Desert Group and with SOE. He says that almost everywhere he went he met Coleshill-trained men, but they never mentioned the organization and neither did he. Today Colonel Croft is the head of the Metropolitan Police Training College, Hendon. Billy Beyts, who had been awarded the M.B.E. for his work at Coleshill, later received the D.S.O. for the part his regiment played in the breakout from the Irrawaddy bridgehead. Shortly after leaving Coleshill he was landed by submarine on the enemy-occupied Andaman Islands for SOE. Today, a civilian, he is employed by the Army to interview prospective officer cadets.

One Auxiliary Units Intelligence Officer went to Madagascar to lead the free forces there, and another, G. R. McNicholl, was sent into Germany to track down the 'Werewolves', a German form of Auxiliary Units which was expected to harass the Allied invading forces, but which fortunately either did not exist or chose not to emerge. And of course many of the civilians in the British Resistance eventually joined up or were conscripted into the regular forces in time to make very good use of their special training.

A FINAL WORD

BRITONS today like to recall their country during the first critical years of the war as a nation united absolutely against the Hun. They forget that at that very time when the nation's future was suspended from the most slender of threads, theirs was still a country in which most people refused to face the realities of the situation, went on strike, took their usual summer holidays, and continued to insist that their women must remain second class citizens and not be allowed the same responsibilities in the war as men. Until the Blitz, British solidarity and that grim national determination to resist the Germans to the death were things that existed for the most part only in Churchillian rhetoric. Fortunately for the British, the Germans did not apparently realize this.

If Operation Sea Lion had been mounted successfully and if the Germans had been able to follow the pattern of occupation laid down in their orders, their presence in Britain would have been as repressive as it was in the Eastern European countries. Instead of being merely shaken at its foundations by bombing and badly scarred by post-war austerity, the British way of life could for a long time afterwards have been contaminated morally, like a house that has been burgled, and the final decontamination might never have been achieved.

The Germans seem never to have settled in their own minds whether they were going to occupy all of Britain or, as in France, occupy the most important areas and then hold the rest to ransom. If the occupation went according to the plans that have been discovered, the British economy would have been destroyed completely, not only by the systematic looting, not only because of the removal of the young male population, but because the nation's industrial machinery was also to have been carried away. However, things may not have gone according to plan; the British made many positive preparations, the effectiveness of which would have depended on the way things worked out when the Germans arrived. And who can say how many of the Germans' original plans might have had to be discarded or altered as a result of what the British were or were not able to do?

Poised to invade and occupy Britain the Germans had no reason to believe that they would be met by a small but highly trained and well-equipped Resistance, for none of the other countries the Germans had invaded in Western Europe had been seeded with such Resistance cells. What effect would this have had on the occupation of Britain?

Probably it would have made the Germans take reprisals and impose tighter and tighter restrictions until, as a number of former Auxiliary Units Intelligence Officers today admit, great numbers of ordinary, decent Britons would have begun to co-operate with the Germans in putting down the Resistance just to bring about a sort of peace. Yet such was the nature of the Resistance that in some parts of the country it might have hung on for months—and if necessary for years—until in the end it succeeded in making the German position untenable or was itself finally destroyed.

Before the 'official' British Resistance had collapsed altogether it would almost certainly have sparked an idea. Ordinary men and women, hearing and seeing the results of the Auxiliary Units' sabotage and not knowing that this was the work of groups set up in the first place by the Regular forces, might well have decided to have a go themselves. In a number of the countries that were occupied the successes of Resistance groups formed by agents sent from London by SOE, and armed by SOE air drops flown out from Britain, inspired individual actions.

In any case, the British Resistance itself had many positive qualities that would have increased its chances of survival. Having been formed along military lines by Regular soldiers, and not having been built around religious groups or political parties, it would probably not have suffered from the inner conflicts that so markedly reduced the overall efficiency of Resistance organizations in the countries that were occupied by the Germans. In all those countries the Resistance cells had to accept almost anyone who drifted into them, but from the beginning the Auxiliary Units organization could pick and choose its men.

In countries that were occupied by the Germans some men drifted away from Resistance groups, often at critical times, simply returning to their above-ground lives. This would have been difficult—and in a number of places impossible—for Resistance men in Britain. Once they had spent a few days or a few weeks in their hideouts, they would have been hard put to account to the German occupation authorities for their absence.

A Resistance organization such as the one planned for Britain could also have had an adverse effect on the character of the country, and not merely because it might have caused reprisals to be taken against the innocent. To invite men into any armed underground movement is in a sense to invite them to place themselves above the law, especially when they must be trained to murder and must be armed with the weapons of assassins— weapons which, if they feel they must, they will turn on any of their neighbours whom they judge to be collaborators. There are no known instances of members of the British Resistance violating the trust put in them, but who can say what they might have done, perhaps with the most honourable of intentions, if they had had to function while their country was occupied? The officers who trained them still express unbounded confidence in them, but might not these men's controlled actions have nevertheless inspired others less controlled—leaving the British a people not even worth liberating?

And in any case, would Britain have been liberated? Europe and North Africa would have been Axis-controlled. The Russian position in 1940 remains an enigma. Certainly British troops abroad at the time could not have achieved this feat, nor could those of the Empire, for their logistical support came mostly from Britain. Almost all the people who provided the information for this book admit that they felt in the first years of the war that had Britain been occupied then, America could not reasonably have been expected to help liberate her, not only because the emotional appeal to Americans of 'Britain standing alone' would have vanished with the occupation, but also because at that time America lacked the means to effect such a liberation. Before the Japanese attack on Pearl Harbor President Roosevelt had steered the American people very gently towards war, ever mindful that neutralist, anti-British and pro-German factions were strong in the United States and could easily become much stronger. America had not yet begun to see herself as the 'great democratic liberator', and the German occupation of Britain would certainly have strengthened the case of American isolationists. Once occupied Britain might have had to go on alone—for ever.

APPENDIXES

APPENDIX A: *British Regional Commissioners, Regions and Headquarters*

Region	Headquarters	Commissioner
Northern	Newcastle	Sir Arthur Lambert
North-Eastern	Leeds	Lord Harlech (until March 1941); General Sir W. H. Bartholomew
North Midland	Nottingham	Lord Trent
Eastern	Cambridge	Sir Will Spens
London		*Senior Commissioner*: Captain Euan Wallace (until January 1941); Sir E. Gowers. *Joint Commissioners*: Sir E. Gowers (until January 1941) and Admiral Sir E. Evans. C. W. Key (from January 1941)
Southern	Reading	Harold Butler (until January 1942); Sir Harry Haig
South-Western	Bristol	General Sir H. Elles (but from April to September 1940, Sir Geoffrey Peto)
Wales	Cardiff	Lord Portal, assisted after January 1940 by two *Joint Regional Commissioners*: Colonel Sir G. Bruce and R. Richards
Midland	Birmingham	Lord Dudley
North-Western	Manchester	Sir Warren Fisher (until April 1940); Sir Harry Haig (until January 1942); Lord Geddes (until July 1942); Hartley Shawcross
Scotland	Edinburgh	T. Johnston (until February 1941); Lord Rosebery
South-Eastern	Tunbridge Wells	Lord Geddes (until July 1941); Lord Monsell

O FFICIAL records of the Auxiliary Units organization are not available for inspection, and most of the unofficial ones that have survived are sketchy personal accounts of local activities. Fortunately, before he relinquished command at Coleshill Brigadier C. R. Major took the trouble to write down in code and then to hide away a number of facts which were at the time very secret but which, if he had not recorded them then, would undoubtedly have been forgotten. Among other things the Brigadier compiled a list of the addresses at which it was possible to contact the individual operational Intelligence Officers in the forward areas late in 1941, when there were more of these officers in the field than at any other time during the existence of the official Resistance organization.

The military addresses on the list are accommodation addresses, for at the time that the list was compiled none of the actual Resistance headquarters was inside military establishments. The list does not include the original area headquarters that were used before each coastal county was assigned its own Intelligence Officer (such as the headquarters in Fort Austin, Plymouth, that originally covered the south-west, and the one in the vicarage in Kelvedon, Essex, that originally covered all East Anglia), nor, of course, does it include the addresses of the area headquarters after the Brigadier's time, when once again there were area rather than county headquarters (Framlingham, Suffolk, for example, became the headquarters for East Anglia, and Ashburton, in Devon, for all the South-west and also for a part of Wales).

The list does not include the headquarters of the various Special Duties Section Intelligence Officers around the country, or of the Special Duties Signals Section which was at Bachelors Hall, a large farmhouse with a Georgian façade, on the outskirts of Hundon, Suffolk, until sometime in 1942 when the personnel there were moved to Coleshill House and Hannington Hall.

The order in which the addresses are given is not, of course, the order in which Resistance groups were formed; it merely follows clockwise round the coast, starting in the north-west of Scotland.

[157]

Area	*Address used*
Outer Hebrides, Sutherland, Caithness, Ross	Initially: Berriedale, Caithness. Later: Golspie Sutherland
Inverness, Nairn, Moray, Banff, Aberdeenshire, Kincardine	Blairmore House, Glass, Aberdeenshire
Angus, Fife	Melville House, Ladybank, Fifeshire
Lothian, Berwick,	c/o G.Q. Border Sub Area
Roxburgh, Dumfries	c/o G.P.O. Melrose
Northumberland	*No address on Brigadier Major's list, but known to have been in Seahouses for a time and also at Scremerston, just south of Berwick-on-Tweed*
Durham, North Riding of Yorkshire	Danby Lodge, Danby, North Yorks.
Lincolnshire	Blankney Hall, Lincoln
Norfolk	Beeston Hall, near Neatishead, Norfolk
Suffolk	The Mill House, Cransford, near Woodbridge, Suffolk
Essex	River House, Earls Colne, near Colchester, Essex
Kent	The Garth, Bilting, near Ashford, Kent
Sussex	Totting Manor, Small Dole, near Steyning, Sussex
Hampshire	Initially: St Peter's Street, Bishop's Waltham, Hants. Later (possibly): Mayes Cottage, Swanmore, Hants (but may merely have been the Intelligence Officer's own residence)
Dorset	Initially: Langton House, Blandford, Dorset. Later: Bingham's Melcombe House, near Dorchester, Dorset
Devon	Polhilsa House, Stoke Climsland, near Callington, Cornwall
Cornwall	(Same as for Devon)
Somerset	68 Monmouth Street, Bridgewater, Somerset
Worcester	(Not recorded)
Hereford, Monmouth	Eye Manor, Eye, near Leominster, Hereford
Glamorgan	Newcastle House, Bridgend, Glamorgan
Carmarthen, Pembroke	H.Q., Carmarthen Sub-Area, Penllwyn Park, Carmarthen

APPENDIX C: *Auxiliary Units Operational State, 1941*

THE following chart has been compiled by Brigadier Major from his personal diaries. It shows the approximate state of the operational side of the Auxiliary Units organization late in 1941. No similar records are in existence for any earlier or later period. There were, of course, other Intelligence Officers in addition to those listed below. The names on this chart are all that appear in the brigadier's notes.

Areas—in clockwise order around the coast	Intelligence Officers	Patrols Formed	Patrols to be Formed	Numbers	Group Commanders	Hideouts Built	Hideouts being Built	Hideouts Wanted
Outer Hebrides, Sutherland, Caithness, Ross	Captain A. G. Fiddes-Watt	26	3	138	2	15	3	9
Inverness, Nairn, Moray, Banff, Aberdeen-shire, Kincardine	Captain R. A. C. Gordon-Lennox	32		220	4	26	4	2
Angus, Fife	Captain W. D. Clark	25		121	4	25		
Lothian, Berwick, Roxburgh, Dumfries	Captain P. R. A. Forbes	17	4	117	3			21
Northumber-land	Captain Anthony Quayle	15	5	66	3		1	19
Durham, North Riding, Yorkshire	Captain G. C. L. Atkinson, M.C.	25		159	4	16	8	3
East Riding, Yorkshire	Captain P. Hollis	34		214		26	3	5

Areas—in clockwise order around the coast	Intelligence Officers	Patrols Formed	Patrols to be Formed	Numbers	Group Commanders	Hideouts Built	Hideouts being Built	Hideouts Wanted
Lincolnshire	Captain Lamb, formerly Captain H. D. Hamilton-Hill	31		187	9	41		1
Norfolk	Captain G. Woodward, formerly Captain N. V. Oxenden, M.C.	35		201	11	40	2	6
Suffolk	Captain J. W. Holberton	28	1	180	5	28	1	1
Essex	Captain R. F. H. Darwall Smith	28		169	5	24	3	1
Kent	Captain G. R. McNicoll, formerly Captains Norman Field and Peter Fleming	33	3	208	10	30	6	4
Sussex	Captain C. G. F. Bond, formerly Captain J. N. W. Gwynn	21		134		28	1	1
Hampshire	Captain E. B. Clive	47		301	10	50	7	
Dorset	Captain R. J. V. Goss, formerly Major the Lord Tony Ashley	32		177	5	36	2	
Devon	Captain J. W. S. Edmundson	23	6	150	6	19	3	7
Cornwall	Captain J. Dingley	28		195	7	27	2	
Somerset	Captain I. Fenwick	44		287	9	50	4	
Worcester	Captain Bucknall	6	1	37	2	8		3
Hereford, Monmouth	Captain C. Sandford	14		93	5	15	2	
Glamorgan	Captain K. W. Johnson	17		89	3	13	1	2
Carmarthen, Pembroke	Captain J. C. Crawley	15		81	1	18		
Totals		576	23	3524	106	534	53	85

APPENDIX D: *Auxiliary Units Group Leaders*

THE following list of civilian group leaders in the British Resistance and the ranks that they were *told* they held in the Home Guard was kept by one of the officers on the staff at Coleshill. The list was compiled at a time when, for administrative purposes, the organization was divided into four regions. The arrangement of the list is not alphabetical but geographical, according to the areas covered by each of the groups.

No. 1 Region
Captain A. J. Thomson, Golspie. Sutherland
Lieut. J. Coghill, Thurso. Caithness
Captain W. A. Coutts, Wick. Caithness
Captain R. Jones, Invergordon. Ross and Cromarty
2/Lieut. G. Macdonald, Golspie. Sutherland
2/Lieut. A. Lehury, Stornoway. Isle of Lewis
Captain K. A. D. Niven, St Andrews. Fife
Major R. O. Ramsay, Arbroath. Angus
Major Sir Torquil Munro, Bt., Kirriemuir. Angus
Captain H. A. Ferrier, Brechin. Angus
Captain R. E. Cathcart, St Monance. Fife
Lieut. W. Pratt, St Monance. Fife
Lieut. A. Crowe, St Andrews. Fife
Captain W. A. Mustard, Muirton, Lossiemouth. Moray
Captain W. F. Smart, Kirktown of Maryculter. Kincardineshire
Lieut. G. S. Fisher, Crossroads, Keith. Banff
Lieut. A. H. Budge, Aberlour. Banff
Captain L. G. Cochrane, Spey Bay. Moray
Lieut. J. L. Low, Old Deer. Aberdeenshire
Lieut. A. Fraser, Ellon. Aberdeenshire
Lieut. J. F. Leslie, Monifieth. Angus
Lieut. A. D. Allison, Coupar Angus. Perthshire
Lieut. J. A. Mackie, Laurencekirk. Kincardineshire
Captain W. S. Wight, Grants house. Berwick
Captain J. Carruthers, Dalry, by Castle Douglas. Kircudbrightshire
Lieut. G. Balfour-Kinnear, Duns. Berwickshire
Lieut. J. Featherstone, Newton St Boswells. Roxburghshire
Lieut. J. Baird, Galashiels. Selkirkshire

Lieut. W. Bourne, Thornhill. Dumfriesshire
2/Lieut. A. Macdonald, Lossiemouth. Moray
2/Lieut. H. Collie, Kinloss. Moray
2/Lieut. R. Cook. Banff
2/Lieut. J. Forsyth, Cairnie, by Huntly. Aberdeenshire
2/Lieut. L. Hutchison, Craigellachie. Banff
2/Lieut. J. Thorburn, Dunbar. East Lothian
2/Lieut. J. A. Hastie, Duns. Berwickshire
2/Lieut. A. Forbes, Kirktown of Maryculter. Kincardineshire
2/Lieut. A. Forbes, Fraserburgh. Aberdeenshire
2/Lieut. J. Reid, Ellon. Aberdeenshire

No. 2 Region
Captain C. V. Colley, Bridlington. Yorks
Lieut. J. N. Woodward, Bridlington. Yorks
Lieut. H. Towse, Rillington. Yorks
Lieut. R. Sisterson, Settrington, Malton. Yorks
Lieut. F. F. Byass, Bainton, Driffield. Yorks
Captain W. Kitching, Aldbrough, Hull. Yorks
Captain H. N. Dixon, Sunk Island, Hull. Yorks
Captain J. M. Wilston, Boldon Colliery. Co. Durham
Captain C. Carrington, Beverley. Yorks
Captain S. Holmes, Hull. Yorks
Lieut. W. H. Cross, Brough. E. Yorks
2/Lieut. J. M. Harrop, Brough. E. Yorks
Captain E. R. Dixon, Redcar. Yorks
2/Lieut. A. Stephenson, Redcar. Yorks
Captain T. H. Robson, Bishopton, Stockton. Co. Durham
Captain A. C. Burningham, Low Fell. Co. Durham
2/Lieut. J. West, Hetton-le-Hole. Co. Durham
Captain H. W. R. Mitchell, Kirby Bedon. Norfolk
Captain R. W. Eades, Norwich. Norfolk
Lieut. C. H. Buxton, Norwich. Norfolk
Lieut. P. N. Neave, North Walsham. Norfolk
Lieut. A. G. Able, Aylsham. Norfolk
Lieut. H. Wharton, Mautby. Norfolk
Lieut. W. W. Ward, Fritton, Great Yarmouth. Norfolk
Captain W. G. Gentle, Brandon. Suffolk
Captain E. J. Robinson, King's Lynn. Norfolk
Lieut. G. F. Rutterford, Brancaster. Norfolk
Lieut. R. R. Stanton, Dersingham, King's Lynn. Norfolk
Captain J. L. Hardy, D.S.O., M.C., Rougham, King's Lynn. Norfolk

Lieut. M. Newngs, King's Lynn. Norfolk
Lieut. R. F. St B. Wayne, East Dereham. Norfolk
Lieut. D. C. Carey, East Dereham. Norfolk
Lieut. E. G. Field, Brandon, King's Lynn. Norfolk
Lieut L. N. Brock, Walsingham. Norfolk
Captain G. Scott Moncrieff, Hacheston, near Woodbridge. Suffolk
Captain L. W. O. Turner, Kenton. Suffolk
Lieut. T. H. Denney, Leiston. Suffolk
Lieut. J. K. Field, Woodbridge. Suffolk
Captain W. D. G. Bartram, Beccles. Suffolk
Captain H. Rusted, Metfield. Suffolk
Captain H. E. Mellor, Ipswich. Suffolk
Captain D. W. Beeton, Woodbridge. Suffolk
Captain E. G. Pawsey, Ipswich. Suffolk
Captain D. S. Parker, Cadbourne Parva, near Caistor. Lincs
Lieut. H. Marshall, Saxby All Saints. Lincs
Lieut. S. Fisk, Kirmington. Lincs
2/Lieut. W. Riggall, Grimsby. Lincs
2/Lieut. E. Halmshaw, Grasby. Lincs
Captain F. Dawson, Spilsby. Lincs
Captain L. I. Clark, Boston. Lincs
Captain W. Greenwood, Butterwick. Lincs
Captain C. N. King, M.C., Wisbech. Cambs
Lieut. W. J. Ground, Spalding. Lincs

No. 3 Region
Captain W. K. Seabrook, Great Leighs, Chelmsford. Essex
Captain C. G. Ford, Hockley. Essex
Captain R. L. Sennitt, Dengie, near Southminster. Essex
Captain G. H. Smith, Colchester. Essex
Lieut. J. Harper, Colchester. Essex
Lieut. H. G. Dennis, Colchester. Essex
Lieut. H. R. Gadsby, Kelvedon. Essex
Lieut. D. G. Drake, Bures. Suffolk
Captain H. C. Berry, Margaretting, Chelmsford. Essex
2/Lieut. D. M. Tarlton, Terling. Essex
Lieut. G. E. Tuker, Danbury. Essex
Lieut. W. G. Heath, Rochford. Essex
2/Lieut. R. Baptie, Rayleigh. Essex
Captain T. Neame, Faversham. Kent
Captain J. O. Foreman, Headcorn, Ashford. Kent
Captain W. G. Gardner, Birchington. Kent

Captain A. W. Marchant, Ash, near Canterbury. Kent
Lieut. F. G. Forster, Oare, Faversham. Kent
Lieut. A. Chester Beatty, Charing. Kent
Lieut. W. G. Johnson, Queenborough, Sheppey. Kent
Lieut. H. J. Highwood, Horsmonden. Kent
Lieut. F. R. F. Luke, Tenterden. Kent
Lieut. J. E. Graves, Crundale, near Canterbury. Kent
2/Lieut. G. Graves, Ashford. Kent
Lieut. G. F. Steed, Deal. Kent
Lieut. C. G. Lines, Wooton, Canterbury. Kent
Captain A. Bailey, Northiam. Sussex
Captain R. B. Edmondson, Lewes. Sussex
Captain A. Cooper, Small Dole. Sussex
Captain A. J. Champion, Ringwood. Hants
Captain A. C. Boyd, Titchfield. Hants
Captain H. C. A. Blishen, Arreton. I.O.W.
Lieut. L. D. C. Ayles, Ringwood. Hants
Lieut. G. B. Ash, Brockenhurst. Hants
2/Lieut. G. Forward, Fritham. Hants
Lieut. D. L. Brownlee, Cosham. Hants
Captain H. H. Gaunt, Puddleton. Dorset
2/Lieut. F. A. Sawtell, Horndean. Hants
2/Lieut. S. G. Taylor, Arreton. I.O.W.
Lieut. J. T. W. Fisk, Brighstone. I.O.W.
2/Lieut. C. W. Burt, Shalfleet. I.O.W.
Lieut. G. Stokes, Southampton. Hants
2/Lieut. W. Bignall, Bitterne. Hants
Lieut. A. G. Dallow, Longwood. Hants
2/Lieut. V. L. Petersen, Droxford. Hants
Lieut. A. A. Hilton, Locks Heath. Hants
Lieut. E. F. Talbot-Ponsonby, Petersfield. Hants
Captain R. C. H. Wilson, D.S.O., M.C., Pimperne, Blandford. Dorset
Captain H. R. N. Charter, Wimborne. Dorset
Lieut. W. B. Williams, Canford Magna, Wimborne. Dorset
Captain G. L. J. Fortnum, Bloxworth, near Wareham. Dorset
Lieut. P. B. Saunders, Broadmayne, Dorchester. Dorset
Lieut. C. J. Quick, Wareham. Dorset
Captain E. B. Sparkes, Langton Herring. Dorset
Lieut. V. Boon, Dorchester. Dorset
Lieut. A. J. Trenchard, Dorchester. Dorset
Lieut. R. G. Walker, Chickerell. Dorset
Captain L. O. Brown, Little Pitt, Whitchurch. Hants

Lieut. J. Woodward, Little Pitt, Whitchurch. Hants

No. 4 Region

Captain C. H. Young, Neath Abbey, Neath. Glam
Lieut. O. G. Knight, Skewen, Neath. Glam
Captain N. Ll. Barker, Ystalyfera, Swansea. Glam
Lieut. T. Smallman, Cwmgors. Carms
Captain J. G. Protheroe-Beynon, Whitland. Carms
Captain J. R. Richards, Carmarthen. Carms
Lieut. F. G. C. Goddard, Whitland. Carms
Lieut. R. L. Yorath, Conwyl Elfed. Carms
Captain J. B. Ebsworth, Kilgetty. Pembs
Captain T. J. George, Letterston. Pembs
Lieut. S. M. Davies, Llanfyrnach. Pembs
Lieut. W. G. Smith, Velindre, Crymmych. Pembs
Lieut. W. R. Sandow, Hayle. Cornwall
Lieut. W. Evan, Manaccan. Cornwall
2/Lieut. L. Bawden, Manaccan. Cornwall
Captain H. W. Abbiss, Truro. Cornwall
Lieut. F. J. Yeo, Truro. Cornwall
2/Lieut. E. K. F. Harte, Truro. Cornwall
Lieut. R. Drew, Padstow. Cornwall
Lieut. A. Harris, St Blazey. Cornwall
Captain G. H. Sergeant, Liskeard. Cornwall
2/Lieut. F. W. J. Mewton, Liskeard. Cornwall
Captain G. W. Slee, Bideford. Devon
Captain W. Falcon, Ivybridge. Devon
Captain C. H. Wellington, Plympton. Devon
Captain A. W. Robertson, Ivybridge. Devon
Captain A. J. Smith, Paignton. Devon
Lieut. J. C. Linscott, Paignton. Devon
Lieut. A. W. Eardley, Dawlish. Devon
Captain S. B. Wood, Seaton. Devon
Captain L. G. Howes, Colytford, Colyton. Devon
2/Lieut. A. W. Pope, Newton Poppleford. Devon
Captain J. G. Spearman, Bath. Somerset
Lieut. W. R. Hornett, Bath. Somerset
Captain A. H. Hunt, Bruton. Somerset
Lieut. E. E. G. Loder, Podimore, Yeovil. Somerset
Captain T. A. Baird, North Petherton, Bridgewater. Somerset
Lieut. J. S. Bent, Shoreditch, Taunton. Somerset
Sgt. F. M. Hepper, Blue Anchor, Washford. Somerset

[165]

Captain B. I. Chambers, Washford. Somerset
2/Lieut. T. H. Down, Watchet. Somerset
Captain H. Radford, Axbridge. Somerset
Lieut. E. A. Harrison, Wells. Somerset
Lieut. C. W. Trusler, Pensfold. Bristol
Captain L. E. van Moppes, Pershore. Worcs
Lieut. E. M. van Moppes, Pershore. Worcs
2/Lieut. R. G. Smith, Crowle. Worcs
Captain G. S. E. Lacon, Leominster. Herefords
Captain J. H. Hall. Hereford
Captain C. F. Bates, Newport. Mon
Lieut. E. Charles-Jones, Newport. Mon
Lieut. B. H. Lyon, Newport. Mon
Captain W. H. L. Chattin, Cardiff. Glam
Lieut. J. H. Bevan, Cardiff. Glam
2/Lieut. N. A. Richards, Cardiff. Glam
Lieut. L. Owen, Bridgend. Glam
2/Lieut. W. S. Smith, Bridgend. Glam

THE *Sonderfahndungsliste G.B.* makes more sense when the reader understands the meaning of the letters and the numerals following each entry. These indicate which offices of the RSHA wanted which people. For example, the first person on the list, J. Aalten, was wanted by RSHA Amt IV E.4. *Amt* means 'department'; Amt IV, the Gestapo, was devoted to combating the opponents of Germany; its sub-section E dealt with 'Matters relating to defence and the Armed Forces'; and the sub-section's office 4 concentrated on the 'North'.

The word *täterkreis* which appears after a number of entries means, roughly, 'ring'. Moya Stevens, for example, is listed as belonging to the 'Täterkreis Stevens/Best'.

The breakdown on the following pages will enable the reader to work out which RSHA departments wanted which people in Britain. The names opposite the main headings are those of the departments' chiefs. German-speaking readers may prefer to consult the original RSHA list of *ämter*, printed alongside the English listing.

The reader should bear in mind that the organizational structure of the RSHA was altered several times after the Arrest List for Britain was published. Dr Six's own strange department, Amt VII, *Weltanschauliche Erforschung und Auswertung* (Ideological Research and Evaluation), was not formed until 1 March 1941. The function of his old department, Amt II, was taken over by Amt IV, under Müller, the head of the Gestapo, and Amt II was then given control of administration and budgeting problems of the RSHA so that Amt I could concentrate on personnel matters and training.

The Reichssicherheitshauptamt, 1939–1940

Amt I Administration and Law [SS Brigadeführer Dr Best]:	*Amt I* Verwaltung und Recht:
I. General office	I. Hauptbüro und Geschäftsstelle
IA(a). Legal matters	IA(a). Recht
IA(b). Passport control and aliens police	IA(b). Passwesen und Ausländerpolizei
IB. Organization of the SIPO [Security Police] and the SD [Security Service]	IB. Organisation der SIPO und des SD
IC. Personnel records of the SIPO and SD	IC. Personalien der SIPO und des SD
ID. Disciplinary matters	ID. Dienststrafsachen
IE. Budget and finance	IE. Haushalt und Wirtschaft
IF. Education and training	IF. Erziehung
IG. Technical questions [Communications and transport]	IG. Technische Angelegenheiten
Amt II Investigation of the Opposition [SS Standartenführer Dr Six]:	*Amt II* Gegnerforschung:
II. General office	II. Geschäftsstelle
IIA. Basic research	IIA. Grundlagenforschung
IIB. Ideological opposition[Freemasonry, the Jews, the churches, Marxism, liberalism]	IIB. Weltanschauliche Gegner
IIC. Internal problems	IIC. Inlandsprobleme
IID. External problems [East, South-East, South, France, the English 'Imperium', Colonies and Pacific area]	IID. Auslandsprobleme
Amt III Spheres of German Life [SS Standartenführer Ohlendorf]:	*Amt III* Deutsche Lebensgebiete:
III. General office	III. Geschäftsstelle
ES. Immigration and settlement	ES. Einwanderung und Siedlung
IIIA. Cultural spheres	IIIA. Kulturelle Gebiete
IIIB. Communal life	IIIB. Gemeinschaftsleben
IIIC. Economic life	IIIC. Wirtschaftsleben

Amt IV Combating the Opposition [SS Oberführer Müller]:

IV. General office

IVA. Communism, Marxism, Popular Front, illegal propaganda
Anti-sabotage and counter-intelligence measures
Right-wing opposition, legitimism, insidious activity
Ecclesiastical-political matters
Emigrants

IVB. Party measures, special cases
Security measures
Attempted assassinations
Economic affairs
Press questions

IVC. Card index, files on individuals, organization of information
Matters concerned with protective custody
Reports
Details of incidents
Information collecting centre
Surveillance and special tasks

IVD. Matters concerned with the Protectorate [i.e. Bohemia and Moravia]
Matters concerned with the Government General [i.e. German-occupied Poland]
Minorities, confidential information centres, Jews
Emigration, evacuation
Communications with foreign police forces

Amt IV Gegnerbekämpfung:

IV. Geschäftsstelle

IVA. Kommunismus, Marxismus, etc.,

Sabotagebekämpfung und Abwehr
Opposition, Reaktion, etc.

Kirchenpolitische Angelegenheiten

Emigranten

IVB. Parteiangelegenheiten

Schutzangelegenheiten
Attentatsmeldungen
Wirtschaftsangelegenheiten
Presseangelegenheiten

IVC. Kartei, Personenakten, Auskunftswesen

Schutzhaftangelegenheiten

Berichterstattungen
Ereignismeldungen
Nachrichten Sammelstelle

Überwachungen und Sonderaufträge

IVD. Protektoratsangelegenheiten

Gouvernementsangelegenheiten

Minderheiten, Vertrauensstellen, Juden
Auswanderung, Räumung
Verkehr mit ausländischen Polizeien

IVE. Matters relating to defence and the Armed Forces Aliens Defence: West, North, East, South	IVE, Allg. Abwehr und Wehrmachtsangelegenheiten Ausländer Abwehr, West, Nord, Ost, Süd

Amt V Criminal Investigation [SS Oberführer Nebe]:

Amt V Verbrechensbekämpfung

V. General office	V. Geschäftsstelle
VA. Structure, tasks, and legal questions relating to the Criminal Police	VA. Aufbau, Aufgaben und Rechtsfragen der Kriminalpolizei
VB. Crime prevention	VB. Vorbeugung
VC. Operations	VC. Einsatz
VD. Identification service and search	VD. Erkennungsdienst und Fahndung
VE. Institute of criminal technology of the Security Police	VE. Kriminaltechnische Institut der Sicherheitspolizei
VF. Economic questions, special training and equipment	VF. Wirtschaftsangelegenheiten, Sonderbeschulung und Ausrüstung der KRIPO

Amt VI Foreign Intelligence [SS Brigadeführer Jost]:

Amt VI Ausland

VI. General office	VI. Geschäftsstelle
VIA. General tasks	VIA. Allgemeine Aufgaben
VIB. Transmission of information and intelligence operations in foreign countries	VIB. Nachrichtenübermittlung und nachrichtentechnische Einsatz im Ausland
VIC. East [Russia, Border States, Far East]	VIC. Ost
VID. South-East [Hungary, Slovakia, the Balkans, Turkey and the Middle East]	VID. Südost
VIE. South [Italy, the Iberian Peninsula, Central and South America]	VIE. Süd
VIF. West [France, Luxemburg, the Low Countries, Switzerland, Liechtenstein]	VIF. West

VIG. North-West [Great Britain,   VIG. Nordwest
      U.S.A., Scandinavia]
VIH. Information on the ideolo-   VIH. Erkündung weltanschau-
      gical opposition abroad   licher Gegner im Ausland
      [Freemasons, Anti-Free-
      masons, Semitism, Anti-
      Semitism, the churches,
      Communism, Marxism,
      liberalism, emigration,
      legitimism and right-wing
      movements]

*

The complete *Sonderfahndungsliste G.B.* runs to 350 pages. These
include a number of ruled blank pages on which extra names
could be written. There was a list of 171 large and small commercial
firms in which the Gestapo were interested, 389 addresses of trade
union offices, of political, religious and social organizations, and a
town-by-town cross-index. I have chosen to reproduce only the
113 pages which I believe will be of the greatest interest to readers.

1. Aalten, J., zuletzt: Holland, vermutl. England (Täterkreis: Dijisen), RSHA IV E 4.
2. Abbassi, Mohamed Oma, 21.9.94 Junagort/Indien, London, RSHA IV E 4.
3. Abbotts, Maude, 19.7.06 Liverpool, RSHA IV E 4.
4. Abercrombie, Lascelles, 9.1.81, Prof. u. Dichter, wohnh. Oxford, Merton College, RSHA VI G 1.
5. Abrahamczijk, Louis Markus Heinz, 15.4.00 Berlin, zuletzt: Holland, vermutl. England, RSHA IV E 4.
6. Abrahamer, Isidor, 16.5.01 Mährisch-Ostrau, Kaufm., Arzt, zuletzt: Teschen, vermutl. Engl., RSHA IV E 5.
7. Abraham, brit. ND-Offizier, vermutl. England, RSHA IV E 4.
8. Abramowicz, Bruno, 2.6.95 Berlin, Redakteur, RSHA IV E 5.
9. Abramowitz, Simon, 23.6.87 Ruß, Kr. Heydekrug, früher Min.-Rat, Wohng.: London, RSHA IV A 1.
10. Abrasimos, Irma geb. Michelson, 12.9.01 Riga, Kontoristin, Bardame. Deckn.: Michalowski, RSHA IV E 5, Stapo Königsberg.
11. Abt, Gottfried, 10.5.92 Heinsberg, (Täterkreis: Christian van Houdt), RSHA IV E 4.
12. Ackermann, Ernst, 25.5.95 Gnarrenberg, Gewerkschaftsangestellter, RSHA IV A 1.
13. Ackermann, Manfred, 1.11.98 Nikolsburg, ehem. Gewerkschafts-sekretär, Deckn.: „Maadl" u. „Martin", RSHA IV A 1 b.
14. Acland, Richard, Antifaschist, liberaler Abgeordneter, RSHA VI G 1.
15. Adams, David, 23.2.75, Labour-Abgeordneter, Wohng.: London, 8 Southill Street Poplar E. C. 4, RSHA VI G 1.
16. Adams, R. A., Major, Gehilfe d. Luftattaché, RSHA IV E 4.
17. Adams, Vyvyan Samuel, 22.4.00. konsul. Abgeordn., Wohng.: London, 3. Gloucester Gate, U. W. 1, RSHA VI G 1.
18. Adamski, Stanislaus, Dr. phil., Gymnasialprof., 5.4.90 Wezerow i. Polen, RSHA IV E 5, Stapo Danzig.
19. Adamson, Jennie, Vertreterin d. 2. Internationale, RSHA VI G 1.
20. Addison, Christopher, 19.6.69 Hogsthorpe, Wohng.: Bucks bei Great Missenden, Peterley Farm. RSHA VI G 1.
21. Adler, Friedrich, Dr., 9.7.79 Wien, Schriftsteller, Sekr. d. II. Internationale, RSHA IV A 1.
22. Adler, Leonhard, Dr., 1882 geb., Dozent, Emigrant, RSHA III A 1.
23. Adler, Max, Dr., 1907 geb., Assistent, Emigrant, RSHA III A 1.
24. Adler, Nettie, London W. 14, 121 A, Sinclair Rd. Edison Gardens, RSHA II B 2.
25. Adolf, Alfred Fritz Berthold Adolf, 30.7.95 Sommerfeld, Dreher (Am-Apparat), RSHA IV A 2.
26. Adolph, Alfred, 30.7.95 Sommerfeld, Dreher (Am-Apparat), RSHA IV A 2.
27. Aenderl, Franz Xaver, 25.11.83 Steinweg, Versicherungs-Insp., Wohng.: London, RSHA IV A 1, Stapo Nürnberg.
28. Alaeddin, Jusuf, brit. Agent, zuletzt: Ankara, vermutl. England, RSHA IV E 4.
29. Agnew, Andrew, Verw.-Dir., Wohng.: London E C 2, St. Helen's Court, Leadenhall Street, RSHA IV E 2.
30. Albania, Johann William, 5.6.77 Leeuwarden, ehem. holl. Minister, zuletzt: Holland, vermutl. England, RSHA III B.
31. Albot, H., Frl., zuletzt: Brüssel, vermutl. Engl. (Täterkreis: Karel Machacek), RSHA IV E 4.

32. Albrecht, Alfred, 2.7.04 München, Vertr., zuletzt: Zagreb/Laibach, vermutl. Engl. (Täterkreis: I. E. Roos), RSHA IV E 4.
33. Albrecht, Otto, 19.3.05 Dirschau, Mechaniker, poln. Provokateur, RSHA IV E 5.
34. Alecander, Kurt, Deckname: Freeman, Schriftsteller, Emigrant, London N 2. 38 Vivian Way, RSHA II B 5.
35. Alexander, Albert Victor, 1.5.85 Weston-Super-Mare, Minister, Wohnung: London, 1 Viktoria Street, RSHA VI G 1.
36. Alexander, John Alexis, engl. Kousul, Wohng.: London (Täterkreis: Eric Eissler), RSHA IV E 4.
37. Allerino (Täterkreis: Werner Mikkelsen), RSHA IV E 4.
38. Allina, Heinrich, 24.11.78 Schaffa/CSR, Nationalrat, RSHA IV A 1 b
39. Mac-Alpine, Charles B., RSHA VI G 1.
40. Altmann, Viktor, Dr., 7.3.00 Wien, Schriftst., Kompon. (Osterr. Legitimit.) RSHA IV A 3.
41. d'Alton, Leiter d. Intellig. Serv. i. Rotterdam (Täterkreis: Egon Rohr, RSHA IV E 4.
42. Ambridge, Mill, Wohng.: Dawigdor-rand-Hove, RSHA IV E 4, Stapol. München.
43. Amery, Leopold, 22.11.73 Gorakhpur (Indien), Minister, Wohng.: London S. W. 1, 112 Laton Square, RSHA VI G 1 II D 5.
44. Ammer, Karl, 5.5.98 Pettenbach, Schlossergehilfe, Wohng.: Jersey, RSHA IV A 1.
45. Amsling, Emigrant, evgl. Geistlicher (Vikar), London (Täterkreis: Hildebrand-Boeckheler-Roger-Freudenberg), RSHA II B 32, VI B 3.
46. Anders, Friedrich, 19.3.99 Barmen (Am-Apparat), RSHA IV A 2.
47. Anderson, Fargus, 9.2.09 Vallington, Rennfahrer, Wohng.: London SW 1, Viktoria-Street 36. RSHA IV E 4.
48. Anderson-Foster, G. Herbert, 30.5.90 Liverpool, brit. Agent, zuletzt: Riga, vermutl. Engl. (Täterkreis: Maundry Gregory), RSHA IV E 4, VI G 2.
49. Anderson, William Albert, 4.3.83 Spezia/Italien, zuletzt: Rom, vermutl. Engl. RSHA IV E 4.
50. Andriessen, Mildnh. d. Bankfirma Pierson u. Co., Amsterdam, vermutl. jetzt in England (Täterkreis: Stevens, Best), RSHA IV E 4.
51. Angell, Normann, 26.12.74, Präs. d. Weltkomitees gegen Krieg u. Faschismus, Wohng.: London, Temple L. C., 4, King's Bench Walk, RSHA VI G 1.
52. van Angeren, Mr. Dr., J.R.M. Generalsekr. in Justizmin., zuletzt: Holland, vermutl. Engl., RSHA III D Holl.
53. Antal, Friedrich, Dr., 1892 geb., Dozent, Wohng.: London, Universität, Emigrant, RSHA III A 1.
54. Antonczyk, Erich, a.10.99 Biel-chowitz, Kaufm., poln. N-Agent, RSHA IV E 5, Stapo Oppeln.
55. Appel, Herbert, Dr., Assistent, II. K. A., 1907 geb., Wohng.: Birmingham, Universität. Emigrant, RSHA III A 1.
56. Appel, Karl, 29.1.92 Hamburg, Seemann, in Engl. intern. (Schiffs-sabotage), RSHA IV A 2, IV A 1.
57. Arcy-Cooper, F. D., Wohng.: London, Unilever Haus, Blackfriars, RSHA IV A 2.
58. Arenz, Heinrich, 3.9.01 Köln, ehem. Straßenb.-Schaffner (Am-Apparat), RSHA IV A 2.
59. Arian, Alexander, 28.1.96 Warschau, poln. Offizier, RSHA IV E 5.
60. Arijs, Franz, RSHA VI G 1.

61. Aris, Reinhold, 1904 geb., Dr., Wohng.: Cambridge, Univers., Emigrant, RSHA III A 1.
62. Armann, Josef, Wohng.: High Cross, Castle Windemen, Westmorland, RSHA IV A 1.
63. Armann, Otto, 6.8.10 Elisenthal, Arbeiter, Wohng.: High Cross, Castle Windemen, Westmorland, RSHA IV A 1 b.
64. Armbruster, Theodor, 22.06 Gnibel, Krs. Tübingen, Schuhmacher (Am-Apparat) RSHA IV A 2.
65. Arnold, Fritz, richtig Kleine, Fritz, 7.3.91 Apolda, RSHA IV E 4, Stapo Prag.
66. Arnold, Robert, Wohng.: London?, richtig Narr, Adolf Paul RSHA VI G 1.
67. Arnold-Forster, William Edward, polit. Schriftsteller, RSHA IV G 1.
68. Arnold, Oberst, Chef d. Nachr.-Abt. d. engl. Gen.-Stabes, RSHA IV E 4.
69. Arnthal, Eduard, 3.2.93 Hamburg, Kunstmaler, zuletzt: Zagreb, vermutl. Engl., RSHA IV A 4, Stapo Graz.
70. Artischewski, Kasimir, 23.4.15 Rundfließ, Krs. Lyck, Reichsw.-Angeh., RSHA IV E 5, Stapo Allenstein.
71. Arter, Mary, 2.7.14 Hamburg-Gr. Flottbeck (Am-Apparat), RSHA IV E 4.
72. Arton, Henry Rolf, 28.10.12, brit. Leutn., RSHA IV E 4, Stapo Frankf./O.
73. Aschaffenburg, Rudolf, Dr., 1902 geb., Wohng.: Edinburgh, Universität, Emigrant, RSHA III A 1.
74. Corbett-Ashby, Frau, Führerin d. lib. Partei, RSHA VI G 1.
75. van Asselt, A. J., zuletzt: Rotterdam-Arnheim, vermutl. England, RSHA IV E 4, Stapol Hamburg.
76. Astbury, Herbert Parcel, 13.11.07 Leeds, Ingenieur, Wohng.: London . W 4, The Lodge Bedfort Park (Täterkreis: Rudolf Köppel), RSHA IV E 4.
77. Astor, John, 20.5.86, Abgeordn., Wohng.: London SW 1, 18, Carlton House Terrace, RSHA VI G 1.
77a. Astor, Lady, London, deutschfeindlich, RSHA IV E 4.
78. Atherton-Smith, Alice Sybil, 13.11.75 Hyde, Wohng.: Chantrya, RSHA IV A 1.
79. Atholl, Duchess of, Katharine, Wohng.: London SW 10, Elm-Park Gardens u. Blair Castle, Blair Atholl, Perthshire, RSHA VI G 1.
80. Atkins, Clement Richard, 3.1.83, Major, Wohng.: Heywood, Stanmore (Middlesex), RSHA VI G 1, II D 5.
81. Attlee, Clemens, Führer d. Labour-Party, Wohng.: London SW 1, Smith Square, Transport House, RSHA II B 4.
82. Aue, Werner Karl Rudolf, 21.98 Albion Villas, brit. Vize-Konsul, zuletzt: Antwerpen, vermutl. Engl., RSHA IV E 4, Stapol. Hannover.
83. Auerbach, Walter, 22.7.05 Hamburg, Archivleiter, Deckn.: Dirksen (Am-Apparat), RSHA IV A 2, IV A 1 b.
84. Avigdor, Rifat (Jude), 9.8.95 Konstantinopel, Konstruktionsleiter (286), RSHA IV E 3.
85. d'Avigdor-Goldsmith, Henry Joseph, 1909 geb., Wohng.: London E C 2, 7, Throgmorton Ave., RSHA II B 2.
86. d'Avigdor-Goldsmith, Sir Osmond Elim, zuletzt: London SW 1, Somerhill, Tonbridge, 47 Hans Place, RSHA II B 2.
87. Azria, Alfonso, zuletzt: Brüssel, vermutl. Engl. (Täterkreis: Hendrik Peter Kreuzenkamp), RSHA IV E 4.

1. Basten, Bernhard Franz, richtig: Donkers, Bernhard Franz, 21.5.03 in Duisburg geb. Arbeiter, 1938 Nymwegen, Kroonstr. 18, vermutl. England (Täterkreis: Pfaffhauren.) RSHA IV E 4 P. 2601.
2. Bast, M. G., London, Unilever House, Blackfriars. IV E 2 – 130/40.
3. Bast, Kurt, 10.10.97 in Langsitz, Krvis-Sekretär der KPC. England, RSHA IV A 1.
4. Bach, Stefan, Dr., geb. 1897, Assistent (Emigrant), Cambridge, III A 1.
5. Beckhouse, Geoffrey, 1899 in Green, Garden-Birmingham, Stettin III A 4380/39, RSHA IV E 4 B. 4506.
6. Bademann, Ludwig, Mitarb. d. Merton, London RSHA III D.
7. Badenoch, Lord, RSHA IV E 4, Gründer der Boy-Scout-Bewegung.
8. Baer, F. 2. Schriftsteller/Emigrant, London E. C. 8, 7 Gracechurch Street, RSHA II B 5.
9. Ba Bär, Karl, Mitarb. d. Merton, London, RSHA III D.
10. Baginski, Oberst, Mitglied der poln. Résistance, RSHA IV D 2.
11. Bagusy, Guillaume Edouard, geb. 17.4.83, wohnh. zuletzt Holland, früh vermutl. England (Täterkreis Stevens-Best), RSHA IV E 4 – B. Utrecht-Stedt Münster.
12. Bahnik, Wilhelm, 15.5.00 in Gnesen, Deckname: Martin, Dicker. Nasenheranmann (Am-Apparat), RSHA IV A 2.
13. Baier, Adolf, 30.9.07 in Oberkirch/B., Schlosser (Am-Apparat), RSHA IV A 2.
14. Baier, Dora, 6.6.04 in Berlin (Am-Apparat), RSHA IV A 6.
15. Baier, Josef, 24.1.79 in Atschau, Bez. Reaken, Konsumbeamter, Manrbeater 39, Palatine Road 4 a, RSHA IV A 1.
16. Bayer, Aloys, 21.6.04 in Wittlich, Schriftsteller (Am-Apparat), RSHA IV E 4.
17. Baker, G. H., britischer Visekonsul, vermutlich England, RSHA IV E 4.
18. Baker-Noel, Philipp, 2.1. 1889 geb. Abgeordneter, Professor, London SW 1, 43 South Eaton Place, RSHA VI G 1.
19. Baker, britischer N.D.-Offizier, Colonel (British Legion), London (Täterkreis: White Baker), RSHA IV E 4 5501 W, 1820/72, 34.
20. Bakken, Dr., richtig Maland Kera, 3.6.05 in Magdeburg, Redakteur, vermutl. England (Täterkreis: Kern-Kreis), RSHA IV A 1.
21. Bakken, geborene Bauer, Margot, 67.12.06 in Hamburg, 1940: Oslo, Hanstrengate 5, vermutlich England (Täterkreis: Hugo Bentscher), RSHA IV A 1.
22. Baldwin, Eva Lewis, brit. Journalistin, 1939: Portugal, vermutl. England, RSHA IV E 4.
23. Barab, Gustav, richtig Dückwald, britischer N.-Agent, 1939: Brüssel, rue de Houblonière 64 (Täterkreis: Kurt Foleenthal), vermutl. England RSHA IV E 4.
24. Barbe, Johann, 18.7.90 Hochweller, Chemiker, 1989 in England, RSHA IV E 4.
25. Barton, Hans, 16.12.97, Deckname: Hans Ober, Karl Mertens, Dr. Wolfheff, Karl Reichard, Adolf Steinmann, Großdülmchenheim, Oberstadtrektor, (Am-Apparat), RSHA IV A 6.
26. Barton, Ernst, 25.5.92, Professor in Cambridge, 17, Cranmer Road, RSHA IV G 1.
27. Barley, britischer Nachrichtenofizier, vermutl. England (Täterkreis: Berkeley), RSHA IV E 4.

27. **Baross, George Nicoll,** 2.1.39 Delegierter bei der Friedenskonferenz London E. C., 76 Basse Hill, RSHA VI G 1.
28. **Baross, Hugh S.,** Direktor, London E. C. 2, Britannic House, Anglo-Iranian-Oil Co., RSHA IV E 2.
29. **Barnett, Lawrence,** Beamter des brit. Konsulates in Panama, vermutl. England, RSHA IV E 4 61 165, Auswärtiges Amt Pol. IX 658/40.
30. **Barntoft, C. W.,** London, Unilever House, Blackfriars, RSHA IV E 2.
31. **Baron, E.** (Antifaschistische Liga), RSHA VI G 4.
32. **Baron, Hans,** Dr., 1900, Privatdozent, London (Emigrant), RSHA III A 1.
33. **Barry, Gerald,** 30.11.98, Journalist (Direktor bei „News Chronicle"), London S. W. 7, 43 Cheval Place, RSHA VI G 1.
34. **Barry,** britischer N.-Agent, vermutl. England, RSHA IV E 4.
35. **Barski, Franciszek** (Franz), 18.6.91 Jablone, Krs. Wollstein, polnischer Kreissekretär, RSHA IV E 5, Stapostelle Schneidemühl.
36. **Barstow, George L.,** Vertreter der Britischen Regierung, London E. C. 2, Britannic House, Anglo-Iranian-Oil Co., RSHA IV E 2.
37. **Barth, Willi,** 25.9.99 Ingersleben, Tischler, vermutl. Sowjetrußland, RSHA IV A 1, Stapostelle Weimar.
38. **Barthel, Alfred,** 4.12.07 Berlin, Deckname: Friedrich Förstel, 19.2.99 geboren, Elektromonteur, vermutl. England (Am-Apparat), RSHA IV A 2.
39. **Bartholdy-Mendelssohn, Albrecht,** Oxford, Balliol College, RSHA VI G 1.
40. **Bartik, Josef,** 8.6.97 Stachau, Deckname: Josef Baranek, Beta, London 53, Lexham, Gardens Kensington W 8, RSHA IV E 4.
41. **Bartik, Josef,** 30.6.97 Stachny-Saice, ehem. tschechischer Major, London (Täterkreis: Frantisek Moravec), RSHA IV E 6.
42. **Bartiszewski, Leonhardt,** 31.8.16 Berlin, Uffz., RSHA IV E 5, Stapostelle Breslau.
43. **Bartlett, Vernon Werner,** 30.4.94 Westbury, Dipl. Korrespondent v. „News Chronicle", Abgeordneter, Liotead Sure, The old Farm House, RSHA IV E 4 2019/E u. VI G 1.
44. **Baruch, Bernhard,** London S. W. 1, 1, Carlton Gardens, RSHA II B 2.
45. **Basch, Anton,** Dr., 5.6.96 Deutsch-Brod, Direktor, RSHA IV E 4 31236, Stapostelle Prag.
46. **Bashford, R. F. O. N.,** Pressattaché, England, RSHA IV E 4.
47. **Bates-Jones, Reginald,** vermutl. England, RSHA IV E 4.
48. **Bauer, Margarete,** 12.11.01 Königswarth, Lagerhalterin, Ashbourne-Derby, Bau-Haus?, RSHA IV A 1 b, Stapostelle Karlsbad.
49. **Bauer,** vork. Balduen, Margot, 27.12.03 Hamburg, 1940: Oslo, Hansteen-gate 4, jetzt: vermutl. England (Täterkreis: Hugo Bentscher), RSHA IV A 4, 6836.
50. **Bauer,** Dr., Beauftragter d. Potschek-Gruppe, London, 458/0 Salisbury House, RSHA IV E 4.
51. **Bauerfeind, Adolf,** 24.5.04 Eibenberg, Deckname: Karallbra, David, Manrov, England, Attentäter, RSHA IV A 2 — 02141/39 g.
52. **Bauerfeind, Robert,** 14.6.12 Markhausen, England, RSHA IV A 1.
53. **Bauhart, Johann,** Schnäldirektor, 1940: Luttenberg/Jugosl., vermutlich England, RSHA IV E 4, Stapoleitstelle Graz.
54. **Baumeister, Alfred Ottomar,** 16.11.07 Plauen, Deckname: Reichenberger, Erich, Bäcker (Am-Apparat), RSHA IV A 2.
55. **Baumgärtel, Elise,** Dr., 1898, London (Emigrantin), RSHA III A 1.

66. **Baumgardt, David,** Dr., 1880, a. o. Professor, Birmingham (Universität), (Emigrant), RSHA III A 1.
57. **Baumgartner, Rupert,** 20.5.10 München, Former (Am-Apparat), RSHA IV A 2.
58. **Baxa, Paul,** Dr., tschechischer Rundfunksprecher, London (Täterkreis: Benesch), RSHA IV D 1 a.
59. **Baylis, L. G.,** britischer Vizekonsul, vermutlich England, RSHA IV E 4, Stapoleitstelle Hamburg.
60. **Bearsted, Viscount,** Präsident, London E. C. 3, St. Helen's Court 22, Shell Transport und Trading Co., RSHA IV E 2.
61. **Bearsted, Viscount Walter Horace Samuel,** 13.3.82, Industrieller, London, Carlton House Gardens, und Banbury, Upton House, RSHA VI G 1.
62. **Beaton, Grace N.,** London, Sekretärin des Internat. Rates der Internat. Kriegsdienstgegner, RSHA VI G 1.
63. **Beaumont,** geborene Vanek, Emilie, 20.3.94 Wien, Agentin, Prag, vermutl. England, RSHA IV E 4 — B. 684.
64. **Beaumont, Frank,** 10.5.96, britischer N.-Offizier, London, RSHA IV E 4 — B. 3996.
65. **Beaverbrock, Lord,** 25.5.79, Zeitungsmagnat, Minister, Cherkley, Leatherhead (Surrey), RSHA VI G 1.
66. **Bebensee, Hans Heinrich,** 11.2.17 Kiel, Schütze, RSHA IV E 5, Stapostelle Allenstein.
67. **Beck,** Redakteur, vermutlich England (Täterkreis: Jens Dons), RSHA IV E 4, Stapostelle Kiel.
68. **Bechbolt, Peter,** 2.7.73 Gelsenkirchen (Am-Apparat), RSHA IV A 2.
69. **Beck, Adolf,** Dr., 1905, Assistent, Greenwich (Emigrant), RSHA III A 1.
70. **Beck, Eugen,** 29.3.07 Stuttgart, Kaufmann (Am-Apparat), RSHA IV A 2.
71. **Beck, Francis,** Schriftsteller (Emigrant), Paignton (Devon), Shorton Coottage, RSHA II B 5.
72. **Beck, Stephan,** Dr., 1695, Assistent, Glasgow (Emigrant), RSHA III A 1.
73. **Beck, Walter,** Dr., Direktor, Boston (Universität), (Emigrant), RSHA III A 1.
74. **Becke, Jan** (Emigrant), London, RSHA II B 5.
75. **Becker, Jerome Sidney,** 20.8.81 New York, Korrespondent, angebl. England, RSHA IV E 4 u. II A 6.
76. **Becker, Karl,** 19.11.94 Hannover, Deckname: Karin, Schriftsteller, zuletzt Prag, jetzt vermutlich England, RSHA IV A 1.
77. **Beckert, Friedrich,** 22.11.97 Giengen, wohnh. in England, RSHA V V 2 c — St. A. Berlin 1 Ma. 52/36.
78. **Becke, Johann Jan,** 16.11.89 Hannover, ehem. sozialdemokratischer Abgeordneter, 1940: London, RSHA IV E 4, IV D 1 a — Stapoleitstelle Prag.
79. **Becvar, Gustaf,** 18.9.94 Neu-Jetschin, Privatbeamter, London, RSHA IV E 4, Stapoleitstelle Prag.
80. **Beekhorst,** britischer Agent, 1939: Rotterdam, vermutlich England, RSHA IV E 4.
81. **Graf Beenstorff** (Täterkreis: Siegfried Franke), RSHA IV E 4.
82. **Beer, Arthur,** Dr., 1900, wohnh. Cambridge, Physikalisches Observatorium, Universität (Emigrant), RSHA III A 1.

2

83. **Beer, Friedrich** (Fritz), 15.6.09 Schweinfurt, Deckname: Heinrich Gruslav, Schriftsteller, vermutl. England (Schwarze Front), RSHA IV A 8.
84. **Beer,** ehem. britischer Konsul in Preßburg, vermutl. England, RSHA IV E 4.
85. **Begall, Siegfried,** 5.2.96 Lucow/Polen, poln. Zollkomm., RSHA IV E 5, Stapo Schneidemühl.
86. **Behrens** vork. Spiegel, Annemarie, 25.7.04 Altona, England, RSHA IV A 1.
87. **Behrovic, Max,** 22.1.18 Roermond, Radiohändler, zuletzt: Holland, vermutl. England (Täterkreis: Theo Hespers), RSHA IV E 4.
88. **Beilen, Normann John,** britischer Agent, vermutlich England, RSHA IV E 4.
89. **Beiner, Rudolf,** 6.11.05 München (Jude), 1939: Brüssel, vermutlich England (Täterkreis: Leo Heymann), RSHA IV E 4.
90. **Beichembra, Harald,** Agrarprofessor, Oxford, RSHA IV A 1.
91. **Heva-Beliska, Leslie,** London S. W. 14, The Close Sheen Conawon, RSHA VI G 1.
92. **Bellisha, Albert L,** London E. C. 3, 15, St. Helens Place, RSHA II B 2.
93. **Below, Ludwig,** 24.9.15 Ruda, Krs. Schwientochlowitz, Grubenarbeiter, polnischer Deserteur, RSHA IV E 5, Stapostelle Oppeln.
94. **Bell, Nancy,** Völkerbundsbewegung, RSHA VI G 1.
95. **Bell,** britischer Agent, zuletzt: Belgrad, vermutl. England, RSHA IV E 4.
96. **Bende, Clemens Ernst,** Dr., 1898, Assistent, Universität Cambridge (Emigrant), RSHA III A 1.
97. **Bender, Josef Theo,** 25.8.06 Wuppertal-Elberfeld, Arbeiter (Am-Apparat), RSHA IV A 1.
98. **Benes, Eduard** Dr. phil., 28.5.84 (?) Koslenech, Exprdsident der CSR., RSHA VI G 1, IV D 1 a, IV E 4, Stapoleitstelle Prag.
99. **Benes,** geb. Vlcek, Hanna, 16.7.85 Deutschdorf, vermutlich London, RSHA IV E 4, Stapoleitstelle Prag.
100. **Benesch, Edward,** Emigrant, Vorsitzender d. tschech. Nationalkomitees in Frankreich und England, London S. W. 16, Gwendolo Ave. 27, RSHA II B 5.
101. **Benges, Davis,** 68.7.04 in London, vermutl. London, RSHA IV E 3 — Stapoleitstelle München.
102. **Benningham, Walter,** 25.1.98 in Kirpee (SPD-Funktionär), England, RSHA IV A d. b.
103. **Benscher, Hugo Israel,** 17.6.03 in Hamburg, vermutlich England, RSHA IV E 4, Stapostelle Kiel.
104. **Bentley, J. W.,** RSHA VI G 1.
105. **Bentwich, Norman,** 1883, Rechtsanwalt und Schriftsteller, Professor, Hollyoot, Vale of Health, N. W. 3., RSHA IV A 1.
106. **Benz, Theodor,** 19.7.80 Köln-Mühlheim, Arbeiter (Am-Apparat), RSHA IV A 2.
106a. **Berendsson, Helene,** Mitarb. d. Merton, London, RSHA III D.
107. **Bergh, van den, Cläve,** Kaufmann, London NW 6, Eton Avenue, Eton Court 50, Unilever Konzern, RSHA III D 2.
108. **Bergh, van den, Albert,** 1875 in London, London W. 1, Alderbrook Park, Cranleigh, Surrey, Flat 64, 30 Grosvenor Square, RSHA II B 2.
109. **Bergh, van den, James Paul,** London, Unilever House, Blackfriars, RSHA IV E 2.

110. **Berg, van den, Jakob Hermann,** 11.9.00 Viersen, 1939: Blerick, Holland, Spoorstr. 36, vermutlich England (Täterkreis: Gerrit Spruijtenburg), RSHA IV E 4.
111. **Berg, van den, Matthias,** 22.8.05 in Viersen, 1939: Blerick/Holland, Spoorstr. 36 (Täterkreis: Gerrit Spruijtenburg), RSHA IV E 4.
112. **Bergh, van den, Sidney** (Jude), Kaufmann, Owlands Mere, Weybridge Surrey (Unilever-Konzern), RSHA III D 2.
113. **Bergh, van den, Sam,** London, Unilever House, Blackfriars, RSHA IV E 2.
114. **Bergh, van den,** Kapitän d. niederl. Armee, Margarinefabrikant, zuletzt Holland, vermutl. England, RSHA III R.
115. **Berg** geborene Schmiedt, Martha, 4.7.97 in Fiel/Süderdithmarschen, Fabrikarbeiterin (Am-Apparat), RSHA IV A 2.
116. **Berg, Wolfgang,** Dr., 1908, Assistent (Emigrant), London, RSHA III A 1.
117. **Bergel, Franz,** Dr., geb. 1900, Privatdozent, Edinburgh, Universität (Emigrant), RSHA III A 1.
118. **Berger, Max Bernhard,** 2.8.95 Wüstenbrand-Nadelrichter, RSHA IV E 4.
119. **Berger, Richard,** britischer Polizeiagent, Deckname: C. Siemens, Simmons, und James Upson, London SW, Brixton Stockwall Road 83, RSHA IV E 4.
120. **Berkeley,** britischer Oberst u. Militärattaché, Budapest, vermutlich England, RSHA IV E 4.
121. **Berkenheim,** London, RSHA IV E 4.
122. **Berlin, Paul Wilhelm Karl,** 2.4.14 Petersdorf, Dienstpflichtiger, London E. C. 4, 29 Barbican, RSHA V D 2 f, und Gericht der Kommandantur Berlin v. 26.3.39.
123. **Bernal, John D.** Professor (Einkreisungspolitiker), RSHA VI G 1.
124. **Bernegau, Wilhelm,** 27.2.03 Werdohl, Arbeiter, Deckname: „Der rote Graf" (Am-Apparat) RSHA IV A 2.
125. **Bernstein, Alex** (Einkreisungspolitiker), RSHA VI G 1.
126. **Berry, George William,** 25.8.96 Jelgava/Lettland, Chef der Paßabtlg. im brit. Kons. Wien, vermutlich England, RSHA IV E 4, Stapoleit Wien.
127. **Berthoud,** Angestellter d. AJOC, London E. C. 2, Britannic-House, RSHA IV E 2.
128. **Berti, Georg,** 12.12.04 Prag, Journalist, 1939: Bukarest (Täterkreis: Bretislav Kika), RSHA IV E 4.
129. **Best,** geborene van Rees, Maria Margareta, 9.1.92 Hellevoetsluis, London NW. 3, Hampstead 3, Holford Road (Täterkreis: Stevens-Best), RSHA IV E 4.
130. **Beser, Otto,** 25.9.98 Reichenberg, Geschäftsführer, Putney bei London SW. 15, 24, Egliston Road, RSHA IV A 1.
131. **Bevis, Ernest,** Minister (Einkreisungspolitiker), Gewerkschaftler, RSHA VI G 1.
132. **Beyer, Martha,** 2.11.06 Hamburg, Schneiderin (Am-Apparat), RSHA IV E 4.
133. **Beyll,** britischer Agent, Belgrad, vermutl. England, RSHA IV E 4.
134. **Bharu, James,** britischer Agent, vermutlich England, RSHA IV E 4.
135. **Bieberstein, von, Hans Bodo,** vermutlich England (Täterkreis: Siegfried Franke), RSHA IV E 4.
136. **Biedermann, Lorenz,** 27.7.10 Haslau, Ashbourne-Denby, Ham Hall RSHA IV A 1 b.

2*

187. **Biecemann, Leo,** 17.3.03 Emmerich, Kapitän a. D., Deckname: Jupp Leo (Am-Apparat), RSHA IV A 2.
188. **Biesterfeld, Bernhard,** holländischer Prinz, RSHA IV E 4.
189. **Bikerman, J. J., Dr.,** 1898 Manchester Universität (Emigrant), RSHA III A 1.
140. **Bileckl, Dr. Jur, Tadeusz,** Mitglied des polnischen Nationalrates. RSHA IV D 2.
141. **Bing, Gertrud, Dr.,** 1692, Assistent, London, Emigrantin, RSHA III A 1.
142. **Birch, Julius Guthlac,** 8.4.84 London, britischer Oberst und ND-Offizier, vermutlich England, RSHA IV E 4.
143. **Birch, Natan** (Antifaschistische Liga), RSHA VI G 1.
144. **Birkenmayer, Alfred,** 28.3.92 Krakau, poln. Konsulatsbeamter, Leiter des poln. ND, RSHA IV E 5, Stapoleit Danzig.
145. **Birkett, W. E.,** d.1.1.82 Blackburn, Botschaftssekretär, 1939: Den Haag, vermutl. England, RSHA IV E 4.
146. **Birnbaum, Gerhard,** britischer Agent, 1936 Warschau, vermutlich England, RSHA IV E 4.
147. **Blaazer, J. N.-**Agent, vermutlich England (Täterkreis: Waldemar Pötsch), RSHA IV E 4.
148. **Black, Deckname: Simpson,** 45 Jahre alt, britischer Agent, England, RSHA IV E 4.
149. **Blackett, P. M. S.,** 18.11.97, Professor, London E. C. 4, Birchbeck Colledge, Breams, Buildings, Felber Lane, RSHA VI G 1.
150. **Blackwood,** Angestellter der AJOC., London E. C. 2, Britannic House, RSHA IV E 2.
151. **Blalkle, E. R.,** London, 32 Fleet Lane E. C. 4, (Jude, Emigrant), RSHA VI G 1.
152. **Blanche-Koelensmid, Gerardus Adrianus Everhard,** 8.4.84, 1939: Amsterdam, vermutl. England (Täterkreis: Snatager), RSHA IV E 4.
153. **Bloch, Robert, Dr.,** 25.9.98 London, Leiter der Kreditanstalt „Bernia" in Buchs/Schweiz, London, Folkestone 18, Grinston-Gardens, RSHA IV E 3, IV A 1, Stapoleit München.
154. **Blankenhagen,** 50 bis 60 Jahre alt, Doorn/Holland, vermutl. England (Täterkreis: Stevens-Best), RSHA IV E 4.
155. **Blankenstein, van, Markus,** 3.6.80 Oderkark, Redakteur (Nieuwe Rotterdamsche Courant), vermutl. England (Täterkreis: Karl Nihom), RSHA IV E 4.
156. **Blaschke, Hermann, Dr.,** 1900, Assistent, Cambridge Universität (Emigrant), RSHA III A 1.
157. **Bloch, Alfred M. Se., Dr.,** 1904, Assistent, London (Emigrant), RSHA III A 1.
158. **F ck, Berthold,** 5.7.00 Randegg bei Konstanz, Kaufmann, Gibraltar, I x A 1, RSHA IV E 4.
159. **Bloch, Max,** richtig Katzenellenbogen, 12.06 Leipzig, Chemiker, vermutl. England (Am-Apparat), RSHA IV A 2.
160. **Bloch, Robert, Dr.** Professor, 1898, Leeds, Universität (Emigrant), RSHA III A 1.
161. **Blochmann, Elisabeth, Dr., Prof.,** 1692, Oxford, (Emigrant), RSHA III A 1.
162. **Blohm, Edgar Georg,** Kaufmann, 1936 London, Cromwell Road 168, RSHA IV E 3, Stapoleit Berlin.
163. **Bloss, Christian,** 24.5.98 Asch, Laborant, England, RSHA IV A 1, Stapostelle Karlsbad.

164. **Blume, Franz, Deckname: Michel,** 26.9.05 Hamburg, Tischler (Am-Apparat), RSHA IV A 2.
165. **Blumenberg, Werner,** 21.12.00 Hülsede, (Redakteur, vermutlich Er z land, RSHA IV A 1.
166. **Blumenfeld, Ralph D.,** 1864 USA., Muscombs, Little East.- Dunmow, RSHA II B 2.
167. **Bodenheimer, Wolf, Dr.,** d.905 geb., London (Emigrant), RSHA III A 1.
168. **Bodenstein, verh. Masur, Annemarie,** 18.11.09 Gronau, RSHA IV A 1, Stapoleit Hamburg.
169. **Böhm, Dr. Ing., 2.7.94** Zaborze (Hindenburg), London, RSHA IV A 1.
170. **Boeckheler, evg. Pfarrer,** London S. E. 23, 23 Manor Mount Forest Hill (Täterkreis: Amaling-HBdobrand-Freudenberg), RSHA II B 32, VI B 3
171. **Boeijen von, Hendrik,** 29.5.89 Putten, ehem. holl. Innenminister, England, RSHA III B.
172. **Boekelman,** britischer Agent, 1939: Den Haag, vermutlich England, RSHA IV E 4.
173. **Boerana, August,** vermutl. England (Täterkreis: August de Fromery), RSHA IV E 4.
174. **Bogard, van den, holl.** Autovermieter, Bergen-Daal/Holland (Täterkreis: Wilhelm Willemse, RSHA IV E 4.
175. **Bogdoll, Karol,** 4.11.96 Zawadzki, Gr. Strehlitz, ehem. poln. Insurgentenführer, ND.-Agent, RSHA IV E 5, Stapo Oppeln.
176. **Bogomolets, Viktor, Dr.,** 8.6.96 Kiew, Journalist, London, RSHA IV A 1.
177. **Bohn, Jans,** 1939: Kopenhagen, vermutl. England (Täterkreis: Brijnen), RSHA IV E 4.
178. **Boland, H,** britischer Agent, 1939: Den Haag, vermutlich England, RSHA IV E 4.
179. **Boland, kath.** Schwester, 1940 vermutlich England, RSHA IV E 4.
180. **Bolkestein, Gerrit,** 9.10.71, Amsterdam, ehem. holl. Unterrichtsminister, vermutlich England, RSHA III B.
181. **Boller, Robert,** Büro-Inhaber, 1940: Yokohama/Japan, vermutlich England, RSHA IV E 4, IV D 5.
182. **Bonham-Carter, Lady, Violet,** London W. 2, 40 Gloucester Square (Linksemannopolitikerin), RSHA VI G 1.
183. **Bonk, Wladislaus,** 24.11.08 Sokohowo, Kurzwarenhändler, RSHA IV E 5, Stapoleit Schneidemühl.
184. **Bonn, Moritz, Dr.,** 1878 geb., Professor, London, Emigrant, RSHA III A 1.
185. **Bonneau, Madelene,** 1939: Paris, vermutl. England (Täterkreis: Albert Albeeit), RSHA IV E 4, Stapoleit Wien.
186. **Bonneau, Susanne,** 1939: Paris, vermutl. England (Täterkreis: Albert Albeeit), RSHA IV E 4, Stapoleit Wien.
187. **Boon, Kammerabgeordneter,** Rechtsanwalt, 1939: Den Haag, vermutlich England (Täterkreis: Prins), RSHA IV E 4.
188. **Boothby, Robert,** 1900, Sekretär von Winston Churchill, London S. W. 1, 17. Tall Mall, RSHA VI G 1.
189. **Borinski, Friedrich, Dr.,** 17.6.08 Berlin, London, 44. Lemsford-Lane, Welwyn Garden, City 1 Blakomer Road, Schwarze Front, RSHA IV A 3.
190. **Borkenau-Pollak, Franz, Dr.,** 1900, London, RSHA III A 1.
191. **Borlinski, Ludwig, Dr.,** 1910, Cambridge, Emigrant, RSHA III A 1.

192. **Borsonwald, Georg,** 29.12 Schwientochlowitz, Wehrpflichtiger, zuletzt: Südafrika, RSHA V—D 2 f., Reichskriegsgericht St. P. L. (RKA.).
193. **Böttlinger, Theodor,** 28.11.04 Schwartau, Kesselschmied, Deckn.: Josef Fleblg, Kurt Richter, Arthur, Kurt, vermutl. England, (Am-Apparat), RSHA IV A 2.
194. **Bouvard, Hugo,** Hauptmann, London, RSHA IV A 2.
195. **Bove, Charles,** London W8. 14 Paterstreet, RSHA IV E 4.
196. **Bower, Philipp George,** England, RSHA IV E 4.
197. **Boyce, Ernest,** Beamter, zuletzt Reval, vermutl. England, brit. ND.-Agent, RSHA VI C 2.
198. **Bozek, Arka,** Mitgl. d. poln. Nationalrates, vermutl. England, RSHA IV D 2.
199. **Bracken, Brendan,** 1901 Direktor, Abgeordneter, London S W 1, 8 North Street, RSHA VI G 1.
200. **Bracken, Fri.,** zuletzt Kopenhagen, vermutl. England (Täterkreis: Jens Groze), RSHA IV E 4, Stapo Kiel.
201. **Brady, Robert A., Prof.,** 12.5.01, London, RSHA IV A 1.
202. **Bragg, William, Sir, Prof.,** 61.3.90 Australien, Windy House Alderley Ledwe Cheshire, RSHA VI G d.
203. **Bragius, Borris, Deckn.: Johannil,** zuletzt: Antwerpen, vermutl. England (Täterkreis: Waldemar Pötsch), RSHA IV E 4.
204. **Brailsford, Henry Noel, geb.** 1873, Journalist, London N. W. 3, Belsize Park Gardens, RSHA VI G 1.
205. **Brakensiek, Leo,** 23 Jahre alt, zuletzt: Amsterdam, vermutl. England (Täterkreis: Prins), RSHA IV E 4.
206. **Bramley, Ted, Or,** unisator, vermutl. England, RSHA VI G 1.
207. **Brandl, Franz,** 24.12.98 Tachau, Coln Cöed bei Merthyr Tydfil, 28 Field Street South Wäles, RSHA IV A 1.
208. **Brandon, Albert Ernest Acton,** 18.9.89 London, brit. Cpt., zuletzt: Genf, vermutl. England (Täterkreis: Burnell), RSHA IV E 4.
209. **Brandt, Arthur, Dr.** med., Jude, 26.5.89 Posen, London (Abtreibung), RSHA IV E 4.
210. **Brandt, Johann,** 17.7.98 Geestemünde, brit. Agent, vermutl. England, RSHA IV E 4.
211. **Brauns, Jan,** Mitgl. d. poln. Regierung, zuletzt: Ohornow, vermutl. England, RSHA IV D 2.
212. **Brauwers, Leon,** zuletzt: Holland, vermutl. England (Täterkreis: J. Hermans), RSHA IV E 4.
213. **Braun, Hans,** 24.1.06 München, Deckn.: Peter, Georg, Angestellter, vermutl. London, RSHA IV A 2.
214. **Braun, Hugo,** 12.2.01 Johanngeorgenstadt, vermutl. England, RSHA IV A 1.
215. **Braun, Matthias,** 18.9.92 Neuß/Rhein, Deckn.: Matz, Schriftsteller, vermutl. England, RSHA IV A 1.
216. **Brantierger, Anton,** 15.8.94 Falkenau, England, RSHA IV A 1 b.
217. **von Brodow, Hans,** vermutl. England (Täterkreis: Siegfried Franke), RSHA IV E 4.
218. **Groljsen, Pieter,** Journalist, zuletzt: Holland, vermutl. England, RSHA IV A 1.
219. **Bruens, Agent,** zuletzt: Boest, vermutl. England (Täterkreis: Prins), RSHA IV E 4.
220. **Breltscheid, Rudolf, Dr.,** Emigrant, 2.11.74 Köln, Schriftsteller, RSHA II B 5.

221. **Braun, Helmut,** 26 Jahre alt, zuletzt: Riga, vermutl. England, RSHA IV E 4, Stapo Tilsit.
222. **Brendel, Otto, Dr., geb.** 1901, vermutl. England, Emigrant, RSHA III A 1.
223. **Brewer,** 35 Jahre alt, brit. Agent, zuletzt: Den Haag, vermutl. England, (Täterkreis: Stevens-Best), RSHA IV E 4.
224. **Brieger, Ernst, Dr.,** Cambridge, Emigrant, RSHA III A 1.
225. **Brinkhof,** brit. Agent, zuletzt: Holland, vermutl. England (Täterkreis: Arende), RSHA IV E 4., Stpkt.-Düsseldorf.
226. **Brittain, Vera, verh. Catlin,** Journalistin, London SW 3, 19 Glebe Palace, RSHA IV E 4.
227. **Brock, Werner, Dr.,** 1901, Cambridge, Emigrant, RSHA III A 1.
228. **Brockway, Archibald Fenner,** 1888 Calcutta, The Spinney Londwater, Hickmansworth Herts, RSHA VI G 1.
229. **Brod, Leise, verh. Obil,** 29.10.07 München, Deckn.: Erna Christel, Hausangestellte, vermutl. England (Am-Apparat), RSHA IV A 2.
230. **Brodetsky, Selig,** 10.2.88 Rußld., Prof., Headingley (Leeds), 3 Grosvenor Road, RSHA VI G 1.
231. **Brodziewicz, Stanislaus,** ehem. pol. Komm., vermutl. England, RSHA IV E 5.
232. **Brönstein, Walter, Dr.,** geb. 1890, vermutl. England, RSHA III A 1.
234. **Brond, Max, Dr.,** 1882, Prof. Edinburgh, RSHA III A 1.
235. **Broumer, Theodor,** 22.6.92 Münster/W., richtig Theodor Frausen, Ing., zuletzt Amsterdam, vermutl. England, RSHA IV E 4.
236. **Brousson, E. F,** Aufsichtsratmitgl., London EC 3, St. Helens Court, Shell-Max and B. P. Ltd., RSHA IV E 2.
237. **Brown, H. Ruskan, Gen.-Sekretär,** vermutl. England, RSHA VI G 1.
238. **Brown, J,** Schriftsteller, vermutl. England, RSHA IV B 4.
239. **ten Brucker richtig Harry Richter,** zuletzt: Den Haag, vermutl. England, (Täterkreis: Karl Nihom), RSHA IV E 4, StPL: Münster.
240. **Brücker, Erna, verh. Owen,** 21.12.04 Oberhausen, vermutl. England, RSHA IV A 1.
241. **v. d. Brug, J. J. H.,** zuletzt: Utrecht/Holland, vermutl. England (Täterkreis: Brijnen), RSHA IV E 4.
242. **Flesch-Brun, Hans,** vermutl. England, RSHA IV G 1.
243. **Brunert, Helene Elisabeth, verh. Robinson,** 27.2.97 Martenau/Frankr., vermutl. England, RSHA IV E 5, Stapoleit Breslau.
244. **Brusa, Josef,** 8.5.08 Herne/W., Arbeiter, vermutl. England, RSHA IV E 5, Stapoleit Breslau.
245. **Brussuwansky, Viktor,** 27.7.15 Charinopol, Student, vermutl. England, RSHA IV E 4, Stapoleit Prag.
246. **Bryan, Carter Ray,** Korrespondent, vermutl. England (Täterkreis: Sigrid Schulz), RSHA IV E 4.
247. **Brzezinski, Franziszek,** 14.9.95 Gardschau, Krs. Dirschau, Nachrichtenoffizier, vermutl. England, RSHA IV E 5, Stapo Schneidemühl.
248. **Buchardt, Fritz, Dr.,** geb. 1902, Oxford, Emigrant, RSHA III A 1 b.
249. **Budberg, Maria,** geb. Sakrewska, Baronin, Deckn.: Mura, London, brit. ND.-Agentin, RSHA VI C 2.
250. **Budzislawski, Hermann,** 11.2.01 Berlin, vermutl. England, Jude, RSHA II B 5.
251. **von Bülow, Horst,** 33.02 Berlin, vermutl. England (Täterkreis: Siegfried Franke), RSHA IV E 4.
252. **Bürger, Hans,** Schriftst., Emigrant, London W. C. 1, 8 Mecklenburgh Square, RSHA II B 5.

228. Bittner, Gottfried, 22.8.14 Offenbach, Wehrpfichtiger, England, Mosolsy, RSHA VD2t, Ger. d. Kommandantur Berlin.
254. Bubieck, Harry, brit. Vizekonsul, vermutl. England, RSHA IV E4.
255. Burell, Robert, 13.8.55, vermutl. England, RSHA VI G1, IIB5.
256. Burovoy, Gurlatno, Dr., geb. 1896, Emigrant, RSHA III A1.
257. Burch, William Isaak, London, RSHA IV E4.
258. Burckart, Egon Karl, 4.6.10 Botzingen, Krs. Aalen, Lehrer, vermutl. England, RSHA IV A1, Stl. Stuttgart.
259. Burde, Friedrich, 23.9.01 Bla.-Schöneberg, Deckn.: Adolf Edgar Schwarz, Dr., Schlosser (Am-Apparat), RSHA IV A2.
260. Burgh, R. B. St. London, RSHA VI G1.
261. Burghley, Lord, London, St. James Court, Buckingham Gate, RSHA VI G1.
262. Burknack, A., London (Täterkreis: H. Snoevliet), RSHA IV E4.
263. Burn, Erika, geb. Kersets, 9.4.14 Berlin, London, 4 Alrington Gardens Chiswick, RSHA IV A1.
264. Burnell, Albert Ernest Aston, 12.9.89 London, brit. Cpt., Deckn.: Bernstein, zuletzt Genf, vermutl. England, Kraftw. GE 21351 GB, RSHA IV E4.
265. Burnham, William Lawson, Lord, 19.2.64 Barton Court Kintbury, Berkss, RSHA VI G1.
266. Burt, Ronald, 27.10.90 Leichester, Ringstead, Kaigton, RSHA IV E4. Stapo Frankfurt/M.
267. Burton, brit. Major, vermutl. England, RSHA IV E4.
268. Burton, brit. Cpt., zuletzt Riga, vermutl. England, RSHA IV E4.
269. Buttinger, Josef, 30.4.06 Reichersberg, Deckn.: Herbert, Gustav Richter, Handelsangestellter, vermutl. England RSHA IV A1.
270. Buxton, Kenneth Ernest, 16.9.16 London, Pilot, England, RSHA IV E4, Stapo Köln.
271. Byron, brit. ND-Agent, England, (Täterkreis: Jens Dons), RSHA IV E4, Stapo Kiel.
272. Bytel, Simon, York, 5 South View, Accomb Road, RSHA VI G1, II B5.
273. Bodyl, Piotr, 13.6.96 Polen, Geistlicher, zuletzt Holland, vermutl. England, RSHA IV E4, Stapo Aachen.

1. Cable, Eric, 1897 Helsingfors, brit. Konsul, vermutl. England, RSHA IV E4.
2. Cadbury, Elisabeth, RSHA VI G1.
2a Sir Cadogan, Leiter des brit. ND., vermutl. England, RSHA IV E4.
3. Calderwood, James, 13.10.11 Glasgow, vermutl. England, RSHA IV E4.
4. Calergii-Coudenhove, Richard, 17.11.94 Tokio, Schriftsteller, vermutlich England, Österr. Legitimist, RSHA IV A3.
5. Camber, Theodor, 28.11.94 Kowno, brit. ND.-Agent, zuletzt Wilna, vermutl. England, RSHA IV E4, Stapo Tilsit IIE4.
6. Cameron, Marian Ellene Mabel, 15.9.96 London, England, RSHA IV A1, IV E4.
7. Campbell, Angus, 6.8.01 London, Beamter d. brit. Passport-Office Berlin, zuletzt Oslo, vermutl. England, RSHA IV E4.
8. Campbell, Anjus, 10.2.61 Norel/Canada, Rentier, England, Deckn. Finkelstein, Steen, RSHA IV E4, Stapoleit Berlin.
9. Camrose, Lord, William E. Berry, 23.6.79, Eigentümer d. „Daily Telegraph Morning Post", Barrow Hills Long Crose, Surrey, London, 25 St. James Place, RSHA VI G1.
10. Mc. Cann, John, zuletzt Wallasey (Cheshire), 4 Meddoecroft Road Täterkreis: Ignatz Petschek, RSHA III D4.
11. Gordon-Canning, Robert, England, RSHA IV E4.
12. Capper, David, 23.01 London, Lehrer, London, RSHA IV A1.
13. Cargill, John T., Direktor, London E.C.2, Britannic House, Anglo-Iranian Oil Co., RSHA IV E2.
14. Carlton, W. J., London, RSHA VI G1.
15. Carner-Cohen, Mosco, Dr., geb. 1904, Dozent, London, RSHA III A1.
16. Caro, Walter Heinz Bubi Anton, Dr. phil., 19.6.09 Berlin, Deckn.: Dr. Kurt Glanz, Chemiker, vermutl. England (Am-Apparat), RSHA IV A2.
17. Carstens, Friedrich, 25.9.03 Erfde, Geschäftsführer d. Firma Page Wate Farrer, London, vermutl. London, RSHA IV E3, Stl. Kärlsruhe.
18. Carter, Henry, Geistlicher, RSHA VI G1.
19. Carter-Bonham, geb. Asquith, Violet, London W.2, Glouchester Square, RSHA VI G1.
20. Mc. Carthy, G. M., Mitarb. d. „Sunday Referee Ld.", RSHA VI B4.
21. Carton, Maxwell, Deckname: Rogersen, London, Vauxhall Bredge 176, RSHA IV E4.
22. Carvell, J. E. M., brit. Generalkonsul, England, RSHA IV E4.
23. Caslavka, Alois, 9.9.99 Böhmisch-Skalitz, Deckname: Cisek, ehem. Stabskapt. d. tschech. Heeres (ND.-Offizier), zuletzt: Prag-Device, Vevarska 49, vermutl. England, RSHA IV E4, Stapoleit Prag.
24. Caslavsky, Karl, Deckname: Rotenstein, zuletzt: Olmütz, vermutl. England, RSHA IV E4.
25. Caspari, Johann, Dr., 16.2.88 Berlin, Landeshauptmann, vermutl. England, Deckname: Weiß, Pick, Dr. Jakobi (Schwarze Front), RSHA IV A3.
26. Cassau, Theodor, 1884, Direktor, London, RSHA III A1.
27. de Castejar, Conde, zuletzt: Lissabon, vermutl. England, RSHA IV E3.
28. Castelchomond, Graf de, O. Brien, brit. Cpt., zuletzt: Kitzbühl, vermutl. England (Täterkreis: O.-Brien French), RSHA IV E4.
29. Catlin, George Edward Cordos, 29.7.96, Politiker. London S.W.3, 19 Glebe Place, RSHA VI G1.

30. Catlin, geb. Brittain, Vera, Journalistin, London SW3, 19 Gleve Place, RSHA VI G1.
31. Causlet, Victor Alexander, 27.12.96, Offizier, London W1, 66 Grosvenor Street, RSHA VI G1.
32. Cebular, Alfred, zuletzt: Novi Sad, vermutl. England, RSHA IV E4.
33. Cecil, Lord, Robert, geb. 1864, London, 16 South Eaton Place, RSHA VI G1.
34. Le Coup, Frederik, 22.3.96 New York, Advokat, England (Kraftw.: AMO 289 GB), RSHA IV E4.
35. Cahn, Ernst Dr., 1906, zuletzt Oxford, RSHA III A1.
36. Chalosor, Thomas, 18.8.99 Wiltshire, brit. Cpt., England, RSHA IV E4.
37. Chamberlain (Arthur) Neville, 18.3.69, Politiker, ehemaliger Ministerpräsident, London S.W.1, 10 Downing-Street, Westbourne, Edgbaston, Birmingham, RSHA II D5 – VI G1.
38. Chandler, Fred William, 8.4.76 Stanmore b. Syney, Dr. d. Staatswissenschaft, England, RSHA IV E4.
39. Chapman, Sir Sidney John, 29.1.88, Prof., London S.W.7, The Imperial College, RSHA VI G1.
40. Charles, E., brit. Agentin, zuletzt: Brüssel, vermutl. England (Täterkreis: Josef Mennecken), RSHA IV E4.
41. Charoux geborene Treffz, Margarete, 25.5.95, Wien, Reisende, London, RSHA IV A1.
42. Charroux, Siegfried, 15.10.96 Wien, Bildhauer, London W.4, Riverside 54, British Grove, RSHA IV A1, III A.
43. Chidson, H. Romey, 13.4.93 London, Militärattaché, brit. Oberstlieuts. zuletzt: Den Haag, vermutl. England (Kraftw.: HZ 36 927 GB.), RSHA IV E4.
43a Chien, John, Edwin, 21.1.01 Braddington, zuletzt: Kopenhagen, vermutl. England, RSHA IV E4.
44. Chingford, Charles, Vertreter, London W.d, Cambridge 510, RSHA IV E4.
45. Chrostomanias, Andreas, Arzt, zuletzt Athen, vermutl. England (Täterkreis: Crawford), RSHA IV E4.
46. Chukhonit-Chudhin, Leon, zuletzt: Kowno, vermutl. England (Täterkreis: Th. Camber), RSHA IV E4, Stapo Tilsit.
47. Churcher, Segrue John, 7.1.84, Liverpool, Journalist, England, RSHA IV E4.
47a Christie, brit. Nachrichtenoffizier, London, RSHA IV E4.
48. Church, Archibald George, 1886 London, Major, Reuturver, Selsdon-Road, Sanderstreet, RSHA VI G1.
49. Churchill, Winston Spencer, Ministerpräsident, Westerham/Kent, Chartwell Manor, RSHA VI A1.
50. Chrystal, Johann, 16.5.92 Sachenthal, vermutl. England, RSHA IV A1.
51. Chrystal, Silvester, 25.11.94 Sachenthal, vermutl. England, RSHA IV A1.
52. Chudak, Gerhard, 12.11.03 Bursim, London N.W.6, 47 Blenheim Gardens, RSHA IV A1.
53. Cielly, Georg, 29.9.14 Scharley/Ostoberschlesien, Obergefreiter, vermutl. ...
54. Cissin, Wanda, 6.1.95 Chmelno, ... vermutl. ..., Stabsspt., London, 49 Lazae Gardens, Kensington W.8 (Täterkreis: Prusohak/Morawa), RSHA IV E4, IV E6.

55. Citrine, Sir, Walter, geb. 1887, Generalsekretär, London S.W.1, Smith Square, RSHA VI G1.
56. Cizek, richtig Caslavka, RSHA IV E4, Stapoleit Prag.
57. Clark, Charles, brit. Agent, zuletzt: Lüttich, vermutl. England (Täterkreis: Kurt Felsenthal), RSHA IV E4.
58. Clark, Herta, geb. Braunthal, 1.2.87 Wien, vermutl. England, RSHA IV A1.
59. Clark, Hilda, Dr., RSHA VI G1.
60. Clark, John, Sekretär, London E.C.2, Britannic-House, Anglo-Iranian Oil Co., RSHA IV E2.
61. Clark, R. T., Schriftsteller, RSHA III A5.
62. Clark, William, 13.8.85 London, Redakteur, London, RSHA IV A1.
63. Clarke, Eric Allan, brit. Hauptmann, England, RSHA IV E4.
64. Clavering, Sir, Albert, Deckname: Closenburg, Reklameagent, vermutl. England, RSHA VI G1.
65. Cleyg, Charles, brit. Leutnant, zuletzt: Dänemark, vermutl. London (Täterkreis: John Hugill), RSHA IV E4.
66. Clutterbuk, geb. Kant, Lina, 15.8.98 Pforzheim, London, Übersetzerin der ITF., RSHA IV A1b.
67. Coockaert, Martha, verh. Mckenna, England, RSHA IV E4.
68. Coatts, W. P., Schriftsteller, vermutl. England, RSHA VI G1.
69. Corbett-Ashby, Frau, Führerin der liberalen Partei, RSHA VI G1.
70. Cockburn, Claude, 56 Jahre alt, Korrespondent, London S.W.J, 34 Victoria Street, Deckname: Frank Pitcain, RSHA IV A1, VI G1.
71. Cockerill, John, brit. General, zuletzt: Antwerpen, vermutl. England, RSHA IV E4.
72. Cocks, Seymour, 1882, Politiker, RSHA VI G1.
73. Coenen, Peter, 6.3.88 Stettin, Gewerkschaftssekretär, vermutl. England, RSHA IV A1.
74. Cohen, Abraham, Dr., Rev., Wohnung: Birmingham 16, 2, Highfield Rd. Edg. Baston, RSHA II B2.
75. Cohen, Engus, Journalist, vermutl. England, RSHA VI G1.
76. Cohen, Israel, Politiker, vermutl. England, London N.W.6, 29 Pattison Road Child's Hill, RSHA IV G1.
77. Cohen-Carner, Mosco, Dr., 1904, Dozent, London, RSHA III A1.
78. Cohen, Lionel Leonard, 1888 geb, Bankier, Wohnung: London W.2, Orme Sq., 3, RSHA II B2.
79. Max Cohen, richtig Nickelche, vermutl. England, RSHA IV D3a.
80. Cohen, Emanuel, 20.1.76 Langenberg, vermutl. England, RSHA IV A1.
81. Cohen, Robert Waley, Verw.-Direktor, London E.C.3, St. Helens Court, Shell Transport u. Trading Co., RSHA IV E2.
82. Cohn, Ernst, Prof., vermutl. London, RSHA III A1.
83. Cohn, Walter, 3.9.04 Chemnitz, Kaufmann, England, RSHA IV A1.
84. Cohn, George, Lektor, Univ. Oxford, RSHA III A1.
85. Collin, Norman, Direktor, RSHA VI G1.
86. Collin, brit. Agent, vermutl. England, RSHA IV E4.
87. Conn, Edward, Dr., 1888, Prof., London, RSHA III A1.
88 Hartley-Cook, Colonel u. Leiter v. M.I.5 (Military-Intelligence), London, RSHA IV E4.
89. Cooper, Duff Alfred, Informationsminister, London S.W.1, Chapel Street 34, RSHA II D5, VI G1.
90. Cooper, P. D'Arcy, Kaufmann, Westbridge Reigate Surrey, Unilever House, Blackfriars, RSHA IV E6, III D5.

90. **Cooper, Ivor,** Mitgl. d. brit. Rüstungswesenausschuss, London, The Old School House, Rudgewick (Sussex), RSHA III D 2.
91. **Copeland, Fred,** RSHA VI G 1.
92. **Coralfleet, Pierre,** richtig: Frank Davison, vermutl. England, RSHA IV E 4.
93. **Cormack, Georges,** Direktor, zuletzt Riga, vermutl. England, RSHA IV E 4.
94. **Coudenhove-Calerghi, Richard,** 17.11.94 Tokio, Schriftsteller, vermutl. England (Österr. Legitimist), RSHA IV A 3.
95. **Courbois,** brit. Agent, zuletzt Brüssel, vermutl. England, RSHA IV E 4.
96. **Coward, Noel,** vermutl. London, RSHA VI G 1.
97. **Mc. Cracken, C.,** 18.7.90 London, brit. Oberleutn., zuletzt Brüssel, vermutl. England, RSHA IV E 4.
97a **Craig, Noel,** 11.11.86, zuletzt Kopenhagen, vermutl. England, RSHA IV E 4.
98. **Cranborne, R.,** Unterstaatssekretär, England, RSHA VI G 1.
99. **Crawford, Janet,** 14.4.77, zuletzt Bukarest, vermutl. England, RSHA IV E 4.
100. **Crawford,** Leiter d. brit. ND., zuletzt Athen, vermutl. England, RSHA IV E 4.
101. **Creighton, T. M.,** vermutl. England (Täterkreis: Algernon Slade), RSHA IV E 4.
102. **Crick, Siegfried,** 40 Jahre alt, England, Deckname: Krik, RSHA IV E 4.
103. **Cripps, Sir Stafford,** Botschafter in Moskau, London E. C. 4, 3 Elm Court, Temple. RSHA II B 4, VI G 1.
104. **Cromwell, William,** England, RSHA IV E 4.
105. **Crooks,** Angehöriger des brit. ND., England, RSHA IV E 4.
106. **Crossfield, B. F.,** 1886, Direktor der New Chronicle, RSHA VI G 1.
107. **Crossman, R. H. S.,** RSHA VI G 1.
108. **Crowther, Goffrey,** 1907, Direktor; England, RSHA VI G 1.
109. **Crozier, W. P.,** Hauptschriftleiter, England, RSHA VI G 1.
110. **Cummings, A. J.,** Mitarb. d. News Chronicle, RSHA IV B 4, VI G 1.
111. **Cunard, Nancy,** England, RSHA VI G 1.
112. **Curtis, David Nathaniel,** Wohnung: Cardiff, Four Winds Penisely Rd, RSHA II B 2.
113. **Curnbull, John,** England (Täterkreis: Stevens/Best), RSHA IV E 4.
114. **Curtis, Frederick F. C., Dr.,** Privatdozent, vermutl. England, RSHA III A 1.
115. **Czogalla, Stanislaus, Dr.,** 23.4.98 Zawade b. Ratibor, Vertreter vermutl. England, RSHA IV E 5, Stapo Oppeln.
116. **Czoska, August,** 1.4.85 Soppieschin, poln. Zollinspektor, vermutl. England, RSHA IV E 5, Stapo Graudenz.

1. **Dabrowski,** verh. Runge, Maria, 18.7.96 Zeznitzere, ehem. Sekretär i. ehem. poln. Konsulat, RSHA IV E 5.
2. **Dahlmann, Johann,** 2.8.94 Thorn, Bergmann, poln. ND-Agent, RSHA IV E 5.
3. **Dallas, George,** 1878, Labour-Abgeordneter, RSHA VI G 1.
4. **Dale-Herbst,** richtig Dale-Long, zuletzt: Brüssel, jetzt: vermutl. England, RSHA IV E 4.
5. **Dale-Long, Herbert,** Deckname: Loog, Lessing, Lane, Lennox, 15.12.75 London, brit. Agent, vermutl. England, RSHA IV E 4.
6. **Dalton, Hugh,** Wirtschaftler (Universität London), RSHA VI G 1.
7. **Daly,** brit. Oberst, zuletzt: Lissabon, vermutl. England, RSHA IV E 4.
8. **Daly, T. D.,** Oberst, Mil.-Attaché, vermutl. England, RSHA IV E 4.
9. **van Damm,** vermutl. England (Täterkreis: Albert Albseit), RSHA IV E 4.
10. **Damm,** Deserteur, brit. Agent, vermutl. England, RSHA IV E 4.
11. **Daniel, de Luce,** 8.6.11 USA, Journalist, vermutl. England (Täterkreis: Sagrue Chrisoston), RSHA IV E 4.
12. **Danckwerts,** brit. Captain, Leiter d. Sp.-Abteilung, vermutl. England, RSHA IV E 4.
13. **Dansey, Claude,** brit. Oberstleutnant a. D., brit. Hauptagent, London, RSHA IV E 4.
13. **Darwin,** vermutl. England, RSHA IV E 4.
14. **Dassau, Robert,** Deckname: Munki, Max, 1.5.09 Hamburg, Arbeiter (Am-Apparat), RSHA IV A 2.
15. **Daube, David, Dr.,** geb. 1909, Assistent, Cambridge (Universität), Emigrant, RSHA III A 1.
16. **Davison,** geb. Boday, Käthe, 25.8.05 Fürstenwalde, Sekretärin, vermutl. London, RSHA II A 1.
17. **Davidson, R.,** Verleger d. „News Chronicle", RSHA VI G.
18. **Davidson, Theodora,** vermutl. England (Täterkreis: Algernon Slades), RSHA IV E 4.
19. **Davies, C. E.,** vermutl. London, Unilever House, Blackfriars, RSHA IV E 2.
20. **Davies, David,** Lord. Bank- u. Eisenbahndirektor (Völkerbundsbewegung Einkreisungsfront gegen Deutschland), RSHA VI G 1.
21. **Davies, Randolph S.,** Schriftsteller, Verfasser d. Buches „Hitler's Spy Ring", RSHA IV B 4.
22. **Davies, Stephan,** 1886, Labourabgeordneter, Förderer der Einkreisungsfront, RSHA VI G 1.
23. **Davies,** brit. Captain u. N.-Agent, London NW 2, 64 Crewys Road Child Hill, Golden Green, RSHA IV E 4.
24. **Davis,** zuletzt Riga. jetzt vermutl. England, brit. ND. Lettland, RSHA IV E 4.
25. **Davisohn-Spencer, Frank Ch.,** 10.8.89 Montabu, Rechtsanwalt, vermutl. England, RSHA IV E 4.
26. **Dawson, Horace Cortland,** 11.11.01 London, Ingenieur, zuletzt Berlin-Grunewald, vermutl. England, RSHA IV E 4, Stapoleit Berlin.
27. **Dawson of Penn,** Lord, Mitunterzeichner der engl. Rundfunkbotschaft an das deutsche Volk im Jahre 1939, RSHA VI G 1.
28. **Day, Donald,** USA-Staatsangehöriger, Vertreter der „Chicago Tribune", zuletzt Riga, brit. ND. Lettland, RSHA VI C 2.
29. **Day,** zuletzt Den Haag, vermutl. England (Täterkreis: Vyth), RSHA IV E 4.

30. **van Deep,** brit. Oberleutnant, vermutl. England, RSHA IV E 4.
31. **Delchmüller, Karl,** 3.11.79 Lichow, Musiker, Southampton, RSHA IV E 4.
32. **Delahaye, J. V.,** Führer der Labour-Party, RSHA VI G 1.
33. **Delmer, Sefton,** Pariser Vertreter d. „Daily Express", London, RSHA IV E 4.
34. **Demikowski, Stanislaus, Dr.,** brit. Agent, vermutl. England (Täterkreis: Fray Strong), RSHA IV E 4.
35. **Demmer, Aneta,** 1940: 24 Jahre, Journalistin, zuletzt Den Haag, vermutlich England (Täterkreis: Stevens/Best), RSHA IV E 4.
36. **Denget, Georg,** 17.9.08 Marktheidenfeld, Seemann, zuletzt Antwerpen, vermutl. England (Täterkreis: Waldemar Pötzsch), RSHA IV E 4.
37. **Dennys, Rodney,** zuletzt Den Haag, vermutl. England (Täterkreis: England), RSHA IV E 4.
38. **Derby (Lord Derby),** Mitunterzeichner der engl. Rundfunkbotschaft 1939, London, RSHA VI G 1.
39. **Derkow, Willi,** 17.11.06 Charlottenburg, Bankangestellter, vermutl. England, RSHA IV A 1 b.
40. **Demauer, Marie, Dr.,** geb. 1901, Ass., London, Emigrant, RSHA III A 1.
41. **Detras-Schweitzer, Alfred,** Bankprokurist, zuletzt Basel, vermutl. England, RSHA IV E 4, Stapoleit Karlsruhe.
42. **Deutsch, Adam, Dr.,** 1907, Ass., Edinburgh, Emigrant, RSHA III A 1.
43. **Deutsch, Julius, Dr.,** 2.2.84 Lackenbach, ehem. österr. Staatssekretär, vermutl. England (Arbeiter-Sport-Internationale), RSHA IV A 1.
44. **Deutsch, Oscar,** Birmingham 15, 5, Baston, Augustus Rd. Edg RSHA II B 2.
45. **Deutsch, Walter, Dr.,** 1894, Privatdozent, vermutl. Universität Manchester, Emigrant, RSHA III A 1.
46. **Devereux, Roy,** vermutl. England (Täterkreis: Algernon Slades), RSHA IV E 4.
46a **Dewald, Walter,** ehem. Pförtner d. brit. Gen.-Konsulats Rotterdam, zuletzt Rotterdam, vermutl. England (Täterkreis: Walter Ewald), RSHA IV E 4.
47. **Dewhurst, Norman,** 29.9.87 Southport, brit. ND.-Offizier, Schriftsteller, zuletzt Riga. jetzt London, RSHA IV E 4, VI C 2.
48. **Dey, W.,** brit. Agent, zuletzt Stockholm, vermutl. England, RSHA IV E 4.
49. **Diamond, A. S.,** London E. C. 4, 1 Temple Gardens, Temple, RSHA II B 2.
50. **Dible,** brit. Konsul, zuletzt: Amsterdam, vermutl. England (Täterkreis: Theo Hespers), RSHA IV E 4.
51. **Dick, Albin,** 24.4.18 Tiss, vermutl. England, RSHA IV A 1.
52. **Dick,** geb. Horn, Lisa, 19.6.19 St. Joachimsthal, vermutl. England, RSHA IV A 1.
53. **Dick, Rudolf,** richtig: Baron von Gerlach, vermutl. England (Täterkreis: Stevens/Best), RSHA IV E 4.
54. **Dicken, Ellen,** ca. 29 Jahre, Krefeld, Kunstgewerbelehrerin, früher in Düsseldorf, vermutl. England, RSHA IV E 4.
55. **Dickinson, Baron,** 1859 geboren, Pazifist, RSHA VI G.
56. **Dickson, Aloe,** Journalist, London SW, Struan-Wimbledon-Park, RSHA IV E 4, III 2, Stapo Reichenberg.

57. **Dickwell,** Deckn.: Gaston Barbé, brit. Agent, zuletzt Brüssel, vermutlich England (Täterkreis: Kurt Felsenstahl), RSHA IV E 4.
58. **Spiegel-Diesenberg, Graf von, Felix,** 19.1.91 Iglau/Mähren, zuletzt Mißlitz, vermutl. England (Täterkreis: von Gerlach), RSHA IV E 4.
59. **Dietzschold, Kurt,** 9.1.88 Leipzig, Bürgermeister, Bristol 8, Pembroke Road Clifton, RSHA IV E 4.
60. **Dijkhooren, A. Q. H.,** früherer holl. Verteidigungsminister, zuletzt Den Haag, vermutl. England, RSHA III B.
61. **Dill, Erhard,** 26.4.10 Selb, Student, vermutl. England, RSHA IV A 1.
62. **Dill, Johann,** 25.6.87 Brand, Parteisekretär, RSHA IV A 1 b.
63. **van Dillen, H.,** brit. Agent, vermutl. England (Täterkreis: Waldemar Pötzsch), RSHA IV E 4.
64. **Dimasaki, Hermann,** 16.11.10 Berlin, zuletzt Antwerpen, vermutl. England, RSHA IV E 4.
65. **Dinhorn, Ruth,** 1908 geb., vermutl. England (Täterkreis: Lukapello), RSHA IV E 4.
66. **Dirksen, Walter,** richtig: Auerbach, Walter, vermutl. England, RSHA IV A 1 b.
67. **van Dittmar,** zuletzt Rotterdam, vermutl. England, RSHA IV E 4.
68. **Dittmar,** ehem. russ. Leutnant, zuletzt Amerika, vermutl. England, RSHA IV E 4.
69. **Divish, Anna,** 8.5.02 Pilsen, Ehefrau des Alfred Frank, vermutl. England, RSHA IV A 1 b.
70. **Dix,** brit. Captain, früher Kopenhagen, vermutl. England, RSHA IV E 4.
71. **Dixen,** brit. Agent, vermutl. England, RSHA IV E 4.
72. **Dixey, Neville,** Antifaschist, Vorsitzender von Lloyds, Mitglied d. IPC u. Lib. P., RSHA VI G.
73. **Djordjewic, Dragi,** Holzhändler, zuletzt Zagreb, vermutl. England (Täterkreis: Lukapello), RSHA IV E 4.
74. **Dlouhy, Dominik,** Großkaufmann, zuletzt Zagreb, vermutl. England, RSHA IV E 4, III A, Stapo Graz.
75. **Doberer, Kurt,** 11.9.04 Nürnberg, Ingenieur, vermutl. England, RSHA IV A 1 b.
76. **Dobeleit,** Radiohändler, brit. ND-Agent, zuletzt: Leibach, vermutl. England (Täterkreis: J. C. Ross), RSHA IV E 4.
77. **Doby,** brit. Captain, vermutl. England, RSHA IV E 4.
78. **Docharly,** London, White Hall (Täterkreis: Allan Graves), RSHA IV E 4.
79. **Dodds, Eric Robertson,** Professor, Oxford, Propagandist gegen Franco, Einkreisungsfront gegen Deutschland, RSHA VI G.
80. **Dörfler, Franz,** 16.4.09 Schwaderbach, vermutl. England, RSHA IV A 1 b.
81. **Dörin, F. P.,** Emigrant, RSHA VI G 1, II B 5.
82. **Doerig, Friedrich,** 4.3.82 Tobertitz, Leutner, vermutl. London, RSHA IV A 1.
83. **Dohrn, Nikolaus,** 26.6.06 Dresden, Schriftsteller, vermutl. England, Öster. Legitimist, RSHA IV A 1.
84. **Dolive, Myra (Irma),** Musiklehrerin, zuletzt: Bukarest, vermutl. England (Täterkreis: Janet Crawford), RSHA IV E 4.
85. **Dolphin, Major,** Leiter brit. Mil. Sp. in Wiesbaden, vermutl. England, RSHA IV E 4.

85a Donald, Mac, James Richards, 31.1.81, brit. N.-Agent, zuletzt: Kop :
hagen, vermutl. England, RSHA IV E 4.
86. Donaldson, richtig: Clement Arnold de Haas, zuletzt: Den Haag.
vermutl. England, RSHA IV E 4.
87. van der Donk, Hector, brit. Leutnant, zuletzt: Brüssel, vermutl. England, RSHA IV E 4.
88. Dookers, Bernhard Franz, Deckname: Baalen, 21.6.05 Duisbu : :,
Arbeiter, zuletzt: Nymwegen, vermutl. England (Täterkreis: P.::
hausen), RSHA IV E 4.
89. Dookers, Franz, 11.7.10 Duisburg, Händler Arbeiter, zuletzt: Nymwegen, vermutl. England (Täterkreis: Pfaffhausen), RSHA IV E 4.
90. Dookers, Johanna Sofia, geb. Schleess, 18.6.06 Baderich, zuletzt:
Nymwegen, vermutl. England (Täterkreis: Wilhelm Willemse), RSHA
IV E 4.
91. Dookers, Kornelius, 5.10.75 Horsen, zuletzt: Duisburg-Wanheim-a.r.,
vermutl. England (Täterkreis: Wilhelm Willemse), RSHA IV E 4.
92. Dookers, Wilhelm, 2.4.12 Duisburg, zuletzt: Nymwegen, vermutl.
England (Täterkreis: Wilhelm Willemse), RSHA IV E 4.
93. Donoghue, J. K., ehem. Mitglied der brit. Botschaft in Berlin, vermutl. England, RSHA IV E 4.
94. Doric, Vlado, Dr., brit. Agent, vermutl. England (Täterkreis: Lukapello), RSHA IV E 4.
95. Dorsill-Möller, Rudolf, London W. C. 1, Bedford-Place 12, RSHA
VI G 1.
96. Douglas, J., Journalist, Herausgeber kommunistischer Schriften,
RSHA VI G.
97. Dowden, A. E., früherer brit. Vizekonsul, RSHA IV E 4.
98. Drage, Sir, Benjamin, London N. W. 3, 28 Eton Ave., RSHA II B 2.
99. Draper, B., vermutl. England, RSHA IV E 4.
100. Dresel, Karl, 18.2.87 Reitendorf, kommunistischer Senator, England,
RSHA IV A 1.
101. Droses, J. J. K., 16.3.92 Maastricht, Portier, zuletzt: Den Haag, vermutl. England (Täterkreis: Arthur Bastin), RSHA IV E 4.
102. Drobnik, Jerzy, Pole, Mitarbeiter der Schrift „Free Europe", vermutl. London, RSHA VI G 1.
103. Drtina, Prokop, Dr., Referent in der Kanzlei des Expräsidenten
Benes, RSHA IV D 1 a.
104. Drucker, Peter, 1909, Prof., Dr., vermutl. London, Emigrant, RSHA
III A 1.
105. Drummond, Lord, Deckname: Grove Spiro, vermutl. England, RSHA
IV E 4.
106. Drummond, R. I. D. Alex, 12.3.79, brit. Fliegeroffizier, vermutl.
England, RSHA IV E 4.
107. Dubicz, Charles, 2.6.92 Warschau, Major, poln. N.-Offizier, RSHA
IV E 5, Stapo Danzig.
108. Dubie, vermutl. England, RSHA IV E 4.
109. Dubinski, D., vermutl. England (Täterkreis: H. Sneevliet), RSHA
IV E 4.
110. Duchacek, Ivo, Dr., 27.2.13 Prößnitz, Redakteur, vermutl. England,
RSHA IV E 4, Stapoleit Prag.
111. Rosenbaum-Ducommun, Vladimir, Rechtsanwalt, vermutl. England,
RSHA IV E 4.
112. Noble-Dudley, Henry, 41.10.01 London, Direktor, vermutl. England,
RSHA IV E 4.

113 Duff, Charles, Schriftleiter, vermutl. England, betrieb rotspanische
Propaganda in England, RSHA VI G.
114. Duff-Cooper, Alfred, Informationsminister, England, RSHA VI G 1.
115. Dukker, D., zuletzt: Antwerpen, vermutl. England (Täterkreis: Hermann Knüfken), RSHA IV E 4.
116. Dulkeit, Erwin, brit. Agent, zuletzt: Riga, vermutl. England, RSHA
IV E 4, Stapoleit Hannover.
117. Dumas, brit. Agent, zuletzt: Brüssel, vermutl. England, RSHA IV E 4.
118. Dumont, Angehöriger des brit. N. D., vermutl. England, RSHA
IV E 4.
119. Dumphy, Peddy, brit. Offizier, vermutl. England, RSHA IV E 4.
120. Dumpi, Leiter eines brit. N.-Büros, vermutl. England, RSHA IV E 4.
121. Duncan, Oliver, Sir, London E. C. 2, 7/8 Princts Street (Täterkreis:
Lautz Potschek), RSHA III D 4.
122. Dunkan-Sendys, Abgeordneter, Schwiegersohn von Winston
Churchill, RSHA VI G.
123. Dunker, Karl, Dr., 1903, Ass., vermutl. London, Emigrant, RSHA
III A 1.
124. Dunderdale, brit. Leutnant, vermutl. England (Täterkreis: Stevens/
Best), RSHA IV E 4.
125. Dunham. S. P. R., brit. Agent, zuletzt Riga (brit. N.-D. Lettland),
vermutl. England, RSHA IV E 4, VI C 2.
126. Dunk, Edgar, Direktor des Linksbuch-Clubs, Antifaschist, RSHA VI G.
127. Dunstan, Mary, Schriftstellerin, RSHA IV B 4.
128. Durban, Edward Charles, 27.3.91 Birmingham, brit. Oberst, vermutl.
England (Täterkreis: Lew Trofimow), RSHA IV E 4.
129. Durrell, richtig Porter, Leiter d. sowj.-russ. Sp.-Abteilung, vermutl.
England, RSHA IV E 4.
130. Dutsh, brit. Captain, vermutl. England, RSHA IV E 4.
131. Dutt, Eric, brit. Major, Leiter d. 13 in Valencia, zuletzt: Valencia,
vermutl. England, RSHA IV E 4.
132. Dutt, Palme R., 15.4.93 (96) Cambridge, Journalist, London, Antifaschist, RSHA IV A 1, VI G.
133. Dyks, Paul, Deckn.: Pavel Pawlowitsch, brit. Oberst, vermutl. England, RSHA IV E 4.

---

1. Eastermann, Alexander Levvey, Journalist, London N. W. 1, 15 Regent's Court, Hanover Gate, RSHA II B 2.
2. Ebbutt, Norman, Berl. Korresp. der Times, RSHA IV B 4 b.
3. Ebeling, Hans, Dr., 29.97 Krefeld, Kaufmann, London (Täterkreis:
Les Ben), RSHA IV E 4, IV E 2.
4. van Eck, Baron, Direktor, London E. C. 5, St. Helens Court, RSHA
IV E 2.
5. Ecker, Fritz, 5.3.92 Fürth i. W., England, RSHA IV A 1 b.
6. Eden, Robert Anthony, 12.6.97, Kriegsminister, London W. 1, Fitz-
hardinge Str. 17, RSHA II D 5, VI G.
7. Eden, Chef d. Fa. Einkaufshaus für Kanada in Zürich, vermutl. England, RSHA IV E 4.
8. Ederheimer A., Dr., Mitarbeiter d. „Merton", London, RSHA III D.
9. Edmonds, brit. Oberst, England, RSHA IV E 4.
10. Edmondson, brit. Vizekonsul, Dairen/Ostasien, vermutl. England
(Täterkreis: Klingmüller), RSHA IV E 4, Stapo Köln.
11. Edwards, Sir Charles, Labour-Abgeordneter, RSHA VI G.
12. Edwards, Hendrik, richtiger Name: Stein, Kurt, 23.2.00 London, England, RSHA IV E 4.
13. Edwards, richtig Moscow, Leiter d. brit. ND. in Amsterdam, zuletzt:
Amsterdam, vermutl. England, RSHA IV E 4.
14. Eeman, Harald, richtig Watson, dipl. Beamter, vermutl. England,
brit. ND. in Lettland, RSHA VI C 2.
15. Eegerden, Frieda, Kent, RSHA IV E 4, Stapoleit Prag.
16. Ehm, Franz, 21.1.01 Zwodau, England, RSHA IV E 4.
17. Ehrenfried, Daniel, 3.9.81 (6.10.83) Gotzdowo/Mühle, Rennstallbesitzer,
Prag, vermutl. England (Täterkreis: von Einem, Gerta, Luise),
RSHA IV E 4.
18. Eichelberg, L., Schriftsteller, Emigrant, Oxford, 159 Woodstock Road,
RSHA II B 5.
19. Eichler, Wilhelm, 7.1.96 Berlin, Leiter des ISK., London, RSHA
IV A 1 b.
20. Eigler, Josef, 22.8.04 Bärringen, Hope Wiew, Castleton, Derbyshire,
RSHA IV A 1 b.
21. op't'Einde, Deckname: van der Heide, vermutl. England RSHA.
IV E 4.
22. Einsenschitz, Robert, Dr., 1906, Emigrant, London, RSHA III A 1.
23. Einstein, Alfred, Dr., 1880, Emigrant, London, RSHA III A 1.
24. Einzig, Paul, Dr., Redakteur, RSHA III A 5, VI G.
25. Merling-Eisenberg, Kurt, 1899, Priv.-Doz., London, RSHA III A 1.
26. Eisenberg, Margarethe, verh. Nußbaum, 23.2.06 Wien, Den Haag,
vermutl. England, RSHA IV E 4.
27. Ekblom, Gustav, 50—55 Jahre alt, Seemann, Stockholm, Köpman-
gatan 18, vermutl. England, RSHA IV E 4, III A 1, Stapo Hamburg.
28. Ekrosher, zuletzt: Kopenhagen, vermutl. England, RSHA IV E 4,
Stapo Kiel.
29. Eliot, brit. N.-Agent, England, RSHA IV E 4.
30. Elissen, brit. Major, England, RSHA IV E 4.
31. Ellerman, Sir, John Reeves, 21.12.09, London W. 1, South Audley
Str. RSHA II B 2.
32. Ellinger, Arthur, Mitarb. d. „Merton", London, RSHA III D.
33. Ellinger, Philipp, Dr., 1887, o. Prof., Emigrant, London, RSHA III A 1.
34. Ellinger, Walter, Mitarb. d. „Merton", vermutl. England, RSHA III D.

35. Ellis, Eunice (Earis), 22.9.90 Cheffield, brit. od. franz. Agentin, England, RSHA IV E 4.
36. Ellis, brit. Journalist, England, RSHA IV E 4.
37. Ellwood, M., brit. Beamtin, England, RSHA IV E 4.
38. Elsas, M. J., 1881, Dozent, Emigrant, London, RSHA III A 1.
39. Eltroy, Rudolf, 1.1.04 Hamm, Umwalzer, England, RSHA II A, Stapo
Potsdam.
40. Elvin, Herbert Heary, RSHA VI G.
41. van Emden, Fritz, 1906, Kurator im Brit. Museum, Emigrant, London, RSHA III A 1.
42. Emmering A., richtig: Vristen, 13.11.95 Loon op Zand, brit. N.-Agent
zuletzt: Rotterdam, vermutl. England (Täterkreis: Stevens-Best)
RSHA IV E 4, Stapo Köln.
43. Emmers, Karl, 14.10.89 Eupen, Gewerkschaftssekretär, vermutl. England, RSHA IV A 1.
44. Endt, Aloisia, verh. Meixner, 14.3.05 Bärringen, Norfolk Falken-
hamm, Thorpland Hall b. Miss Savary, RSHA IV A 1 b.
45. Enfrees, brit. Hauptmann u. ND.-Offizier, England, RSHA IV E 4.
46. Engel, Stefan, Dr., 1878, a. o. Prof., Emigrant, London, Gru-
Ormonde Street, RSHA III A 1.
47. Engelmann, Ludwig, 24.3.08 Iserlohn, Heizer, England, Internierungslager, RSHA IV A 1.
48. Engemann, Herbert, 16.7.01 Berlin, Dipl.-Ing., vermutl. England,
RSHA IV E 4.
49. English, brit. Cpt., vermutl. England, RSHA IV E 4.
50. Enoc, Mitarb. d. Chefs des brit. Nachrichtendienstes, vermutl. England (Täterkreis: Walter Oehme), RSHA IV E 4.
51. Epstein, Fritz, Dr., 1898, Assistent, Emigrant, London, Univ., RSHA
52. Epstein, Jacob, 1880 New York, Bildhauer, London S. W. 7, 18 Hyde
park Gate, RSHA II B 2.
53. Erban, früh. Presseattaché d. techech. Gesandtschaft, vermutl. England (Täterkreis: Stevens/Best), RSHA IV E 4.
54. Erdmann, Erich, vermutl. England (Täterkreis: Wilhelm Willemse),
RSHA IV E 4.
55. Erlanger, Richard, Mitarb. d. Merton, London, RSHA III D.
56. Ernst, brit. Vizekonsul, zuletzt: Zagreb, vermutl. England, RSHA
IV E 4, Stapo Graz.
57. Ernst, Aloisi, Dr., Deckname: Schwarz, 6.11.01 Neurode, Schriftsteller
London, evtl. nach Schottland verzogen, RSHA IV A 3.
58. Eschka, Hermann, 16.5.09 Voigtagrün, England, RSHA IV A 1 b.
59. Eschka, Karl, 15.7.90 Voigtagrün, Leeds, RSHA IV A 1 b.
60. Esser, Eugenie, brit. Agentin, zuletzt: Riga, vermutl. England, RSHA
IV E 4.
61. Etherington-Smith, R. G. A., Botsch.-Sekr., England, RSHA IV E 4
62. Everett, Motoreningenieur, London E. C. 2, Britannic House, RSHA
IV E 2.
63. Evea, H. B. Heath, Direktor, London E. C. 2, Britannic House, RSHA
IV E 2.
64. Ewing, Alfred, England, RSHA IV E 4.
65. Evingham, brit. Captain, England, RSHA IV E 4.
66. Ewert, brit. General, England, RSHA IV E 4.
67. Ewinger, Margarete, geb. Schenk, Dr. phil., 23.3.21 Gotha, Sekretär
England, RSHA IV E 4, Stapo Nürnberg.

65 Ewinga, Elisabeth, 31.7.90 Brüssel, Konzertpianistin u. Sprachlehrerin, vermutl. England, RSHA IV E 4, 9 V 7, Gestapoleit München.
66 Ewald, Walter, 29.11.05 Kiel, Deckname: Papageien-Walter, England (Südengland interniert), (Insel), RSHA IV A 1.
67 Eyre, ehemaliger brit. Konsul in Holland, Revisor, London, Unilever Haus, RSHA IV E 4, IV E 2.

1. Fabian, Dora, geb. Heinemann, Dr. phil., 28.5.01 Berlin, RSHA IV A 1 b.
1a Fabius, H. A. C., General, Leiter d. holl. ND., vermutl. England, RSHA IV E 4.
2. Fachreddin, Osman, brit. Agent, vermutl. England, RSHA IV E 4.
3. Fairholme, W. E., brit. Brigadegeneral, England, RSHA IV E 4.
4. Fajans, Edgar, Dr., geb. 1911, Bristol (Univers.), Emigrant, RSHA III A 1.
5. Falk, Werner, Dr., Dozent, geb. 1906 Oxford (Univers.), Emigrant, RSHA III A 1.
6. Falk, Deserteur, brit. Agent, vermutl. England, RSHA IV E 4.
7. Fallowfield, Algernon Gordon, Vizekonsul, England, RSHA IV E 4.
8. Falter, Alfred, 25.7.80 Ropa b. Gorlice, Industrieller, Mitglied der poln. Emigrantenregierung in England, RSHA III B 15.
9. Falter, Mitglied d. poln. Nationalr., Stellvertr. d. Finanzmin., RSHA IV D 2.
10. Fanshawe, brit. Kommandeur, vermutl. England, RSHA IV E 4.
11. Farell, John, England (Täterkreis: Engemann), RSHA IV E 4.
12. Farkas, Adalbert, geb. 1906 Cambridge (Univers.), Emigrant, RSHA III A 1.
13. Farlane, F. N. Mason Mac, ehemaliger brit. Militärattaché in Berlin, vermutl. England, RSHA IV E 4.
14. Featherston, brit. Capitain, vermutl. in England, RSHA IV E 4.
15. Fechner, Max, 3.10.05 Charlottenburg, Gemälderestaurator (Am-Apparat), RSHA IV A 2.
16. Feddersen, Fritz, Deckname: Fred Karlssen, 10.9.14 Hamburg, Matrose, Emigrant, zuletzt Stockholm, vermutl. England, RSHA IV E 4, Stapoleit Hamburg.
17. Feierabend, Ladislaus, Dr., 14.6.99 Kostelec, Staatsmin. d. csl. Auslandsregierung, Emigrant, RSHA IV D 1 a.
18. Feilding, R. C., Oberst, London, Stoke House bei Slough (Täterkreis: Julius Petschek), RSHA III D 4.
19. Feiler, Erich, geb. 1882, a. o. Prof., Emigrant, London, RSHA III A 1.
20. Feldmann, Egon, 21.7.09 Hamburg, zuletzt Amsterdam, vermutl. England (Täterkreis: Karl Nihom), RSHA IV E 4, Stapoleit Münster.
21. Felstead, S. Theodore, Schriftsteller, RSHA IV B 4.
22. Fenston, Joe, 40 J. alt, brit. ND.-Agent, London 77, Ourtney-Court Maida Vale W. 9, RSHA IV E 4.
23. Ferguson, C. H., London, Unilever Haus, Blackfriars, RSHA IV E 2.
24. Ferguson, Mary, Journalistin, RSHA VI G.
25. Ferl, Gustav, Deckn.: Rachel Clerk, 23.12.90 Gr. Ottersleben, ehem. SPD.-Parteisekr., vermutl. England (Sopade), RSHA IV A 1 b.
26. Fern, Rose, Hotelangestellte, Yokohama/Japan, vermutl. England, RSHA IV E 4.
27. Feuchtwanger, Franz, Deckname: Hugo Boenecke, 6.6.08 München, Student (Am-Apparat), RSHA IV A 2.
28. Feuchtwanger, Lion, 7.7.84 München, Schriftsteller, Emigrant, London W.C.6, Henriette Street, RSHA VI G 1, II B 5.
29. Feuermann, Emanuel, Emigrant, London, RSHA III A 1.
30. Fewster Arnold, 6.3.12 Newcastle, Student, RSHA IV E 4, Stapoleit Stettin.
31. Fichter, Oskar, Deckname: Oskar, 30.1.98 Furtwangen/Baden, Steindrucker (Am-Apparat), RSHA IV A 2.
32. Ficker, Hermann, 4.10.93 Friedrichsreuth, RSHA IV A 1 b.
33. Fildes, J. V., London, Unilever House, Blackfriars, RSHA IV E 2.

34. Piligiewicz, Tytus, Mitgl. d. poln. Nationalrates, RSHA IV D 2.
35. Pilliter, D. F. S., brit. Gen.-Konsul, vermutl. England (Täterkreis: Werner Aue), RSHA IV E 4.
36. Finmon, Edo (Edu), 16.6.81 Amsterdam, Generalsekr. d. ITF, London (Täterkreis: Stevens/Best), RSHA IV E 4, IV A 1 b, IV A 5.
37. Findlay, brit. ND.-Agent, RSHA IV E 4.
38. Fink-Trier, Trools, Zeitungsangestellter, zuletzt: Apenrade, vermutl. England (Täterkreis: Jens Dons), RSHA IV E 4, Stapo Kiel.
39. Finkelstein, Anjus, richtig Campbell, 10.2.61 Sorel/Kanada, Rentier, vermutl. England, RSHA IV E 4, Stapoleit Berlin.
40. Firis, Gustav, 1.7.00 Opama, Konsulatssekr., Pressereferent, RSHA IV E 5, Stapo Leipzig.
41. Fischbach, Anton, 14.7.99 Rotau, Osmondthorpe (Leedsg.), bei Rev. A. A. Hoskings, St. Philips, Vicarage, RSHA IV A 1.
42. Fischer, Louis, Mitarbeiter d. „Union d. demokratischen Kontrolle", RSHA VI G.
43. Fischer, Marie, 23.5.98 Elbogen, Barry (Glan), 17. Castel Street, RSHA IV A 1 b, Stapo Karlsbad.
44. Fischer, Mitarbeiter d. Militärattachés Kala, Emigrant, Jude, London, RSHA II B 5.
45. Fischer, RSHA VI G 1.
46. Fischer, brit. Feldwebel, vermutl. England, RSHA IV E 4.
47. Fisher, William, 14.8.96 Lodz, vermutl. England, RSHA IV E 4.
48. Fisher, Sergeant bei Scotland-Yard, vermutl. England, RSHA IV E 4.
49. Fisher-Sarasin, brit. Major, Leiter d. brit. Spionagebüros in Bern, vermutl. England, RSHA IV E 4.
50. Fischgold, Harry, Dr., geb. 1903, Emigrant, Ass. am City Mental Hospital in Nottingham, RSHA III A 1.
50a Fizdigaar, brit. N.-Agent, vermutl. England, RSHA IV E 4.
51. Fleck, Josef, geb. 1901, vermutl. England, RSHA IV E 4, Stapo Brünn.
52. Fleck, Karl, 5.11.90 Simbim, vermutl. England, RSHA IV A 1 b.
53. Fleck, Karl, 5.12.90 Selbitz b. Teplitz, Sekr. d. Keramarbeiterverbandes, vermutl. England, RSHA II A, Stapo Karlsbad.
54. Fleischhacker, Hans, Dr., geb. 1898, Ass., Emigrant, London, Maudsley Hospital, RSHA III A 1.
55. Fleischmann, Karl, 15.6.90 Wasserruppen, vermutl. England RSHA IV A 1 b.
56. Fleischmann, Paul, Dr., geb. 1879, a. o. Prof., Emigrant, London, RSHA III A 1.
57. Fleming, Edward L., RSHA IV D 4.
58. Flemming, Edward L., Schriftsteller, RSHA III A 5.
59. Flesch-Brun, Hans, Vorstandsmitglied d. „Freien deutschen Kulturliga in England", Emigrant, RSHA VI G, II B 5.
60. Fletcher, Reginald, geb. 1885, Offizier, Abgeordneter, RSHA VI G.
61. Floid, Marguerite, vermutl. England, RSHA IV E 4.
62. Florent, brit. Auftraggeber, vermutl. England (Täterkreis: Franzius Janssens), RSHA IV E 4.
63. Flower, Clement, 14.9.78 England, vermutl. England, RSHA IV E 4.
64. Fodor, M. W., Schriftsteller, RSHA IV B 4, VI G 1.
65. Förstel, Friedrich, 19.2.99 Elektromonteur, richtig Barthel, Alfred, vermutl. England, RSHA IV A 2.
66. Förster, Max, Dr., geb. 1869, o. Prof., Emigrant, New Haven, Yale Universität, RSHA III A 1.

67. Fehrmann, Nikolaus, Johannes, Präsident d. lux. Gewerkschaften, früher Luxemburg, vermutl. London, RSHA IV A 1 b.
68. Pollen, William J., Beamter d. brit. Konsulats in Panama, vermutl. England, RSHA IV E 4.
69. Folley, Frank Edward, Kapitän, ehemaliger Leiter d. brit. Paßbüros in Berlin, vermutl. England, RSHA IV E 4.
70. Fomfera, Heinrich, 10.11.95 Essen-Schonnebeck, Deckname: Franz, Maurer (Am-Apparat), RSHA IV A 2.
71. Foot, Dingle, geb. 1905, Abgeordneter d. liberalen Partei, RSHA VI G 1.
72. Footman, David, London, 25 Collingham Place, RSHA VI G 1.
73. Forbarth, A., Schriftsteller, RSHA IV B 4.
74. Forbes, Dita, 27.10.05 Düsseldorf, Erzieherin, vermutl. England (Täterkreis: Gustav Weber), RSHA IV E 4.
75. Forbes, Ogilvie George, 47 Jahre alt, Botschaftsrat, vermutl. England, RSHA IV E 4.
76. Forbes, Agent im brit. ND., vermutl. England (Täterkreis: Gustav Weber), RSHA IV E 4.
77. Ford, Josef Alfred, 26.7.64 Darlington, brit. Journalist, England, RSHA IV E 4.
78. Forêne, brit. Agent, England, RSHA IV E 4.
79. Forester, W. B. C. W., brit. Vizekonsul, vermutl. England, RSHA IV E 4.
80. Forst, Josef, 21.7.95 Prag, chem. tschech. Oberleutnant, London (Täterkreis: Frantisek Moravec), RSHA IV E 6.
81. Forster, Edward Morgan, geb. 1879, Schriftsteller, RSHA VI G 1.
82. Forster, G., brit. Agent (Täterkreis: James Haymes), RSHA IV E 4.
83. Forster-Arnold, William Edward, politischer Schriftsteller, RSHA VI G 1.
84. Fort (Forst), Josef, 21.7.95 Ziakow, chem. tschech. Stabskapitän, London, 53 Lexham Gardens Kensington W. 8, RSHA IV E 4.
85. Foster-Anderson, G. Herbert, 60.5.90 Liverpool, brit. Agent, zuletzt: Kaunas, vermutl. England (Täterkreis: Gregory Maundry), RSHA IV E 4.
86. Foulds, brit. Konsul i. Ostasien, vermutl. England (Täterkreis: Klingmüller), RSHA IV E 4.
87. Fraenkel, Eduard, Dr., geb. 1888, o. Prof., Oxford (Universität), Emigrant, RSHA III A 1.
88. Fraenkel, Ernst, geb. 1896, a. Prof., Emigrant, London, RSHA III A 1.
89. Fraenkel, Gottfried, Dr., geb. 1901, Priv.-Doz. u. Prof. d. Zoologie, Universität London, RSHA III A 1.
90. Fränkel, Hermann, Dr., geb. 1888, a.-o. Prof. a. d. Stanford-Universität, Emigrant RSHA III A 1.
91. Franco, brit. Konsul, zuletzt: Den Haag, vermutl. England, RSHA IV E 4.
92. Frank, Alfred, 3.6.97 Brüssel, ehemaliger Beamter d. British Passport-Control-Office, vermutl. England, RSHA IV E 4.
93. Frank, Alois, 3.6.97 Schekuroch, ehem. tschech. Major, London (Täterkreis: Frantisek Moravec), RSHA IV E 4.
94. Frank, Karl, Dr., 31.5.98 Wien, Schriftsteller, Deckname: Willi Müller, vermutl. England, RSHA IV A 1.
95. Frank, Kurt, Angestellter, zuletzt: Den Haag, vermutl. England (Täterkreis: Stevens/Best), RSHA IV E 4.

96. **Frank, Steven,** 20.9.05 London, Sekretär i. brit. Paßbüro, zuletzt: Kopenhagen, vermutl. England, RSHA IV E 4, Stapo Kiel.
97. **Frank,** chem. techech. Major, London, 53 Lexham Gardens, Kensington W. 8, RSHA IV E 4.
98. **Franke, Ludwig,** richtig: **Kleine, Fritz,** 7.3.01 Apolda, RSHA IV E 4, Stapoleit Prag.
99. **Franke, Otto,** 15.9.77 Berlin-Neukölln, London, RSHA IV A 1.
100. **Frankel, Dan,** Abgeordneter der Labour Party, Jude, RSHA VI G 1.
101. **Frankenstein, George (Georg),** Schriftsteller, RSHA IV B 4.
102. **Frankenstein, Georg,** Baron, 18.3.78 Wien, London, RSHA VI G 1, II B 5.
103. **Franssen,** geb. **Gentsch, Elisabeth,** 1.9.91 Ruhla/Thür., zuletzt: Amsterdam, vermutl. England, RSHA IV E 4.
104. **Franssen, Gerhard,** 31.8.96 Rysen/Holland, zuletzt: Amsterdam, vermutl. England, RSHA IV E 4.
105. **Franssen, Leo,** zuletzt: Amsterdam, vermutl. England, RSHA IV E 4, Stapo Osnabrück.
106. **Franssen, Ruth,** 6.3.20 Dortmund, zuletzt: Amsterdam, vermutl. England, RSHA IV E 4, Stapo Lüneburg.
107. **Franssen, Theodor,** 22.6.92 Münster/W., Ing., Deckname: **de Jong, de Friessen, Brouwer,** zuletzt: Amsterdam, vermutl. England, RSHA IV E 4.
108. **Fraser, Harald Dareton,** Deckname: **Geoffrey,** 8.10.89 Chicago, berichterstatter d. Chicago Tribune, vermutl. England, RSHA IV E 4.
109. **Fraser, William,** stellvertretender Präsident, London, E. C. 2, Britannic House Anglo-Iranian Oil Co., RSHA IV E 2.
110. **Freeman-Horn,** Leiter der brit. Aluminium-Comp., London, RSHA IV E 4.
111. **de Fremery, August,** Deckname: **John,** 7.5.95 's Gravenhage, zuletzt: 's Gravenhage, vermutl. England (Täterkreis: Steven/Best), RSHA IV E 4.
112. **French, Marquis de Casteichomond,** O'Brien, brit. Agent, Kapitän, vermutl. England, RSHA IV E 4, Stapoleit München.
113. **French,** brit. Nachrichtenoffizier, vermutl. England (Täterkreis: Steven/Best), RSHA IV E 4.
114. **Freud, Sigmund, Dr.,** Jude, 6.5.56 Freiburg (Mähren), London, RSHA II B 5.
115. **Freudenberg, Alexander,** 11.1.98 Colombo auf Ceylon, Kaufmann, vermutl. England, RSHA IV E 4.
116. **Freudenberg, Dr.,** chem. Legationssekr., Emigrant, zuletzt: Berlin, jetzt: London, W. C. 1, 26, Bedford Way, RSHA VI G 1, II B 3, II B 5, VI H 3.
117. **Freudenberg, Frau,** London, W. C. 1, 26 Bedford Way, Jüdin, RSHA III A, VI H 3.
118. **Freudenthal, Walter,** geb. 1898, Priv.-Doz., Emigrant, London, RSHA III A 1.
119. **Freund, Ernst, Dr.,** Prof., zuletzt: Wien, jetzt: London, RSHA VI G 1.
120. **Freund-Kahn, Otto,** Schriftsteller/Emigrant, London N. W. 6. 1 Fawley Road, RSHA II B 5.
121. **Freund, Richard,** Schriftsteller, RSHA III A 5.
122. **Freundlich, Herbert, Dr.,** geb. 1880, o. Prof., Emigrant, London (Universität), RSHA III A 1.

123. **Freyhan, Robert, Dr.,** geb. 1901, Prof., Emigrant, London (Universität), RSHA III A 1.
124. **Fricer, Alexander,** 3.5.94 Pilsen, chem. techech. Major, RSHA IV E 4, Stapoleit Prag.
125. **Fricke, Otto,** London, E. C. G., Broadstreet Place, RSHA IV E 4.
126. **Friedberg, Carl,** geb. 1901, Assistent, Emigrant, vermutl. London, RSHA III A 1.
127. **Friedjger, Karl,** 21.5.06 München, vermutl. England, RSHA IV A 3.
128. **Friedl, Karl,** 3.4.84 Auschowitz, England, RSHA IV A 1 b,
129. **Friedländer, Erich, Dr.,** geb. 1897, Assistent, Emigrant, zuletzt Berlin, vermutl. England, RSHA III A 1.
130. **Friedländer, Ernst,** d5.8.08 Posen, Ing., London. (Am-Apparat), RSHA IV A 2.
131. **Friedmann, Ernst Joseph, Dr.,** geb. 1877, a. Prof., Emigrant, Cambridge (Universität), RSHA III A 1.
132. **Friedmann, Hans,** 26.6.94 Berlin, Kaufmann, London, RSHA IV A 1.
133. **Friedmann, Dr.,** früherer techech. Minister, Jude, zuletzt Prag, jetzt in London, RSHA VI G 1, II B 5.
134. **Friedrich, Gerhard,** 4.2.16 Graudenz, Dienstpflichtiger, London, RSHA V D 2 f.
135. **Friedrich, Josef,** 25.8.95 Orpur/Sudetengau, Tischler, Liverpool, RSHA IV A 1.
136. **Fries, Reeltje,** Vertr. d. brit. Fa. Royal Mail Steamship Comp., vermutl. England, RSHA IV E 4.
137. **Fries, Herbert Friedrich,** 30.6.09 Markneukirchen, Bekenntnis-(luter, St. Leonards-On Sea, Sussex/England, RSHA IV A 5 b.
138. **Fries, geb. Volz, Hildegard Wilhelmine Else Margarete,** 3.7.07 Wüstegiersdorf/Schl., St. Leonards-On Sea Suxex/England, RSHA IV A 5 b.
139. **de Friessen, Theodor,** richtig **Theodor Franssen,** 22.6.92 Münster/Westf., Ing., zuletzt Amsterdam, vermutl. England, RSHA IV E 4.
140. **Friags, Josef,** Deckname: **Taxi-Friags,** 24.9.95 Vaals/Holland, Taxi-unternehmer, zuletzt Vaals/Holland, vermutl. England (Täterkreis: Stevens/Best), RSHA IV E 4.
141. **Frinten, Adrianus Johannes Josephus,** richtig **Vrinten,** 13.11.93 Loon op Zand, brit. N.-Agent, zuletzt Rotterdam, vermutl. England (Täterkreis: Stevens/Best), RSHA IV E 4.
142. **Frischauer, Willi,** Schriftsteller, österr. Emigrant, vermutl. London, RSHA VI G 1, II B 5.
143. **Fritsch (Frye), Franz,** 23.12.95 Prag, chem. techech. Stabskapitän, London 53, Lexham Gardens, Kensington W. 8, RSHA IV E 4.
144. **von Fritz, Kurt, Dr.,** geb. 1900, Priv.-Doz., Emigrant, Portland, Reed College, RSHA III A 1.
145. **Fröhlich, Hans,** 30.3.90 Johannisburg/Transvaal, vermutl. England, RSHA IV E 4.
146. **Fröhlich, Herbert, Dr.,** geb. 1905, Priv.-Doz., Emigrant, Bristol (Universität), RSHA III A 1.
147. **Fröhlich, Paul,** 7.8.64 Neusellerhausen, Redakteur, vermutl. England, RSHA IV A 1.
148. **Frommer, Leopold, Dr.,** geb. 1804, Assistent, Emigrant, London, RSHA III A 1.
149. **Fry, A. Ruth,** Schatzmeisterin d. Intern. Rates der Internationale der Kriegsdienstgegner, London, RSHA VI G 1.

150. **Fry, Maxey Sarah,** geb. 1874, Direktorin d. Rundfunkgesellschaft, RSHA VI G 1.
151. **Frye, Franz,** 23.12.95 Prag, chem. techech. Stabskap., London (Täterkreis: Frantisek Moravec), RSHA IV E 4.
152. **Fuchs, Hans J., Dr.,** geb. 1897, Assistent, Emigrant, London, RSHA III A 1.
153. **Fuchs, Martin, Dr.,** 26.9.03 Wien, franz. dipl. Beamter, vermutl. England (österr. Legitimisten), RSHA IV E 4.
154. **Fulman, Frank,** brit. Vizekonsul, RSHA IV E 4.
155. **Fullfeon, Francis,** 16.1.95 Crewe-Chesh, engl. Vizekonsul, vermutl. England (Täterkreis: C. E. King), RSHA IV E 4.
156. **Furmanek, Joseph,** 20.8.85 Botsche, Krs. Meseritz, Angestellter, pola. Offizier, RSHA IV E 5, Stapo Schneidemühl.

1. **Gaihede, Jams,** Kaufmann (Fischexportgeschäft), vermutl. England, RSHA IV E 4.
2. **Gainer, St. Clair D.,** 18.10.91 Tarapoto, chem. Brit. Gen.-Konsul in Wien, vermutl. England, RSHA IV E 4.
3. **de Gay,** verh. **Roster,** London, RSHA IV E 4.
4. **Gallacher, William,** Dez. 1881 Paisley, Metallarbeiter, England, RSHA IV A 1, VI C 1.
5. **Gallienne, Wilfred Hansford,** brit. Gesandter in Estland, zuletzt: Reval, vermutl. England, RSHA VI C 2.
6. **Gamma-Stocker, Gustav,** 22.10.04 Zürich, Hotel-Sekretär, zuletzt: Zürich, vermutl. England, RSHA IV E 4, Stapoleit Karlsruhe.
7. **Gapocznik, S. TH, Dr.,** Emigrant, Cambridge, RSHA III A 1.
8. **Garbett, Reginald,** Schriftsteller, RSHA IV B 4.
9. **Garratt, Geoffrey, Theodor,** Journalist (Zig. „Manchester Guardian"), RSHA VI G 1.
10. **Garston, Lancelot Cyril Brewster, Dr.,** 6.9.09 Bramley, England (Kraftw. GB. EYH. 670), RSHA IV E 4, Stapo Kiel.
11. **Gartner, Josef,** 17.7.88 Tuchau, Süd-England, RSHA IV A 1.
12. **Garvin, James Louis,** 12.4.68, Dir. der Zig. „Observer", London, RSHA IV B 4.
13. **de Gaulle,** ehemaliger französischer General, London RSHA VI G 1.
14. **Gawlina, Josef,** Bischof, Mitgl. d. poln. National-Rat, RSHA IV D 2.
15. **Gawronski, Sigismund Dr.,** Deckname: **Dr. Rawita-Gawronski,** 9.12.86 Genf, Handelsrat, Poln. Botsch. Berlin, RSHA IV E 5.
16. **de Gay** verh. gew. **Roster,** Angestellte d. Fa. General Trading u. Shipping Co., London, RSHA IV E 4.
17. **de Geer, D. J.,** 14.12.70 Groningen, chem. holl. Ministerpräsident, zuletzt: Den Haag, vermutl. England, RSHA III B.
18. **Geijsendorfer,** Flieger, England, RSHA III B.
19. **Gellert, Ernst,** 7.1.00 Hannover, vermutl. England, RSHA IV A 1.
20. **Gellert, Grete,** Ashot-Berks/London, RSHA III D.
21. **Gellert, Mitzi,** Mitarbeiterin d. Petschoks, Ashot-Berks, bei London, RSHA III D.
22. **Gellert, Oswald, Dr.** Askot Berks b. London (Täterkreis: Julius Petschek), RSHA III D 4.
23. **Gengel, Andreas, Dr.,** 1895, Privatdozent, Emigrant, Oxford (Universität), RSHA III A 1.
24. **Genkaleyel, Anton,** 4.4.94 Wittskowitz, Büroangestellter, RSHA IV E 5, Stapo Troppau.
25. **Gens, Adolf,** 11.10.06 Eibenberg, Wilmslow, Provinz Cheshire, High-Bank-Fulschaw Park, RSHA IV A 1.
26. **Gentsch, Elisabeth,** verh. **Franssen,** 1.9.91 Ruhla/Thür., zuletzt: Amsterdam, vermutl. England, RSHA IV E 4.
27. **Gérard, Roger,** Deckname: **Leather, Henri Jean,** ND.-Agent, England, RSHA IV E 4.
28. **Gerarde, Eugenie,** geb. **Menter,** verw. **Lösch, Ehefrau,** früher Sittart/Holl., vermutl. England (Täterkreis: Stevens/Best), RSHA IV E 4.
29. **Gerarde, Josef Heinrich Arnold,** 19.8.89 Haarlem, holl. Oberleuta. d. R., zuletzt: Sittart/Holl., vermutl. England (Täterkreis: Stevens/Best), RSHA IV E 4.
30. **Gerasimov, Georg,** 15.7.00 Odessa, vermutl. England, RSHA IV E 4.
31. **Gerbrandy, Pieter, Sjoerds,** 10.4.85 Goengamieden, chem. holl. Justizminister, England, RSHA III B.

72

32. **von Gerlach, Baron, Rudolf**, 12.7.56 Baden-Baden, Privatmann, Deckname: „Dick", vermutl. England (Täterkreis: Best/Stevens), RSHA IV E 4.
33. **Germens**, brit. Major, England, RSHA IV E 4.
34. **Gessner, Rudolf**, Emigrant, London, RSHA VI G 1.
35. **Geurts, Jakob**, brit. Agent, zuletzt: Basel, vermutl. England, RSHA IV E 4.
36. **Gewittzsch, Serge**, 9.11.92 Nikiforowka, ehem. russ. Rittmeister, vermutl. England, RSHA IV E 4.
37. **Geyer, Kurt**, Dr. phil., 19.11.91 Leipzig, vermutl. England, RSHA IV A 1.
38. **Geyer, Richard**, 29.10.96 St. Joachimsthal, England, RSHA IV A 1.
39. **Gibb, C.**, brit. Agent d. Secr. Service, zuletzt: Shanghai, vermutl. England, RSHA IV E 4.
40. **Gibbs, Philipp**, Schriftsteller, RSHA IV B 4.
41. **Gibbons, Harold C. L.**, 13.5.97 London, brit. Hauptmann, Major, zuletzt: Prag, vermutl. England. RSHA IV E 4.
42. **Gibson, Harald**, brit. Agent, vermutl. England (Täterkreis: Borris Sobinoff), RSHA IV E 4.
43. **Gibson, England**, Major, zuletzt: Libau, RSHA VI C 2.
44. **Gibson, Korrespondent der Ztg. „Times"**, zuletzt: Bukarest, vermutl. England, RSHA IV E 4.
45. **Giddings**, brit. Cpt., vermutl. England, RSHA IV E 4.
46. **Gieseck, Willi (Wilhelm)**, 14.7.01 Berlin, Maurer, RSHA IV A 2.
47. **Giffey, England**, Major, Sekr. an engl. Gesandtsch. in Reval, Chef des Passport-Office, ND.-Agent, Freimaurer, zuletzt: Reval/Estl., vermutl. England RSHA IV E 4, VI C 2.
48. **Gilbert**, simon, London EC 2, 47 Moorlane, RSHA II B 2.
49. **Giles, G. C. T.**, Sekretär, RSHA VI G 1.
50. **Gilewicz, Waclaw**, 10.1.09 Maciegiew, Poln. Konsulatssekretär, RSHA IV E 5.
51. **Gilles, William**, Mitgl. d. Unters.-Komm. London SW 1, Transport House, Smith Square RSHA II B 4.
52. **Gillies**, Sekretär d. Labour-Party, London, Smith Square Transport House, Trade Union, RSHA IV E 5.
53. **Ginsberg, Morris**, Prof., London WC 2, Houghton Street, RSHA II B 2.
54. **Gistrowind, Waclaw**, 26.9.94 Czempin, Elektromonteur, poln.-N. Agent, RSHA IV E 5, Stapo Schneidemühl.
55. **Girling, Charles John**, brit. Vizekonsul, vermutl. England, RSHA IV E 4.
56. **Gittner, Franz**, 4.11.97 Staab/Bez. Mies, Maurer, London, RSHA IV A 1.
57. **Gladstone, Dorothy**, Viscountess, Präsidentin, RSHA VI G 1.
58. **Glass, Kurt**, Dr., richtig: Walter Caro, 19.6.09 Berlin, Dr. phil. Chemiker, vermutl. England. RSHA IV A 2.
59. **Glaser, Ludwig**, 4.3.93 Elm, Kreis Karlsbad, Bergmann, Neat-Inverness-Schottland, RSHA IV A 1 b, Stapo Karlsbad.
60. **Glawill, Vincent**, vermutl. England. RSHA IV E 4.
61. **Glöckner, Anton**, 18.2.00 Trinksaifen, Edinburgh, RSHA IV A 1.
62. **Glöckauf, Eugen**, Dr., 1906, Emigrant, London (Univers.), RSHA III A 1.
63. **Glücksmann, Alfred**, Dr., 1904, Assistent, Emigrant, Cambridge, RSHA III A 1.
64. **Glückstein, L. H.**, konservativer Abgeordneter, RSHA VI G 1.
65. **Glückstein, Morris**, Stadtrat, RSHA VI G 1.

72 G

66. **Godber, Frederick**, Verw.-Direktor, London E. C. 3, 29 St. Helens Court. Great St. Helen's (Shell Transport u. Trading Co.), RSHA IV E 2.
67. **Goder, Fritz**, 2.7.08 Grünberg, Schlosser, RSHA IV A 2.
68. **Godfrey**, verh. Stevens, Moya, 16.2.95 London, Schriftstellerin, London (Täterkreis: Stevens/Best), RSHA SV E 4.
69. **Götz, Martin**, Dr. phil., 13.9.06 Nürnberg, Emigrant, London, RSHA IV A 1, III A 1.
70. **Götze, Albrecht**, Dr., 1697, o. Prof., Emigrant, New Haven, Yale Universität, RSHA III A 1.
71. **Gold, Barbara**, RSHA VI G 1.
72. **Goldsmith, Cecil C.**, ehem. Lehrer, London, RSHA IV E 4.
73. **Goldsmith**, engl. Major, Direktor, vermutl. England (Täterkreis: Hans Schönfeld), RSHA IV E 4.
74. **Gollancz, Ruth**, Leiterin des Linksbuch-Clubs, London, 14 Henriette Street, RSHA VI G 1.
75. **Gollancz, Viktor**, 0893, Verleger, London, 14 Henrietta Street, RSHA VI G 1, IV B 4.
76. **von Goissenau Arnold, Vieth**, Deckname: Ludwig Renn, 22.4.89 Dresden, Polizeioberleutnant a. D., RSHA IV A 2.
77. **Golton, Mary**, vermutl. Agentin d. brit.N.-D., Liverpool, RSHA IV E 4.
78. **Gomolla, Karl**, 7.14.16 Burghof, Flieger, RSHA IV E 5.
79. **Gooch, George Peabody**, geboren 1876, Historiker, London W. 8, 76 Campden Hill Road, RSHA VI G 1.
80. **Goodall, Dora**, London, S. W. 4, The Old Corner House, Paradise Road, RSHA IV A 1.
81. **Goodmann, Paul**, London N. W. 11, Hatikvah The Rich Way, RSHA II B 2.
82. **Goossenaerts, Miel**, zuletzt: Brüssel, vermutl. England, RSHA IV E 4.
83. **Gordon-Canning, Robert**, RSHA IV E 4.
84. **Gostynski, Erich**, Dr., 1904, Emigrant, Manchester, RSHA III A 1.
85. **Gotelee, Emily**, 1.8.14 Medstead/England, Sprachlehrerin, vermutl. England, RSHA IV E 4.
86. **Gottfried, Nelly Katharina**, 7.7.02 Stolberg, zuletzt Holland, vermutl. England, RSHA IV E 4.
87. **Gottfurcht, Fritz**, Emigrant, London, RSHA IV A 1.
88. **Gottfurcht, Hans**, 7.2.96 Berlin, Handlungsgehilfe, RSHA IV A 1 b.
89. **Gottheil, Herta**, Schriftstellerin, Emigrantin, London W. 2, 120 Sussex Gardens, RSHA II B 2.
90. **Gouffier-Choiseul, Louis**, zuletzt: Kowno, vermutl. England (Täterkreis: Th. Camber), RSHA IV E 4, Stapo Tilsit.
91. **Gough, Fritz Herbert Charles Gerald**, 20.12.99 London, brit. Kolonialbeamter, Nevin, Northwales, Gosse Chliff/Engl., Kraftw. CHU 64 099, RSHA IV E 4.
92. **Gouat, Reginald Gye**, brit. Admiral a. D., Mitarbeiter d. Intelligence Service. RSHA IV E 4.
93. **Grabowski, Felix**, 19.11.05 Culmsee, Poln. Deserteur, RSHA IV E 5, Stapo Schneidemühl.
94. **Grabowski, Jan (Johann)**, Deckname: Lomkowski, 26.1.99 Lessen, Kr. Graudenz, Poln. N.-Offz., RSHA IV E 5, Stapo Graudenz.
95. **Gräf, Hugo**, 10.10.92 Rebstädt, Schlosser, Sekretär, London, RSHA II A 1.
96. **Graetzer, Rosa**, 28.5.99 Berlin, Angestellte, London, RSHA IV A 1.
97. **Grafly, J. A.**, ehem. Kriegsgefangener, Essex/Engld., 95 Devon Road Barking. RSHA IV E 4.

74

98. **Graham, A.**, Lord. Beauftragter der Petschek-Gruppe, Woodbridge Suffolk, RSHA III D.
99. **Graham, Ronald**, Priv.-Detektiv, London, RSHA IV E 4.
100. **Grallasky, Justizm.**, Mitgl. d. poln. Nation.-Rates, RSHA IV D 2.
101. **Grant, Leiter der Sabot. Abtlg. des S. I. S. i. London, (Täterkreis: Stevens/Best), RSHA IV E 4.
102. **Grant, Leslie Remvik**, 8.1.93, brit. Cpt., vermutl. England, RSHA IV E 4.
103. **Graves, Allan**, 19.8.91 New Ross/Engl., Attaché d. brit. Botsch., Dublin, 44 Stuphens Green, RSHA IV E 4.
104. **Gray, Margarete**, Gesellschafterin, zuletzt: Paris, vermutl. England, RSHA IV E 4.
105. **Greegor, Übersetzer**, zuletzt: Yokohama/Jap., vermutl. England, RSHA IV E 4.
106. **Green**, etwa 57 Jahre alt, brit. ND.-Agentin, RSHA IV E 4.
107. **Greenberg, Ivan Marion**, London E. C. 2, 47/49 Moor Lane, RSHA II B 2.
108. **Greenhalgh, H. R.**, London, Unilever House, Blackfriars, RSHA IV E 2.
109. **Greenwood, Arthur**, 1880, Minister, London S. W. 1, 28 Old Queen Street, RSHA VI G 1.
110. **Gregory, J. D.**, Schriftsteller, RSHA IV B 4.
111. **Greil, Walter**, 30.6.11 Wien, Ingenieur, RSHA IV A 2.
112. **Grenfeld, A. D. Thomas**, 14.8.69 St. Ives, engl. Major, England, RSHA IV A 1.
'13. **Grenson, William**, brit. ND.-Offizier, vermutl. England, RSHA IV E 4.
114. **Grigg, Edward**, RSHA VI G 1.
115. **Grenenberg, Elsa**, 4.1.00 Königsberg, Stenotypistin, vermutl. England, RSHA IV A 1.
116. **Gross, Fabius**, Dr., 1906, Assistent, Emigrant, Plymouth, RSHA III A 1.
117. **Gross, Fritz**, Schriftsteller, Emigrant, London W. C. 1, 8 Regent Square, RSHA II B 5.
118. **Gross, Emil**, 6.8.04 Bielefeld, vermutl. England, RSHA IV A 1.
119. **Gross-Mayer, Willy**, Dr., 1889, a. o. Prof., Emigrant, London, Maudsley Hospital, RSHA III A 1.
120. **Gross, Wilhelm**, Dr., 1883, o. Prof., Emigrant, zuletzt: Breslau, RSHA III A 1.
121. **Grossmann, Emil**, 24.5.80 Essen-Borbeck, Zeitungshändler, England, RSHA IV A 2.
122. **Grossmann, Henryk**, Dr., a. o. Professor, 1881, Emigrant, London. RSHA III A 1.
123. **Grossmann, Kurt**, 21.5.97 Berlin, Präsident der deutschen Liga für Menschenrechte, vermutl. England, RSHA IV A 1.
124. **Grove-Spiro, Stanley**, Deckname: Lord Drummond, George Saville, 18.1.00 Cap Town/S.-Afrika, ehemaliger engl. Fliegerleutnant, Kaufmann, Bankier, Makler, London-Kensington, W. 8, Cottes more Gardens 18, Büro: London V., Suffolk-Street, Pall-Mall S. W. 1, RSHA IV E 4.
125. **Grünberg, Hans**, Dr., 1907, Assistent, Emigrant, London, RSHA III A 1.
126. **Grüner, H. E.**, 1916: 28 Jahre alt, brit. Agent, vermutl. England RSHA IV A 1.
127. **Grünfeld, Hans**, 25.5.99 Neudorf, Student, RSHA IV A 2.

75 G

128. **Grunov, Heinrich**, 15.8.00 Schweinfurt, richtig: **Friedrich Beer**, Schriftsteller, England, RSHA IV A 3.
129. **Grunwald, Max**, 3.1.03 Friedenau, London 170, Goswell-Road C. 1, RSHA IV A 1.
130. **Gruschwitz, Max**, 9.10.92 Breslau, Redakteur, England, RSHA IV A 3.
131. **Gryning, James**, 27.11.99 Stammvvore/Engl., Privatier, vermutl. England, RSHA IV E 4.
132. **Grzonka, Maria**, Deckname: Kutwitz, Helene, 6.11.97 Heydebreck O. S., RSHA IV E 5, Stapo Oppeln.
133. **Guedalla, Herbert**, RSHA VI G 1.
134. **Günther, August**, vermutl. England, RSHA IV E 4.
135. **Gunther, John**, Schriftsteller, RSHA IV B 4.
136. **Gupta, Dilip Kumar**, 9.7.07 Kalkutta, Sekretär, England, RSHA IV A 1.
137. **Gutkind, Curt Sigmar**, Dr., 1896, a. o. Prof., Emigrant, London, Bedford College, RSHA III A 1.
138. **Gutmann**, vermutl. England (Täterkreis: Stevens/Best), RSHA IV E 4.
139. **Guttmann, Bernhard**, Schriftsteller, Emigrant, Hindhead (Surrey), Winiwhistle England, RSHA II B 5.
140. **Guttmann, Erich**, Dr., 7.2.80 Berlin, Arzt, England, RSHA VO 3 c.
141. **Guttmann, Erich**, Dr., 1896, Priv.-Dozent, Emigrant, London, Maudsley Hospital, RSHA III A 1.

1. de Haas, Clement Arnold, zuletzt: Den Haag, vermutl. England, RSHA IV E 4.
2. de Haas, S.S.11 Uckel, zuletzt: Den Haag, vermutl. England, RSHA IV E 4.
3. Habsburg, Erzherzog von, Robert, 1915 geb., London, RSHA VI G 4.
4. Hackin, brit. Agent, RSHA IV E 4.
5. Haefner, Victor, 18.5.96 Brenden, Bez. Waldshut, Oberitz. a. D., Flugzeugf., London W. 2, 24 Norfolk-Square, RSHA IV E 6, Stapolei Stuttgart.
6. Hahn, Karl, 27.8.09 Hannover, früh. KPD-Funktionär, zuletzt: Amsterdam, vermutl. Engl, RSHA IV E 4.
7. Haide, Paul, 3.10.70 Hohenstein-Ernstthal, kaufm. Angest., RSHA IV A 1 b.
8. Hakin, Wally, j., brit. Agentin, RSHA IV-E 4.
9. Haidane, Charlotte, RSHA VI G 1.
10. Haidane, John E.G., Prof., geb. 6.14.92, RSHA VI G 1.
11. Halder, richtig Strauß, Berthold, Dr., brit. Agent, zuletzt: Den Haag, vermutl. England, RSHA IV E 4.
12. Halevy, Elazar, London E. W. 2, 68 Sarre Road, RSHA II B 2.
13. Halford, F. L., Generalmanager, Wohng.: London E.C.3, St. Helens Court, Shell-Mex and B. P. Ltd., RSHA IV E 2.
14. Halifax, Viscount Edward Frederick, Lindley Wood, 14.4.81, Politiker, London SW d, 66 Eaton Square, u. Garrowby York u. Hickleton Hall, Doncaster, RSHA II D 5.
15. Hall, King, Schriftsteller, RSHA IV B 4.
16. Sir Hall, Reginald, ehem. Leiter d. ND. d. engl. Admiralität (Täterkreis: Rintelen), RSHA IV E 4.
17. Hall, Hatton, brit. Major, brit. ND.-Offizier, RSHA IV E 4.
18. Hall, Lady, RSHA VI G 1.
19. Haller, polit. Org. u. Prop., Mitgl. d. poln. Reg., RSHA IV D 2.
20. Hamacher, Hermann, 29.1.86 Sächteln, RSHA IV A d.
21. Hamburger, Richard, Dr., a. o. Prof., 1894 geb., Priv.-Praxis in London, Emigrant, RSHA III A 1.
22. Hamer, Fritz, 10.10.00 Klenzau, Masch.-Schlosser (Am-Apparat), RSHA IV A 2.
23. Hamilton, Gerald, 4.11.90 Schanghai, RSHA IV A 4.
24. von Hammerstein, Abraham Chaim, 1.10.95 Lods, N-Agent, Deckname: Marguilis, RSHA IV E 5, Stapoleit Danzig.
25. Hammersten, Roeder, zuletzt Holland, vermutl. England, RSHA III B.
26. Hammon, John, 31.12.01 London, Angestellter, RSHA IV A 1 b.
27. Hampel, Franz, 16.2.07 Karbitz, Redakteur, RSHA IV E 4.
28. Hampel, Marie, 27.4.95 Tschau, Wohng.: Margate/Kent, RSHA IV A 1.
29. Hänsel, Jude, Mitinh. d. Fa. Hänsel u. Schmitt, London SW. 1, 13 Viktoria-Street, RSHA IV E 4.
30. Hanfstaengl, Ernst, Dr., 11.2.87 München, Wohng.: London, 36. Gunterstone Road W. 14, West Kensington, RSHA IV C 5.
31. Hanisch, Franz, 9.7.59 Klösterle, Wohng.: New Field-Hall, Bels-Dust bei Kipton/York, RSHA IV A b.
31a Halay, Sir, brit. ND.-Agent, England, RSHA IV E 4.
32. Hans, Heinrich, 25.4.15 Zerbau/Schles., ehem. Schütze I. R. 87, zuletzt: Belgien, vermutl. England, RSHA IV E 4, Stapo Aachen.
33. Harand, Irene, Schriftstellerin, Wohng.: London, RSHA VI G 1, II B 5.

34. Harewood, Earl of, Henry George Ch. (Lascelles), 9.9.82, Wohng.: London, 32 Green Street, RSHA VI G 1.
35. Harford, Lionel Wilfred, zuletzt: Riga, vermutl. England, engl. ND.-Lottleod), RSHA VI C 2.
36. Harms, Hermann, 23.6.86 Leopoldshall, ehem. Gewerkschaftsskr., RSHA IV A 4.
37. Harle, Edwin, brit. Vizekonsul (Täterkreis: Renald Panton), RSHA IV E 4.
38. Harman, Kathleen, Wohng.: London, 82 Lauderdale (Täterkreis: Siegfried Wrzszysky), RSHA IV E 4.
39. Harmann, Lucie, Inh. d. Fa. Binder Handin, zuletzt: Belgrad, vermutl. England, RSHA IV E 4.
40. Harms, Otto Gustav Ernst, 17.11.92 Hamburg, brit. Agent, zuletzt: Amsterdam, vermutl. England (Täterkreis: Theodor Franssen), RSHA IV E 4.
41. Harmar, Maria, verh. Raweck, 28.10.90 Meassmünster, zuletzt: Holland, vermutl. England, RSHA IV E 4.
42. Harper, Mac, 21.9.94 Gloucester, brit. Major, RSHA IV E 4, Stapo Kiel.
43. Harris, Sir, Percy, Alfred, geb. 1876, RSHA VI G 1.
44. Harris, Pierce, London N. W. 2, 149 Anson Road, RSHA II B 2.
45. Harrison, G. W., Botschaftssekr. d. brit. Botschaft in Berlin, RSHA IV E 4.
1. Harrison, Hubert, 22.11.95 Walsall, Journalist, RSHA IV B 4 Stapo Graz.
47. Harting, A., Wohng.: London, Unilever House, Blackfriars, RSHA IV E 2.
48. Hartland, L. H., Wohng.: London, Unilever House, Blackfriars, RSHA IV E 2.
49. Hartmann, Bruno, 22.4.96 Hamburg, Redaktionssekr., RSHA IV A 1 b.
50. Hartmann, Hans, 17.2.07 Biederitz, Braner, London, 8. W. 1, Cranet Court Sloane, Avenue Chelsea, RSHA IV E 4, Stapoleit Magdeburg.
51. Hartner, Willy, Dr., 1905 geb., Dozent, Cambridge, Harvard University, Emigrant, RSHA III A 1.
52. Harvey, John, 2.7.10 Windau, zuletzt: Preßburg, vermutl. England, RSHA IV E 4.
53. Harwood, Kaufmann, zuletzt: Reval, vermutl. England, (engl ND.-Zolland), RSHA VI C 2.
54. Hasselberg, Heinrich, 14.8.90 Holdenstedt, Postsabh. (Am-Apparat), RSHA IV A 2.
55. Hasting, Diener des Stevens (Täterkreis: Stevens/Best), RSHA IV E 4.
56. Hatton-Hall, brit. Major, brit. ND.-Offizier, RSHA IV E 4.
57. Hauck, Walter, 5.5.95 Steinau, Vertreter, London W. 2, Park West, Edgwarraoad (Schwarze Front), RSHA IV A 3.
58. Hauswicked, C. (Täterkreis: H. Snowd/Best), RSHA IV E 4.
59. Hauptmann, Eduard (Edward), 7.2.04 Zgier, poln. N.-Offizier, RSHA IV E 5, Stapoleit Danzig.
60. van Hauts, J., brit. Konsul, zuletzt: Amsterdam, vermutl. England, RSHA IV E 4.
61. Hawkins, ehem. Poln. Kapitän, Mitarbeiter im brit. ND., zuletzt: Windhuk/Südwestafrika, vermutl. England, RSHA IV E 4.
62. Hay, August, 21.5.97 Dudweiler/Saar, Bergarbeiter (Am-Apparat), RSHA IV A 2.
63. Hay, Howard, George, brit. Obernt. i. Gen.-Stab, RSHA IV E 4.

64. Hay, Dr., brit. Militärattaché, RSHA IV E 4.
65. Hayday, Arthur, 1869 geb., RSHA VI G 1.
66. Haywood, Colonel, brit. Botschafter, RSHA IV E 4.
67. Head, George, 17.10.10, Bergbauing., RSHA IV E 4.
68. Hearn, A. C., Direktor, Wohng.: London E.C.2, Britannic House, Anglo-Iranian-Oil-Co., RSHA IV E 2.
69. Heerten, Günun, 21.10.03 Schanghai, Commander d. brit. Armee, RSHA IV E 4.
70. Heartfield, John, 1891 geb., Karikaturist, richtig Hersfeld, Helmut, RSHA VI G 1, III A 5.
71. Heatcote-Quenhardman, Tomas Alexander, brit. Kapit., zuletzt: Esbjerg/Dänemark, vermutl. Engl. (Täterkreis: John Hugill), RSHA IV E 4, Stapo Kiel.
72. Heaton-Armstrong, William Duncan Francis, 29.9.95 Veldes/Jugosl., London, Pall Mall (C. o. Lloyds Bank), RSHA IV E 4.
73. Hecht, Hauptmann, Wohng.: London, RSHA IV A 8 a.
74. Heckmann, Gustav, 22.4.98 Voerde-Niederrhein, Studienassessor, RSHA IV A 1.
75. Hedley, Snowden, fnh. einer Autorep.-Werkst., zuletzt: Sofia, vermutl. Engl., RSHA IV E 4.
76. Heger, Josef, 22.7.07 Weipert, Wohnort: Goldesborough, Yorkshire, RSHA IV A 1 b.
77. Heichelheim, Fritz, Dr., 1901 geb., Privatdozent, Wohng.: Cambridge, Emigrant, RSHA III A 1.
78. van der Heide, richtig: van't Einde, (holl. St.-A.), RSHA IV E 4.
79. Heidelberger, Rudolf, 6.5.01 Trinkassfen, Wohng.: Beech Mount, Selattya Oswestry Salop, RSHA IV A 1 b.
80. Heider, Johann, 29.12.05 Neudeck, RSHA IV A 1 b.
81. Heilborn, Hans-L., Dr., 1906 geb., Assistent, Cambridge (Univers.), Emigrant, RSHA III A 1.
82. Hellbsett, George Henry, London SW 1, 20 Suffolk-Street, RSHA II B 2.
83. Hellfort, Dora Magdalene, 9.12.05 Chemnitz, Sekretärin, Wohng.: verm. Short Hills, Sandy Lodge, Road Moor-Park Herts, RSHA II A, Stapo Chemnitz.
84. Heinann, Betty, Dr., 1695 geb., a. o. Prof., London (Universität), Emigrant, RSHA III A 1.
85. Heimann, Fritz, Dr., 3.2.09 Schöneberg, Jurist (Schwarze Front), RSHA IV A 3.
86. Heimann, Paula Gertrud, geb. Glatzke, Dr. med, 8.2.99 Danzig, RSHA IV A 3.
87. Hein, Josef, 9.12.03 Ottowitz, Wohng.: Brook, Guildford-Surrey, RSHA IV A 1 b.
88. Heine, Friedrich (Fritz), 6.12.04 Hannover, RSHA IV A 1.
89. Heinemann, Fritz, Dr., 1889 geb., a. o. Prof., Privatdozent, Emigrant, RSHA III A 1.
90. Heinrich, Günther Eberhard, 30.10.14 Berlin, Dienstpfl., London W. 1, 65 Grafton Way, RSHA IV E 4, V-D 2.
91. Heinrdorf-Loewinson, Helene, geb. Heindorf, 13.2.99 Gora-Calwarja, Journalistin, RSHA IV A 3.
92. Heintze, Joseph, etwa 45 J., Grenzw.-Beamter, RSHA IV E 6, Stapo Liegnitz.
93. Heiser, Herbert, 20.1.16 Eppendorf, Arbeitsmann, RSHA IV E 5, Stapoleit Königsberg.

94. Heitler, Walter, Dr., 1904 geb., Privatdozent, Bristol (Universität), Emigrant, RSHA III A 1.
95. Hellmann, Reinhard, 1909 geb., Assistent, Emigrant, RSHA III A 1.
96. Hellmers, Arno, 11.1.02 Oberhausen-Sterkrade, zuletzt Rotterdam, vermutl. England, RSHA IV E 4, Stapo Kiel.
97. Helmer-Hirschberg, Olaf, Dr., 1910 geb., London (Universität), Emigrant, RSHA III A 1.
98. Helmers, Anton, 17.1.02 Sterkrade, zuletzt: Rotterdam, vermutl. Engl, Deckname: Hellmann, Jan Smits, RSHA IV E 4, Stapoleit Kiel.
99. Henderson, Arthur, 1893 geb., RSHA VI G 1.
100. Henderson, A, Journalist, RSHA IV B 4 b.
101. Henderson, Neville Meyrick, 1882 geb., ehem. brit. Botschafter in Berlin, RSHA IV E 4.
102. Henderson, Henry Augustus, 20.5.90 Lübbeke, brit. Agent, London Sdwest 7, Kalandergardens, RSHA IV E 4.
103. Hendrika, Harry (Henry), 22.4.73 Oss/Holland, zuletzt: Den Haag, vermutl. England (Täterkreis: Aloisius Porta), RSHA IV E 4.
104. Hendriks, Jan, Deckname des de Fremery, RSHA IV E 4.
105. Hennemann, Kart, 17.9.96 Köln, Tischler (Am-Apparat), RSHA IV A 2.
106. Hennig, Elisabeth, 16.9.00 Düsseldorf, RSHA IV A 1.
107. Henri, Ernst, Schriftsteller, RSHA IV B 4 b.
108. Henriques, Cyril, London W. 8, 4 Capden Hill Square, RSHA II B 2.
109. Mitchell-Henry, Maurlel, 28.3.95 Bradford/England, Reklameleiterin (Täterkreis: Julius Gethias Birch), RSHA IV E 4.
110. Henson, Franz, 28.9.96 Vaalnyk, Kaufm., brit. Agent, zuletzt: Utrecht/Holland, vermutl. England (Täterkreis: Wilhelm Willems), RSHA IV E 4, Stapoleit Düsseldorf.
111. Hepper, Montson Geffry Alarig, 22.10.06 Basingstole/London, brit. Arzneipt., London 10, Warrington Crescent, RSHA IV E 4, Stapo Lüneburg.
112. Herb, Max, Schriftsteller, Emigrant, London N. W. 8, 3—4 Thurlow Road, RSHA II B 5.
113. Herbert, Alfred, Sir, zuletzt: Coventry, RSHA IV E 4.
114. Herbert, Geoffrey, brit. Commander, RSHA IV E 4.
115. Herbschild, Moritz, Mitarbeiter d. Merton, London, RSHA III D.
116. Herlag, Franz Paul Felix, Dr. phil., 22.4.02 Webgeldorf, RSHA IV A 1.
117. Hermann, Johannes, 20.7.96 Venlo, zuletzt: Amsterdam, vermutl. England, Deckname: "Beak" (Stevens/Best), RSHA IV E 4.
118. Herrmann, Max, 25.5.96 Neisse, Schriftsteller, London, Bryanston Court Flat, 82 Upper George Street, RSHA IV A 1, RSHA II A.
119. Hertog, Edgar, Mitarbeiter d. Merton, London, RSHA III D.
120. Hert, Friedrich, Prof., Nationalökonom, London N. W. 14, 27 Corringham Road, RSHA VI G 1.
121. Hertz, Joseph Hermann, 25.9.72, Hauptrabbiner, Wohng.: a) London d. St. Jame Place, b) London N. W. 8, 103 Hamilton Terr, c) London E.C.3, 4 Crecohurch Pl. Aldgate, RSHA IV E 4.
122. Hertz, Moritz, Dr., 1881 geb., Privatdozent, 1891 geb., Cambridge (Universität), Emigrant, RSHA III A 1.
123. Hersfeld, Helmut, 1891 geb., Karikaturist, richtig: Heartfield, John, RSHA VI G 1.
124. Herzfeld, John, richtig: Heartfield, John, RSHA VI G 1.
125. Herzheimer, Rudolf, Mitarbeiter d. Merton, London, RSHA III D.

126. Hornstein, Anna, verh. Neubeck, 20.6.00 Witten/Ruhr (Am-Apparat), RSHA IV A 2.
127. Heepers, Theo (Theodor), 12.12.08 München-Gladbach, kath. Jugendführer (Täterkreis: Stevens/Best), RSHA IV E 4.
128. Tillman-Hessell, Hubert, 2.2.97 Birmingham, brit. Journalist, RSHA IV E 4.
129. Heselton, van, H., Sekretär, zuletzt: Leiden/Holland, vermutl. England, RSHA IV E 4.
130. Heussen, J. H., zuletzt: Heerlebaan/Holland, vermutl. England (Täterkreis: Céline Joosten), RSHA IV E 4, Stapo Aachen.
131. Hevliger, W., Sekretär, zuletzt: Middelburg/Holland, vermutl.: England (Täterkreis: Brijnen), RSHA IV E 4.
132. Hermann, Friedrich, 22.4.00 Brünn, Journalist, Deckname: Franz Walter (Am-Apparat), RSHA IV A 2.
133. Heymann, Gertrud Elisabeth Sarah, 16.9.22 Hamburg, RSHA IV E 4, Stapoleit Hamburg.
134. Heymann, Leo, 24.11.10 (Altenstadt), Vertreter, Kaufm., zuletzt: Brüssel, vermutl. England, RSHA IV E 4.
135. Heywards, J., 2.2.99 Gommorey/England, brit. Cpt., London (Täterkreis: Pacey), RSHA IV E 4, Stapoleit Berlin.
136. Heyworth, Geoffrey, Wohng.: London, Unilever House Blackfriars, RSHA IV E 2.
137. Hicks, George, 1879 geb., Wohng.: London S. W. 4, RSHA VI G 1.
138. Hicks, George, 2.1.96 London, Abgeordneter (Täterkreis: H. Snowliet), RSHA IV E 4.
139. Hicke, Emil, 18.4.94 Böhmisch-Wiesenthal, RSHA IV A 1 b.
140. Hildebrand, Geistlicher, vermutl. London, (illegaler NG. der Bekenntnisfront), RSHA II B 3, VI B 3.
141. Hiller, Kurt, 17.8.85 Berlin, Schriftsteller, Wohng.: London S. W. 2, 196 Fordwich Road London N. W. 6, 7. St. Lawrence Mansions, Priory Park Road (Täterkreis: Schwarze Front), RSHA IV A 6, II B 5.
142. Hillmann, Hermann Christian M. A., 1910 geb., Assistent, Dundee, Emigrant, RSHA III A 1.
143. Himmelwelt, F., Dr., 1908 geb., Assistent, London, Emigrant, RSHA III A 1.
143a Hinchley-Cook, Colonel u. Leiter von M. I. 5 (Military-Intelligence), London RSHA IV E 4.
144. Hinderks, Hermann, 19.12.07 Hamburg, Student (Am-Apparat), RSHA IV A 2.
145. Hintze, Karl, 18.8.84 Putzbus/M., zuletzt: USA, vermutl. England, RSHA IV E 4.
146. Hinze, Gerhard, Wohng.: London, Emigrant, RSHA VI G 1, II B 5.
147. Hirsch, Adolf, 21.3.87 Mandel, RSHA IV E 4, Stapo Koblenz.
148. Hirsch, Emil, 24.12.76 Berlin, London N. W. 4, Elliot-Road Hendon, Deckname: Schwarz, Erich, London N. W. 11, Golders Green Bc, Poste Restante, RSHA IV A 1.
149. Hirsch, Kurt A., Dr., 1906 geb., Cambridge (Universität), Emigrant, RSHA III A 1.
150. Hirsch, Max, 4.2.08 Gleiwitz, Arbeiter, Wohng.: Margate-Kent, Montross 100/2 — Northdown Road Park, Cliftonville, RSHA IV A 1, Stapo Karlsbad.
151. Hirschfeld, Hans, 26.11.94 Hamburg, RSHA IV A 1.
152. Hirschlaff, Ernst, Dr., 1908 geb., Cambridge (Universität), Emigrant, RSHA III A 1.

153. Hitzemann, Johannes, 29.11.05 Glückstadt, Wehrpfl., Okt. 39 in d. Südafr. Union festgen., RSHA V—D 2 f.
154. Hobbys, G. E. J., brit. Visekonsul, RSHA IV E 4.
155. Hobson, John Atkinson, 1868 geb., RSHA VI G 1.
156. Graf Hochberg, Mitgl. d. poln. Reg., RSHA IV D 2.
157. Hodgkins, Tommy, brit. Pol.-Beamter, Sunderland/Engl., Alexander Road 5, Holm Gardens (Täterkreis: Norita), RSHA IV E 4, Stapo Königsberg.
158. Höfer, Johann, 6.9.15 Frauenberg, Bez. Bruck a. d. Mur, Kraftfahrer, Wohng.: London, RSHA IV A 2, Stapo Graz.
159. Höft, Otto, 31.3.07 Plagow, RSHA IV A 1.
160. Höttermann, Karl, 20.2.94 Pirmasens, Schriftsteller, Emigrant, London, RSHA IV A 1, IV E 4, VI G 1, II B 5, IV A 5.
161. Hölzel, Camillo, 6.12.08 Sobnitz, London (Attentäter), RSHA IV A 2.
162. Hoffmann, Simon, 8.8.76 Wien, Generaldir., RSHA IV E 4.
163. Hofmann, Lothar, 16.2.08 Leipzig, Techniker, Deckname: Richter, Haus (Am-Apparat), RSHA IV A 2.
164. Hofmann, Max, 1.3.91 Mülhausen, RSHA IV A 1.
165. Hofmann, Walter, 25.7.07 Pirmasens, Modelleur, Verkäufer, RSHA IV A 1.
166. Fürstin von Hohenberg, Maria, Wohng.: London, Emigrantin, RSHA VI G 1, II B 5.
167. Holler, Emigrant, London, RSHA II B 5.
168. Holman, A., chem. 1. Sekr. d. Botschaft in Berlin, RSHA IV E 4.
169. Holzinger, Arthur, 13.11.98 Gängerhof, RSHA IV A 1.
170. Honigmann, Hans, Dr., 1891 geb., Direktor, London (Zoolog. Gesellschaft), Emigrant, RSHA III A 1.
171. Honnebecke, Jan Harms, 1.5.90 Hoogezand, Arbeiter, RSHA IV E 4.
172. Hoogezand, Angestellter, zuletzt: Den Haag, vermutl. England (Täterkreis: I. A. Rietveld), RSHA IV E 4.
173. Hooper, William John, 23.4.05 Rotterdam, brit. Agent, zuletzt: Scheveningen/Holland, vermutl. England (Täterkreis: Stevens/Best), Deckname: Konrad, RSHA IV E 4.
174. Hope, W. P., 26.3.05 London, Ing., zuletzt: Overschie b. Rotterdam, vermutl. England (Täterkreis: James Haynes), RSHA IV E 4.
175. Hopf, Fritz, 23.7.02 Neudorf, RSHA IV A 1 b.
176. Hopmans, M. J., Sekr., zuletzt: Zwolle/Holland, vermutl. England IV A 1.
177. Hore-Belisha, Leslie, Wohng.: London S. W. 14, The Close, Sheen Common, London S. W. 1, Reform Club, London S. W. d., 104 Pall Mall, RSHA JI B 2, VI G 1.
178. Horn, Wenzl, 17.9.94 Simmer, RSHA IV A 1 b.
179. Freemann-Horn, London d. brit. Alumin.-Comp., London, RSHA IV E 4.
180. Horner, Arthur, Präsident d. Bergarb.-Gewerksch., RSHA VI G 1.
181. Horsing, Eric, Chemiker, London N. W. L., Dorset Square 66, RSHA IV E 4.
182. Horowitz, Phineas, London N. W. 2, 9 Großvenor Garden, RSHA II B 2.
183. Horrabin, James Francis, 1884 geb., Abgeordnete d. lib. Partei, RSHA VI G 1.
184. Horsemann, Dorothy, Direktorin vom „Linksbuch-Club", RSHA VI G 1.

185. Horstmann, Hermann, 12.9.93 Osnabrück, Rechtsanw. (Am-Apparat), RSHA IV A 2.
185. a. Houser, brit. ND.-Agent, früh. Kopenhagen, vermutl. England, RSHA IV E 4.
186. Houtermans, Fritz, Dr., 12.2.03 Danzig, Assistent, RSHA IV A 1.
187. Howard, Elisabeth, 6.3.78 London, Leiterin d. engl. Quäker, RSHA IV A 1.
188. Howard, Stanley, brit. Cpt., Wohng.: Aston Clinton, Park-Hotel, RSHA IV E 4, Stapoleit Hamburg.
189. Howard, brit. Cpt., London S. W. 1, Sloane Street 144, Deckname: Hughes, auch S. C. Tavlor, RSHA IV E 4.
190. Howe, Robert, Diplomat, zuletzt: Riga, vermutl. England (engl. ND-Lettland), RSHA VI C 2.
191. Hubmann, Josef, 13.11.10 Pernegg, Schlosser (Am-Apparat), Deckname: Josef Lustig, RSHA IV A 2.
192. Hudson, brit. ND-Offizier (Täterkreis: Jens Dons), RSHA IV E 4, Stapo Kiel.
193. Hüfler, Johann, 20.1.11 Pechbach, London, RSHA IV A 1 b.
194. Hüsgen, Ernst Hugo, 3.3.14 Wiescheid, zuletzt: Rotterdam, vermutl. England (Täterkreis: Julius Rogosch), RSHA IV E 4.
195. Huetling, L., Sekr., zuletzt: Holland, vermutl. England (Täterkreis: Brijnen), RSHA IV E 4.
196. Hütgens, Louis, 9.11.85 Venlo/Holland, Gärtner (Täterkreis: Stevens/Best), RSHA IV E 4.
197. Hütter, Helmut, d.5.99 Krems, Nachr.-Agent (Österr. Legitimist), RSHA IV A 3.
198. Hugh, Isabell, 29.4.04 Dublin, London, Clampham Park, 72 Rodenhurst Road, RSHA IV E 4.
199. Hughes, James Mogurk, richtig: Howard, brit. Cpt., London S. W. 1, Sloane Street 144, RSHA IV E 4.
200. Hughes, W. R., Wohng.: Herts Welwyn Garden City (Täterkreis: von der Ropp), RSHA IV E 4.
201. Hugill, John Michael, 6.11.15 (17) Banderstead, Student, Wohng.: Treford-Purley (Kraftw.: „HPB" 231 GB), RSHA IV E 4, Stapo Kiel.
202. Hummel, Georges, Mitgründ. d. Investment Comp. Luxemburg, einer Petschekschen Holding-Ges., London (Täterkreis: Ignatz Petschek), RSHA III D 4.
203. Hummel, Sidney, Mitgründ. d. Investment Comp. S. A. Luxemburg, einer Petschekschen Holding-Ges., London (Täterkreis: Ignatz Petschek), RSHA III D 4.
204. Humphrey, brit. Major, Abt.-Leiter im brit. N.-D., London (Täterkreis: M. King), RSHA IV E 4.
205. Hurwitz, Max, Leeds 7, 56 Harehills Avenue, RSHA II B 2.
206. Husband, Patrick, Bücherrevisor, Angest. d. brit. N.-D., Middleton-Sea (Sussex), Yapton Road, RSHA IV E 4.
207. Huston, brit. Major, zuletzt: Bukarest, vermutl. England (Täterkreis: Elbing), RSHA IV E 4.
208. Hut, S., Sekr., zuletzt: Veendam/Holland, vermutl. England (Täterkreis: Brijnen), RSHA IV E 4.
209. Huxley, Aldous, 26.7.94, Schriftsteller, RSHA VI G 1.
210. Huxley, Julian Sorell, 22.6.87 Prof., London N. W. 8, Regents Park (Zoological Society), RSHA VI G 1.
211. Graf v. Haya, Hans, Schriftsteller, London, Emigr., RSHA VI G 1, II B 5.

212. Hyamson, Albert, London N.W. 2, 32 Teignmouth Road, RSHA II B 2.
213. Hymans, Maurice, brit. Agent, Deckname: de Leeuw u. Dr. Haas, RSHA IV E 4.

1. Ide, W. H., Agent, zuletzt: Amsterdam, Toldwaarstr. 6, vermutl. England, brit. ND-Agent, (Täterkreis: Prinz), RSHA IV E 4.
2. Iedema, J., Sekretär, zuletzt: Holland, Laan 1, brit. ND.-Agent, vermutl. England, (Täterkreis: Breijnen, RSHA IV E 4.
3. Ignatieff, A., Angeh. d. brit. ND, London, Shell Max House, Strand, RSHA IV E 4.
4. Ilbin, Ladislaus Deczka. Fritz Theo Otto, 15.5.03 Mannheim, Redakteur, RSHA IV A 2.
5. Ingr, Sergej, Div.-General, Minister für nat. Verteidigung der tschech. Regierung in London, RSHA IV D 1 a.
6. Ingrams, Leonhard, London, (Täterkreis: Julius Petschek), RSHA III D 4.
7. Ingron, Sergej, tschech. Minister f. nationale Verteidigung, RSHA II B 5.
8. Inkpin, Albert, Zeitungsverleger, RSHA VI G 1.
9. Intsch, Max, Deckn.: Macintosch, Café-Boektzer, zuletzt: Rotterdam, vermutl. England, RSHA IV E 4.
10. Iraver, Keith, Major, zuletzt: Reval (Estland), RSHA VI C 2.
11. Irmler, Eduard, 9.9.80 Dottmannsdorf, Direktor der niederl. Handelsgesellschaft, zuletzt: Amsterdam, vermutl. England, RSHA IV E 4, Stapoleit Berlin.
12. Irmer, Erich, 26.8.08 Berlin, Vertreter, London, RSHA IV A 1, Stapoleit Berlin.
13. Isaac, Gerald Rufus, richtig: Reading, Lord, RSHA VI G 1.
14. Isaacs, George Alfred, 1883, Sekr. d. Nationalunion d. Drucker, RSHA VI G 1.
15. Isaacs, Morris, RSHA VI G 1.
16. Isherwood, Henry, 28.10.98 Wimborne, Beamter d. brit. Luftfahrtmin., London W. C. 1, Russel Square, Hotel Royal, RSHA IV E 4, Stapoleit Berlin.
17. Israel, Wilhelm James, Dr., 1886, Privatdozent, Emigrant, London (seit 1933 Privatpraxis), RSHA III A 1.
18. Israelski, Martin, Dr., 1901, Emigrant, seit 1936 in Glasgow, RSHA III A 1.

1. Jablonski, Robert, 29.4.09 Paris, vermutl. England, RSHA IV A 1.
2. Jabotinsky, Vladimir, London N. W. 8, 47 Finchley Road, RSHA II B 2.
3. Jacks (Jaksch), Eisel, 16.7.91 London, Schiffssabotage, RSHA IV A 2.
4. Jacobi, gesch. Honig, Johanna, 17.8.96 Thorn, Photographin, London, RSHA IV A 1, IV A 2.
5. Jacobs, von, G. H., richtig: Jacobes, 17.9.96 Hettin/Rum., Direktor, RSHA IV E 4.
6. Jacobs, Norman Myer, Manchester 7, 86 Upper Park Road, RSHA II B 2.
7. Jacobson, Werner, Dr., 1906, Assistent, Emigrant, Cambridge, RSHA III A 1.
8. Jacobsthal, Paul, Dr., 1880, o. Prof., Emigrant, Oxford (Univ.), RSHA III A 1.
9. Jacobus, M. H., London N. W. 8, 22. Abercon Place (Täterkreis: Long-...t/Jakobus), RSHA IV E 4, Stapoleit München.
10. Jacoby, Fritz, Dr., 1902, Ass., Emigrant, Birmingham (Universität Physiologisches Institut), RSHA III A 1.
11. Jacomb, William, 29.8.08 (96), Brighton, brit. Offizier, London, Pall Mall 116, RSHA IV E 4.
12. Jäckh, Ernst, 22.2.75 Urach, Direktor, Emigrant, RSHA II B 5, III A 1, VI G 1.
13. Jäger, Hans Ferdinand Heinrich, Deckname: Kohout, 10.2.99 Berlin-Friedenau, Redakteur, London N. 7, 21 Anson Road bei Jen. Greening. Schwarze Front, RSHA IV A 3, IV E 6.
14. Jaffe, Gerda Josephine, 21.6.10 Berlin-Charlottenburg, RSHA IV A 1.
15. Jagger, John, Jude, Labour-Abgeordneter, RSHA VI G 1.
16. Jakabos, G. I. (G. H.), 17.9.96 Hettin/Rumänien, Direktor, London, RSHA IV E 4.
17. Jakubeizik, Jerzy, 19.12.10 Strzemieszyl, Student, RSHA IV E 5, Stapo Danzig.
18. Jaksch, Wenzel, 25.9.96 Langstrohnitz, Maurer, London N. W. 3, 35, Park Gardens im Hause Miß Warzinger bei Belsize, RSHA IV A 1, IV A 1 b.
19. Janczak, Johann (Jan), 8.5.11 Hamborn, Arbeiter, RSHA IV E 5, Stapoleit Breslau.
20. Janßer, Barnett, London W. 2, 3 Lancaster Terr., RSHA II B 2.
21. Jansen, Cornelius, 4.8.83 Made in Drimmelen, Leutn. d. Nachr.-Abteil. in Roermond, zuletzt: Roermond, vermutl. England (Täterkreis: Stobbe), RSHA IV E 4.
22. Jansen, zuletzt: Rotterdam, vermutl. England (Täterkreis: J. A. Rietveld), RSHA IV E 4.
23. Jansens, H. J. H., Kunstmaler, zuletzt: Amsterdam, Lijnbaangracht 302, vermutl. England (Täterkreis: J. W. Lousing), RSHA IV E 4.
24. Jaworski, Anton, 15.5.04, RSHA IV E 5.
25. Jaworski, Jan, Dr., Mitgl. d. poln. Nationalrats, RSHA IV D 2.
26. Jelic, Branimir, Dr., 28.2.05 Dolac/Jagoslawien, Arzt, vermutl. im evtl. Internierungslager oder Gefängnis, RSHA IV D 3.
27. Jellinek, Frank, 9.1.08 London, Schriftsteller, vermutl. England, RSHA IV E 4.
28. Jenkins, Muriel, London S. E. 26, 20 Dukesthorpe Road, Sydenham, RSHA IV A 1.

7*

29. Jequier, Richard Adrian, Prokurist der Swiss Bank Corp., London E. C. 2, Gresham Street 99 (Täterkreis: Ignatz Petschek), RSHA III D 4.
30. Jerry, Gregoire, zuletzt: Bayonne, vermutl. England, RSHA IV E 4.
31. Jewelewski, Julius, 6.5.74 Willimpol, Emigrant, London, RSHA II B 5.
32. Jirric, Gerhard, etwa 23 Jahre alt, Student, zuletzt: Troebeek, Troebeekstraat 25, vermutl. England (Täterkreis: Erwin Stroschein), RSHA IV E 4.
33. Joachim, Willy, 17.10.98 Walfischbay/Südwest-Afrika, Steuermann, vermutl. England, RSHA IV A 2.
34. Joad, Cyril Edwin, 12.8.91, Prof. u. Schriftsteller, London N. W. 3, 4 East Heath Road, RSHA VI G 1.
35. John, Fritz, Dr., 1910, Assistent, Emigrant, Lexington, RSHA III A 1.
36. Johnson, Fran W., etwa 42 Jahre, 1934, brit. ND.-Agent, ehem. brit. Offizier, vermutl. England, RSHA IV E 4.
37. Johnson, Leiter des brit. ND. in Jugosl., vermutl. England, RSHA IV E 4.
38. Johnston, Ellen, vermutl. England, RSHA IV E 4.
39. De Jong, Theodor, richtig Theodor Fransen, 22.6.92 Münster/W., Ing., zuletzt: Amsterdam, vermutl. England, RSHA IV E 4.
40. Johnsson, Harcourt, 1895, Leiter d. Publikationsabteilung, RSHA VI G 1.
41. Price-Jones, Alan, London (Täterkreis: Ignatz Petschek), RSHA III D 4.
42. Jones, Edith, 16.2.10 London, Sekr. i. d. brit. Paßabteilung Kopenhagen, vermutl. England (Täterkreis: Steven/Frank), RSHA IV E 4.
43. Jones, Evelyn, RSHA VI G 1.
44. Jones, Frederick Elwyn, Schriftsteller, RSHA III A 5.
45. Jones-Bates, Reginald, vermutl. England, RSHA IV E 4.
46. Jones, Oscar Philipp, 15.10.98 Beckenham/England, Master-Pilot (Aircraft), London, RSHA IV E 4, Stapo Köln.
47. Joseph, Walter, Mitarbeiter d. Merton, London, RSHA III D.
48. Jowett, William Frederick, Abg. der. Labour-Party, RSHA VI G 1.
49. Joye, Harold Cornelis, Direktor, vermutl. England, RSHA IV E 4.
50. Jancsek, Stanislaw, Mitgl. d. poln. Nat.-Rates, RSHA IV D 2.
51. Jubanski, Boris, richtig Braginski, zuletzt: Antwerpen, vermutl. England (Täterkreis: Fritz W. Eger), RSHA IV E 4.
52. Julienborger, Franz, Dr., 1906, London, Emigrant, RSHA III A 1.
53. Jurneck, Felix Franz, 5.10.12 Türschtiegel, RSHA IV E 5, Stapo Schneidemühl.

1. Kabel, E. G., brit. Generalkonsul, England (Täterkreis: E. G. Cable), RSHA IV E 4.
2. Kabollk, Dr., Vorsitzender d. britisch-tschech.-slow. Zentrums in London, London W. 9, 6 Clifton Gardens (Täterkreis: Benesch VI G 1, Telef.: Abercon 6828), RSHA IV D 1 a.
3. Kaczmarczyk, Josef, 2.5.1900 Siemianowitz, poln. Agent, RSHA IV E 5, Stapoleit Breslau.
4. Kadega, Kurt, brit. Offizier, England, RSHA IV—II O 2.
5. Kadi, Abdel, brit. Agent, zuletzt: Kabul, vermutl. England, RSHA IV A 2.
6. Kahn, Ludwig W., Dr., 1910, Assistent, London, RSHA III A 1.
7. Kahn-Freund, Otto, Schriftsteller, Emigrant, London N. W. 6, 1 Fawley Road, RSHA II B 5.
8. Kaiser, Ch., Jude, zuletzt: Kowno, vermutl. England, brit. ND.-Litauen, RSHA VI C 2.
9. Kaiser, Walter, 22.11.09 Barmen, Stukkateur (Am-Apparat), RSHA IV A 2.
10. Kaiser, Arnold Meer, Journalist, London N. 3, 37 North Crescent, RSHA II B 2.
11. Kala, Oberst, London, RSHA VI G 1.
12. Kallin, Anna, 55 Jahre, ehem. Tänzerin, zuletzt: Bukarest, vermutl. England, RSHA IV A 1.
13. Kamaltner, Bernhard, Dr., 25.10.90 Dirschau, London, RSHA IV A 1.
14. Kant, Lina, 15.6.98 Pforzheim, Übersetzerin der ITF, London, RSHA IV A 1 b.
15. Kantorowicz, Hermann, 1877, Prof., England, RSHA III A 1.
16. Kantorowitsch, Miron, Dr., 1895, London, RSHA III A 1.
17. Kantorowicz, Otto, Dr., 1905, London, RSHA III A 1.
18. Karin, richtig: Karl-Becker, vermutl. England, RSHA IV A 1.
19. Karpinski, Marian Vladimir, 6.8.91 Lemberg, poln. Nachrichtenoffizier, RSHA IV E 5, Stapoleit Danzig.
20. Karplus, Kurt, 1907, Assistent, vermutl. England, Emigrant, RSHA III A 1.
21. Kaspar, Jaroslav, 12.08 Alt Paka, ehem. tschech. Stabsopt., vermutl. England, RSHA IV E 4, Stapoleit Prag.
22. Kasper, Wilhelm, 8.8.92 Neustadt b. Freiburg, Kaufmann (Am Apparat), RSHA IV A 2.
23. van Kasteel, Piet A., Dr., Journalist, zuletzt: Den Haag, vermutl. England, RSHA II B 2.
24. Kastner, Rudolf, Schriftsteller, Emigrant, London N. W. 6, South Lodge Grove End Road, RSHA II B 5.
25. Katas, Alada, Journalist, Budapest, vermutl. England (Täterkreis: Lukapello), RSHA IV E 4, Stapo Köln.
26. Katz, David, 1884, Prof., London, Emigrant, RSHA III A 1.
27. Katzenellenbogen, Max, 1.2.06 Leipzig, Deckname: Bloch, Chemiker (Am-Apparat), RSHA IV A 2.
28. Kaufmann, Boris, Dr., 1904, London, Emigrant, RSHA III A 1.
29. Kaufmann, Fritz, Dr., 1891, Emigrant, Privatdozent, Oxford, RSHA III A 1.
30. Kaufmann, Robert, Dr., Jude, London, RSHA VI G 1.
31. Kaufmann, 19.12.97 Großbeisheim, richtig: Hans Barben, Oberstadtsekretär, vermutl. England (Am-Apparat), RSHA IV A 2.
32. Kay, G. R., Schriftsteller, RSHA IV E 4.

88. Kaye, G., Führer d. Union d. demokr. Kontrollen, vermutl. England, RSHA VI G 1.
84. Keenan, brit. Major, London, RSHA IV E 4.
85. Keenan, Officier, England, brit. ND.-Esthand, RSHA VI C 2.
86. Kellwerth, Ernst, 29.7.09 Graslitz, vermutl. England, RSHA IV A 1 b.
87. Keizer, L. A., Sekretär, zuletzt: Holland, vermutl. England, RSHA IV E 4.
88. Kellner, Lotte, Dr., 1904, vermutl. London, Emigrant, RSHA III A 1.
89. Kemmerling, Jacob, 23.6.95 Kerkrade, vermutl. England, RSHA IV E 4.
40. Kempt, Johann, 12.5.98 St.Joachimsthal, Winagombe, Cleusield, Road EXT., Leichester, RSHA IV A 1 b.
41. Kendrick, Thomas, 26.11.85 Cape Town (Capstadt), brit. Cpt., England, RSHA IV E 4.
42. Kennard, brit. Major, zuletzt: Windhuk/Südwestafrika, vermutl. England, RSHA IV E 4.
42a. Kenney, Rowland, brit. N.-Agent, zuletzt: Kopenhagen, vermutl. England, RSHA IV E 4.
43. Kenny, Francis, 6.2.00 Kongston/England, Beamter, Hull, 72 Langstoft Grave Cottingham Road, RSHA IV A 1.
44. Kenny, brit. Cpt., England, RSHA IV E 4.
45. van Kerkhoff, Christian, 31.1.85 Leiden, Zigarrenfabrikant, zuletzt: Holland, vermutl. England (Täterkreis: Albert Steigers), RSHA IV E 4.
46. Kern, Alfred, richtig Helmut Kern, 3.6.05 Magdeburg, Redakteur, vermutl. England (Täterkreis: Kern-Kreis), RSHA IV A 1.
47. Kern, Helmut, 3.6.05 Magdeburg, Redakteur, vermutl. England (Täterkreis: Kern-Kreis), Deckname: Alfred Kern und D. Bakker, RSHA IV A 1.
48. Kernroy, brit. Pol.-Beamter, Deckname: Bromsley, RSHA IV E 4.
49. Kerr, Alfred, Berichterstatter d. Pariser Tageszeitung, vermutl. England, RSHA IV E 4.
50. Korras, Ferdinand Louis, 18.8.83 Framere/England, Parlamentsmitgl., London W.C.1, First Avenue House, 45 High-Holborn, RSHA IV E 4, Stapoleit Wien.
51. Kessler, J. B. A., Direktor, London E.C.3, 22 St. Helens Court, Shell Transport u. Trading Co., RSHA IV E 4.
52. Keyser, Edward G., Angestellter, zuletzt: Brüssel, vermutl. England (Täterkreis: Waldemar Pötsch), RSHA IV E 4.
53. Kibble, Mill, K., Manchester (Täterkreis: Walter Becker), 12 Newton Street, RSHA IV E 4.
54. Kick, Egon Erwin (Jude), Emigrant, London, RSHA II B 5.
55. Kidd, Ronald, vermutl. England, RSHA VI G 1.
56. Kiewitz, Helene, 6.11.97 Heydebreck/OS., Deckname: Maria Graoeka, RSHA IV E 5, Stapo Oppeln.
57. Kika, Bretislav, 25.11.08 Zablate, ebem. tschech. Militärattaché, vermutl. England, RSHA IV E 4, Stapo Kiel.
58. Kiliey, Kenneth, 24.4.89 London, brit. Cpt., zuletzt: Kopenhagen, vermutl. England, RSHA IV E 4, Stapo Kiel.
58a. Kiley, Kenneth, 24.4.89, brit. N.-Agent, zuletzt: Kopenhagen, vermutl. England, RSHA IV E 4.
59. King, M., brit. Cpt., London, White-Hall, RSHA IV E 4.
60. King-Hall, Stephen, 21.3.93, Herausgeber der „K.-H.-Briefe", London, Headfield House, Hadley Hants, RSHA VI G 1.

61. Kingborg, R., Kaufmann, zuletzt: Reval, vermutl. England, brit. ND.-Estland, RSHA VI C 2.
62. Kinlay, K. G., London, RSHA VI G 1.
63. Kinsey, George William Ernest, 8.9.01 London, Elektriker, London, 51 Revelstokera, RSHA IV E 4, Stapo Köln.
64. Kirchner, Wilhelm, 6.1.20 Düsseldorf, Arbeitsdienstmann, RSHA IV E 5, Stapoleit Breslau.
65. Kirkpatrik, Leonard, 6.11.90 Woodbidge, Commender d. Royal Nay Admiralty, London (Täterkreis: George Campbal), RSHA IV E 4, Stapo Kiel.
66. Kirsch, Hans, Ingenieur, London, RSHA IV E 4.
67. Kirschmann, Emil, 13.11.88 Oberstein/Nahe, vermutl. England, RSHA IV A 1 b.
68. Kirschneck, Christof, 29.11.12 Haslau, Handlungsgehilfe, vermutl. England, RSHA IV A 1, Stapo Karlsbad.
69. Kiss, Paul Alfred, 1.3.94 Greiz-Dölau, London N. 14, 62 The Woodland, RSHA IV A 1, Stapoleit Dresden.
70. Klaas, Rudolf Jesse, 19.2.15 Beddington/England, Dienstpflichtiger, Beddington Croydon, The First Hilliers Lane, RSHA V D 2 f.
71. Klausmann, Robert, 15.5.96 Essen, ebem. komm. Landtagsabgeordneter (Am-Apparat), RSHA IV A 2.
72. Klee-Rawidowicz, Esther E., Dr., geb. 1900, Assistent, London, RSHA II A 1.
73. van Kleffens, Mr. E. N., ebem. holländ. Außenmin., zuletzt: Den Haag, vermutl. England, RSHA III D.
74. Klein, Heinz (Jude), Emigrant, zuletzt: Brüssel, vermutl. England (Täterkreis: Karl Machacek), RSHA IV E 4.
75. Klein, Steffan, vermutl. England (Täterkreis: Albert Albeelt), RSHA IV E 4, Stapoleit Wien.
76. Kleine, Fritz, 7.3.01 Apolda, Maschinenmeister (Am-Apparat), RSHA IV A 2.
77. Kleine, Fritz, 7.3.01 Apolda, Werkmeister, Decknamen: Fritz Arnol, Rudolf Ludwig ,Franke, Wagner, vermutl. England, RSHA IV E 4, Stapoleit Prag.
78. von Kleist, richtig: Franz Rintelen, 19.8.78 Frankfurt/O., deutscher Korvettenkapitän, England, RSHA IV E 4.
79. Klepper, Otto, 17.8.88 Brotierode, Deckname: Charles Reber, Rechtsanwalt, vermutl. England (Deutsche Freiheitspartei), RSHA IV A 1.
80. Klibansky, Raymond, Dr., 1905, Privatdozent, Oxford, Emigrant, RSHA III A 1.
81. Klienberger, Emma, Dr., 1692, Priv.-Dozent, London, RSHA III A 1.
82. Klimpl, Resle, 3.4.09 Fischern, vermutl. London, RSHA IV A 1 b.
83. Klinger, Eugen, 30.5.06 Rosenberg, Redakteur, London, 14. Kingsroad Rugboy Mansiona Flat 18, RSHA IV E 4, Stapoleit Prag.
84. Klvana, Franz, 80.1.00 Drahotus, ebem. tschech. Stabshpt., vermutl. England, RSHA IV E 4, Stapoleit Prag.
85. Kniefke, Hans, Deckname: Haas, brit. Agent, zuletzt Antwerpen, vermutl. England (Täterkreis: Waldemar Pötsch), RSHA IV E 4.
86. Kniefke, Kurt, Deckname: Haas, brit. Agent, zuletzt: Holland, vermutl. England, RSHA IV E 4, Stapo Wilhelmshaven.
87. Knight, Jaspar, führend i. Unilever-Konzern, Wohng.: Oxoa, Bolney Court, RSHA III D.
88. Knoblauch, Louis, Leith, Baltic Street 18, RSHA IV E 5, Stapo Trier.

89. von Kaiseringer, Waldemar, 8.10.06 Rochlesburg, vermutl. England, RSHA IV A 1.
90. Kanp, Werner, 29.12.14 Cuxhaven, Journalist, London E. 1, Pine Cottage Poyebell Hall 23, Commercialstr., RSHA IV E 4.
91. Knowlin, James Metcalfe, 8.9.11, Halifax, Architekt, London S.W.7, 150 Cromwell Road, RSHA IV E 4, Stapoleit München.
92. Knowlin, M., 25.11.91 Askorn, brit. Cpt., London, (Täterkreis: Werner Pohl), RSHA IV E 4.
93. Kor, Adam, 61.8.91 Suwalken, polnischer Minister, vermutl. England, Decknamen: Witold, Krajewski, Warninski, Adam, RSHA III B u. IV D 2.
94. Kochanski, Theodor, 29.5.00 Makowansk, poln. Sergeant, vermutl. England, RSHA IV E 5, Stapoleit Danzig.
95. Koebel, Eberhard, 22.6.07 Stuttgart, Schriftsteller, Deckname: Tusk, London S.W. 20, 284 Coombe Lane (bündische Jugend), RSHA IV B 1 b.
96. Köhler, Franz, 12.9.17 Silberbach, England, RSHA IV A 1 b.
97. Koehler, Hans Jürgen, 21.2.05 Frankfurt/M., richtig Pfeiffer, Heinrich, Schriftsteller, vermutl. England, RSHA IV B 4.
98. Koch, Joh. M., Sekretär, zuletzt: Amsterdam, vermutl. England (Täterkreis: Brijnen), RSHA IV E 4.
99. Blanche-Koolemans, G. A. E., zuletzt: Amsterdam, vermutl. England (Täterkreis: Prins), RSHA IV E 4.
100. Koenen-Wessel, Heinrich, 7.4.86 Hamburg, Redakteur, vermutl. England, RSHA IV A 1, Stapo Halle.
101. König, Ernst, 20.6.97 Halle (Am-Apparat), RSHA IV A 2.
102. Körbel, Josef, Dr. jur., 20.9.09 Geisenberg, Leg. Attaché, vermutl. England, RSHA IV E 4, Stapoleit Prag.
103. Körner, Tibor, 26.4.89 Santiago/Chile, Journalist, zuletzt: Den Haag, vermutl. England, RSHA IV E 4.
104. Köves, Anton, 8.6.16 Altroiau, England, RSHA IV A 1 b.
105. Mac Kagan, richtig Makabis, vermutl. England, RSHA IV D 3 a.
106. Mac Kohen, richtig Makabis, vermutl. England, RSHA IV D 3.
107. Kohl, Marie, verh. Wagner, 1.6.05 Haslau, Strickerin, vermutl. England, RSHA IV A 1.
108. Kohn, Hans, Dr., 1891, Prof., Northamton, RSHA III A 1.
109. Kohnert, Hans, 10.2.99 Berlin-Friedenau, richtig Jäger, Hans, Redakteur, London N. 7, 51 Ascoa Road (Schwarze Front), RSHA IV A 1.
110. de Kok, J. E. F., Direktor, zuletzt: 's-Gravenhage, vermutl. England, RSHA IV E 2.
111. Kohsschka, Oskar, 8.10.06 Pöschlarn, Emigrant, Vorstandsmitgl. d. freien dtsch. Kulturliga i. England, London, RSHA IV A 1, II B 5.
112. Kolbe, F., Bankier, London W. 1, Vollbeckstreet 17 (Schwarze Front), RSHA IV A 6.
113. Kollibau, Mats, 45 Jahre alt, Dobrownik, Konsulatssekretär, zuletzt: Zagreb, vermutl. England, RSHA IV E 4, Stapo Graz.
114. Kolodziejczyk, Julian, 46 Jahre alt, poln. Kpt., Deckname: Kolodziejczak, vermutl. England, RSHA IV E 5, Stapo Oppeln.
115. Kolodziejczyk, Julian, 54 Jahre alt, poln. Kpt., Deckname: Krzysowski, Kolodziejczyk, vermutl. England, RSHA IV E 5, Stapo Oppeln.
116. Konrad, Josef, 18.9.91 Schönwald, Oxford, RSHA IV A 1 b.
117. Koening, H. G., Sekretär, zuletzt: Amsterdam, vermutl. England (Täterkreis: Brijnen), RSHA IV E 4.

118. Kopeta, Josef, 19.2.92 Mies, Furlay Hall, Ankomovo Staffordsh, RSHA IV A 1.
119. Korda, Alexander, 16.9.98 Turkeve, Ungarn, Direktor d. Korda Film-Productions Ltd., London N. W. 81, Avenue Road, St. John's Wood, RSHA III D 5.
120. Koren, Ludwig, 4.2.96 St. Martin-OStr., vermutl. England, RSHA IV E 5, Stapoleit Wien.
121. Kornaszewski, Wladislaw, 2.7.09 Strelno, Krs. Mogilno, Kaufmann, vermutl. England, RSHA IV E 5, Stapo Grandenz.
122. Kossack, Imogen, 12.4.13 Glasgow, richtig: Veit, Spmehlehnenia, London, RSHA IV E 4.
123. Kossak, Ling, richtig: Hermann Pavelleg, vermutl. England, RSHA IV E 4, Stapoleit Prag.
124. Koster, van Gross Er, M. H., Sekretär, zuletzt: Holland, vermutl. England (Täterkreis: Beijnen), RSHA IV E 4.
125. Koster, Paul, 27.1.98 Heiler/Holland, Decknamen: K. Bakker, Paul Kaiter, Peter Ballin, Nachrichtenagent, zuletzt: Fenfa, vermutl. England, RSHA IV E 4.
126. Kot, Stanislav, 22.10.85 Ruda, O.Schles., Prof., poln. Emigrant, vermutl. England, RSHA III B 15.
127. Kotze, Josef, 12.8.91 Schlon Ostrau, Sekretär, vermutl. England, RSHA IV E 4.
128. Kotting, Gerardus Cornelius, 26.7.80 Rotterdam, Deckname: Klings, brit. Agent, zuletzt: Rotterdam, vermutl. England, RSHA IV E 4.
129. Rooey-Rongal, Jan, 4914 Paigton England, brit. Officier, Old Rectory Codlorf, Wilts, England (Täterkreis: David Peter), RSHA IV E 4, Stapo Innsbruck.
130. Kowalski, Josef, 14.5.04 Laar-Dinsburg, Pächter, vermutl. England, RSHA IV E 5, Stapo Oppeln.
131. Kowoll, Johann Jan 27.12.90 Siemianowitz, Redakteur, London, RSHA IV A 1 b.
132. Kraemer, Wilhelm, 11.2.90 Duisburg, Decknamen: Kraemel, Kraenel, Kroni, Lageriet, zuletzt: Holland, vermutl. England (Täterkreis: Wilhelm Willemse), RSHA IV E 4, Stapoleit Düsseldorf.
133. Krafft, Jerzy, Grenzwachtkommissar, vermutl. England, RSHA IV E 5, Stapo Schneidemühl.
134. Krajewski, richtig: Kor, Minister, vermutl. England, RSHA III B 15.
135. Kraus, Otto, 1.1.83 Platten, Krs. Neudeck, Leichester, 67 Sparkenhoe Street, RSHA IV A 1.
136. Kraus, Wolfgang, geb. 1905, Assistent, Cambridge, RSHA III A 1.
137. Krause, Arno, Agent, London S.W.5, Black Friars Road, RSHA IV E 4.
138. Kraushaar, geb. Seapanski, Luise, Decknamen: Trude, 13.2.05 Berlin, (Am-Apparat), RSHA IV A 2.
139. Krause, Max, Mitarbeiter des Merton, London, RSHA III D.
140. Krautter, Kurt, 27.11.04 Neukölln, Arbeiter, vermutl. England (Am-Apparat), RSHA IV A 2.
141. Krayer, Otto, Dr., 1900, Privatdozent, vermutl. England, RSHA III A 1.
142. Krebs, Hans Adolf, 1900, Privatdozent, Sheffield, RSHA III A f.
143. Kreglich, brit. Agent, zuletzt: Rotterdam, vermutl. England, RSHA IV E 4.
144. Krulhisk, Karl, 14.9.88 Ootkow, vermutl. England, RSHA IV A 1.

145. Krejei, Ludwig, 17.8.90 Brünn, ehem. tschech. General, vermutl. England, RSHA IV E 4, Stapoleit Prag.
146. Kroll, Johann, 16.6.98 Christophhammer, Eisendreher, Leichester/ England, RSHA IV E 4, Stapo Chemnitz.
147. Krausmann, Willi, 6.10.07 Berlin, vermutl. England, RSHA IV A 1 b.
148. Krenkel, Werner, 18.6.22 Christophhammer, vermutl. Leichester, RSHA IV A 1 b.
149. Krothovski, Franzisek, 5.2.97 Jakalos Kpt., vermutl. England, RSHA IV E 5, Stapo Oppeln.
150. Krausinger, geb. Sabbe, Maria, z1.11.05 Pivola/Jugosl., zuletzt: Belgrad, vermutl. England, RSHA IV E 4.
151. Kruyscig, Gerhard, 25.12.90 Krossen, Gewerkschaftsfunktionär, London, RSHA IV A 1 b.
152. Kalessa, Jan, 5.3.93 Cicie, Kra. Warschau, Landwirt, vermutl. England, RSHA IV E 5.
153. Krier, geb. Becker, Lily, Ehefrau, London, RSHA IV A 1 b.
154. Krier, Peter (Pierre), 18.95 Bonneweg, Luxemb., Minister, London, RSHA IV A 1 b.
155. Kris, Karl, Dr., 28.10.05 Bilin, techn. Beamter, London 8. W. 5, Trebovir Road, RSHA IV E 4, Stapoleit Prag.
156. Kolgate, Jan, 42 Jahre, Grenzwachtbeamter, vermutl. England, RSHA IV E 5, Stapo Frankfurt/O.
157. Kroll, Josef, 16.11.05 Lazare, Kra. Kalisch, Arbeiter, vermutl. England, RSHA IV E 5, Stapoleit Breslau.
158. Krauchassky, Wenzel, 5.6.76 Prag, Redakteur, London, RSHA IV E 4, Stapoleit Prag.
159. Krüger, Emil, 19.11.08 Braunschweig, vermutl. England, RSHA IV A 1.
160. Krayorwski, Julian, Deckname: Kniedziejczak, 54 Jahre alt, poln. Kpt., vermutl. England, RSHA IV E 5, Stapo Oppeln.
161. Krzyzanowski, Winfried, Deckname: Lädecka, 14.5.96 Neustettin, Schriftsteller, vermutl. England, RSHA IV E 5, Etapo Innsbruck.
162. Kalasek, brit. Agent, zuletzt: Ungvar, vermutl. England (Täterkreis: R. Kukla), RSHA IV E 4.
163. Kubis, Prag, 22.3.12 Rüntha, Kra. Hamm, Molkor, vermutl. England, RSHA IV E 5, Stapo Allenstein.
164. Kusedzuki, geb. Grudewitz, Berta, 30.6.79 Kottbus, London, RSHA IV A 1.
165. Kuczynski, Robert, 1876, Direktor, London, Emigrant, RSHA III A 1, IV A 1.
166. Kugler, Josef, 22.1.87 Schönfeld, Bes. Ellbogen, Arbeiter, Inverness/ Nord-Scotland, Culloden House, RSHA IV A 1, Stapoleit Karlsbad.
167. Kühndorf, Karl-August, Emigrant, zuletzt: Riga, vermutl. England, brit. ND. in Lettland, RSHA VI C 2.
168. Kühnl, Franz, 13.11.91 Saaz, Albury/England, RSHA IV A 1 b.
169. Kühnl, Oskar, 18.5.13 Rothau, Margate/Kent, 25 Northdown Road, RSHA IV A 1 b.
170. Kürti, Nicholas, Dr., 1908, Assistent, Oxford/England, Emigrant, RSHA III A 1.
171. Kuhn, Heinrich, Dr., 1904, Privatdozent, Oxford, Emigrant, RSHA III A 1.
172. Kuhnt, Mitgl. d. poln. Regierung, vermutl. England, RSHA IV D 2.
173. Kukla, Rudolf, 29.6.00 Sukowsko/Kra. Ganok, brit. Agent, vermutl. England, RSHA IV E 4.

174. Kampeet, Prokop, 18.7.94 Hnevkovize, ehem. tschech. Oberst, England, RSHA IV E 4, Stapoleit Prag.
175. Kunslik, Anton, 14.4.00 Staab, vermutl. England, RSHA IV A 1 b.
176. Kupfer-Sachs, Rudolf, 22.5.97 Berlin, richtig: Sachs, Graphiker, vermutl. England, RSHA V-C 3 a, Stapoleit Berlin.
177. Kupka, Franz, 2.1.01 Rosenberg/O.-Schles., Kellner, vermutl. England, RSHA IV E 5, Stapo Oppeln.
178. Kaplest, Wenzl, 22.6.97 Eleonorenhain, vermutl. England, RSHA IV A 1 b.
179. Kurz, Jaroslav, 7.4.99 Klattau, ehem. tschech. Major, vermutl. England, RSHA IV E 4, Stapoleit Prag.
180. Kurz, Otto, Dr., 1908, London, Warburg-Institut, RSHA III A 1.
181. Kutschker, Franz, 26.11.16 Groß Endersdorf, Dienstpflichtiger, Manchester, 14 Wimislay Grove 3, RSHA V D 2 f, Ger. d. 22. Div.
182. Kuttner, Erich, 27.5.87 Berlin-Schöneberg, Redakteur, vermutl. England, IV A 1 b.
183. Kysilewskyj, Wladimir, Dr., Schriftsteller, vermutl. England, RSHA IV D 3 a.

1. Laberthe, André, London, Mitglied der illeg. frances. Regierung, RSHA VI G 1.
2. Laborski, Karl, ca. 45 Jahre, Fellhändler, vermutl. England (Täterkreis: Fred Schidloff), RSHA IV E 4.
3. Lagarde, Leo, 25.11.92 Zamin, vermutl. England, RSHA IV A 1 b.
4. Lambert, Charles Albert, 14.10.00 London, Berichterstatter, RSHA IV A 1.
5. Lambert, Charles A., ehemaliger Berliner Korrespondent d. "Manchester Gardian", vermutl. England, RSHA IV B 4.
6. Lamkowski, Jan (Johann), Deckname: Grabowski, 26.1.23 Lessen, poln. N.-Offizier, RSHA IV E 5, Stapo Graudenz.
7. Lamm, Arnold, brit. N.-Agent, zuletzt: Antwerpen, vermutl. England, RSHA IV E 4.
8. Lampertsberger, Josef, 16.9.12 Degerndorf, Kellner, vermutl. England, RSHA IV A 1, Stapoleit München.
9. Landau, Hans, Dr., 1802, a. o. Professor, London, Emigrant, RSHA III A 1.
10. Landau, Josef, Dr. phil., 30.4.77 Litzmannstadt, Bankier, vermutl. England, poln. Emigrantenregierung, RSHA III B.
11. Landau, Max (Jude), Bankbeamter, London (Täterkreis: Ignatz Petschek), RSHA III D 4.
12. Landsberi, F. H., Dr., vermutl. London, RSHA II B 5.
13. Lane, brit. Captain, London, RSHA IV E 4.
14. Lange, Gerhard, 2.7.92 Rhede, Werftzeichner, vermutl. England (Täterkreis: Aloisius Porta), RSHA IV E 4.
15. Lange, Robert, 21.5.92 Magdeburg, Werkmeister, vermutl. England, RSHA IV E 4.
16. Lange, Willy, 20.5.99 Öderan, vermutl. England, RSHA IV A 1 b.
17. Langer, Felix, Dr., Schriftsteller, Emigrant, London N. W. 3, 16. Rosmplay Road, RSHA II B 5.
18. Langhammer, Karl, 26.3.85 Schwaderbach, vermutl. England, RSHA IV A 1 b.
19. Langner, Adolphe Maximilian, Dr. Dr., 14.7.98 Woronlenka, Agent, vermutl. England, RSHA IV E 4.
20. Langrührdt, Erich, Dr., geb. 1910, Prof., Cambridge, Emigrant, RSHA III A 1.
21. Lauzer, V., "Internationaler Friedensfeldzug", RSHA VI G 1.
22. Lansbury, George, 1859, London E. 3, 39 Bow Road, fördert deutsche Emigranten und Einkreisungspolitik, RSHA VI G 1.
23. Lareida, Jean, Deckname: Victor, Voucher, 17.4.03 Zürich, ND.-Agent, RSHA IV E 4, Stapo Bremen.
24. Lasalle, Raffael, 10.5.87 Köln, brit. ND.-Agent, vermutl. England, RSHA IV E 4.
25. Laser, Hans, Dr., 1899, Privatdozent, Cambridge, Molteno-Institut, Emigrant, RSHA III A 1.
26. Laski, Harold J., 30.6.93 Prof., London W. 14, Devon Lodge, Addison Bridge Place, Antifaschistische Liga, RSHA II B 2.
27. Laski, Nathan, Manchester, Antifaschist, RSHA VI G 1.
28. Laski, Neville, Jonas, Rechtsanwalt, London N. W. 3, 10. Wedderburn Rd., jüdische Abgeordneten-Kammer, Völkerbundsanhänger, RSHA VI G 1, II B 2.
29. Laskowski, Ladyga, 15.2.94 Rossenberg, poln. Major, Kaufmann, RSHA IV E 5, Stapo Oppeln.

30. Lasnitski, Arthur, Dr., geb. 1896, Ass., Manchester Universität, Emigrant, RSHA III A 1.
31. Last, Samuel, Dr., 1902, Ass., Northampton, Mental-Hospital, Emigrant, RSHA III A 1.
32. Latham, George, 1875, Abgeordneter, Gewerkschaftler, RSHA VI G 1.
33. Lauger, Heinrich, Dr., 1899, Privatdozent, Emigrant, London, RSHA III A 1.
34. Laun, geb. Zettl, Marie, 1.10.84 Neuhammer, RSHA IV A 1.
35. Laurence, Martin, richtig: Adolf Paul Narr, London, RSHA VI G 1.
36. Laurence, Robert, richtig: Adolf Paul Narr, London, RSHA VI G 1.
37. Lasthew, verh. Webb, geb. Sellheim, Magda Antonowna, Russin, zuletzt: Reval, vermutl. England, brit. ND.-Estland, RSHA VI C 2.
38. Postdick-Lawrence, Frederic William, 1871, Abgeordneter, RSHA VI G 1.
39. Lawrence, George, Reverend, Prediger, vermutl. England, RSHA IV E 4.
40. Lawrenzon, brit. Agent, zuletzt: Petrinja, vermutl. England, RSHA IV E 4, III A, Stapo Graz.
41. Lawson, E. F., Jude, brit. Hauptmann, RSHA VI G 1.
42. Lawther, Will, Rotspanienpropagandist, RSHA VI G 1.
43. Layton, Dorothey, London, Anhänger der Harand-Bewegung, RSHA VI G 1.
44. Layton, Walter Thomas, Sir, 15.3.94, Vorsitzender "News Chronicle", London 8. W. 15, 108 West Hill, Putney, Antifaschist, RSHA VI G 1.
45. Lazarus, Abraham, Kommunistenführer, Jude, RSHA VI G 1.
46. Lazarsfeld-Jahoda, Marie, Dr., 26.1.07 Wien, Schriftstellerin, Jüdin (Täterkreis: SPÖ.-Auslandszweigstelle), London N. W. 1, 40 Regents Park Perrace, RSHA II B 5, IV A 1 b, VI G 1.
46 a. O'Leary, brit. N.-Agent, zuletzt: Kopenhagen, vermutl. England, RSHA IV E 4.
47. Leather, Henryk, vermutl. England (Täterkreis: Fisher), RSHA IV E 4.
48. Leather, Henry Jens, Deckname: Roger Gerard, 45 Jahre, brit. Offizier, vermutl. England, RSHA IV E 4.
49. Leairy, Leiter d. brit. Pass. Office, zuletzt: Kopenhagen, vermutl. England (Täterkreis: G. M. Bjerring), RSHA IV E 4, Stapo Kiel.
50. Lecwicz, Zygmunt, 25.3.96 Warschau, Kunstreiter (ehem. poln. Oberst), RSHA IV E 5, Stapo Schneidemühl.
51. Lederer, Richard, 6.5.05 Asch, RSHA IV A 1.
52. Loeb, Rudolf, 7.5.02 Berlin, vermutl. England, RSHA IV A 1.
53. de Loeuw, Maurice, Deckname: Heymann, brit. ND.-Agent, vermutl. England (Täterkreis: Tinsley), RSHA IV E 4.
54. Lefontaine, Dick (Edward), brit. Konsulatsbeamter, N.-Offizier, zuletzt: Istanbul, vermutl. England, RSHA IV E 4.
55. Leftwich, Joseph, Journalist, London N. 6, 24 Shepherds Hill High Gate, RSHA II B 2.
56. Legh-Jones, George, Direktor, London E. C. 3, 22. St. Helens Court, Shell Transport u. Trading Co., RSHA IV E 4.
57. Lehmann, Hans Leo, Dr., 1907, Ass., London (Universität), Emigrant, RSHA III A 1.
58. Lehmann, Kurt, 20.8.06 Barmen, Seemann, RSHA IV A 1, Stapoleit Hamburg.
59. Lehmann-Rußbüldt, Otto, 1.1.71 Berlin, London, RSHA II B 5.

60. **Lehmann**, Werner, 22.5.04 Bochum, Seemann, vermutl. London, RSHA IV A 1.
61. **Leichentritt**, Bruno, Dr., 1866, a. o. Prof., vermutl. London, Emigrant, RSHA III A 1.
62. **Leichter**, Otto, Dr. jur., Deckname: Kearns Huber, 22.2.97, vermutl. England, RSHA IV A 1.
63. **Leiper**, Henry, Dr., Methodistenpfarrer, vermutl. England, Anhänger der „Friends of Europe", RSHA VI G 1.
64. **Leiser**, Arthur, brit. N.-Agent, vermutl. England (Täterkreis: Fray Strong), RSHA IV E 4.
65. **Leißler**, Rudolf, 20.3.11 Nieder-Ramstedt, Heiser, Internierungslager, RSHA IV A 1, Stapoleit Hamburg.
66. **Lengborne**, brit. Oberstleutnant, vermutl. England, RSHA IV E 4.
67. **Lengyel**, Emil, Schriftsteller, vermutl. England, RSHA IV B 4.
68. **Lennox**, John Robert, 22.10.96 London, Architekt, London, S. E., 14 Courtside, RSHA IV E 4.
69. **Lennox**, V. C. H. Gordon, Korrespondent d. „Daily Telegrafo", London, RSHA IV A 2.
70. **Lenz**, Friedrich, 14.10.02 Saarbrücken, Installateur (Am-Apparat), RSHA IV A 2.
71. **Leonhard**, Leo, 21.1.16 Frankfurt/M., Dienstpflichtiger, London N. W. 6, 260 Finchley Road oder 70 Westend Lane, RSHA Amt V D 2 f.
72. **Leslie**, I. R. P., Kaufmann, zuletzt: Reval, vermutl. England (Brit. ND-Estland), RSHA VI C 2.
73. **Lesser**, J., Dr., Schriftsteller, Emigrant, London N. W. 6, 56 Fairhazel Gardens, RSHA II B 5.
74. **Lessig**, Herbert, Deckname: Bert, Ping-Pong, Tilly, 5.7.02 Dresden, Buchdrucker (Am-Apparat), RSHA IV A 2.
75. **Leubuscher**, Charlotte, Dr., a. o. Prof., 1888, Oxford, Emigrant, RSHA III A 1.
76. **Leubuscher**, Walter, 9.1.09 Marburg, Techniker, vermutl. England, Schwarze Front, RSHA IV A 3.
77. **v. Reichenau-Leuchtmar**, Ernst, 23.5.96 Berlin, Privatlehrer, vermutl. England (Am-Apparat), RSHA IV A 2.
78. **von Leusden**, D. M., Holländer, Sekretär, zuletzt: Holland, vermutl. England (Täterkreis: Brijnen), RSHA IV E 4.
79. **Leusing**, I. W., 22.5.02 Mettmann, brit. Agent, zuletzt: Rotterdam, vermutl. England, RSHA IV E 4.
80. **Leverhulme**, Viscount, London, Unilever-House, Blackfriars, RSHA IV E 2.
81. **Levi**, Adolf, Mitarbeiter d. Merton, London, RSHA III D.
82. **Levinthal**, Walter, Dr., Assistent, 1886 Bath, Emigrant, RSHA III A 1.
83. **Levisohn**, Ida, Dr., Prof., 1901, London, Emigrant, RSHA IV A 1.
84. **Levy**, Hermann, a. o. Prof., 1881 London, Emigrant, RSHA III A 1.
85. **Levy**, Hyman, Prof., Einkreisungsfront - Anhänger, Jude, RSHA VI G 1.
86. **Lewandowski**, Leon, 2.2.99 Lissa, Radiohändler, RSHA IV E 5, Stapo Liegnitz.
87. **Lichfield**, Jack, 10.9.84 London, Kaufmann, vermutl. England, RSHA IV E 4.
88. **Lichtenstaedter**, Ilse, Dr., 1901 geb. Oxford (Universität), Emigrant, RSHA IV A 1.

89. **Lieberamann**, Hermann, 6.1.70 Drohobycz, Rechtsanw., Jude, politischer Sejm-Abgeordneter, RSHA III B, IV D 2.
90. **Liebmann**, Gerhard, Deckname: Meier, Werner, 29.6.06 Charlottenburg, Konstrukteur, Cambridge (Am-Apparat), RSHA IV A 1, IV A 2.
91. **Liebmann**, Hermann, Dr., 1907, Edingburgh (Universität), Emigrant, RSHA III A 1.
92. **Liepmann**, Hederik, Dr., 1904, Dozent, vermutl. London, Emigrant, RSHA III A 1.
93. **Liepmann**, Leo, Dr., 1900 geb., Privatdozent, vermutl. London, Emigrant, RSHA III A 1.
94. **Lincoln**, Ashe, Jude, vermutl. London, Anglo-Ukrainisches Komitee, London 1, Essex Court Temple E. C. 4, RSHA D S a.
95. **Lindsay**, Alexander, Dunlop, 1871, Oxford (Universität), Volksfrontanhänger, RSHA VI G 1.
96. **Lindsay-Scott**, vermutl. England, Angehöriger des Nationalrats d. Arbeiterbewegung, RSHA VI G 1.
97. **Lindstädt**, Erich, 5.11.05 Rixdorf, vermutl. England, RSHA IV A 1 b.
98. **Lionell**, Wiette, vermutl. England (Täterkreis: Fisher), RSHA IV E 4.
99. **Lis**, Josef, Major, N.-Offz., vermutl. England, RSHA IV E 5, Stapo Grandenz.
100. **Lisbeths**, brit. Hauptmann, N.-Offz., vermutl. England, RSHA IV E 4.
101. **Lisicki**, vermutl. London (Free Europe), Emigrant, RSHA VI G 1, II B 5.
102. **Lissmann**, Hans, Werner, Dr., 1909, Cambridge (Universität), Emigrant, RSHA III A 1.
103. **Listerwall**, brit. Journalist, vermutl. England, RSHA IV E 4.
104. **Listowel**, William, London-Kensington 6. W. 7, 96, Onslowgardens, Anhänger gegen Deutschland gerichteter Organisationen, RSHA VI G 1, IV A 6.
105. **Lizycky**, Karl, 26.3.96 Hotteschau, ehem. Sekr. d. tschech. Außenministeriums, vermutl. London, RSHA IV E 4, Stapoleit Prag.
106. **Litgeber**, Boleslaw, vermutl. London (Free Europe), RSHA VI G 1.
107. **Liticky**, Karl, Dr., 23.3.96 Hotteschau, OSR.-Legationsrat, RSHA IV D 1.
108. **Liverman**, Maurice Gordon, geb. 1892, London N. W. 2, 45 Coverdale Rd., RSHA II B 2.
109. **Livingstone**, Adelheid, Leiterin d. brit. Gräberkommission, N.-Agentin, vermutl. England, RSHA IV E 4.
110. **Lloyd**, J. B., Direktor, London E. C. 2, Britannic House, Anglo-Iranian-Oil Co., RSHA IV E 2.
111. **Lloyd**, George Megan, 1902, lib. Abgeordneter, London, (Völkerbundsbewegung), RSHA VI G 1.
112. **Lord Lloyd**, Chef d. British Council, London, RSHA IV E 4.
113. **Lobkowicz**, Max Erwin, 29.12.88 Bilin, Gesandtschaftsrat, London, tschech. Emigrant, RSHA IV E 4, Stapoleit Prag.
114. **Lobkowicz**, Max Ernst, Fürst, CSR.-Attaché, vermutl. London, RSHA IV D 1 a.
115. **Lockhart**, Bruce, 2.9.87, Journalist, London, RSHA IV E 4.
116. **Loeb**, Otto, Dr., 30.5.96 Trier, London N. W. 6, 6 Eton Rise, RSHA IV E 4, Stapo Koblenz.
117. **Loeser**, Alfred, Dr., vermutl. London (Privatpraxis), Emigrant, RSHA III A 1.
118. **Löwe**, Adolfo, 1893, Professor, Emigrant, Manchester, RSHA III A 1.

119. **Löwe**, Eberhard, 24.02.90 Berlin, Major, vermutl. England, RSHA IV E 5, Stapo Tilsit.
120. **Loewe**, Linnell, brit. ND.-Offizier, zuletzt: Den Haag, vermutl. England (Täterkreis: Stevens/Best), RSHA IV E 4.
121. **Löwenbach**, Jan, Dr., Emigrant, Welwyn Garden City (Hertfordshire), 36 Digswellroad, RSHA II B 5.
122. **Loewenson**, Leo, 1894, Assistent, London, Emigrant, RSHA III A 1.
123. **Löwenstein**, Otto, Dr., 1906, Assistent, Birmingham (Universität), Emigrant, RSHA III A 1.
124. **Loewenthal**, Hans, Dr., 1899, Assistent, London, Emigrant, RSHA III A 1.
125. **Löwi**, Siegmund, 5.4.88 Barneidorf, Gewerkschaftssekretär, vermutl. London, RSHA IV A 1 b.
126. **Löwy**, Siegmund, 5.4.88 Warnsdorf, vermutl. England, RSHA IV A 1, Stapol Dresden.
127. **Loggin**, Estelle, vermutl. England (Emigrantenzeitschrift „Die Zukunft"), RSHA VI G 1.
128. **London**, Heinz, Dr., 1907, Bristol (Universität), Emigrant, RSHA III A 1.
129. **Lorenz**, Charlotte Elisabeth, geb. Helde, 6.11.04 Dresden, RSHA IV A 1, Stapoleit Dresden.
130. **Lorenz**, Ludwig, 6.3.17 Altrohlau, vermutl. England, RSHA IV A 1 b.
131. **Lorentz**, Roman, 20.7.10 Troppau, ehem. estn. Offizier, vermutl. England, RSHA IV E 4, III E 4, Stapo Tilsit.
132. **Lorimer**, Emily, Overend, Schriftstellerin, vermutl. England, RSHA IV A 6.
133. **Loscelles**, Henry George Ch., richtig: Harewood, Earl of, Henry George Ch., RSHA VI G 1.
134. **Losch**, Johann, 66.12.00, Anstreicher, RSHA IV A 1, Stapoleit Karlsbad.
135. **Lothar**, Hans, Mitinh. d. Fa. „Secker u. Warburg", Emigrant, London W. C. 2, 22, Essex Street, RSHA II B 5.
136. **London**, Direktor, zuletzt: Wassenaar, vermutl. England, RSHA IV E 5.
137. **Low**, David, 7.4.91, Karikaturist des „Evening Standart", London N. W. 11, 3 Rodborough Road, RSHA IV B 4, VI G 1.
138. **Lubszynski**, Gerhard Hans, 26.8.04 Berlin, Ingenieur, vermutl. London, RSHA IV A 1.
139. **Lucas**, F. L., Prof., Cambridge (Universität), (Emigrantenzeitschrift: „Die Zukunft"), RSHA VI G 1.
140. **Ludwig**, A. H., brit. N.-Agent, zuletzt: Den Haag, vermutl. England, RSHA IV E 4.
141. **Lübeck**, Hans, 12.7.06 Bremen, Handlungsgehilfe, vermutl. England, RSHA IV E 5.
142. **Lüdecke**, Winfried, Deckname: Krzyzanowski, 14.5.96 Neustettin, Schriftsteller, RSHA IV E 5, Stapo Innsbruck.
143. **Lukapello**, Ljubomir, Dr., brit. N.-Agent, vermutl. England, RSHA IV 4.
144. **Lund**, F. W., Direktor, London E. C. 2, Britannic House, Anglo-Iranian-Oil-Co., RSHA IV E 2.
145. **Lund**, R. T., Secretary des Boy-Scout I. B., London S. W. 1, 25 Buckingham Palace Road, Internationales Büro der Boy-Scouts, RSHA IV B 4.

146. **Layton**, May (Frau), Sekretärin, vermutl. England (Täterkreis: Brijnen) RSHA IV E 4.
147. **Lyall**, George, brit. Generalkonsul, vermutl. England, RSHA IV E 4.
148. **Lyon**, George Ernest, 14.4.88 London, Ingenieur, vermutl. London (Täterkreis: Henry Noble-Dudley), RSHA IV E 4, Stapoleit Königsberg.
149. **Lyttelton**, Oliver, Captain, vermutl. London, Personenkreis: Merton, RSHA III D 6.

1. v. Maassen, Maj. C., zuletzt: Breda/Holl, vermutl. England (Täterkreis: Brijnen), RSHA IV E 4, Stapo Osnabrück.
2. Maas, F., zuletzt Burgan-Schoorl, Leauweg C 126 Schoorl, vermutl. England (Täterkreis: Brijnen), RSHA IV E 4, Stapo Osnabrück.
3. Macadam, Fri., RSHA VI G 1.
4. Mac-Alpine, Charles D., RSHA VI G 1.
5. Macaulay, Rose, Schriftstellerin, RSHA VI G 1.
6. Mac-Coun, Mr. Wallasey (Cheshire), 4 Meddescroft Road (Täterkreis: Ignatz Petschek), RSHA III D 4.
7. Max-Carthy, G. M., Mitesh. v. "Sunday Referee Ltd.", RSHA IV B 4.
8. Macoaun, Alexander, Deckname: Macoaun, Macoaun, 5.12.95 Petersburg, Prof. d. Chemie, England, RSHA IV A 2.
9. Mac-Coun, zuletzt, vermutl. England, RSHA IV D 3 a.
10. Mac-Cracken, C., 13.7.90 London, brit. G.-Leutnant, zuletzt: Brüssel, vermutl. England, RSHA IV E 4.
11. Mac-Kagan, richtig: Makshin, vermutl. England, RSHA IV D 3 a.
12. Mc-Mahon, Direktor, London S. W. 1, 5 Wilton Place, RSHA IV E 2.
13. Macklewise, Stanisław, Mitgl. d. poln. Nat.-Rates, RSHA VI G 1.
14. Mackay, Ronald, RSHA VI G 1.
15. Mc-Mahon, Henry, Direktor, London S. W. 1, 5 Wilton Place, RSHA IV E 2.
16. Macmillan, Harold, 1894, Politiker u. Verleger, Haywards Heath/Sussex, Chelwood Gate, RSHA VI G 1.
17. Macmillan, Lord, RSHA VI G 1.
18. Macmurray, Major, M. J., Oboe-Sekre., RSHA VI G 1.
19. Macshen, richtig: Makshin, vermutl. England, RSHA IV D 3 a.
20. Macnara, Edward Henri, 6.6.11 London, Steward (Flaggeschloch. "Imperial Airways"), London, RSHA IV E 4.
21. Major, Hans, 12.2.16 Berlin, Jahresd. Soldat, England, RSHA VD 2 f.
22. Magwean, J. H., Handelsrat b. einer Botschaft, England, RSHA IV E 4.
23. Maier (Maier-Hochsetzken), Johannes, Redakteur, Emigrant, London N. W. 2, Belsize Park Gardens, RSHA II B 5, IV A 2.
24. Maier-Hochsetzken, L. G., Schriftleiter, Emigrant, London N. W. 2, 22 Belsize Park Gardens, RSHA II B 5.
25. Mayer, Gustav, Dr., 1871, a. o. Prof., Emigrant, London, RSHA III A 1.
26. Mayer, Peter, Schriftleiter, Emigrant, London W. 9, 34 Lanhill Road (Maida Hill), RSHA II B 5.
27. Mayer-Groß, Willy, Dr., 1889, a. o. Prof., London, Maudsley Hospital, Emigrant, RSHA III A 1.
28. Maier, Johannes C., 2.5.01 Ostrog, Krs. Ratibor, Chefredakteur, RSHA IV E 4.
29. Maier, Karl, 20.5.97 Königstein, Krs. Pirna, Schlosser, Liverpool, RSHA IV A 1.
30. Meyer, Alfred, Dr., 1895, a. o. Prof., Emigrant, London, Maudsley Hospital, RSHA III A 1.
31. Mayer, S., 61., Emigrant, London, RSHA VI G 1.
32. Mayer, Ernst-Wilhelm, 2.4.89 Leobschütz, RSHA IV A 1 b.
33. Mayer, Gerhard, Dr., 1904, Emigrant, Manchester, RSHA III A 1.
34. Mayer, Herbert, 1911, Ass., Emigrant, London, RSHA III A 1.
35. Mayer, Martin, London, RSHA III D.
36. Mayer, Otto, Deckname: Otto, d.7.11.08 Poine (Am-Apparat), RSHA IV A 2.
37. Mayer, 30.6.01 Leyden, zuletzt: Den Haag, vermutl. England (Täterkreis: de Haas), RSHA IV E 4, Stapo Aachen.

38. Maine, W., Abteilter b. brit. ND., London, RSHA IV E 4.
39. Maier, Martin, 13.11.15 Frankfurt/M., Kaufmann, zuletzt: Den Haag, vermutl. England (Täterkreis: Meijer, Arnold), RSHA IV E 4, Stapoleit Münster.
40. Maix, Anton, Redakteur, London, RSHA II B 5.
41. Maixner, Jos., brit. Agent, zuletzt: Brüssel, vermutl. England (Täterkreis: Kurt Petschek), RSHA IV E 4.
42. Maixner, Anna, 30.8.91 Weisserdorf/England, Witwe, Sevenoaks-Kent, Hazelbourne/England (Täterkreis: Holden), RSHA II B 5, Mahassi), RSHA IV E 4, Stapo Neustadt/W.
43. Maixner, Hedden Hill, 22.7.09 Broadstaira, Student, Sevenoaks-Kent, Hazelbourne/England, RSHA IV E 4, Stapo Neustadt/W.
44. Makabin, Jakob, Deckname: Mac-Cohen, Mac-Kohen, Rammoovky, Maccben, Mac-Kagan, Matrivasky, Mossya-Rammoovky, 67.9.80 Wien oder Wien, vermutl. England, RSHA IV D 3 a.
45. Maksain, R. W., Direktor, London K. C. 2, 28 Great St. Helen's (Shell Transport u. Trading Co.), RSHA IV E 2.
46. Malcolm, S., Angestellter d. Fa. Harries Scarbo Limited, London, — 4 Lloyd's Av. Fenchurch Street, RSHA IV E 2, Stapo Karlsruhe.
47. Malock, Lord, 21.4.65, RSHA VI G 1.
48. Mallon, James Joseph, 1880, Soziologe, Fab.-Soz., RSHA VI G 1.
49. Malone, Cecil, L'Estrange, Oberst, Mitgl. d. Parlaments, London, RSHA IV D 3 a.
50. Mandelbaum, Kurt, Dr., d.3.11.04 Schweinfurt, London, RSHA IV A 1.
51. Mander, Geoffrey, geb. 1882, Politiker, Abgeordneter, London S. W. 1, d. Barton Street, RSHA VI G 1.
52. Mannheim, Ernst, Dr., 1900, Ass., Emigrant, London, RSHA III A 1.
53. Mannheim, Karl, Dr., 1868, o. Prof., Emigrant, London, RSHA III A 1.
54. Mannheim, Dr., 1868, a.-o. Prof., Emigrant, London, RSHA III A 1.
55. Mann, Heinrich, 27.3.71 Lübeck, Schriftsteller, Emigrant, RSHA II B 5.
56. Mann, Jakob, 21.4.44 Schuhe/Polen, Student, RSHA IV E 5, Stapo Köslin.
57. Mannet, Josef, 27.2.19 Karlsbad, Sad Sari, RSHA IV A 1 b.
58. Mannin, Ethel, 1900, Journalistin, RSHA VI G 1.
59. Manning, Leah, Politikerin, RSHA VI G 1.
60. Mannten, 4898, Aufsichtführer, RSHA VI G 1.
61. Mannteiagur, geb. Hartwig, Stenotypistin, RSHA IV A 1 b.
62. Manthey, Stanislaus, poln. Krim-Beamter, RSHA IV E 5, Stapo Liegnitz.
63. de la Mar, A., Leiter d. Büro Reuter in Amsterdam, zuletzt: Amsterdam, vermutl. England, RSHA IV E 4, Stapo Münster.
64. Marchband, John, Generalsekr. d. engl. Eisenbahnerverb., vermutl. England, RSHA IV A 1 b.
65. Marchbank, John, 1883, Gewerkschaftler, vermutl. England, RSHA VI G 1.
66. Margaies, Rudolf, Deckname: Stachs, Stach u. Stochert, RSHA Parvus, Parkasbelter, vermutl. England (Am-Apparat), RSHA IV A 2.
67. Margulies, Abraham Chaim, Deckname: von Hammerstein, 1.13 Lodz, poln. N.-Agent, RSHA IV E 5, Stapo Danzig.

68. de Marich, A. H., (Agostono), 19.1.88, Grenzpolizeimajor a. D., zuletzt: Utrecht, vermutl. England (Täterkreis: Verhoeven), RSHA IV E 4, Stapo Aachen.
69. Marks, Simon, London S. W. 7, 48 Hyde Park Gate, South-Kensington, RSHA II B 2.
70. Markschoffel, Günther, 16.11.08 Gleiwitz, vermutl. England, RSHA IV A 1.
71. Marley, Lord, 16.4.84, Fab.-Soz., Toronto, 417 Bloor Street West, RSHA VI G 1, IV A 5.
72. Marmorek-Schlitter, Dr., 60.11.78 Wien, Redakteur, vermutl. England, RSHA IV A 1.
73. Marschetti, Baron, 22.7.94 Youse, angebl. engl. Offizier, London, 15. Emperorgate, RSHA IV E 4.
74. Marrack, Prof., London, RSHA VI G 1.
75. Mars, Hans, 1896, Dozent, Emigrant, Birmingham, RSHA III A 1.
76. Marschak, Jacob, 1898, Priv.-Dozent, Emigrant, Oxford, RSHA III A 1.
77. Martin, Hans, Direktor d. holl. Lebd.-Ges. E. L. M., Den Haag, zuletzt: Den Haag, vermutl. England, RSHA IV E 4.
78. Martin, Kingsley, 28.7.97, Journalist, London W. C. 1, 16. Great James Street, RSHA VI G 1.
79. Martin, Robert, richtig: Narr, Adolf Paul, vermutl. London, RSHA VI G 1.
80. Martin, Leiter d. Intern. Büros d. intern. Pfadfinderbewegung in London, vermutl. London, Emigrant, London, RSHA IV E 4.
81. Marx, A., Bankdirektor, zuletzt: Amsterdam, vermutl. England, RSHA IV E 4.
82. Marx, Fritz M., Dr., 1900, Ass., Emigrant, Cambridge (Universität), RSHA III A 1.
83. Masaryk, Jan, tr. tschech. Gesandter in London, Außenmin. d. csl. Regierung in London, Emigrant, RSHA IV D 1 a II B 5.
84. Masaryk, Johann, Emigrant, London, RSHA VI G 1.
85. Maschler, Kurt, Schriftsteller, Emigrant, Stanmore b. London, 1 Woodcroft Avenue, RSHA II B 5.
86. Mass, Simon, richtig: Jakob, richtig: Makshin (Prinz), vermutl. England, RSHA IV D 3 a.
87. Massoun, Alexander, Deckname: Massoun, Massoun, Alexander, 5.12.95 Petersburg, Prof. d. Chemie, RSHA IV A 2.
88. Mason-MacFarlane, F. N., Oberst, Attaché f. Luftfahrt, England, RSHA IV E 4.
89. Mastel, Frau, vermutl. England, RSHA VI G 1.
90. Masterson, brit. Capt. u. Generaldirektor d. Phönix Oil in London, London/Bukarest (Täterkreis: Dr. Fritz Rauth), RSHA IV E 4.
91. Masson, Alexander, richtig: Massoun, 5.12.95 Petersburg, Prof. d. Chemie, England, RSHA IV A 2.
92. Mauer, Erwin, 22d.32, Friedrichstadt, Prokurist, vermutl. England, RSHA IV A 1, Stapoleit Hamburg.
92a. Mauer, geb. Bachmann, Annemarie, 18.11.09 Gronau, vermutl. England, RSHA IV A 1, Stapoleit Hamburg.
93. Matkou, Kommandant, zuletzt: Brüssel, vermutl. England, RSHA IV E 4, Stapoleit Münster.
94. Matten, Richard, 20.12.96 Neuwied, Metzger, London, Hendon Pure Mansion Flat 34, RSHA IV A 1.

95. Mattuck, Israel, Geistlicher, vermutl. England, RSHA IV G 1.
96. Matuschek, Josef, 19.2.97 Radwanitz, Redakteur, vermutl. England, RSHA IV A 1.
97. Maude, Charles R., 27.2.82 England, Leiter d. Berl. Spionageabteil. d. engl. Mission, Colonel, vermutl. England, RSHA IV E 4.
98. Mazza, Ernst G. B., Sir, engl. Generalkonsul i. Rotterdam, zuletzt: Rotterdam, vermutl. England, RSHA IV E 4.
99. Maxton, James, 22.6.85, Politiker, Abgeordneter, Greenwood Barhead Renfrewshire, RSHA VI G 1.
100. May, Edward, Dr., 1905, London, Privatpraxis, Emigrant, RSHA III A 1.
101. May, J. Henry, 1867, Wirtschaftler, RSHA VI G 1.
102. Maynard, John, Sir, vermutl. England, RSHA VI G 1.
103. Mazome, Alexander, Deckname: Alexander Massoun, 5.12.95 Petersburg, Prof. d. Chemie, RSHA IV A 2.
104. McKenna, Martha, vermutl. England, RSHA IV E 4.
105. Meisel, Hans, Emigrant, Princeton, 65 Stockton Street, RSHA II B 5.
106. Meißner, Ferdinand, Dr., 26.3.95 Olmütz, fr. Hauptschriftleiter des Preßburger „Grenzboten", London S. W. 7, 8 Mason Place, RSHA IV E 4.
107. Meixner, geb. Endt, Aloisia, 14.3.05 Bärringen, b. 2018 Savvary Thorpland Hall, Norfolk Falkenham, RSHA IV A 1 b.
   3. Melchert, Willi, Schriftsteller, vermutl. England, RSHA III A 5.
   J. Meichett, Henry, 10.5.98 London, Bankdirektor, London S. W. 1, 6 Chelsea Embankment, RSHA II B 2.
110. Meller, William, 1898, Journalist, RSHA VI G 1.
111. Mellors, Taddy, engl. Rennfahrer, vermutl. England (Täterkreis: Kurt Felsenthal), RSHA IV E 4.
112. Mendelssohn-Bartholdy, Albrecht, Dr., 1874, o. Prof., Emigrant, Univers. Oxford, RSHA VI G 1.
113. Mense, Bernhard, Schriftsteller, London W. 9, 67. Warrington Crescent, Emigrant, RSHA III A 5, II B 5.
114. Mennicke, Carl, Dr., 1887, Prof., Emigrant, Amersfoort, RSHA III A 1.
115. Menzies, Frederick, London, RSHA IV E 4, Stapo Darmstadt.
116. Mörling-Eisenberg, Kurt, 1899, Priv.-Dozent, Emigrant, London, RSHA III A 1.
117. Merry, a. F., Handelssekr., RSHA IV E 4.
118. Merteus, Kurt, richtig: Hans Barteus, 19.12.97 Großbüllesheim, Oberstadtsekr., vermutl. England (Am-Apparat), RSHA IV A 2.
119. Merten, Alfred, Dr., London, RSHA III D.
120. Merton, Israel Richard, 1.12.81 Frankfurt/M., Kaufmann, Emigrant, Jude, London (Brit. Metallcorporation Ltd.), RSHA IV E 4, Stapo Frankfurt/M.
121. Merz, Josef, 12.2.14 Rotenfels, Eisendreher, zuletzt: Utrecht/Holland, vermutl. England, RSHA IV E 4, Stapoleit Karlsruhe.
122. Mesham, Taddy, 2.2.09 Frankfurt/M., London, RSHA IV A 1.
123. Messe, Le, Worthing-Sussex, 25. Bulkington Ounte, RSHA IV E 4.
124. Messer, Lord, 12.6.65, Frhr. d. Mb. Part. Hurst Place, Cookham Dene Berks, RSHA VI G 1.
125. Metal, Julie, 26.5.79, Jarow, Bankier, London, RSHA IV A 1.
126. Messel, Alfred, Dr., 1896, a. o. Prof., Emigrant, London, RSHA III A 1.

127. **Meynsberg, Friedrich, Dr.**, 1875, a. o. Prof., Emigrant, Sheffield, RSHA III A 1.
127a. **Meyer, Martin**, Mitarbeiter d. Merton, London, RSHA III D.
128. **Meynen, Hermann**, Deckname: Meynen-Seilerbeck, 7.5.95 Mülheim, fr. Wirtschafts-Schriftsteller, vermutl. England (Schwarze Front), RSHA IV A 3.
129. **Meyrowitz, Paul**, 22.11.88, Frankfurt/M., Bankier, London (Täterkreis: Frank Beaumont), RSHA IV E 4, Stapolt Berlin.
130. **Mevering, E.**, zuletzt: Hilversum/Holl., vermutl. England (Täterkreis: Breijnen), RSHA IV E 4.
131. **Michael, Siegfried E., Dr.**, 1898, Birmingham, Emigrant, RSHA III A 1.
132. **Michalowski, Günther Isidor**, Deckname: Joachim, 7.8.11 Düsseldorf, Student, vermutl. England (Am-Apparat), RSHA IV A 2.
133. **Michalowski, Irma**, richtig: Abrasimow, Irma, geb. Michelson, 12.9.01 Riga, Kontoristin, Bardame, vermutl. England, RSHA IV E 5, Stapolt Königsberg/Pr.
134. **Michealis, Lorenz, Dr.**, 1902, Ass., Emigrant, Glasgow, RSHA III A 1.
135. **Michelson, verheiratete Abrasimow, Irma**, Deckname: Michalowski, 12.9.01 Riga, Kontoristin, Bardame, RSHA IV E 5, Stapolt Königsberg.
136. **Middelton-Peddelton**, richtig: Ustinow, London, RSHA IV E 4.
137. **Middleton, James Smith**, 1878, Politiker, vermutl. England, RSHA VI G 1.
138. **Migawa, Antos**, Arbeiter, vermutl. England, RSHA IV E 5, Stapo Schneidemühl.
139. **Mijer, brit. Agent**, vermutl. England (Täterkreis: Oberst Gibson), RSHA IV E 4.
140. **Mikolajczyk, Stanislaw**, Mitgl. d. poln. Nat.-Rat., vermutl. England, RSHA IV D 2.
141. **Miles, Dr.**, vermutl. England, RSHA VI G 1.
142. **Miller, Cyrill**, Lehrer, zuletzt: Riga, vermutl. England, engl. ND.-Leitland, RSHA VI O 2.
143. **Mills, David**, Abteilungsleiter d. Völkerbundsliga u. 18.-Mann, London, RSHA IV E 4.
144. **Mills, John Kenneth**, 1908: etwa 26 Jahre, Kensington geb., Reisender, London, RSHA IV E 3.
145. **Mitchell, John George**, 19.11.05 Blekchley. Arzt, Biddonkam bei Bedfort (Kraftw. BPO 450 GB), RSHA IV E 4.
146. **Mitchell, Pete~ Chalmers, Sir**, 23.11.64, Wissenschaftler, vermutl. England, RSHA IV E 4.
147. **Mitchell, William Foot**, Direktor, Essex, Quendon Hall, RSHA IV E 2.
148. **Mitchell, Angestellter der AJOC**, London E.C. 2, Britannic House, RSHA IV E 3.
149. **Mitchison, G. R.**, vermutl. England, RSHA VI G 1.
150. **Mitchison, Naomi**, 1.11.97, Novellistin, River Court, Hammersmith Mall, RSHA VI A 1.
151. **Mitchell-Henry, Muriel**, 26.8.98 Bradford, Reklameleiterin. vermutl. England, (Täterkreis: Julius Guthlac Birch), RSHA IV E 4.
152. **Modrze, Annelise, Dr.**, geb. 1901, Emigrantin, Oxford (Universität), RSHA III A 1.
153. **Möckel, Wilhelm**, 20.2.96 Asch, Scherer, London N. 8, SS-Prince 40, Church Linci, RSHA IV A 1, Stapo Karlsbad.

154. **Möller-Dostall, Rudolf**, Journalist, Emigrant, London W. C. 1, Bedford-Place 12, RSHA VI G 1, III B 5.
155. **Möser, Hertha**, 26.9.11 Berlin, Schneiderin, vermutl. England, Am-Apparat, RSHA IV A 2.
156. **Mohrer, Rose**, 11.6.12 Frankfurt/M., stud. med., London, RSHA IV A 1.
157. **Mokriwsky, richtig: Makohin**, vermutl. England, RSHA IV D 3 a.
158. **Molitor, Willi**, 25.5.02 Essen, Schlosser, London, RSHA II A 1, Stapoleit Düsseldorf.
159. **Moncrieff, A., Dr.**, vermutl. England, RSHA VI G 1.
160. **Monk, Herbert**, brit. Vizekonsul, vermutl. England, RSHA IV E 4.
161. **Monks, Noel**, Korresp. des „Daily Express", vermutl. England, RSHA VI G 1.
162. **Monolovici, Sandu**, zuletzt: Bukarest, vermutl. England, RSHA IV E 4.
163. **Montagu, Lionel Samuel**, geb. 1883, Bankier, London W. 1, 5 Saville Row, RSHA II B 2.
164. **Montague, Frederick**, geb. 1876, Politiker, vermutl. England, RSHA VI G 1.
165. **Montague, Soor**, Schriftsteller, vermutl. England, RSHA VI G 1.
166. **Montefiori, L. G.**, London W. 1, 37 Weymouth St., RSHA VI G 1, II B 2.
167. **Montresor, John**, 1912 Captown/Südafrika, angebl. engl. Offizier, Borthmouth, Gun House (Täterkreis: David Peter), RSHA IV E 4.
168. **Moszar, Ferdinand**, 12.7.96 Mlady-Smoliwec, chem. tschech. Oberstleutnant, vermutl. England, RSHA IV E 4, Stapoleit Prag.
169. **Moore, Taddy**, engl. Motorradrennfahrer (Täterkreis: Felsenthal), RSHA IV E 4.
170. **Moos, Siegfried**, 19.9.04 München, Bankangestellter, London, RSHA IV A 1.
171. **Mooseberg, Fritz**, 16.5.02 Lippstadt, Kaufmann, zuletzt: Holland, vermutl. England, RSHA IV E 4, Stapo Dortmund.
172. **Moravec, Franz**, 23.7.95 Caslau, chem. tschech. Oberst, London W. 8, 53 Lexham Gardens, Kensington, RSHA IV E 4, Stapoleit Prag.
173. **Moravec, Frantisek**, 23.7.95 Tschaslan, chem. tschech. Oberst, London, RSHA IV E 6.
174. **Morgan, David**, Herausgeber des „Youth at Work", RSAH VI G 1.
175. **Morris**, Angestellter der AJOC, London E. C. 2, Britannic House, RSHA IV E 2.
176. **Morton**, zuletzt: Libau, vermutl. England (engl. ND.), RSHA VI C 2.
177. **Morton, brit. Major**, vermutl. England (Täterkreis: Oberst Gibson), RSHA IV E 4.
178. **Morrison, Herbert**, Stadtpräsident v. London, London (Täterkreis: Treviranus), RSHA IV E 4.
179. **Morrison, Herbert Stanley**, 3.1.88, Minister, London S. E. 9, 55 Archery Road, RSHA VI G 1.
180. **Morrison, R. M. S.**, West Lychett, East Lane, engl. ND., RSHA VI C 2.
181. **Morrison, Stanley**, Direktor d. Londoner Rundfunkges., London, RSHA VI G 1.
182. **Morton, S. Guy (Stanley), Dr.-Ing.**, 2.1.85 London, Journalist, RSHA IV E 4, Stapoleit Prag.

183. **Moscow, Edward**, 1909 etwa 40 Jahre, Leiter des brit. ND. in Amsterdam, zuletzt: Amsterdam, vermutl. England, Kraftw. G 34697, RSHA IV E 4.
184. **Mosenthal, Elise**, 23.1.20 Berlin, London S. W. 15, Putney Lane, RSHA IV E 4, Stapoleit Hamburg.
185. **Moses, Arthur**, Vorsteher, zuletzt: Heerlen/Holl., vermutl. England, RSHA IV E 4, Stapo Aachen.
186. **Moser, Alfred**, 13.5.05 München, Schriftleiter, RSHA IV A 1.
187. **Mrosowski, Felix**, 18.5.96 Krakau, poln. Hptm. N.-Offizier, RSHA IV E 5, Stapo Graudenz.
188. **Müller, Josef**, 22.8.08 Zuflucht, England, RSHA IV A 1 b.
189. **Müller, Stephan**, 6.1.16 Schwaderbach, London, RSHA IV A 1 b.
190. **Münster, Hedwich**, 1888, a. o. Professor, Emigrant, Oxford, RSHA III D.
191. **Münzenberg, Wilhelm**, Emigrant, 14.8.89 Erfurt, Schriftsteller, RSHA II B 5.
192. **Muir, Ramsay**, 1872, Historiker u. Politiker, RSHA VI G 1.
193. **Muir, R. H.**, führend i. Unilever-Konzern, Bracknell, Pop's House, RSHA III D.
194. **Munelt, J. H. D.**, zuletzt: Enschede/Holland, jetzt vermutl. England (Täterkreis: Breijnen), RSHA IV E 4.
195. **Murs, richtig Bamberg**, geb. Berneis Sakrewska, engl. ND. Estland, RSHA VI C 2, B 369.
196. **Murphie, John Thomas**, 9.12.88 Manchester, Journalist, London 5, Crossroad Highbury, New Park 145, RSHA IV A 1.
197. **Murray, Barbara**, London, RSHA VI G 1.
198. **Murray, Gilbert**, geb. 1866, Prof. der Univers. Oxford, Oxford, RSHA VI G 1.
199. **Murray, Rodney Margarethe**, 18.9.94 Gramond/Schottland, zuletzt: Buchschlag/Hessen, vermutl. England, RSHA IV E 4, Stapo Darmstadt.
200. **Murry, Mary**, vermutl. England, RSHA VI G 1.
201. **Musil, Josef**, London, Rosendaal Road, RSHA IV E 4.
202. **Myer, Morris**, Journalist, London N. W. 11, 63 Ashbourn-Avenue, RSHA II B 2.
203. **Mykura, Franz**, 9.9.96 Trnovan, England, RSHA IV A 1 b.

1. **Nabakowski, Josef**, 27.1.10 Broczynow/Kr. Stargard, Arbeiter, poln. N.-Agent, RSHA IV E 5.
2. **Nagelschmidt, Franz, Dr.**, 1875, Manchester, Emigrant, RSHA III A 1.
3. **Nagelschmidt, Günther, Dr.**, 1908, ledig, Ass., Emigrant, London, RSHA III A 1.
4. **Najdowski, Zygmunt Stanislaus**, 22.2.10, Hamborn, Student, poln. N.-Agent, RSHA IV E 5.
5. **Narr, Agnes**, 13.5.04 Andernach, zuletzt: Brüssel, jetzt vermutl. England (Täterkreis: Leo Heymann), RSHA IV E 4, III A, Stapo Aachen.
6. **Narr, Adolf Paul**, 18.2.92, Kunstmaler, Schriftsteller, Deckname: Arnold, Robert, Laurenze, Robert, Martin, Robert, Laurenze, Martin, London, RSHA IV E 4.
7. **Nathan, Harry Louis**, geb. 1889, Rechtsanw. u. Politiker, RSHA VI G 1.
8. **Naumann, Hans, Dr.**, geb. 1901, Emigrant, Greenwich, Hospital, RSHA III A 1.
9. **Necsa, Jaromir**, 17.9.89 Neustadt, chem. Minister d. CSR., London, RSHA IV D 1, II B 5.
10. **Nebede, Min. d. chem. CSR.**, Emigrant, London, RSHA IV E 4.
11. **Neubeck, Anna**, geb. Hernstein, 20.5.00 Witten/Ruhr (Am-Apparat). RSHA IV A 2.
12. **Neubeck, Hans**, 20.6.97 Essen/Ruhr (Am-Apparat), RSHA IV A 2.
13. **Neuberger, Albert, Dr.**, 1908, Emigrant, London, RSHA IV A 1.
14. **Neudert, Franz**, 26.11.12 Eibenberg, England, RSHA IV A 1.
15. **Neudert, Franz**, 16.6.20 Poschotzan, Kaufmann, England, RSHA IV A 1.
16. **Neudert, Josef**, 10.8.02 Eibenberg, England, RSHA IV A 1.
17. **Neugroschel, Dr.**, Rechtsanwalt, London (Täterkreis: Ambert Albedt), RSHA IV E 4, Stapoleit Wien.
18. **Neumann, Bernhard Hermann, Dr.**, geb. 1909, Cambridge, Univers., Emigrant, RSHA III A 1.
19. **Neumann, Ernst**, 1.5.09 Breslau, Kaufmann, RSHA IV E 5, Stapoleit Breslau.
20. **Neumann, Franz, Dr.**, Mitarbeiter i. d. Labour Party, London W. C. 1, 59 Dorthy Street, Telefon: Holborn 0747, RSHA IV A 1-IV A 5.
21. **Neumann, Otto Reinhold Gustav**, 4.4.09 Saabor, Kr.- Grünberg, Arbeiter, komm. Funktionär u. brit. N.-Agent, RSHA IV E 5.
22. **Nevinson, Henry Woodd**, Journalist, RSHA VI G 1.
23. **Newbiggin**, RSHA VI G 1.
24. **Newbold, J. T. Walton**, RSHA IV G 1.
25. **Newby, Kenneth**, 11.9.08 Bradford, RSHA IV A 1 b.
26. **Newhouse, Peter Henry**, 14.3.04 Barrackpore/Indien, England, RSHA IV E 4.
27. **Nichel, Mac.**, führend im Unilever Konzern, London E. C. 4, Unilever-House, Blackfriars, RSHA III D.
28. **Nicholson, H. W.**, Mitarb. des „Manchester Guardian", London, RSHA IV B 4.
29. **Nicholson, England**, dipl. Beamter (engl. ND.-Lettland), zuletzt: Riga, RSHA VI G 1.
30. **Nickisson, Arthur George**, Flieger, London, RSHA IV E 4, Stapo Köln.
31. **Nickel, Wilhelm**, 24.12.01 Schwerta, Schauspieler, England, RSHA IV A 1.
32. **Nickolls, Harold**, geb. 1886 Teheran, Schriftsteller u. Politiker, London S. E. 1, 4 King's Bench-Walk, RSHA VI G 1.

32. **Nisbergall, Otto**, 5.1.04 Kusel, Sekretär (Am-Apparat), RSHA IV A 2.
33. **Nissen, Karel**, 6.10.00 Winterswijk, zuletzt: Holland, jetzt vermutl. England, RSHA IV E 4, Stapoleit Münster.
34. **de Nijs, H.**, zuletzt: Schagen/Holland, vermutl. jetzt England (Täterkreis: Breijnen), RSHA IV E 4.
65. **Nitkewitsch, Otto**, 60 Jahre alt, vermutl. England, RSHA IV E 4, Stapoleit Stuttgart.
36. **Noble Dudley, Henry**, 11.10.01 London, Direktor, London (Kraftwg.: DDU 460" GB), RSHA IV E 4, Stapoleit Königsberg.
37. **Noel-Baker, Philipp J.**, geb. 1689, Abgeordneter, Professor, London S. W. 1, 49 South Eaton Place, RSHA VI G 2.
38. **Norbeck, geb. Norbeck, Hannie Marie**, 14.11.99 Budin/Norw., poln. Agentin, RSHA IV E 6.
69. **Norreys, früher Newton**, London W. 1, 41 Hertford Street Mayfair, RSHA IV E 2, Stapoleit Wien.
70. **Norris, F. R. V.** (Francis Benedikt), 6.6.66 London?, engl. Lt. Col. (S. L.), J. M. K. X., London, RSHA IV E 4, Stapo Kiel.
41. **Norriz, Franzisca**, Oberst a. d. d. engl. Armee, RSHA VI G 1.
42. **Nortes, Michael**, London, RSHA IV E 4, Stapo Innsbruck.
42a. **North, Harald**, früher Kopenhagen, vermutl. England, brit. ND. Agent, RSHA IV E 4.
43. **Novotny, Anton**, 13.7.91 Wrschowitz, Arbeiter, Maurer, RSHA IV A 1.
44. **Novy, Wilhelm**, 20.2.92 Zuckmantel, Parteisekretär, RSHA IV A 1.
45. **Nowack, Gerda**, 22.1.15 Schmiedeberg i. Hirschberg, Stenotypistin, Grove-Meadow b. Beaconsfield, RSHA IV A 1.
46. **Nowak, Peter**, 29.6.16 London, Dienstpflichtiger, RSHA V — D 2 f —, A. O. Hamburg.
47. **Nowakowski-Tempka, Siegmund, Dr.**, 1891 Krakau, Journalist, Schriftsteller, Mitglied der poln. Emigrantenregierung i. England, RSHA III 2.
48. **Nowakowski, Zygmunt, Dr.**, Mitgl. d. poln. Nat.-Rates, RSHA IV D 2.
49. **Nuding, Hermann**, 8.7.02 Oberurbach, Fabrikarbeiter, Deckname: Klaus Hermann Degen (Am-Apparat), RSHA IV A 2.
50. **Nußbaum, geb. Eisenberg, Margarethe**, 28.2.06 Wien, 1939: Den Haag, jetzt: vermutl. England, RSHA IV E 4.
51. **Nußbaumer, A. C.**, London E. C. 2, 49. Gresham Street (Täterkreis: Ignatz Petschek (Bankaschvrstländiger der Petscheks), RSHA III D 4.
52. **Nygrys, S. H. S.**, Agent des brit. ND., London, RSHA IV E 4.

---

1. **Ober, Hans** (richtig: Hans Bartoss), 19.12.97 Großbällschein, Oberstadtsekretär, vermutl. England (Am-Apparat), RSHA IV A 2.
2. **Obermüller, Angestellter d. Shell**, London E. C. 3, 62. St. Helens Court, Shell Transport a. Trading Co., RSHA IV E 3.
3. **Ochocki, Waclaw Wenzel**, 7.9.96 Dolzig, Bürogehilfe, poln. Agent, RSHA IV E 5, Stapo Liegnitz.
4. **Ochs, Felix, Dr.**, Mitarbeiter d. Merton, London, RSHA III D.
5. **Ociemek, Johann**, 29.5.17 Klein-Lassowitz, Arbeitsdienstmann, RSHA IV E 5, Stapo Oppeln.
6. **O'Donoghan, J. K.**, ehem. Angehöriger der brit. Botschaft in Berlin, RSHA IV E 4.
7. **Oehl, geb. Brod, Luise Erna Christl**, 29.10.07 München, Hausangestellte (Am-Apparat), RSHA IV A 2.
8. **Ohm, Emil**, 29.7.07 St. Joachimsthal, RSHA IV A 1.
9. **von Oertzen, Maria**, geb. Stewart, 24.6.78 Rohais/Engl., London, RSHA IV E 4, Stapoleit Hannover.
10. **Ottinghaus, Walter**, 26.2.55 Gevelsberg, Gewerkschaftsbeamter, RSHA IV A 1.
11. **Ogilvie-Forbes, George, Sir**, etwa 45 J. alt, Botschaftsrat, RSHA IV E 4.
12. **Oistros, Schriftsteller**, RSHA IV B 4.
13. **Olden, Rudolf, Dr.**, 14.1.85 Stettin, Rechtsanwalt, Schriftsteller, Cambridge oder Oxford, Yatscombe Cottage Boars Hill, RSHA IV A 1, IV A 1 b, IV A 6, II B 5.
14. **Olden, Rudolf, Sekretär d. "Intern. PEN-Association"**, Oxford, Yatscombe-Cottage Boars Hill, RSHA IV A 1.
15. **Olden, Rudolf, Berichterst. d. "Pariser Zeitung"**, RSHA IV B 4.
16. **Oldenbroek, Jan (Jääpl)**, etwa 45 Jahre, Sekretär der ITF, London, RSHA IV A 1.
16a **O'Leary, brit. ND.-Agent**, zuletzt: Kopenhagen, RSHA IV E 4.
17. **Oigin, Konstantin**, 24.6.04 Orel (Rußland), ehem. russ. Emigrant, London, RSHA IV E 4, Stapoleit Berlin.
18. **Olifiers, C. H.**, holl. Hauptmann im ND., zuletzt: Den Haag, RSHA IV E 4, Stapoleit Düsseldorf.
19. **Oliver, E. T.**, 1939, 49—43 J. alt, Leiter der Schiffmaklerfirma Coubro u. Scrutton, zuletzt: Rotterdam, vermutl. England, RSHA IV E 4.
20. **Oliver, Philippe**, zuletzt: Paris, vermutl. England, RSHA IV E 4.
21. **Olivier, Vic**, jüd. Schauspieler, RSHA VI G 1.
21a **Olivier, Christoph Ardou**, Deckname: Smith, 10.4.00 Cooktown, brit. N.-Agent, früher Kopenhagen, vermutl. England, RSHA IV E 4.
22. **Ollenhauer, Erich**, 27.3.01 Magdeburg, Parteisekretär (SPD.), vermutl. England, RSHA IV A 1.
23. **Olsen, Hyalg**, London, RSHA IV E 4.
24. **Olszar, Karl**, 18.4.14 Neu-Oderberg, Schneider, RSHA IV E 5, Stapo Brünn.
25. **Olszok, Josef**, 12.4.15 Dt.-Leuthen, Schneider, RSHA IV E 6, Stapo Brünn.
26. **Olthof, Jan**, 36 Jahre alt, Sergeant, zuletzt: Holland, vermutl. England, RSHA IV E 4, Stapo Aachen.
27. **van Oerschot, niederl. Oberst u. Leiter des niederländischen ND.**, früher: Den Haag, vermutl. England, RSHA IV E 4, Stapo Aachen.
28. **v. Oosterhout, Gerardus**, 27.3.07 Rotterdam, zuletzt: Rotterdam, vermutl. England (Täterkreis: Breijnen), RSHA IV E 4.

---

29. **Oostervaen, J. W.**, holl. Hauptmann i. holl. Gen. Stab, zuletzt: Den Haag, vermutl. England, RSHA IV E 4, Stapoleit Düsseldorf.
30. **Opl, Adolf**, 12.12.94 Prochomuth, Holowdort bei Sheffield, RSHA IV A 1.
31. **Oppenheim, Arthur**, Mitarbeiter d. Merton, London, RSHA III D.
32. **Oppenheimer, Gertrud, Dr.**, geb. 1898, ledig, Emigrantin, London, RSHA III A 1.
33. **Oppenheimer, brit. Handelsattaché i. Den Haag**, zuletzt: Den Haag. jetzt: vermutl. England, RSHA IV E 4.
34. **Orlowicz, Marian**, 17.9.15 Komarow/Kr. Godecke, Student, RSHA IV E 5.
35. **Ostrer, Isidore**, London W. 1, Upper Brook Fellde, Park Street 47, RSHA II B 2.
36. **Ossuki, Franzke**, geb. Wschova, 31.3.89, vermutl. England, Ehefrau des Stefan Ossuki, RSHA IV E 4, Stapoleit Prag.
37. **Ossuki, Stefan**, 31.3.89 Brezova, ehem. tschech. Gesandter in Paris, vermutl. England, RSHA IV E 4, Stapoleit Prag.
38. **Ossuky, Stefan, Dr.**, 31.3.06 Brezova, ehem. csl. Gesandter in Paris, Staatsminister d. csl. Regierung in London, RSHA IV D 1, II B 5.
39. **Otten, Karl**, 29.7.89 Oberkruechten/Aachen, Schriftsteller, Emigrant, London N. W. 11, 58 Hampstead Way, RSHA II B 5.
40. **Ould, Hermon**, geb. 1886, Schriftsteller, London W. C. 1, 36 Wobern Square, RSHA VI G 1.
41. **Outrata, Eduard, Dr.**, geb. 1898, ehem. Leiter der Brünner Waffenwerke, Finanzmin. d. csl. Regierung in London, RSHA IV D 1.
42. **Outrata, Eduard**, 7.3.98 Caslau, Industrieller, London, RSHA IV E 4, Stapoleit Prag.
43. **Outraty, Eduard, Dr.**, Emigrant, Finanzmin. im tschech. Nationalausschuß, London, RSHA II B 5.
44. **Owen, Erna**, geb. Brückner, 21.12.04 Oberhausen, England, RSHA IV A 1.

---

1. **Packe, Edward H.**, Vertr. d. Brit. Regierung, London E. C. 2, Britannic House, Anglo-Iranian-Oil-Co., RSHA IV E 2.
2. **Padding, A. H.**, zuletzt: Eindhoven, jetzt: vermutl. England (Täterkreis: Breijnen), RSHA IV E 4.
3. **Paderewski, Ignacy**, Musiker, Mitgl. d. poln. Nat.-Rates, RSHA IV D 2.
4. **Padt, De, N.**, zuletzt: Zutfen/Holl., jetzt: vermutl. England (Täterkreis: Breijnen), RSHA IV E 4.
5. **Paetel, Karl-Otto**, 23.11.06 Berlin, Schriftsteller, vermutl. London, Deckname: Olaf Harrasia, Alex Afenda (Boy-Scout International-Büro/Möhringstr. Bergedorf), RSHA IV B 1.
6. **Pagel, Walter, Dr.**, Privatdozent am Papworth, Settlement, Cambridge, RSHA III A 1.
7. **Pain, Peter**, RSHA VI G 1.
8. **Paish, George**, 1867, Wirtschaftler, RSHA VI G 1.
9. **Palacek, Karl**, 28.1.18 Pilsen, ehem. tschech. Major, London, Kensington W. 8, 53. Lexham Gardens, RSHA IV E 4.
10. **Palacek, Karl**, 28.1.96 Pilsen, ehem. tschech. Major, London (Täterkreis: Moravec, Fraodtek), RSHA IV E 4.
11. **Palecek**, 29.1.96 Pilsen, Major OBR., London, Deckname: Zimmer, RSHA IV E 4, Stapo Dortmund.
12. **Palmer, R. A.**, Gen-Sekr. d. Coop. Union Ltd., RSHA VI G 1.
13. **Panafsky, Eugen (Jude)**, London (Täterkreis: Ignatz Petschek), RSHA III D 4.
14. **Pankhurst, Sylvia**, Sekret. Int. Frauenliga Matteotti, Woodford Green/Essex, 3 Charterie Road, RSHA VI G 1.
15. **Pannes, Friedrich Gustav**, 28.9.00 Essen, Hausmeister, zuletzt: Amsterdam, jetzt: vermutl. England, RSHA IV E 4.
16. **Pansch, zuletzt: Kowno**, jetzt: vermutl. England, RSHA IV E 4, Stapo Tilsit.
17. **van Panthaleon, J. H., Dr.**, Direktor, London E. O. 3, St. Helen's Court, The Asiatic Petroleum Co., RSHA IV E 2.
18. **Pares, Bernhard**, 1867, Prof. für Slawische Kultur an der Universität London, RSHA VI G 1.
19. **Parigger, P. H.**, zuletzt: Holland, jetzt: vermutl. England, RSHA IV E 4.
20. **Parker, John**, geb. 1906, RSHA VI G 1.
21. **Parker, S. J., Oberst**, RSHA VI G 1.
22. **Parmentier, ehem. Zivilflieger der KLM.**, Emigrant, England, RSHA III B.
23. **Pasberg, Maximilian Max**, 26.7.98 Ratibor, Student, Volkswirt, RSHA IV E 5, Stapo Oppeln.
24. **Paskal, Sydney**, RSHA IV G 1.
25. **Passfeld, Baron**, RSHA VI G 1.
26. **de Passco, holländ. Major**, zuletzt: Wassenaar, vermutl. England, RSHA IV E 4, Stapoleit Düsseldorf.
27. **Paterson, John**, Leiter des Nachrichteninstitutes I. C. I., London S. W. 1, Buckinghamgate (Täterkreis: a. Informationsheft I. C. I.), RSHA III D 5.
28. **Paty, richtig: Kaspar, Jaroslav**, RSHA IV E 4, Stapoleit Prag.
29. **Paul, Ernst**, 27.4.97 Steinsdorf/Tetschen, Generalsekretär, RSHA IV A 1.

30. Pawlowitsch, Paul, richtig: Paul Dyka, Oberst, England, RSHA IV E 4.
31. Paxton, Geistlicher, RSHA VI G 1.
32. Pearson, I. W., London, Unilever House, Blackfriars, RSHA IV E 2.
33. Pearson, R. G. (Cecil James?), brit. Nachr.-Offz., zuletzt: Genf, jetzt: vermutl. England, RSHA IV E 4.
34. Peartree, Stanley Arthur, 19.11.02 Leytonstone, Tabakssachverständiger, zuletzt: Griechenland, jetzt: vermutl. England, RSHA IV E 4, Stapoleit Dresden.
35. Pecher, Anton, 2.4.90 Neudek, England, RSHA IV A 1.
36. Pecher, Karl, 7.4.86 Neudeck, RSHA IV A 1.
37. Middelton-Peddelton, richtig: Ustinov, RSHA IV E 4.
38. Peethick-Lawrence, Frederic William, geb. 1871, Abgeordneter, RSHA VI G 1.
39. Pekio, Jaroslav, 3.8.01 Wilkischen, Manchester, Birsch Polygon Dickenson Road, RSHA IV A 1.
40. Perabo, Franz, Dr., Assistent, geb. 1910, Emigrant, London, RSHA IV A 1.
41. Pernikar, Johann, 11.1.03 Ober-Cerekwe, ehem. tschech. Stabskapitän (Luftwaffe), vermutl. England, RSHA IV E 4, Stapoleit Prag.
42. Perry, S. F., Sekr. Coop. P., RSHA VI G 1.
43. Peter, Franz, 13.2.15 Märiisch-Lodenice, tschech. Leutnant, ND.-Offz., vermutl. England, RSHA IV E 4, Stapoleit Prag.
44. Peters, Wilhelm, Dr., geb. 1880, o. Prof., Emigrant, Surrey, RSHA III A 1.
45. Petersen, Jan, Schriftsteller, RSHA III A 5.
46. Petigura, Ardeschir, 21.8.05 Kulangsu, Arzt, England, RSHA IV A 1.
47. Petschek, Ernst, Dr. (Jude), London W. 1, Corkstreet (Täterkreis: Ignatz Petschek), RSHA III D 4.
48. Petschek, Eva Elisabeth, Ashot-Berks b London (Täterkreis: Ignatz Petschek), RSHA III D.
49. Petschek, Fritz, Sohn Isidor Petscheks, Ashot-Berks b. London (Täterkreis: Julius Petschek), RSHA III D 4.
50. Petschek, Ina Louise, Ashot-Berks b London (Täterkreis: Julius Petschek), RSHA III D 4.
51. Petschek, Ina Louise, Ashot-Berks b. London (Täterkreis: Ignatz Petschek), RSHA III D 4.
52. Petschek, Karl (Jude), London W. 1, Corkstreet, Mayflair-Hotel, St. Regies (Täterkreis: Ignatz Petschek), RSHA III D 4.
53. Petschek, Paul, Dr. (Jude), Ashot-Berks b. London (Täterkreis: Julius Petschek), RSHA III D 4.
54. Petschek, Rita Madelaine, Ashot-Berks b. London (Täterkreis: Ignatz Petschek), RSHA III D 4.
55. Petschek, Victor (Jude), Ashot-Berks b. London (Täterkreis: Julius Petschek), RSHA III D 4.
56. Petschek, Walter (Jude), Ashot-Berks b. London (Täterkreis: Julius Petschek), RSHA III D 4.
57. Petschek, Wilhelm (Jude), London W. 1, Corkstreet, Mayflair Hotel, St. Regies (Täterkreis: Ignatz Petschek), RSHA III D 4.
58. Pety richtig Kaspar, Jaroslav, RSHA IV E 4, Stapoleit Prag.
59. Peveling, Hermann, 7.8.04 Lippstadt, Schriftsteller, Deckname: Ling Kossak, London, RSHA IV E 4, Stapoleit Prag.
60. Pfaff, Josef, 15.12.95 Ochsenfurt, RSHA IV A 1.
61. Pfefferkorn, Olga, 1.8.16 Frankfurt/M., Liverpool, RSHA IV A 1

62. Pfeifer, Heinrich, 21.3.05 Frankfurt/M., RSHA IV E 5.
63. Pfeiffer, Heinrich, 21.3.05 Frankfurt/M., Schriftsteller, Deckname: Hans Jürgen Koehler, RSHA IV B 4.
64. Pfeiffer, Jan Waclaw, 31.3.18 Warschau, Student, poln. Offizier, RSHA IV E 5, Stapoleit Stettin.
65. Pflüger, Kurt, 12.10.10 Hannover, Student, London (Am-Apparat), RSHA IV A 2.
66. Philipp, Ursula, Dr., geb. 1908, Emigrantin, London (Universität), RSHA III A 1.
67. Philippovitsch, Jochim, 9.1.10 Cladie/England, Dipl.-Ingenieur, Manchester, RSHA IV E 4, Stapo Leipzig.
68. Philips, Christopher John, 30.6.96 Nottingham, vermutl. England, RSHA IV E 4, Stapoleit München.
69. Phillips, Ch. J., brit. Vizekonsul, vermutl. England, RSHA IV E 4.
70. Piasetzki, Karl, 20.1.97 Satorw b. Krakau, Oberst, Leiter der Offen-... Abteilung, RSHA IV E 5, Stapo Kattowitz.
71. Pick, R. H., Schriftsteller, Emigrant, London S. W. 5, 62 West Cromwell Road, RSHA II B 5.
72. Pieniazek, Mieczyslaw, 27.4.96 Sliwacow, Zollinspektor, Kundschaftsoffizier, RSHA IV E 5, Stapo Schneidemühl.
73. Pieper, Prof., Emigrant, vermutl. England, Sozialdemokr. Weltprotestantismus, RSHA VI B 3, II B 3.
74. Pierson, Allard, Bankinhaber, zuletzt: Amsterdam, vermutl. England, RSHA IV E 4.
75. Pietz, Vincenty, 2.7.97 Czarnikau, Gärtner, RSHA IV E 5, Stapo Oppeln.
76. Pietzuch, Emil, 9.3.99 Neurode, Zimmermann, Deckname: Franz Arthur (Am Apparat), RSHA IV A 2.
77. Pioch Albert, 8.4.95 Stewnitz, Krs. Flatow, Landwirt, RSHA IV E 5, Stapo Schneidemühl.
78. Bdyl-Ploto, 13.6.98 Polen, protest. Geistlicher, zuletzt: Holland, jetzt vermutl. England, RSHA IV E 4, Stapo Aachen.
79. Pitcairn, Frank, Korrespondent, London S. W. 1, Viktoria Street 34, RSHA IV A 1.
80. Plasczyk, Paul, 7.10.06 Mikulaschütz, N.-Agent (Polen), RSHA IV E 5, Stapo Oppeln.
81. van der Plasse, J. M. Z., holl. Major, zuletzt: Wassensar, vermutl. England (Täterkreis: Karel Nihom), RSHA IV E 4, Stapoleit Düsseldorf.
82. Plaut, Theodor, geb. 1888, a. o. Prof., Emigrant, Leeds, RSHA III A 1.
83. Plawski, Eugen Josef Stanislaw, 26.3.95 Noworosyjsk/Kaukasus, Konteradmiral der poln. Admiralität in England, RSHA III B.
84. Plesch, Johann, Dr., 1878, a. o. Prof., Emigrant, Privatpraxis in London seit 1934, RSHA III A 1.
85. Plotke, Karl, Mitarbeiter des Merton, London, RSHA III D.
86. Podlipnig, Josef, 21.6.02 Klagenfurt, Redakteur, Deckname: Fritz Valentin, vermutl. England, RSHA IV A 1.
87. Pöschmann, Karl, 7.9.06 Eisenberg, RSHA IV A 1.
88. Potzsch, Gustav, 19.8.98 Rixdorf, Metallarbeiter (Am-Apparat), RSHA IV A 2.
89. Polak, Ernst, Dr., Emigrant, London W. 8, Alma Terrace 7 Allen Street, RSHA II B 5.

90. ...elzy, W. C. LYFI Zerusberger/Holland, zuletzt: Den Haag, vermutl. England, RSHA IV E 4.
91. Polanyi, Michael, Dr., geb. 1891, a. o. Prof., Manchester (Universität, Emigrant, RSHA III A 1.
92. Poldermann, Ir. L. J., zuletzt: Holland, vermutl. England, RSHA IV E 4.
93. Poldermann, M., zuletzt: Zierikzee/Holl., vermutl. England (Täterkreis: Breijnen), RSHA IV E 4.
94. Poliakoff, N., Journalist, London, RSHA IV E 4.
95. Poll, W., zuletzt: Amsterdam, vermutl. England, RSHA IV E 4, Stapo Aachen.
96. Pollack, Oskar, Dr., 7.10.93 Wien, Journalist, Decknamen: Graf Smith, Amann, vermutl. England, RSHA IV A 1.
97. Politt, Harry, geb. 1890, Politiker, RSHA VI G 1, II B 4.
98. Pomeroy, Henry Ernest, brit. Vizekonsul, RSHA IV E 4.
99. Ponsonby, Lord, geb. 1871, Politiker, RSHA VI G 1.
100. Poptonek, Wojciech (Albert), 20.4.96 Trsinice, Maschinenschlosser, Kraftwagenführer, RSHA IV E 5, Stapo Schneidemühl.
101. Poppinger, Konrad, 22.2.04 Wien, Schlosser, London, RSHA V C 1 e.
102. Porter, E. Z., Leiter einer sowjet.-ND-Zentrale i. Warschau, zuletzt: bis Vizekonsul in Riga, RSHA IV E 4, Stapo Tilsit.
103. Posplszony, Jakob, 13.7.87 Chojno, Kr. Samter, Tischler, RSHA IV E 5.
104. Posthuma, A., Vertreter, Angest. des Stevens, vermutl. England (Täterkreis: Stevens-Best), RSHA IV E 4.
105. Potocki, Graf, Josef, Mitgl. d. poln. Reg., hoh. Beamter i. Außenministerium, RSHA IV D 2.
106. Powell, W. Manoel, brit. Vizekonsul, vermutl. England, RSHA IV E 4.
107. Power, Eileen, Prof., RSHA VI G 1.
108. Prager, Emigrant, London, 518 Endeleighcourt, RSHA II B 5.
109. Praha, R., Gewerkschaftsbeamter, RSHA VI G 1.
110. Preussitz, Carl, 1876, a.-o. Prof., Emigrant, Isle of Wight, RSHA III A 1.
111. Preussitz, Otto, Dr., geb. 1904, Privatdozent, Emigrant, London, RSHA III A 1.
112. Prasak, K., London, RSHA IV E 4.
113. Prehals, Leo, 23.8.02 Mährisch-Ostrau, ehem. tschech. General, England, RSHA IV E 4, Stapoleit Prag.
114. Preß, Hans, Dr., London W.O.4, Museumstr. 41 a, Emigrantenbuchhandlung, RSHA IV A 1, IV A 6.
115. Preston, Thomas, Hilderand, Diplomat, zuletzt: Kaunas (engl. ND.-Litauen), RSHA VI C 2.
116. Pretorian, Alfred, 60.30.02 Berlin, Kaufmann, vermutl. England, RSHA IV E 4, Stapoleit Prag.
117. Le Prevost, R. W., Herausgeber der Zeitschrift "Headway", RSHA VI G 1.
118. Prevoser, Nikolaus, Dr., geb. 1902, Priv.-Dozent, Emigrant, London, RSHA III A d.
119. Primorsky, Franz, 27.9.18? Litovel (Hana-Mähren), RSHA IV E 5, Stapo Brünn.
120. Price-Jones, Alaz, London (Täterkreis: Ignatz Petschek), RSHA III D 4.

121. Price, George Ward, 17.2.86 Sonderkorresp. vom "Daily Mail", London. RSHA IV B 4.
122. Price, Morgan, Philip, 1885, Politiker, RSHA VI G 1.
123. Pries, Viktor, 21.8.08 Hamburg, Schlosser (Am-Apparat), RSHA IV A 2.
124. Priestley, John Boynton, geb. 1894, Schriftsteller, RSHA IV B 4.
125. Prince, Edmund Matthew, 31.9.96 London, Geschäftsführer, vermutl. England, RSHA IV E 4, Stapo Wesermünde.
126. Pringsheim, Ludwig, 4.3.16 Halle/Saale, Wehrpflichtiger, London, RSHA V - D 2 f, Ger. d. Kommand. Berlin.
127. Prins, zuletzt: Den Haag, jetzt: vermutl. England, RSHA IV E 4.
128. Pritt, Denis Nowell, geb. 1887, London, L. C. 4, 3 Pump Court, RSHA VI G 1.
129. Prochaska, Karl, 25.4.05 Brünn, ehem. tschech. ND.-Offz., vermutl. England, RSHA IV E 4, Stapoleit Prag.
130. Prochownik, Vilma, Dr., 1904, ledig, Ass., Cambridge (Universität), Emigrant, RSHA III A 1.
131. Proskauer, Arthur, 4.8.80 Bauerwitz-Leobschütz, Apotheker, RSHA IV E 5.
132. Proskauer, Elisabeth, geb. Winter, 28.6.96 Jägerndorf, RSHA IV E 5.
133. Proskauer, Erich, 8.9.89 Kreuzburg, Apotheker, RSHA IV E 5.
134. Przyblski, Jan, 21.3.98 Jaroslaw, poln. N.-Offz., Journalist, RSHA IV E 5, Stapo Danzig.
135. Pucista, Stefan, Rechtsanwalt, RSHA IV E 5, Stapo Bromberg.
136. Pugh, Sir Arthur, geb. 1870, Vorsitzender der Generalrates der Gewerkschaften, RSHA VI G 1.
137. Pulvermann, Heinz (Jude), Generaldirektor d. Julius Petschek Konzerns, London, Grosvenor House, Park-Lane (Täterkreis: Julius Petschek), RSHA III D 4.
138. Puppe, Bruno, 17.1.04 Niederschönbrunn, Ziegeleiarbeiter, Manchester, RSHA IV A 1, Stapoleit Dresden.
139. Gans Edler Herr zu Putlitz, Wolfgang, 16.7.99 Laaske, ehem. Legationsrat b. d. Dtsch. Gesandtschaft, vermutl. England, RSHA IV E 4.

1. Rabinowitsch, Eugen J., Dr., geb. 1896, Ass., Emigrant, London (Univers.), RSHA III A 1.
2. Raczkiewicz, Mitgl. d. poln. Reg., Staatspräsident, RSHA IV D 2.
3. Radatz, Heinrich Hermann Johann, 6.6.09 Krefeld, Matrose (Heizer), RSHA IV A 1.
4. Radbruch, Gustav, Dr., geb. 1878, o. Prof., Emigrant, Oxford (Universität), RSHA III A 1.
5. Raddatz, Heinrich, 2.8.09 Krefeld, in England interniert, Schiffssabotage, RSHA IV A 2.
6. Rademakers, J. M., Schiffskapitän, zuletzt: Holland, vermutl. England, RSHA IV E 4, Stapoleit Düsseldorf.
7. Rado, Richard, Dr., geb. 1906, Sheffield (Universität), Emigrant, RSHA III A 1.
8. Rahle, Hans, RSHA VI G 1, II B 5.
9. Ramsdale, brit. ND.-Agent, zuletzt: Schiebrock b. Rotte, vermutl. England, RSHA IV E 4, Stapoleit Stuttgart.
10. Randal, Norman, Sir, Verbindungsoff. zw. Scotland Yard u. Secret Intell. Service, RSHA IV E 4.
11. Ratcliffe, Herbert James, 18.4.89 London, Jeelong., Direktor, Captain, vermutl. England, RSHA IV E 4, Stapo Köln.
12. Rathbone, Eleonor, geb. 1872, Abgeordnete, Liverpool, Greenbank, Greenbank Lane, RSHA VI G 1.
13. Rauch, Harry, 16.5.13 Berlin, Kürschner, vermutl. England, RSHA IV E 4, Stapo Bremen.
14. Rauschning, Hermann, Dr., 7.8.87 Thorn, ehem. Senatspräsident von Danzig, vermutl. England, RSHA IV A 1, IV A 6, II B 5.
15. Raven, Charles E., Geistlicher, RSHA VI G 1.
16. Rawidowics, Simon, Dr., geb. 1897, London, Emigrant, RSHA III A 1.
17. Rawita-Gawronski, Sigismund (Zygmunt), Dr., 9.12.66 Genf, Handelsrat. Poln. Botsch. Berlin, Deckname: Gawronski, RSHA IV E 5.
18. Rawitzki, Karl, Dr., 21.10.79, Emigrant, Jude, vermutl. England, RSHA II B 5.
19. Masepa-Razumowsky, Jakob, Prinz, richtig: Makohin, vermutl. England, RSHA IV D 3.
20. Razumowsky, Leon, Prinz, richtig: Makohin, vermutl. England, RSHA IV D 3.
21. Reader, Ethel, RSHA VI G 1.
22. Reading, Marquess of Gerald, Rufus, 10.1.89 London (Familienname Isaac), Heathfield/Sussex, Great Broadhust Farm, RSHA VI G 6, II B 2.
23. Reading, Eva Violet, London S. W. 7, 65. Rutland Gate, RSHA II B 2.
24. Reed, Douglas, Schriftsteller, RSHA IV B 4, III A 5.
25. Reed, Georg, Generalsekretär d. ITF., England (Schiffssabotage), RSHA IV A 2.
26. Regnart, Cyril H. (Cyrus), 65—72 Jahre alt, Kptn., Nachr.-Offz. d. brit. Sp.-Büros in Brüssel, vermutl. England, RSHA IV E 4.
27. Regulski, Janusz, 27.12.87 Zawiercie, General, Konsul, Mitglied der poln. Emigrantenregierung i. England, RSHA III B 3.
28. Rehbein, Helmut, 15.2.15 Potsdam, Dienstpflichtiger, zuletzt: Neu-Seeland, RSHA V D 2 f.
29. Rehwald, Franz, 14.8.08 Redakteur, RSHA IV A 1.
30. Reichard, Hans, 28.12.04 Hamburg, Werftarbeiter (Am-Apparat), RSHA IV A 2.

31. v. Reichenau-Leuchtmar, Ernst, 23.5.98 Berlin, Privatlehrer, (Am-Apparat), RSHA IV A 2.
32. Reichenbach, Bernhard, Dr., 12.12.88 Berlin, Schauspieler, Schriftsteller, London, RSHA IV A 1.
33. Reichenbach, Fritz Ernst, 11.7.00 Limbach/Sa., vermutl. England, RSHA IV E 4, Stapoleit Chemnitz.
34. Reichenbach, Hermann, 6.7.96 Hamburg, Musiker, England, RSHA IV A 1.
35. Reichenberger, Emanuel, Pater, RSHA VI G 1, II B 5.
36. Reichenberger, Erich, Deckn. des Alfred Ottomar Baumeister, RSHA IV A 1.
37. Reif, Julius, 5.10.93 Handlawa, London, RSHA IV A 1.
38. Reilly, Sidney Georg, 24.3.74 Dublin, brit. Kapitän u. N.-Offizier, vermutl. England, RSHA IV E 4.
39. Reinhold, Ernst, 16.11.97 Schönfeld, RSHA IV A 1.
40. Reinwarth, Adolf, 26.8.05 Eibenberg, England, RSHA IV A 1.
41. Reisser, Anton, 30.12.90 München, Gewerkschaftssekretär, England, RSHA IV A 1.
42. Reiter, Tiberius, Dr., geb. 1908, seit 1936: Privatpraxis in London, Emigrant, RSHA III A 1.
43. Reitzner, Richard, 69.8.98 Einsiedel, Parteisekretär, vermutl. England, RSHA IV A 1.
44. Remltschka, Ella, 19.12.13 Fischern, RSHA IV A 1.
45. Reul, Hans, 13.4.08 Hof/Bayern, vermutl. England, RSHA IV E 4, Stapo Nürnberg.
46. Reul, Karoline Effi, 14.4.08 London, London, Ealing 5, RSHA IV E 4.
47. Reybekiel, von, Helena, Dr., 1881, Dozentin, Birmingham (Universität), Emigrantin, RSHA III A 1.
48. Reynoulds, England, Antiquitätenhändler (Engl. ND-Lettland). RSHA VI C 2.
49. Rexler, Franz, 23.6.15 Potrelacken, Kapitän, zuletzt: Konstantinopel, vermutl. England, RSHA IV E 4, Stapoleit Wien.
50. Rhodes, Christopher, 30.4.14 Gosport/England, brit. Offiz. d. Paß-Control-Office, zuletzt: Den Haag, vermutl. England (Täterkreis: Stevens/Best), RSHA IV E 4.
51. Rhondda, Margaret Haig, Viscountess, geb. 12.6.83, Journalistin, London N. W. 3, 1 B Bay Tree Lodge, RSHA VI G 1.
52. Richardsohn, John Philipp, 29.11.90 Preston, Matrose, London, RSHA IV A 1.
53. Richter, Harry, 8.5.00 Tischenreuth, Journalist, zuletzt: Den Haag, vermutl. England, RSHA IV E 4.
54. Richter, Lothar, Dr., geb. 1895, Halifax, Emigrant, RSHA III A 1.
55. Rickards, Esther, Dr., RSHA VI G 1.
56. Rickert, Richard Martin, 18.3.07, England, RSHA IV A 1.
57. Riddel (Riddle), James, Kaufmann, zuletzt: Reval (Engl. ND-Estland), RSHA VI C 2.
58. Riddle (Riddel), James, England, Kaufmann, engl. Freimaurer, Wohnsitz zuletzt Reval (Engl. ND-Estland), RSHA VI C 2.
59. Ridley, P. A., RSHA VI G 1.
60. Rieck, Alfred, 4.7.92 Stettin, Adventist, zuletzt: Maastricht, vermutl. England, RSHA IV E 4, Stapo Aachen.

61. Rieger, Julius, Dr., ev. Geistlicher, London S. E. 3, 1 Ulundi Road Blackheath (Täterkreis: Amalng-Hildebrand-Freudenberg), RSHA II B 3, VI B 3.
62. Riehl, Jürgen, 10.10.06 Königsberg, Gerichtsassessor, London (Täterkreis: Boy-Scout Internationales Büro/Bündische Jugend), RSHA IV B 1.
63. Rieß, Erwin, 12.10.07 Mannheim, Schlosser (Am-Apparat), RSHA IV A 2.
64. Rilpma, W. A. F. H., zuletzt: Holland, vermutl. England, RSHA IV E 4, Stapoleit Breslau.
65. Rinke, Heinz, 8.6.19 Remscheid, ehem. RAD-Mann, RSHA IV E 5, Stapoleit Breslau.
66. Rinner, Erich, Dr., 27.7.02 Berlin, vermutl. England, RSHA IV A 1.
67. Rinteten, Franz, 19.8.78 Frankfurt/O., dtsch. Korvettenkapitän a. D. u. Schriftsteller, Deckname: Rintelen v. Kleist, RSHA IV E 4, IV B 4, III A 5.
68. Rintelen v. Kleist, Franz, richtig Rintelen, Franz, 19.8.78 Frankfurt/O., dtsch. Korvettenkapitän a. D. u. Schriftsteller, England, RSHA IV E 4.
69. von Rintelen, Franz, richtig: Rintelen, Franz, 19.8.78 Frankfurt/O., dtsch. Korvettenkapitän, England, RSHA IV E 4.
70. Ripka, Hubert, Dr., 26.7.95 Koderik? Köberwitz? Redakteur, Journalist, Staatssekretär i. Min. f. Ausw. Angel. d. csl. Regierung i. London RSHA IV D 1, IV E 4.
71. Ripka, England, RSHA II B 5.
72. Robak, Josef, 5.11.99, Oberleutnant, RSHA IV E 5, Stapoleit Danzig.
73. Roberts, Frederic Owen, 1876, Parlamentsmitglied, RSHA VI G 1.
74. Roberts, Peter, richtig Dr. Schiller-Marmorek, 10.11.78 Wien, Redakteur, Schriftsteller, vermutl. England, RSHA IV A 1.
75. Roberts, Stephen H., Schriftsteller, RSHA IV B 4.
76. Roberts, Vera, zuletzt: Prag, vermutl. England, RSHA IV A 1.
77. Roberts, Wilfried, 28.8.00 Abgeordneter, London N. W. 3. 75 Flask Walk, RSHA VI G 1.
78. Robertson, H. S., Captain, London, Piccadilly 49, RSHA IV E 4.
79. Robertson, J. M., RSHA VI G 1.
80. Robeson, Paul, Negersänger, RSHA VI G 1.
81. Robinson, Helene Elisabeth, geb. Brumert, 27.2.97 Martenau/Frankr., Ehefrau, vermutl. England, RSHA IV E 4.
82. Robinson, Jos., Rot-Spanienkämpfer, RSHA VI G 1.
83. Robinson, L. B., brit. Gen.-Konsul, vermutl. England, RSHA IV E 4.
84. Robinson, W. A., RSHA VI G 1.
85. Robinson, William Field, Vertreter einer brit. Bankengruppe, vermutl. England, RSHA IV E 4.
86. Robisch, Rudolf, 14.9.02 Nassengrub, Brauereiarb., RSHA IV A 1.
87. Rodd, B. H., Corford-Chiffs-Bournemouth, Bruddernel-Avenue, RSHA IV E 4, Stapoleit Stuttgart.
88. Roddy(le), William, Stewart, 17.12.82 London, brit. Oberstleutn., vermutl. England (Täterkreis: Gerta Leize v. Einem), RSHA IV A 2.
89. Rogers, Frank, London, Clapham-Road #40, Attentäter, RSHA IV A 2, Stapoleit Hannover.
90. Rose, Manderid, London, 4 Carmelit Street, RSHA IV E 4, Stapoleit Hannover.
91. Röhr, Albert, 5.11.04 Halle, Stukkateur, Birmingham, Deckname: Heinz (Am-Apparat), RSHA IV A 2.
92. Röhrer, Adolf, 61.12.98 Georgenthal, RSHA IV A 1.
93. Roetlbeer, P. R., zuletzt: Holland, vermutl. England, RSHA IV E 4.

94. Rösch, Emil, 15.4.81 Hirschenstand, Kr. Graslitz, London od. Lei ... Wentworth Road 14 b. Mosward. RSHA IV A 1.
95. Rötz, Franz, 29.1.87 Altkinsberg, Kr. Eger, RSHA IV A 1.
96. Rötz, Franz, 9.9.09 Altkinsberg, Kr. Eger, RSHA IV A 1.
97. Rohair, 11.6.85 Lingbootem, zuletzt: Den Haag, vermutl. England, RSHA IV E 4, Stapoleit Düsseldorf.
98. Rohm, anders, 31.7.76 Schönfeld, Kr. Eibogen, RSHA IV A 1.
99. Rohrschneider, Hildegard, 17.7.99 Liegnitz, Sekretärin, RSHA ...
100. Rommelau, Ernst, 2.12.06 Heidelberg, Kaufmann (Am-Apparat), RSHA IV A 2.
101. Rosey-Kougel, Jan, geb. 1914 Paigton/England, angebl. brit. Offizier, Old Rectory-Codford, Wilts, England, RSHA IV E 4, Stapo Innsbruck.
102. Rosenbaum, Mitarbeiter d. brit. N.-Dienstes, zuletzt: Den Haag, brit. vermutl. England, RSHA IV E 4, Stapoleit Düsseldorf.
103. Rops, William Sylvester, 7.12.86 Dresden, brit. N.-Agent, London W. 1, 69 Brook-Str., Saville Club, RSHA IV E 4.
104. van der Rops, Freddy, London W. 1, 69 Brook-Str., RSHA IV E 4.
105. Rosenau, Helen, Dr., geb. 1900, London, Emigrantin, RSHA III A 1.
106. Rosenau, Wilhelm, 29.11.16 Graudenz, Arbeiter (ehem. Gefr.), RSHA IV E 5, Stapo Dortmund.
107. Rosenbaum, Eduard, Dr., geb. 1887, London, Emigrant, RSHA ...
108. Rosenbaum-Docoumn, Vladimir, Rechtsanwalt, vermutl. England, RSHA IV E 4.
109. Rosenberg, Arthur, Dr. phil., 19.12.89 Berlin, Privatdozent, a. o. Prof., Liverpool. Emigrant. RSHA III A 1.
110. Rosenberg, Hans, Dr., 1890 geb., a. o. Prof., Emigrant, RSHA III A 1.
111. Rosenberg, Karl, Dr., 1898 geb., Kurator, Cambridge (Harvard Univ.), Emigrant RSHA III A 1.
112. Rosenberg, Marie, 1907 geb., Assistentin, Ambleside, Emigrantin, RSHA III A 1.
113. Rosenthal, Alfred, Dr., 1902 geb., London, Emigrant, RSHA III A 1.
114. Rosenthal, Erwin, Dr., 1904 geb., Prof., Manchester, Emigrant, RSHA III A 1.
115. Rosin, Paul, Dr., 1890 geb., o. Prof., London, Emigrant, RSHA III A 1.
116. Rosner, Ast
eul, 16.1.97 Wien, poln. ehem. Major, RSHA IV E 5, Stapoleit Danzig.
117. van Rossem, Cornelius, 5.4.79 Prätoria/Transvaal, angebl. Komponist, Amsterdam, vermutl. England, RSHA IV E 4, Stapoleit Berlin.
118. Rosner, Emil, RSHA VI G 1.
119. Rossmässl, Rudolf, 6.6.00 Rothau, RSHA IV A 1.
120. Rossel, Paul, Prof., 1905 geb., London, Emigrant, RSHA III A 1.
121. Roth, Cecil, Schriftsteller, RSHA IV B 4.
122. Rotenfeld, Anthony James B., 1897 geb., Bankier, London W 1, 42 Hill-St., Berkeley-Sq., RSHA VI G 1, II B 2.
123. de Rothschild, Leonel Nathan, London W. 8, 18 Kensington Palace Gardens, RSHA II B 2.
124. Rothschild, Paul, Dr., 1901 geb., Ass., Emigrant, RSHA III A 1.
125. Rovers, zuletzt: Holland, vermutl. England (Täterkreis: Antoine). RSHA IV E 4, Stapoleit Münster.

126 Roweck, Maria, geb. Harmler, 26.10.20 Massmünster, zuletzt: Holland, vermutl. England, RSHA IV E 4.
127. Royden, Agnes Maude, Dr., geb. 1876, Publizistin, RSHA VI G 1.
128. Royden, T., Direktor, Liverpool, Cunard Building, RSHA IV E 2.
129. Rozier, geb. de Guy, London, RSHA IV E 4.
130 Rubner, Wenzl, 1.9.86 Oberlohma, Krs. Eger, RSHA IV A 1.
131. Rudinsky, Josef, Dr., 30.7.91 Thurzovska, Journalist, frh. Pfarrer, Deckname: Ing. Thurko, vermutl. England, RSHA IV E 4, Stapoleit Prag.
132. Ruege, Maria, geb. Dobrowski, 18.7.96 Zezmizere, Sekr. i. chem. poln. Konsulat, RSHA IV E 5.
133. Runcke, Georg, Dr., 1900 geb., Assistent, London, Emigrant, RSHA III A 1.
134. Russel, Bertrand, RSHA VI G 1.
135. Rust, Edmund, 24.10.00 Litschkau, RSHA IV A 1.
136. Rychlinski, Stanislaus, 20.4.06 Stocherowo, Arzt, RSHA IV E 5, Stapoleit Königsberg.
137. Ryn, Franz, 28.11.05 Schönbrunn, chem. Hotelier, vermutl. England RSHA IV E 4, Stapoleit Prag.

1 Saar, Fritz, 21.10.87 Minden, vermutl. England, RSHA IV A 1.
2 Sachs, Rudolf, Deckname: Kupfer-Sachs, 22.5.97 Berlin, Graphiker, vermutl England, RSHA V C 3 a.
3 Sachs, Tobias, brit. Agent, zuletzt: Kowno, vermutl. England, RSHA IV E 4, VI C 2, Stapo Tilsit.
4 Sack, Julius, Deckname: Julije Zaks, 26.8.00, brit. Agent, zuletzt: Riga, vermutl. England, RSHA IV E 4, VI C 2.
5 Safrastian, A., brit. N.-Agent, London N. W. 8, 71 Haverstock Hill, RSHA A 1.
6 Sailer, Karl-Hans, 15.10.00, Redakteur, vermutl. England, RSHA IV A 1.
7 Sakrewska, verh. Baronin Budberg, Maria, Deckname: „Mura", in Rußland geboren, vermutl. London (brit. ND.-Estland), RSHA VI C 2.
8 Salinger, Robert, 9.1.93 Weikersdorf, Kaufmann, vermutl. England, RSHA IV E 4, Stapoleit Berlin.
9 Salmon, Sir, Isidore, 1876, London W. 1, 51 Mount Street, RSHA II B 2.
10 Salmond, John Maitland, Direktor, London E. C. 3, 22 St. Helens Court, Shell Transport a. Trading Co., RSHA IV E 2.
11 Salomon, Richard, Dr., geb. 1884, o. Prof., London (Universität), Emigrant, RSHA III A 1.
12 Salomon, Sidney, Rechtsanwalt, London W. C. 1, Woburn House, Upper Woburn Place, RSHA II B 2.
13 Salter, Sir, Arthur, 1881, Prof., Oxford, Parlamentsausschuß für Flüchtlinge, RSHA VI G 1.
14 Samuel, Herbert Louis, London W 2, 32 Porchester Terr., RSHA II B 2.
15 Samuel, P. M., Direktor, London E. C. 3, 22 St. Helens Court, Shell Transport a. Trading Co., RSHA IV E 2.
16 Samuel, Richard, Dr., geb. 1900, Assistent, Cambridge (Universität), Emigrant, RSHA III A 1.
17 Samuel, Viscount, geb. 1670, Mitglied vom Rat für christliches Judentum, RSHA VI G 1.
18 Samuels, Harry, Rechtsanwalt, London N. W. 2, 28 Exeter Road, RSHA II B 2.
19 Sandivnek, zuletzt: Winterswijk, vermutl. England, RSHA IV E 4, Stapoleit Münster.
20 Sander, Wilhelm, 6.5.95 Dresden, RSHA IV A 1 b.
21 Sander, William, 22.2.94 (22.4.84) London, brit. Vizekonsul, vermutl. England, RSHA IV E 4.
22 Sanders, William Stephan, 1871, Politiker („Fabian Society"), RSHA VI G 1.
23 Sankey, Viscount John, 26.10.66, Jurist, London W. 8, 13 Albert Place („Fabian Society"), RSHA VI G 1.
24 Sapieha, Fürst, Mitglied der ehem. poln. Regierung, vermutl. England, RSHA IV D 2.
25 Sarasin-Fisher, brit. Major, N.-Agent, vermutl. England, RSHA IV E 4.
26 Sartori, August, brit. Vizekonsul, vermutl. England, RSHA IV E 4.
27 Sassoon, Ellice Victor, 30.12.81, London EC 6, 86 Grace Church Street, RSHA II B 2.
28 Sattler, Ernst, 16.2.1692 Teplitz, vermutl. England, RSHA IV A 1.
29 Sattler, Josef, 29.10.05 Graslitz, RSHA IV A 1 b.
30 Sattler, Josef, 22.12.12 Eibenberg, vermutl. England, RSHA IV A 1 b.
31 Savill, Geoffrees, 28.8.01 Royston, Ingenieur, East Sheen, Observatory Nr. 50, RSHA IV E 4, Stapoleit Berlin.

32. Saville, George, richtig: Grove-Spiro, RSHA IV E 4.
33. Saxl, Fritz, Dr., geb. 1890, a. o. Prof., London (Warburg Institut), (Emigrant), RSHA III A 1.
34. Scaly, Pastor, zuletzt Hamburg, vermutl. England, RSHA IV E 4.
35. Scott, John Russell, geb. 1879, Vorsitzender d. „Manchester Guardian", „Evening News", RSHA VI G 1.
36. Scott-Lindsay, Sekretär, vermutl. England (Nationalrat d. Arbeiterbewegung), RSHA VI G 1.
37. Schottländer, Baron, Generalvertreter, London (Fa.: Guild Hall Civil Contractes), RSHA IV E 3, Stapoleit Stuttgart.
38. Sedgwice, E. F. H., richtig: Hanfstaengl, Ernst, Dr., 11.2.87 München, London, 69 Gunterstone Road, RSHA IV E 4.
39. Sedkel, Stan, brit. Beamter, zuletzt Riga, vermutl. England (brit. ND Lettland), RSHA VI C 2.
40. Sedlarecek, Karl, 24.9.94 Brüssel, chem. tschech. Stabskapitän, vermutl. England, RSHA IV E 4, Stapolt. Prag.
41. Seed, Chart Harry, 2.4.88 London, London, RSHA IV E 4, Stapo Kiel.
42. Seeger, Gerhard, 16.11.96 Leipzig, Schriftsteller (Emigrant), vermutl. England, RSHA II B 5.
43. Seelig, Louis, 6.7.02 London, Sekretär, Pilot, früher Westerland, Täterkreis: Grove-Spiro, vermutl. England, RSHA IV E 4.
44. Seelig, Paul, 10.8.13 Bandung, zuletzt Holland, vermutl. England, RSHA IV E 4.
45. Seelig, Siegfried Fritz, Dr., 1699 geboren, Privatdozent, Edinburgh Emigrant, RSHA III A 1.
46. Segres, J. C., Korrespondent der „News Chronicle", früher Wien, vermutl. England, RSHA IV B 4.
47. Sakier, Bernhard, 4.5.95 Kolomea, poln. Offizier, RSHA IV E 5, Stapoleit Breslau.
48. Seligmann, Leonore (Lore), 16.5.07 Frankfurt/M., vermutl. London, RSHA IV D 1.
48a Sell, K. G., brit. N. Agent, zuletzt Kopenhagen, vermutl. England, RSHA IV E 4.
49. Sellheim, Magda Antonewna, verh. Webb, gesch. Lasthew, Russin, zuletzt Reval, vermutl. England (brit. ND.-Estland), RSHA VI C 2.
50. Semseff, Z., vermutl. London, 101. Arthur Court Quinsway Nr. 2, RSHA IV E 4, Stapoleit Wien.
51. Watson-Seton, E. Williams, 1679, Prof. (Historiker) vermutl. England (Täterkreis: tschechoslowakisches Komitee „Internationaler Friedensfeldzug"), RSHA VI G 1.
52. Shackleton, London, 175 Piccadilly, Tel.: 2448/9, (Täterkreis: Alabert Albeert), RSHA IV E 4, Stapoleit Wien.
53. Shadworth, Harald Anthony, 28.4.92 Piccadilly-Eye, brit. Botschaftsattaché, vermutl. England (Täterkreis: von Einem), RSHA IV E 4.
54. Shannon, Edmund Cecil, 11.9.98, brit. Major, London W 1, Piccadilly 96, RSHA IV E 4, Stapo Wesermünde.
55. Shenley, Richard, brit. Captain, vermutl. England, RSHA IV E 4.
56. Shepherd, M., brit. Konsul, vermutl. England, RSHA IV E 4.
57. Sheridan, Klara, geb. Wrecke, geb. 1900 in England, Schriftstellerin, vermutl. London, RSHA IV E 4.
58. Shewell, Emanuel, 1884, Politiker, RSHA IV E 4.
59. Sieff, Israel Moses, Präsident der englischen Zionistenorganisation, RSHA VI G 1.
60. Sieff, Rebecca Dora, London W 1, Brook House, Parklane, RSHA II B 2.

61. Sievers, Max, Deckn.: Silke, 11.7.87 Berlin, Verbandssekretär, vermutl. England, RSHA IV A 1.
62. Sigmund, Rudolf, 2.5.02 Drahowitz, Albury Chilworth b. Guildforth Surrey, Surrey guest house, RSHA IV A 1 b.
63. Sik, Alexander, Dr., 20.10.00 Sewastopol, Advokatenkonzipient, London, RSHA IV E 4, Stapoleit Prag.
64. Sikorski, Wladislaw Eugenlusz, 20.5.81 Tuszow Nar, chem. poln. General, vermutl. England, RSHA III B, IV D 2, VI G 1.
65. Silkin, Lewis, Jude, Parlamentsmitglied, Londoner Stadtrat, vermutl. London, RSHA VI G 1.
66. Sillem, James Herbert, 22.5.96 Sunnighill, Kaufmann, zuletzt: Dorpat, vermutl. England (brit. ND.-Estland), RSHA VI C 2.
67. Sillem, Walter Oskar, 16.7.74 Zaber, Fabrikant, zuletzt: Dorpat, vermutl. England (brit. ND.-Estland), RSHA VI C 2.
68. Silley, ca. 50 Jahre, Hoteleinhaberin, Brixham, Nortcliff-Hotel, RSHA IV E 4, Stapo Osnabrück.
69. Lord Cademan of Silverdale, Jude, Präsident, London E. C. 2, Britannic House, Anglo-Iranian-Oil, Co., RSHA IV E 2.
70. Silvermann, Abgeordneter, RSHA VI G 1.
71. Siman, Rudolf, 10.4.98 Jindr-Hradec, chem. tschech. Stabskapitän und Journalist, zuletzt Den Haag, vermutl. England, RSHA IV E 4.
72. Simon, A. P., Abgeordneter, vermutl. London, RSHA VI G 1.
73. Simon, Franz, Dr., 1890, o. Prof., Oxford (Universität), Emigrant, RSHA III A 1.
74. Simon, Sir John Allsebrook, 1873 geboren, Abgeordneter, RSHA VI G 1.
75. Simon, Hugo, 1.9.80 Usch, Bankier, chem. Finanzminister, vermutl. England, RSHA III A 1.
76. Simon, Walter, Dr., 1896, a. o. Prof., London, Emigrant, RSHA III A 1.
77. Simon, belgischer Artillerist, zuletzt: Lüttich, vermutl. England, RSHA IV E 4, Stapo Trier.
78. Simon, Dr., Direktor, London (Legitimist), RSHA VI G 1.
79. Simon, Hellmuth, Dr., 1698, vermutl. London, Emigrant, RSHA III A 1.
80. Simpson, P., etwa 58 Jahre alt, brit. Agent, zuletzt: Brüssel, vermutl. London, RSHA IV E 4.
81. Simpson, I. L., London, Unilever House, Blackfriars, RSHA IV E 2.
82. Simpson, richtig Black, ca. 45 Jahre alt, brit. Agent, vermutl. England, RSHA III A 1.
83. Simpson, Prof., Edinburgh (Universität), (brit. ND-Estland), RSHA VI C 2.
84. Simpson, Stanley, Korrespondent der Londoner „Times", RSHA VI G 1.
85. Sinclair, Sir Archibald, 1890, Führer der liberalen Partei, RSHA VI G 1.
86. Sinclair, Beamter im Answ. Amt in London, vermutl. London, RSHA IV E 4.
87. Singer, H. W., Dr., 1910 geboren, vermutl. London, Emigrant, RSHA III A 1.
88. Singer, Karl, 9.5.90 Wien, vermutl. England, RSHA IV A 1 b.
89. von Sinowjew, ca. 50 Jahre, zuletzt: Köln, vermutl. England, RSHA IV E 4, Stapo Köln.
90. Sionwith, Franz, 9.1.00 Orlowen, Bauer u. Dolmetscher, RSHA IV E 5, Stapo Allenstein.

91. Skrzecki, Taddäus Marian Viktor, 7.8.08 Berlin, poln. Agent, vermutl. England, RSHA IV E 5.
92. Skupiel, Viktor, £9.10.11 Dortmund, Arbeiter, Privatlehrer, RSHA IV E 5, Stapo Schneidemühl.
93. Skorogodski, Dasyto, 13.2.04 Petersburg, Ingenieur, vermutl. London, RSHA IV D 3 a.
94. Skorupa, Wilhelm, 10.11.94 Paruschowitz, Kaufmann, vermutl. England, RSHA IV E 5, Stapo Oppeln.
95. Skoszewski, Wladislaus, 26.4.91 Schiiewitz, poln. Polizeibeamter, RSHA IV E 5, Stapo Schneidemühl.
96. ter Staa, H., zuletzt: Amsterdam, vermutl. England, RSHA IV E 4.
97. Staalos, Alderman, brit. Major, Wentworth/Norfolk-Cottage, Surrav. (Kraftw.: DYL 417 (GB), Marke Röwer), RSHA IV E 4.
98. Stadky, Emil, 11.1.05 Wien, Eisendr..ber, vermutl. England (RSO. Funktionär), RSHA IV A 1 b.
99. Stasna, Wenzel, 24.1.93 Ranna, ehem. tschech. Stabskapitän, London, 53 Lexham Gardens, Kensington W 8, Frantisek Moravec, RSHA IV E 4, IV E 6.
100. Stavlk, Jural, Dr., 28.1.90 Dobrsniva, ehem. tschech. Gesandter (Täterkreis: Benes), vermutl. England, RSHA IV E 4, IV D 1, Stapoleit Prag.
101. Slezak, ehem. tschech. General, (Täterkreis: Benes), vermutl. England, RSHA IV D 1 a.
102. Smalthoues, Robert Townsen, brit. Generalkonsul, vermutl. England, RSHA IV E 4.
103. Smirnoff, Iwan, Flieger, zuletzt: Holland, vermutl. England, RSHA III B.
104. Smith-Atherton, Aline Sybil, 13.11.75 Ryde, Chantrya, RSHA IV A 1.
105. Smith, Bertram A., Direktor, London S. W. 1, Shell Transport & Trading Comp., RSHA IV E 2.
106. Smith, Cyrus, brit. Passport-Offizier, vermutl. England, (Täterkreis: Jene Doos), RSHA IV E 4, III D, Stapo Kiel.
107. Smith, Jackson, Gehilfe des Handelsattachés, vermutl. England, RSHA IV E 4.
108. Walker-Smith, Jonah, London W. C. 1, 21 Russell Square, (Täterkreis: Ignatz Petschek), RSHA III D 4.
109. Smith, Neville A., 1.6.14 Leicester, Börsenmakler, London E. C. 2, 35 Morgate, RSHA IV E 4, Stapo Erfurt.
110. Smith, Ressie (Remy), vermutl. London, RSHA VI G 1.
111. Smith, R. W., Sheffield, 40, 214 Cobden Niew R., RSHA IV E 4, Stapo Kiel.
112. Smith, Wilburn Emmet, 7.4.82 Port Henry, amerikanischer Major, zuletzt: Brüssel, vermutl. England, RSHA IV E 4, Stapo Aachen.
113. Smith, W. Gordon, 16.4.15 England, Geophysiker, Durham, 14 Kitchener Terrace, Garrow Co., RSHA IV E 4.
114. Smits, Jan, zuletzt: Holland, vermutl. England, (Täterkreis: Hel-...), RSHA IV E 4, Stapo Kiel.
115. Smith, Johann, zuletzt: Rotterdam, vermutl. England, RSHA IV E 4, Stapo Kiel.
116. Smogarzewski, Kaz., vermutl. London, (Täterkreis: „Free Europe"), RSHA VI G 1.
117. Smolcic, Franz, £5.5.08 Königsberg, Guildford, Surrey Hills, Guesthouse Chvonthnas, RSHA IV A d b.

118. Smudek, Johann, 8.9.15 Weißenschmid, vermutl. England, RSHA IV E 4, Stapoleit Prag.
119. Smutny, Jaromir, 23.6.92 Bavorov, ehem. Legationsrat, Gesandter, vermutl. London, (Täterkreis: Benes), RSHA IV E 4, IV D 1, Stapoleit Prag.
120. Snejdarek, Josef, 2.4.75 Nepajedla, ehem. tschech. General, vermutl. England, RSHA IV E 4, Stapoleit Prag.
121. Snejdarek, Mme., vermutl. England, RSHA IV E 4, Stapoleit Prag.
122. Snell, Wilhelm, 23.7.94 Oranienburg, Gewerkschaftler vermutl. England, RSHA IV A 1.
123. Snell, Lord, 1866 geboren, Führer d. Arbeiterpartei im Oberhaus, RSHA VI G 1.
124. Snow, C. P., vermutl. England, Cambridge (Universität), RSHA VI G 1.
125. Söllner, Karl, Dr., 1908, Privatdozent, vermutl. London, Emigrant, RSHA III A 1.
126. Sokoloff, Celiwa, London N. W. 6, 43 Compayne Gardens, RSHA II B 2.
127. Sokolov, Celina, geb. Warschau, London N. W. 6, 43 Compayne Garden, RSHA II B 2.
128. Sokolow, Leonid, Russe, Handelsvertreter, zuletzt: Reval, vermutl. England (Brit. ND-Estland), RSHA VI C 2.
129. Soley, Generalvertreter Vickers-Armstrong, vermutl. London, RSHA IV E 4, Stapoleit Berlin.
130. Solmsen, Friedrich, Dr., 1904, Privatdozent, Cambridge (Universität), Emigrant, RSHA III A 1.
131. Soltowski, Adam, Graf, Pole, zuletzt: Kowno, vermutl. England (brit. ND-Litauen), RSHA VI C 2.
132. Sommer, Julius, Mitarbeiter d. Merton, London, RSHA III D.
133. Sommer, brit. Agent, vermutl. England, Täterkreis: Gibson, RSHA IV E 4.
134. Sommerfeld, Martin, Dr., 1894 geboren, ao. Prof., Northampton, Smith College, Emigrant, RSHA III A 1.
135. Sondheimer, Robert, Dr., vermutl. London, Emigrant, RSHA III A 1.
136. Sonikowski, poln. General, vermutl. England, Angehöriger der ehem. poln. Regierung, RSHA IV D 2.
137. Sorensen, Reginald William, vermutl. England (Sozialistische christliche Liga), RSHA VI G 1.
138. Sosnowski, Georg (Jerzy), 4.12.96 Lemberg, ehem. poln. Rittmeister, N.-Agent, vermutl. England, RSHA IV E 5.
139. Southam, Kaufmann, zuletzt: Reval, vermutl. England, brit. ND, Estland, RSHA VI C 2.
140. Southwood, Julius Salter Elias, Lord, 1873 geboren, Direktor von „Odhams Press Ltd.", vermutl. London, RSHA VI G 1.
141. Grove-Spiro, Stanley, Deckname: Lord Drummond, George Saville, 18.1.00 Cap Town, Bankier, Makler, brit. Agent, London 6, Suffolk Street Pall-Mall (Büro), London S. W. 1, Kensingtown, London W. 8, Gottesmore Gardens 18 oder de Vere Gardens 46 (privat), RSHA IV E 4.
142. Spurny, Aneska, 15.1.95 Doubrawice, ehem. tschech. Abgeordneter, vermutl. London, RSHA IV E 4, Stapoleit Prag.
143. Squance, W. R. J., Gewerkschaftsbeamter, vermutl. England (Internationaler Friedensfeldzug), RSHA VI G 1.

144. Sramek, Johann, Dr., 11.8.70 Grygov, vermutl. England, Täterkreis: Benes, RSHA IV E 4, IV D 1 a, Stapoleit Prag.
145. Stadtkoff, E. S. Roman, 9.6.90 Rußland, ehem. russ. Offizier, zuletzt: Riga und Belgrad, vermutl. England, brit. ND-Lettland, RSHA IV E 4, VI C 2.
146. Sudakoff, Viktor, etwa 40 Jahre, Geschäftsführer, zuletzt: Riga, vermutl. England, brit. ND. Lettland, RSHA IV E 4, Stapo Tilsit.
147. Sulzbach, Herbert, Schriftsteller, Emigrant, London N. W. 3, 58 b Belsize Park Gardens, RSHA B 5.
148. Sulzbacher, Max, Dr., 1901, Assistent, vermutl. London, Emigrant, RSHA III A 1.
149. Sunrzuld, Roman, 27.5.02 Kamienskoje, Kaufmann, vermutl. England, RSHA IV E 5, Stapo Bromberg.
150. Sunrzuld, Roman, 27.5.02 Kamienskoje, Kaufmann, vermutl. England, RSHA IV E 5, Stapo Bromberg.
151. Surawski, Chas W., Auslandsredakteur b. „Daily Express", London E. C. 4, Fleetstreet, Täterkreis: Panton. RSHA IV E 4.
152. Swaffer, Hannen, 1879 geboren, Schriftleiter des „Daily Herald", vermutl. London, RSHA VI G 1.
153. Swann, F. T. Frederick Theodor, 22.7.99 St. Petersburg, Kapitän, vermutl. London, RSHA IV E 4, Stapoleit Berlin.
154. Swaything, Gladys Helen Rachel, London W. 8, 28 Kensington Court, RSHA II B 2.
155. Swaything, Stuart Albert Samuel Montagu, Lord, 1898, London S. W. 1, 8 Grosvenor Crescent und Townhill Park, West End bei Southampton, RSHA II B 2.
156. Swindels, Jerzy Wincdenters, 5.4.92, Kalisch, poln. Admiral, vermutl. England, RSHA III B.
157. Syrcka, Franz, 1.1.08 Kurgan, RSHA IV E 5, Stapo Elbing.
158. Szczurkowski, Josef, vermutl. England (Polnischer Nationalrat), RSHA IV D 2.
159. Szeffer, Tadeus, etwa 36 Jahre, ehemal. poln. Hauptmann, RSHA IV E 5, Stapoleit Danzig.
160. Szillard, Leo, Dr., 1898, Privatdozent, Oxford (Universität), Emigrant, RSHA III A 1.
161. Sziminsk, Hanns Maria, geb. Paciorkowska, 17.7.89 Pagow, Angestellte, vermutl. England, RSHA IV E 5, Stapo Leipzig.
162. Sziandak, Henryk, 17.5.05 Bobrownini, Arzt, vermutl. England, RSHA IV E 5, Stapo Leipzig.
163. Szliwitski, Henryk, 21.1.96 Onesen, poln. Oberleutnant, N.-Agent, vermutl. England, RSHA IV E 5, Stapoleit Stettin.
164. Szmidt (Schmidt), Henryk, 2.1.01 Parlin, poln. Hauptmann, N.-Offizier, vermutl. England, RSHA IV E 5.
165. Szdos, Rezzi, Tänzerin, zuletzt: Belgrad, vermutl. England, RSHA IV E 4.
166. Sznos, Gustav, poln. Offizier, RSHA IV E 5.
167. Szwabe (Schwabe), Wawrzyn, 10.9.06 Kopnitz, Tischler, poln. Agent, vermutl. England, RSHA IV E 5.
168. Szwarcbart, Ignacy, Dr., Mitglied des polnischen Nationalrates (Poln. Nationalrat), RSHA IV D 2.
169. Szymanski, Theofil, 10.8.06 Königshütte, Destillateur, Kutscher, vermutl. England, RSHA IV E 5, Stapo Oppeln.

1. Schacloss, vermutl. London, Tel.: 2469/0 (Täterkreis: Albert Albosti), RSHA IV E 4, Stapoleit Wien.
2. Schallamach, Adolf, geb. 1905, Assistent, vermutl. England, RSHA III A 1.
3. Scharf, Alfred, Dr., 1900, Assistent, London, RSHA III A 1.
4. Scharf, Karl, Dr., 1911, London, RSHA III A 1.
5. Schary, August, 26.11.98 Poremba, Km.-Fbd., Hüttenarbeiter, vermutl. England, RSHA IV E 5, Stapo Oppeln.
6. Schauroth, von, Robert, früher Offizier, England, RSHA IV E 4.
7. Scheffer, Hermann, 22.2.88 Reutte/Tirol, England, NW 9, Slough House, Kings Bury, RSHA IV E 4, Stapoleit Stuttgart.
8. Scheitler, Josef, 27.10.99 Chodau, Sheffield, Rastlings Road 149, RSHA IV A 1, Stapoleit Karlsruhe.
9. Schellenberger, H., Vorstandsmitglied der Freien deutschen Kulturliga in England, London, RSHA VI G 1.
10. Scherbauen, Franz, 19.1.00 Graslitz, vermutl. England, RSHA IV A 1 b.
11. Schermaly, Aloula, 14.7.08 Frankfurt/M., Hilfsarbeiter, vermutl. England (Am-Apparat), RSHA IV A 2.
12. Scheuer, Ernst, Dr., Mitarbeiter d. Merton, London, RSHA III D.
13. Schick, George, London, Univer House, Blackfriars, RSHA IV E 2.
14. Schiefer, Fritz, 25.3.89 Obliga, Schleifer, vermutl. England (Am-Apparat), RSHA IV A 2.
15. Schiff, Otto, 1876, London W. 1, 25 Berkeley Square, RSHA II B 2.
16. Schiff, Viktor, Mitarbeiter d. „Daily Herald", London, RSHA I B V 4.
17. Schifrin, Alexander, Dr., Jude, 11.8.01 Charkow/Rußland, vermutl. England, RSHA IV A 1.
18. Schijbal, Josef, 19.6.03 Hrun - Trebinie, ehem. tschech. Stabskpt., vermutl. England, RSHA IV E 4, Stapoleit Prag.
19. Schild, Gotthard, 31.1.98 Wohlau, Kaufmann, vermutl. England (Täterkreis: Hans Jäger), RSHA IV E 6.
20. Schiller-Mascurek, Dr., 10.11.78 Wien, Deckname: Peter Roberts, Redakteur, vermutl. England, RSHA IV A 1.
21. Schilling, Ernst, 25.10.01 Berlin, Bäcker, London (Am-Apparat), RSHA IV A 2.
22. Schlafke, Hermann Erwin Adolf, 2.11.05 Kattowitz, poln. N.-Agent, RSHA IV E 5, Stapo Oppeln.
23. Schleicher, Johannes, 20.2.04 Schwabach, Lehrer, England, RSHA IV A 1.
24. Schlesinger, Max, geb. 1905, Ass. London, RSHA III A 1.
25. Schloßmann, Hans, Dr., geb. 1894, Cambridge, RSHA III A 1.
26. Schmettan, Alfons, 26.4.86 Bukarest, Artist, N.-Agent, Kaufmann, vermutl. England, RSHA IV E 4.
27. Schmidkunz, Andreas, 18.12.97 Eger, vermutl. England, RSHA IV A 1 b.
28. Schmidt, Erich, 4.8.10 Berlin, vermutl. England, RSHA IV A 1.
29. Schmidt, Heinz, 26.11.06 Halle/S., Berichterstatter, RSHA IV A 1, Stapo Halle.
30. Schmidt, Johanna, 24.7.90 Frankfurt/M., vermutl. England, RSHA IV A 1.
31. Schmidt, Ludwig, 7.4.89 Drahowitz b. Karlsbad, vermutl. England, RSHA IV A 1 b.
32. Schmidt, Werner, 18.10.11 Berlin, Photograph, vermutl. England, RSHA IV A 1.

33. **Schmitt, Fritz Eduard**, 11.8.99 Sobernheim/Rhld., Dipl.-Ing., London S. W. 1, Victoria-Street, RSHA IV E 4, Stapoleit Magdeburg.
34. **Schmitz, Edmund**, 16.5.16 Hobscheid, Dienstpflichtiger, zuletzt: Pa llastine, vermutl. England, RSHA V D 2 f.
35. **Schneider, Barbara**, geb. Ripper, 18.1.96 Budapest, London N. W 3, 2 B Winchester Road, RSHA IV A 1.
36. **Schneider, Bruno**, 21.1.04 Adorf/Sachsen, Schlosser, London, RSHA IV A 1.
37. **Schneider, Bruno**, 6.9.04 Adorf, Bez. Olsnitz, N.-Agent, London E. G. 4 35 Bridestreet, RSHA IV E 3, Stapo Halle.
38. **Schneider, Erich**, geb. 1908, Ass., London, RSHA III A 1.
39. **Schneider, Friedrich Wilhelm**, 20.8.19 Köln-Mülheim, Chauffeur, Diener, zuletzt: Den Haag, vermutl. England (Täterkreis: von Put litz), RSHA IV E 4, Stapo Köln.
40. **Schneider, Josef**, 27.6.13 St. Joachimsthal, vermutl. England, RSHA IV A 1 b.
41. **Schuurmann, Robert**, 1904, Ass., Cambridge, RSHA III A 1.
42. **Schönberg, Alexander**, 1892, Prof., Edinburgh, RSHA III A 1.
43. **Schönstein, Karl**, 8.3.88 Haslau, Kr. Asch, vermutl. England. RSHA IV A 1 b.
A. **Scholtyssek, Engelbert**, poln. N.-Agent, vermutl. England, RSHA IV E 5, Stapo Oppeln.
45. **Schramek, Jan**, Dr., Emigrant, Min.-Präs. i. tschechoslow. National ausschuß, vermutl. London, RSHA II B 6.
46. **Schreiner, G.**, zuletzt: Amsterdam, vermutl. England, RSHA IV E 4
47. **Schreiner, Wilhelm Otto**, 16.9.92 Laubach, Redakteur, vermutl. England, RSHA IV A 1.
48. **Schröbel (Schröder)**, vermutl. England (Täterkreis: Stevens/Best RSHA IV E 4.
49. **Schröder**, vermutl. England (Täterkreis: Stevens/Best), RSHA IV E 4
50. **Schubert, Alfred**, 19.8.00 Schmiedeberg, Hope View/England Castleton Derbyshire, RSHA IV A 1.
51. **Schürmann, Stanislaw**, 9.5.00 poln. Beamter, RSHA IV E 5.
52. **Schürrer, Alfred**, 8.5.11 Kobling, vermutl. England, RSHA IV A 1
53. **Schütz, Arthur**, Schriftsteller, Emigrant, London N. W 6, 10 Tarras brae Court, Willesden Lane, RSHA II B 5.
54. **Schütz, Eva**, vermutl. England, RSHA IV E 4.
55. **Schuh, Georg**, 31.8.17 London, Dienstpflichtiger, London, RSHA V — D 2 f, KP-Stelle Braunschweig.
56. **von der Schulenburg**, 13.3.08 Küstrin, zuletzt: s' Gravenhage, vermutl. England, RSHA IV E 4.
57. **Schulz, Gustav**, 7.6.15 Freienhuben, Füsilier, vermutl. England, RSHA IV E 5, Stapo Tilsit.
58. **Schulz, Hans Jürgen**, 6.11.14 Hersfeld, Schlosser, RSHA IV E 4.
59. **Schuster, George**, Sir, 1881, London S. W. 1, 61. James' Pl Nether Worton House Middle Barton Oxon, RSHA II B 2
60. **Schwann, Hans**, 5.7.84 München, Kaufmann, vermutl. England RSHA IV E 5.
61. **Schwarz, Erich**, Deckname: Hirsch, London, RSHA IV A 1.
62. **Schwarz, Ernst**, Dr., geb. 1899, London, RSHA III A 1.
63. **Schwarz, Georg**, Mitarbeiter d. Merton, London, RSHA III D
64. **Schwarz, Richard**, 8.5.91 Fleißen, Margate-Kent/Engld., RSHA IV A
65. **Schwarzenberger, Georg**, geb. 1908, Ass., London, RSHA III A 1.

66. **Schwarzloh, Georg**, 19.12.11 Lübeck, Deckname: Steiner, fr. Pol.-Beamter, vermutl. England (Schwarze Front), RSHA IV A 6.
67. **Schwarzschild, Ernst Lazarus**, 14.12.09 Frankfurt/M., Schriftleiter, London, RSHA IV A 1.
68. **Schweitzer-Detraz, Alfred**, Bankprokurist, zuletzt: Basel, vermutl. England, RSHA IV E 4, III A 1, Stapoleit Karlsruhe.
69. **Schweitzer, Alois**, 1.7.05 Litice, ehem. tschech. Kpt., vermutl. England, RSHA IV E 4, Stapoleit Prag.
70. **Schweitzer**, ehem. evgl. Superintendent, Emigrant, vermutl. England (illegaler Nachrichtendienst der Bekenntnisfront), RSHA VI H 3, II B 3.

1. **Spodrowski, Kasimir Stanislaus**, 1.3.90, poln. Oberstleutn., vermutl. England, RSHA IV E 5, Stapo Oppeln.
2. **Spears, Edward Luis**, 1886, Politiker u. Offizier, vermutl. England, RSHA VI G 1.
3. **Spencer-Davidson, Ch. Frank**, 10.6.99 Montabo, Rechtsanwalt, RSHA IV E 4, Etapoleit Wien.
4. **Spencer, Maurice**, Oberst, vermutl. England, RSHA VI G 1.
5. **Spender, John Alfred**, 1862, Journalist, vermutl. England, RSHA VI G 1.
6. **Spender, Steffan**, 1909, Schriftsteller, vermutl. England, RSHA VI G 1.
7. **Speth, Helmut**, 29.8.11 Szankow, poln. Agent, vermutl. England, RSHA IV E 4, Stapo Schneidemühl.
8. **Speyer, Alexander Nikolaus**, 6.2.87 Amsterdam, Rechtsanwalt, zuletzt: Holland, vermutl. England, RSHA IV E 4, Stapo Osnabrück.
9. **Spiegel, Annemarie**, geb. Behrens, 25.7.01 Altona, vermutl. England, RSHA IV A 1.
10. **von Spiegel-Diesenberg, Felix**, Graf, 19.1.91 Igisa/München, zuletzt: Südmähren, vermutl. England (Täterkreis: von Gerlach), RSHA IV E 4.
11. **Spielero, Karl**, 7.4.98 M.-Gladbach, Min. Direktor a. D., vermutl. London (Deutsche Freiheitspartei, Schwarze Front), RSHA IV A 1, IV A 3.
12. **Spielberg, Isabella**, 13.10.02 England, RSHA IV E 4, Stapoleit Berlin.
13. **Spielbichler, Felix**, 10.1.11 Lendorf, Kr. Spittal, Maurergehilfe, vermutl. England, RSHA IV A 1.
13a **Grove-Spiro, Stanley**, Deckname: Lord Drummond, George Saville, 19.1.00 Cap Town, Bankier, Makler, London S. & Suffolk Street Pall-Mall (Büro), London S. W. 1, Kensington, London W. 8, Gottesmore Gardens 18, oder der Vere Gardens 46 (privat), RSHA II A 5.
14. **Spithost, C.**, zuletzt: Holland, vermutl. England (Täterkreis: Brijnen), RSHA IV E 4.
15. **Speer, Mr., J.**, zuletzt: Holland, vermutl. England, RSHA IV E 4.
16. **Sprenger**, zuletzt: Z. O.-Drente/Holland, vermutl. England (Täterkreis: Brijnen), RSHA IV E 4.
17. **Sprenger, Josef**, 16.8.95 Oporowka, Kr. Lissa, vermutl. England, RSHA IV E 5.
18. **Spriok, Franz**, 20.1.00 Lippstadt, Drahtzieher, vermutl. England (Am-Apparat), RSHA IV A 2.
19. **Spurny, Anezka**, 15.1.95 Donbrawice, ehem. tschech. Abgeordneter. vermutl. London, RSHA IV E 4, Stapoleit Prag.

1. **Stängler, Josef**, 9.5.98 Eibogen, Hilfsarbeiter, Barry Glan, 17 Castel Street, RSHA IV A 1, IV A 1 b.
2. **Stahl, Johannes**, 25.6.00 Heiligenstadt, Deckname: Franz, vermutl. England (Am-Apparat), RSHA IV A 2.
3. **Stampfer, Friedrich**, 8.9.74 Brünn, Schriftsteller, Emigrant, vermutl. England, RSHA II B 5.
4. **Stanczyk**, Mitgl. d. poln. Regierung, vermutl. England (poln. Regierung), RSHA IV D 2.
5. **Staniszewski, Jan**, 16.5.96 Woyak, poln. Agent, vermutl. England, RSHA IV E 5, Stapo Köslin.
6. **Stanton, Edmund**, 21.10.81 Cork in Irland, Kaufmann, London W. 1, Cavendish Court, RSHA IV E 4.
7. **von Starhemberg, Rüdiger Ernst**, 10.5.99 Efsrding, Leiter d. österr. Heimwehr, vermutl. England (Legitimist), RSHA IV A 3.
8. **Starkenborgh, Fürst**, brit. Fliegeroffizier, Emigrant, RSHA II B 5.
9. **Starzynski, Adam**, 10.12.93 Jutrowchin, ehem. poln. Beamter, vermutl. England, RSHA IV E 5, Stapo Dortmund.
10. **Stassen, J. W.**, zuletzt: Holland, vermutl. England (Täterkreis: Brijnen), RSHA IV E 4.
11. **Stedman, P. S.**, Miß, vermutl. England, RSHA VI G 1.
12. **Steel, William**, 10.10.71, Journalist, London, RSHA IV E 4, IV A 5, IV B 4, III B 6, VI G 1.
13. **Steel, C. E**, I. Botschaftssekretär, England, RSHA IV E 4.
14. **Steen**, richtig Campbell, Anton, 10.2.61 Sorel/Canada, Rentier, England, RSHA IV E 4, Stapoleit Berlin.
15. **Steesberghe, Maximilian Paul Leon**, 2.5.99 Leiden, ehem. holländ. Wirtschaftsminister, zuletzt: Den Haag, vermutl. England, RSHA III B.
16. **Stein, G. L.**, vermutl. England, RSHA VI G 1.
17. **Stern, S. S. J.**, zuletzt: Reval/Estland, vermutl. England (brit. ND. Estland), RSHA VI C 2.
18. **Stegemann, B.**, zuletzt: Winterswyk/Holland, vermutl. England (Täterkreis: Brijnen), RSHA IV E 4.
19. **Stein, Anna**, geb. Uhilr, 31.3.02 Wien, Büroangestellte, vermutl. England, RSHA IV E 4.
20. **Stein, H. K.**, Sekretär, London E. C. 3, St. Helen's Court, Shell Mex and B. P. Ltd., RSHA IV E 4.
21. **Stein, Karl**, 20.2.00 London, vermutl. England, RSHA IV E 4.
22. **Stein, Moritz**, 4.3.15 Leipzig, poln. N.-Agent, vermutl. England, RSHA IV E 5, Stapo Danzig.
23. **Stein, Oskar**, poln. Agent, RSHA IV E 5.
24. **Steiner, Josef**, 23.12.12 Altenmark, Brotausträger, London, RSHA IV A 1, Stapo Salzburg.
25. **Steinfels, Hugo**, 17.8.05 Birkenfeld, vermutl. England, RSHA IV A 1.
26. **Stempel, Baron**, Mandatsinspektor, vermutl. England, RSHA IV E 4.
27. **Stepanek, Paul**, Filmschauspieler, Emigrant, vermutl. England, RSHA II B 5.
28. **Stephen, Campbell**, 1884, Politiker, vermutl. England, RSHA VI G 1.
29. **Stephens David**, brit. Beamter, vermutl. England, RSHA IV E 4, Stapo Insb.?
30. **Stephens, Philipp Pembrocke**, 23.9.03 Little, Missenden/England, Journalist, England, RSHA IV A 1.
31. **Stercka, Pierre**, zuletzt: Brabant, vermutl. England, RSHA IV E 4.
32. **Stern, Karl**, Dr., 1906, London, RSHA III A 1.

28. Stern, Kurt, 1902, Privatdocent. England, Rochester, RSHA III A 1.
34. Stevens, Maya, geb. Godfrey, 16.2.95 London, Schriftstellerin, L..:!:- (Täterkreis: Stevens/Best), RSHA IV E 4.
35. Stewart, Margaret, Schriftstellerin, vermutl. England, RSHA VI G 1.
36. Stewart, Marie, verh. von Oertzen, 24.8.78 Rehain/Engl., L..:!:- (Täterkreis: von Oertzen), RSHA IV E 4, Stapoleit Hannover.
37. Gamms-Stocker, Gustav, 22.10.04 Zürich, Hoteloecretär, zul..::- Zürich, vermutl. England, RSHA IV E 4, Stapoleit Karlsruhe.
38. Stockinger, Fritz, 21.9.94 Wien, früherer Handelsminister, vermut'. England (österr. Legitimist), RSHA IV A 3.
39. Stoddart, H. N., zuletzt: Riga, vermutl. England, brit. ND.-Lettland. RSHA VI C 2.
40. Stooter, Walter Donk, 5.7.15 London, London, RSHA IV A 1, Stap- Lübeck.
41. Stohwasser, Adolf, 21.5.07 Altrohlau, vermutl. England, RSHA IV A 1b.
42. Stocker, R. R., Abgeordneter, vermutl. England, RSHA VI G 1.
43. Stokvis, Zadek, 19.3.76 Den Haag, zuletzt: Holland, vermutl. England, RSHA IV E 4.
44. Stoll, Fritz, 20.7.96 Breslau, Prokurist, zuletzt: Amsterdam, vermutl. England (Täterkreis: Kurt Wechselmann), RSHA IV E 4, Stapoleit Breslau.
45. Stolper, Gustav, Schriftsteller, 25.7.98 Wien, Jude, Emigrant, vermutl. London, RSHA II B 5.
46. Stoltcrfoht, Hermann Gustav, brit. Visekonsul, England, RSHA IV E 4.
47. Stopford, Frederic Viktor, 6.7.00 Wymuth, Commandeur, zuletzt: Prag, vermutl. England, RSHA IV E 4.
48. Storwasser, Otto, 19.2.98 Altrohlau, vermutl. England, RSHA IV A 1b.
49. Stowitz, Hederlak, 16.10.08 Pockbach, vermutl. England, RSHA IV A 1b.
50. Strabolgi, Lord, 1886, vermutl. England, RSHA VI G 1.
51. Strachey, John, Schriftsteller, vermutl. England, RSHA IV B 4.
52. Strachey, Lytton, 1901, Schriftsteller, vermutl. England, RSHA VI G 1.
53. Strastenau, Gustaf, 14.6.08 Maastricht, Schiffsfunker, zuletzt: Holland, vermutl. England (Täterkreis: Stevens/Best), RSHA IV E 4.
54. Strachmüller, Emil, 25.2.02 ehem. tschech. Major, London, 65 Lexham Gardens, Kensington W.8 (Täterkreis: Frantisek Moravec), RSHA IV E 4, IV E 6.
55. Strasser, Otto, 10.9.97 Windsheim, Schriftsteller, vermutl. England (Schwarze Front), Decknamen: Baumann, Dr. Berger, Leerbrocks, Otto Bouatena, RSHA IV A 3.
56. Strasser, Paul, 21.2.95 Windsheim, Kapuziner-Pater, vermutl. England (Schwarze Front), Deckname: Pater Bernhard, RSHA IV A 3.
56a. Strauß, Bert, jod. Emigrant, zuletzt: Den Haag, vermutl. England, RSHA IV E 4.
57. Strauß, Bertold, richtig: Dr. Halder, brit. Agent, zuletzt: Den Haag, vermutl. England, RSHA IV E 4.
58. Strauß (Strawson), Frank, Direktor, vermutl. England, RSHA VI G 1.
59. Strauß, Georg Russell, Politiker, vermutl. England, RSHA VI G 1.
60. Strawson-Strauß, Frank, Direktor, vermutl. England, RSHA VI G 1.
61. Strecker, H. A. Puller, Dr., 1864, Privatdocent, England, RSHA III A 1.
62. Strelka, Karl, 68.9.96 Prag, ehem. tschech. Major, vermutl. England, RSHA IV E 4, Stapoleit Prag.

26. Strong, Pray, brit. Hauptagent, vermutl. England, RSHA IV E 4, Stapoleit München.
44. Strong, N. W. D., Korr.-Kpt., England RSHA IV E 4.
45. Strong, Nic, zuletzt: Amsterdam, vermutl. England, RSHA IV E 4.
46. Stroomil, Miggl d. poln. Regierung, vermutl. England, RSHA IV D 2.
47. Stuart, Barbara, brit. Obent, zuletzt: Wien, vermutl. England, RSHA IV E 4.
68. Stuffkens, A. P., zuletzt: Holland, vermutl. England (Täterkreis: Brijnen), RSHA IV E 4.
69. Stutzig, Ernst, 6.6.05 Pockbfen, vermutl. England, RSHA IV A 1b.
70. Styczonowski, Franz, Kraftfahrer, poln. Feldwebel, vermutl. England, RSHA IV E 6.

T

1. Tacke, Richard, 11.8.77 Berlin, Kunstmaler, zuletzt: Holland, vermutl. England, RSHA IV E 4, Stapo Hamburg.
2. Tatlow, Charles Edmund, London, Unilever House, Blackfriars, RSHA IV E 2.
3. Tauer, Jaroslaw, 24.2.96 Bela (Weißwasser), ehem. tschechischer Hauptmann, London, Lexham Gardens, Kensington W.8 (Täterkreis: Frantisek Moravec), RSHA IV E 4, IV E 6.
4. Tautz, Max, 28.6.96 Goldbach, Krs. Glatz, Glasschleifer, RSHA IV E 4, zuletzt: Kattowitz.
5. Taylor, Rees Lewell, RSHA IV E 4.
6. Taylor, S. W., Major im Kriegsamt, London, RSHA IV E 4, Stapoleit Hannover.
7. Taylor, ca. 50 Jahre alt, brit. N.-Agent, zuletzt: Rotterdam, vermutl. England (Täterkreis: Hooper), RSHA IV E 4, Stapoleit Hamburg.
8. Tcharth, Wilhelm, Deckname: Schimmel, Schonck, Michelski, Schneider, Georg Humbold, Hermann, Fritz, 6.8.02 Düsseldorf, Schiffsstauer, RSHA IV A 2.
9. Tebbe, Else Johanna, 7.12.13 Mühlheim, zuletzt: Den Haag, vermutl. England (Täterkreis: Wilhelm Willmse), RSHA IV E 4, Stapoleit Düsseldorf.
10. Tempel, Hermann, 29.11.89 Dietrum, Schriftsleiter, vermutl. England, RSHA IV A 1.
11. van den Tempel, Jan, Dr., d.8.77 Willemstad (N. Br.), ehem. holl. Sozialminister, zuletzt: Amsterdam, vermutl. England, RSHA III B.
12. Temperley, Raleigh, 50 Jahre alt, brit. Militärattaché in Holland, vermutl. England (Täterkreis: Stevens/Best), RSHA IV E 4.
13. Tempka-Nowakowski, Siegmund, Dr., geb. 1891 Krakau, Journalist, vermutl. England, poln. Emigrantenregierung, RSHA III B.
14. Tergit-Reißenberg, Gabriele, Schriftstellerin, Emigrantin, London NW.3, 21 Belsize Avenue, RSHA II B 5.
15. Tester, A. A. Artus, Dr., London S. W., James Place 14, RSHA IV E 4, Stapoleit Stettin.
16. Tester, Arthur, Dr., Emigrant, 29.8.95 Stuttgart, Schauspieler, Bankdirektor, RSHA II B 5, VI G 1.
17. Tester, Ingeborg, 22.12.18 Wiesbaden, zuletzt: Berlin-Halensee, vermutl. England, RSHA IV E 4, Stapoleit Hamburg.
18. Tewson, H. V., geschäftl. Sekretär des Gewerkschaftsausschusses, RSHA VI G 1.
19. Thalheimer, August, Dr., 18.3.84 Affaltrach/Württ., Schriftsteller, zuletzt: London, RSHA IV A 1.
20. Thomsen, Maj. Du C. P., zuletzt: Gouda/Holl., vermutl. England (Täterkreis: Breijnen), RSHA IV E 4.
21. Thompson, George Paget, geb. 1892, Prof. d. Physik 1. London, RSHA VI G 1.
22. Thompson, John, 2.10.13 Bradford, RSHA IV A 1b.
23. Thompson, Leiter engl. Agenten, zuletzt: Wien, vermutl. England, RSHA IV E 4, Stapoleit Wien.
24. Thomson, David Yalden, London N. W. 1, 8 St. George's Terrace, RSHA IV B 1b.
25. Thorndike, Sybil, Nationalrat für zivile Freiheit, RSHA VI G 1.
26. Thorner, Hans, Dr., geb. 1905, Assistent, London, Peckham House (Mental Hospital), RSHA III A 1.
27. Thortes, James, Journalist, London, Lexington Road 4, RSHA IV E 4, Stapoleit Karlsruhe.

28. Thornton, brit. Kapitän, zuletzt: Brüssel, vermutl. England (Täterkreis: Waldemar Pötsch), RSHA IV E 4.
29. Thurbe, richtig: Dr. Josef Rudinsky, Ing., RSHA IV E 4, Stapoleit Prag.
30. Thurswald, Albert, 27.2.07 Wilkischen, Krs. Mies, RSHA IV A 1.
31. Thurtle, Ernest, geb. 1884, Vertreter der Labour Party, RSHA VI G 1.
32. Tiarks, Frank C., Direktor, London E. C. 2, Britannic House, Anglo Iranian-Oil Co., RSHA IV E 2.
33. Tichy, Oldrich, 30.1.98 Nechanicich (Netbanicich), ehem. tschech. Oberstltn., London W.6, 65 Lexham Gardens, Kensington (Täterkreis: Frantisek Moravec), RSHA IV E 4, IV E 6.
34. Tille, Gustav, 7.6.90 Schelkau, Krs. Weißenfels, Schuhmacher, Lagerverwalter, RSHA IV A 4.
35. Tillett, Ben, geb. 1860, Gewerkschaftsführer, RSHA VI G 1.
36. Tinsom-Hassan, Hubert, 22.07 Birmingham, engl. Journalist, London, RSHA IV A 1.
37. Timperley, Harold J., Journalist, RSHA VI G 1.
38. Tinsley, Rabian Richard, 14.21.75 Liverpool, zuletzt: Rotterdam, vermutl. England, RSHA IV E 4.
39. Tischkowies, Stefan, Graf (Täterkreis: Camber), RSHA IV E 4, Stapo Tilsit.
40. Todd, Judith, RSHA VI G 1.
41. Tomaszewski, Tadeusz, Miggl d. poln. Nationalraten, RSHA IV D 2.
42. Tomezak, Ludwig, 30.7.94 Miemierzyce/Grodzisk, poln. Grenzbeamter, RSHA IV E 5, Stapo Liegnitz.
43. Tonnhuon, William, 4.6.05, brit. Agent, vermutl. England, RSHA IV E 4, Stapo Tilsit.
44. Tompson, Alfred, 29.6.01 London, zuletzt: London (Täterkreis: Johns Kreus), RSHA IV E 4, Stapo Koblenz.
45. Tompeon, Gordon, Dr., RSHA VI G 1.
46. Toot, Jak, zuletzt: Holland, vermutl. England, RSHA IV E 4.
47. Tops, Jak. Eisenbahnbeamter, zuletzt: Blerik/Sportstraat, vermutl. England, RSHA IV E 4.
48. Tarr, Donn, Schriftsteller, RSHA VI G 1.
49. Toov-Werax, Sylvie, Schriftstellerin, RSHA VI G 1.
50. Träger, Eva, 16.10.05 Neulohle, Kinderhortseude, RSHA IV A 2.
51. Traube, kolitor, Dr., 1880, geb., a.o. Prof., Emigrant, Edinburgh (Universität), RSHA III A 1.
52. Trautsch, Walter Ehrcgott, Deckname: Erich Schubert, 16.3.05 Langefeld, Metallarbeiter, RSHA IV A 2.
53. Treiburn, J., zuletzt: Holland, vermutl. England, RSHA IV E 4.
54. Trebil, Johann, 21.6.10 Guslitz, Krs. Kgur (Krs. Falkenau), Fabrikarbeiter, Faversham-Kent, 54 Abbey-Fields, RSHA IV A 1b, IV A 1.
55. Trenchard, Burnett Harta, Lord, Marshall der RAF, Dancer's Hill House, Barnett Herts, RSHA III D 2.
56. Tressl, J. A., Prof., RSHA VI G 1.
57. Treskin, Robert, 17.11.05, Purtwangen, Polizeibeamter, vermutl. England, RSHA IV E 4.
58. Trestbum, E. N. S., Finanzrat der brit. Botschaft in Berlin, RSHA IV E 4.
59. Trevelyan, Sir, Charles, 1870 geb., RSHA VI G 1.

60. Treviranus, Gottfried Reinhold, 20.2.91 Schleiden/Lippe, Reichsminister a. D., Sekretär b. Flüchtlingskomitee im Völkerbund, London, RSHA IV E 4, IV 5 a, IV B d, IV A 1 b, VI G 1, II B 5.
61. Trebitsch, geb. Liemmer, Witwe, Voctmori-of-Wight, Mittcholl-Avenue, RSHA IV A 1.
62. Trösk, Otto, 16.5.05 Tyczyn, Dipl.-Ing., RSHA IV E 4, Stapoleit Danzig.
63. Trenkhardt, Arthur, 10.7.87 Gelsenkirchen, poln. Redakteur, RSHA IV E 3, Stapo Oppeln.
64. Tropplowitz, Renom, 14.8.01 Gradacae, Bosnien, Kaufmann, RSHA IV E 5, Stapo Liegnitz.
64a Turnhall, ca. 60 Jahre alt, brit. N.-Agent, früh. Kopenhagen, vermutl. England, RSHA IV E 4.
65. Turner, dipl. Beamter, zuletzt: Roval/England, RSHA IV C 2.
66. Türkheim, Hans, geb. 1869, a. o. Prof., Emigrant, London, RSHA III A 1.
67. Twoja, Alexa, zuletzt: Kutno, vermutl. England (Täterkreis: Norman John Reiles), RSHA IV E 4.
68. Tyzan, Anna H., Sekretärin, London, 55 Grosvenor Crescent, RSHA VI G 1.

1. Ucko, Hans, Dr., geb. 1900, Privatdozent, Emigrant, London, Guys Hospital, RSHA III A 1.
2. v. Uden, W. D., zuletzt: Holland, vermutl. England, RSHA IV E 4.
3. Uhllr, Anna, verh. Stein, 31.3.02 Wien, vermutl. England, RSHA IV A 1.
4. Uhlmann, Fred, Vorstandsmitgl. d. „Freien deutschen Kulturliga" in England, London, RSHA VI G 1, II B 5.
5. Ulich, Robert, Dr., zuletzt: 1890, Emigrant, Cambridge, o. Prof. und Dozent an der Universität, RSHA III A 1.
6. Ullrich, Erwin, Deckname: Basil Herbert, 9.8.08 Berlin, RSHA IV A 2.
7. Unwin, Stanley, geb. 1884, Verleger, Vorsitzender und Direktor, RSHA C I G 1.
8. Uppington, A. H., Somerset/England, 38 Marlborough, Buildings, RSHA IV E 3, Stapo Trier.
9. Urch, Thomas, Journalist, zuletzt: Riga, vermutl. England, RSHA VI C 2.
10. Ustinov, Journalist, London, Deckname: Middelton-Peddelton, brit. N.-Agent, RSHA IV E 4.
11. Utley, Freda, Journalistin, RSHA VI G 1.

14*

1. Vachell, J. L., Oberst, Att. für Luftfahrt, England, RSHA IV E 4.
2. Vahrenhorst, Frieda, 27.2.15 Hannover, vermutl. England, RSHA IV A 1.
3. Valentin, Veit, Dr., 1885, a. o. Prof., Emigrant, London (Universität), RSHA III A 1.
4. Vandenheed, Matheus Otto, 14.10.92 Amsterdam, franz. Agent, zuletzt: Rotterdam, vermutl. England, RSHA IV E 4, Stapo Aachen.
5. Vseck, verh. Beaumont, Emilie, 20.3.94 Wien, Agentin, zuletzt: Prag, vermutl. England (Täterkreis: Beaumont), RSHA IV E 4.
6. Vansittart, Robert, führend im brit. ND., Dipl. Hauptberater des Aussenministe., London W. 1, 44 Park Street, RSHA IV E 4.
7. Varga, Josef, 29.9.07 Berlin, Arbeiter, London, Deckname: Karl, RSHA IV A 1, IV A 2.
8. Vasicek, Josef, 16.3.96 Tritschein, Handelsreisender, RSHA IV A 1, Stapo Troppau.
9. Vastelabend, Bram, etwa 56 Jahre alt, zuletzt: Holland, vermutl. England (Täterkreis: Prins), RSHA IV E 4.
10. Vaucher, Victor, richtig: Jean Lareide, RSHA IV E 4, Stapo Bremen.
11. Vaughan, Janet, Dr., RSHA VI G 1.
12. Vedral, Jaroslav, 17.11.95 Melnik, ehem. tschech. Oberst, vermutl. England, RSHA IV E 4, Stapoleit Prag.
13. Veit, geb. Kneznack, Imogen, 12.4.13 Glasgow, Sprachlehrerin, London RSHA IV E 4.
14. Velthuis, Jan Gerrit, zuletzt: Rotterdam, vermutl. England, RSHA IV E 4, Stapoleit Düsseldorf.
15. Veltmann, Mj. J. A., zuletzt: Haarlem, vermutl. England (Täterkreis: Breijnen), RSHA IV E 4.
16. Venzl, Georg, 31.7.98 Eger, RSHA IV A 1 b.
17. Vergeossen, zuletzt: Holland, vermutl. England RSHA III A, Stapo Aachen.
18. Verhoef, J., zuletzt: Den Haag, vermutl. England (Täterkreis: Breijnen), RSHA IV E 4.
19. Verona, Hilda, RSHA VI G 1.
20. Verrat, Hochschullehrer, England, RSHA III B.
21. Vevers, G. M., Dr., Vize-Vorsitzender der Cult. Rel. USSR., RSHA VI G 1.
22. Viertel, Berthold, London, Emigrant, RSHA VI G 1.
23. Vlest, Rudolf (Dr. ?), 24.9.90 Revuca, ehem. tschech. General, Staatssekretär im Min. für nat. Verteidigung d. csl. Regierung in London, London, RSHA IV E 4, IV D 1, Stapoleit Prag.
24. Vinke, H. L., holl. Hauptmann d. R. im ND., zuletzt: Holland, vermutl. England, RSHA IV E 4.
25. Vitold, richtig: Kos, Minister (poln. Emigrantenregierung), vermutl. England, RSHA IV E 4.
26. Vive, Arthur, Ang. d. belg. Militär-Büreau, zuletzt: Brüssel, vermutl. England (Täterkreis: Bastian), RSHA IV E 4, Stapo Köln.
27. Vivien, fr. Offizier d. ind. Polizei, zuletzt: London (Täterkreis: Wolfgang zu Putlitz), RSHA IV E 4.
28. Vleugels, vermutl. England, RSHA IV E 4.
29. Völki, Anton, 12.7.03 Neuenbrand, Krs. Asch, RSHA IV A 1 b.
30. Völki, Josef, 20.3.95 Neuenbrand, Krs. Asch, London, 88 Pacro Park, S. E. 13, RSHA IV A 1, Stapo Karlsbad.
31. Vogel, Johann, 16.2.91 Oberartelshofen, Vorsitzender der SPD., vermutl. England, RSHA IV A 1.

32. Vogel, Wilhelm Hans 11.12.10 Fürth, Parteisekretär (SPD.), vermutl. England, RSHA IV A 1.
33. Vogelser, 15.8.16 Utrecht, Student, zuletzt: s'Gravenhage, vermutl. England, RSHA IV E 4, Stapoleit Düsseldorf.
34. Vogelsesang, P., zuletzt: Gorinchem/Holl., vermutl. England (Täterkreis: Breijnen), RSHA IV E 4.
35. Veit, Franz, 6.9.06 Lichtenstadt, Krs. Karlsbad, Porzellandreher, Keawig/England, Haus End Cumberlandstr., RSHA IV A 1 b, Stapo Karlsbad.
36. Voltisck, Ingenieur, London, RSHA VI G 1, II B 5.
37. Volak, Otokar, 31.3.02 Zlin, ehem. tschech. Stabskpt., vermutl. England, RSHA IV E 4, Stapoleit Prag.
38. Vollerth, Max, 26.8.03 Hamburg, Nieter, RSHA IV A 2.
39. Vomberg, Josef, 11.8.16 Brauweiler, RAD-Mann, London, RSHA V D 2 f.
40. Voeck, Willem Frederik, 29.8.96 Sido-Hardjo/Nl. Ind., Kapitän, zuletzt: Den Haag, vermutl. England, RSHA IV E 4, Stapo Aachen.
41. Voedracek, Karl, 21.1.80 Prag, ehem. tschech. Oberstltn., vermutl. England, RSHA IV E 4, Stapoleit Prag.
42. Voorbourgh, Albert Peter, 20.5.17 Rotterdam, Sekretär, zuletzt: Den Haag, vermutl. England (Täterkreis: Best), RSHA IV E 4, Stapoleit Düsseldorf.
43. Vorstman, Mr. L. D., zuletzt: Holland, vermutl. England, RSHA IV E 4.
44. Vraas, Fritz, 12.4.15 Türmitz, Krs. Aussig, RSHA IV A 1 b.
45. de Vries, Adrianus Johannes Josephus, 13.11.93 Loon op Zand. brit. N.-Agent, richtig: Vristen, zuletzt: Rotterdam, vermutl. England, RSHA IV E 4.
46. de Vries, holl. Gastwirt, zuletzt: Nijmegen/Holl., vermutl. England (Täterkreis: Wilhelm Willemse), RSHA IV E 4, Stapoleit Düsseldorf.
47. de Vries, zuletzt: Holland, vermutl. England (Täterkreis: Meyerdorf), RSHA IV E 4, Stapo Lüneburg.
48. de Vriessen, zuletzt: Amsterdam, vermutl. England (Täterkreis: Theodor Prasssen), RSHA IV E 4, Stapo Lüneburg.
49. Vristen, Adrianus Johannes Josephus, 13.11.93 Léon op Zand. brit. N.-Agent, Decknamen: Zwarr, A. Emmering, Fristen, de Vries, Kraftw. „H. 79640" (Täterkreis: Stevens-Best), RSHA IV E 4, Stapoleit Düsseldorf.
50. Vygren, Ferdinand Hubert Josef, 29.12.97 Heerlen/Holl., Kaufmann, zuletzt: Heerlen/Holl., vermutl. England, RSHA IV E 4, Stapo Aachen.
51. Vyth, zuletzt: Den Haag, vermutl. England, RSHA IV E 4.

. Wachova, Pauline, verehel. Ossuski, 31.3.89, vermutl. England (Täterkreis: Stefan Ossuski), RSHA IV E 4. Stapoleit Prag.
2 Wachsmann, Klaus, Dr. geb. 1907. Emigrant, London, RSHA III A 1.
. Wagner, Albert Malte, Dr., geb. 1886, Privatdozent, Emigrant,
London. RSHA III A 1.
4. Wagner, Fritz, richtig Knleffke, Karl, Agent, zuletzt: Amsterdam, ver-
mutl. England, RSHA IV E 4, Stapo Wilhelmshaven.
. Wagner, Linda, 13.11.13 Asch, vermutl. England, RSHA IV A 1 b.
6 Wagner, Mark, geb. Kohl, 1.8.08 Haslau, Strickerin, RSHA IV A 1.
. Wagner, Rudolf, richtig Kleine, Fritz, 7.3.01 Apolda, RSHA IV E 4,
Stapoleit Prag.
. Wale, engl. Oberstltn., RSHA VI C 2.
9. Walcken, Alexander George, geb. 1873, Gewerkschaftsbeamter,
RSHA VI G 1.
. Walker-Smith, Sir, Jonah, London, W. C. 1, 21. Russell Square
Täterkreis: Ignatz Petachek), RSHA III D 4.
11. Walter, Franz, richtig Hermann, Fridrich, 28.4.00 Brünn,
vermutl. England, RSHA IV A 2.
12. Walter, Friedrich, 8.4.15 London, Wehrpflichtiger, Heath (Kent),
73 Broadway Brexley, RSHA V D 2 f.
13. Walsh, H., zuletzt: Holland, vermutl. England, RSHA IV E 4, Stapo
Bremen.
14. Walzer, zuletzt: Heerlen, vermutl. England, RSHA IV E 4, Stapo
Aachen.
15. Wanka, Franz, 14.7.98 Oberleutensdorf, RSHA IV A 1 b.
16. Wanka, Marie, 30.12.02 Furth i. W., vermutl. England, RSHA IV A 1 b.
17. Wanner, Johann, 23.1.19 Seefeld/Tirol, RAD-Mann, vermutl. England,
RSHA V D 2 f, KP-Stelle Innsbruck.
18. Warburg, G., Schriftleiter, RSHA IV B 4, IV A 5.
19. Wardle, W. L., Oberhaupt der Methodistenkirche, RSHA VI G 1.
20. Wardrop, E., brit. Konsul, vermutl. England, RSHA IV E 4.
21. Wark, Nikolaus, Dr., 18.1.81 Böwen (Luxemburg), Dozent, zuletzt:
Heerlen/Holland, vermutl. England, RSHA IV E 4, Stapo Aachen.
22. Warminski, Adam, richtig Koc, Minister der poln. Emigrantenregierung, vermutl. England, RSHA III B.
23. Warner-Townsend, Sylvia, Schriftstellerin, RSHA VI G 1.
24. Wassermann, Albert, Dr., geb. 1901, Emigrant, London, Privatdozent an der Universität, RSHA III A 1.
25. Watkins, Olga, Schriftstellerin, RSHA IV B 4.
26. Watson, Johnried, Deckname: Harald, Esman, 26.4.93 Brüssel, geb.
1895 Glasgow, dipl. Beamter, zuletzt: Riga, Stockholm und Kaunas,
vermutl. England, RSHA VI C 2.
27. Watson, Robert I., Direktor, London E. C. 2, Britannic House, Anglo-
Iranian-Oil-Co., RSHA IV E 2.
28. Watson - Seton, R. Williams, geb. 1879, Historiker, Prof. f. Zentral-
europäische Geschichte, vermutl. England, RSHA VI G 1.
29. Webb, Beatrice, geb. 1859, Ehrenpräsidentin, RSHA VI G 1.
30. Webb, Magda Antonowna, geb. Seilbein, gesch. Lauthew, zuletzt:
Reval/Estland (Täterkreis: M. Budberg), RSHA VI C 2.
31. Weber, Alois, 27.7.97, Arbeiter, vermutl. England, RSHA IV A 1.
32. Weber, August Karl Wilhelm, Dr., 4.2.71 Oldenburg, Bankdirektor
a. D., London, RSHA IV A 1 b.

33. Weber, Editha, 27.10.05 Düsseldorf, Erzieherin, vermutl. England,
RSHA IV E 4.
34. Weber, Ludwig, 22.5.02 Pfungstadt/Darmstadt, RSHA IV A 1, IV A 2.
35. Wechselmann, Kurt, 3.2.88 Mieckobitz, Kaufmann, zuletzt: Den Haag,
vermutl. England, RSHA IV E 4. Stapoleit Breslau.
36. Weck, Kurt, 30.11.92 Werdau/Sa., vermutl. England, RSHA IV A 1.
37. Weckel, Kurt, 15.3.77 Schedewitz, Volksschullehrer, RSHA IV A 1 b.
38. Wedgwood, Josiah Clement, 1872. brit. Oberst, RSHA VI G 1.
39. van Weegen, Wilhelm, 1.2.04 Urden/Holland, zuletzt: Renkum b.
Arnheim, vermutl. England, RSHA IV E 4.
40. Weidmann, Friedrich Wilhelm, 8.11.02 Erlangen, Arbeiter, London,
RSHA II B 3. Stapo Nürnberg.
41. Weil, Hans, Dr., 1905 geb., Assistent, Emigrant, Newcastle-on-Tyne.
RSHA III A 1.
42. Weiler, Gerhard, Dr., 1899 geb., Emigrant, Oxford. RSHA III A 1.
43. Weinberger, Martin, Dr., 1893, verh., Emigrant, London, Dozent a. d.
Universität, RSHA III A 1.
44. Weinhart, Josef, 17.6.97 Gfell, Glas Y Mor, Y. M. G. A., Barry i. Glam.
RSHA IV A 1 b.
45. Weinmann, Fritz, Emigrant (Jude), London. RSHA III D 4.
46. Weinmann, Hans, Hauptaktionär d. Westböhmischen Bergbauaktien-
vereins. London. RSHA III D.
47. Weinstein, Alexander, Dr., geb. 1897, London, Privatdozent a. d.
Universität. Emigrant. RSHA III A 1.
48. Weisenfeld, Nathan, Arzt, London. RSHA IV A 2.
49. Weiß, Bernhard, 30.7.80 Berlin, ehem. Pol.-Vize-Präs., RSHA IV A 1,
VI G 1.
50. Weiß, Harry, Dr., 1906 geb., Emigrant, London, RSHA III A 1.
51. Weiß, Joseph, Dr., 1906 geb., London, Emigrant, Assistent an der
Universität, RSHA III A 1.
52. Weißenberg, Kart, Dr., 1893 geb, Emigrant, a. o. Professor, Southampton. RSHA III A 1.
53. Weizmann, Chaim, 1873 oder 1874 in Motyli bei Pinsk, Professor
der Chemie, Führer der gesamten Judenvereine Englands, London
S. W. 1. 104 Pall Mall, Reform-Club. RSHA II B 2, VI G 1.
54. Welker, Helene, 13.12.94 Berlin. RSHA IV A 2.
55. Wells, Herbert George, 1866 geb., Schriftsteller, London N. W. 1.
Regents Park 13, Hanover Terrace, RSHA VI G 1. III A 5, II B 4.
55a Weish, brit. N.-Agent, zuletzt: Kopenhagen, vermutl. England, RSHA
IV E 4.
56. Welter, Charles Joseph Ignace Marie, 6.4.80 Den Haag, ehem. holl.
Kolonialminister, zuletzt: Den Haag, Statenplein 10, RSHA III B.
57. de Werdestuyn, de Wijkersloot, Robert, 21.9.12 Utrecht, Student,
zuletzt: Nymwegen, vermutl. England, RSHA IV E 4, Stapoleit
Düsseldorf.
58. Wenzel, Johann, Deckname: Hermann und Bergmann, 9.3.02 Niedau,
Schlosser, Schmied, RSHA IV A 2.
59. Werner, Heinz, Dr., 1890 geb., Cambridge, Emigrant, a. o. Prof. an
der Universität. RSHA III A 1.
60. Werner, Hermann, 27.9.93 Rückwa, vermutl. England, RSHA IV A 1 b.
61. Werner, Paul Robert, 16.5.15 Scheidewitz, Gefreiter, RSHA IV E 4.
Stapoleit Breslau.
62. Wertheimer, Lydia, Mitarbeiterin d. Merton, London, RSHA III D.
63. West, Rebeca, 1892 geb., Journalistin, RSHA VI G 1.

64. Westhoff, Dr., richtig: Hans Berkos, 19.12.97 Großhöllenheim, Oberstadtsekretär, vermutl. England, RSHA IV A 2.
65. Westerlaken, zuletzt: Holland, vermutl. England, RSHA IV E 4.
66. Wetzel, Rudolf Paul, 30.1.09 Rechenberg, Büroangest., Student, London N. 6, 89 Hornsey Lane Highate, RSHA IV A 1, Stapoleit Dresden.
67. Weyer, D., F., zuletzt: Aalsmeer/Holland, vermutl. England (Täterkreis: Breijnen), RSHA IV E 4.
68. Whately, Monica, Schriftstellerin, RSHA IV B 4.
69. White, H. Graham, 1880 geb., Politiker, RSHA VI G 1.
70. White-Baker, John, 12.8.02 W.-Malting-Kent, Captain, N.-Offizier,
London, Fracanti Lane, RSHA IV E 4.
71. Wickenden, Leonard (Waverin), 15.6.95 Mischinow, Schuhmacher, poln.
N.-Agent, RSHA IV E 5, Stapoleit Breslau.
72. Wiersma, A., zuletzt: Heiloo/Holland, vermutl. England (Täterkreis:
Breijnen), RSHA IV E 4.
73. Wigham, Gilbert C., Direktor, London E. C. 2, Britannic House,
Anglo-Iranian-Oil-Co, RSHA IV E 2.
74. Wigner, Eugen, Dr., Emigrant, Madison, a. o. Prof. an der Universität, RSHA III A 1.
75. de Wijkersloot, de Werdestuyn, Robert, 21.9.12 Utrecht, Student,
zuletzt: Nymwegen, vermutl. England, RSHA IV E 4, Stapoleit
Düsseldorf.
76. Wildman, B., brit. Konsul, vermutl. England, RSHA IV E 4.
77. Wildman, Direktor d. brit. Gesellsch., "Becos" in Riga, vermut.
England RSHA IV E 4.
78. Wiles, Ph., RSHA VI G 1.
79. Williams, engl. Offizier, London 17, West Bury Avenue, Wordgreen 22
(Täterkreis: Williuse), RSHA IV E 4, Stapoleit Münster.
80. Wilkinson, Ellen, Abgeordneter, London W. C. 1, Universität College,
Cower Street, RSHA IV A 6, VI G 1.
81. Willam, D (Täterkreis: Willms), RSHA IV E 4.
82. Willems, Gerardus Hubert, 14.4.08 Kessel, Krs. Limburg, Kraftfahrer,
Verkäufer, zuletzt: Venlo/Holland, vermutl. England (Täterkreis:
Gerhard Willms), RSHA IV E 4.
83. Williams, A. M., brit. Vizekonsul, RSHA IV E 4.
84. Williams, Francis, Herausgeber d. "Daily Herald", RSHA VI G 1.
85. Williams, James, Händler, brit. N.-Agent in Litauen, zuletzt: Kaunas,
RSHA VI C 2.
86. van der Willik, Piet, 22.7.90 Den Haag, Direktor, vermutl. England
(Täterkreis: Best), RSHA IV E 4.
87. Willis, Ted, Vorsitz. d. Jugendliga Arbeiterpartei, RSHA VI G 1.
88. Willms, Gerhard, 14.4.08 Kessel, Krs. Limburg, Verkäufer, zuletzt:
Venlo/Holland, RSHA IV E 4, Stapoleit Düsseldorf.
89. Wilmerlk, Johann, 5.1.09 Hradzen, Krs. Mies, Tagarbeiter, Watford,
83. the Harebrauds, RSHA IV A 1, Stapo Karlsbad.
90. Wilsarik, Wilhelm, 10.11.10 Hradzen, Krs. Mies, Maurer, RSHA IV A 1,
Stapo Karlsbad.
91. Wilson, Florence, brit. N.-Agent, zuletzt: Kopenhagen, vermutl.
England RSHA IV E 4.
92. Wilson, H. J., London E. C. 1, 15 Barnstaple, Mansions, Roosbery
Avenue, RSHA IV E 4, Stapo Halle.
93. Zimmer, Paul, 28.11.08 Gablonz, RSHA IV A 1.
94. Wind, Edgar, Dr., 1900 geb., Emigrant, Privatdozent, London, RSHA
III A 1.

94. Winter, verh. Proskauer, Elisabeth, 23.6.96 Jägerndorf, RSHA IV E 4.
95. Winterstein, Arthur, Dr., RSHA VI G 1.
96. Winiicki, Leo, Dr., 1901 geb., Emigrant, Ass., Privatpraxis in Manchester, RSHA III A 1.
97. Wisniewski, Kurt Heinz, 22.8.10 Schleusenau, Arbeitsdienstmann,
RSHA IV E 5, Stapoleit Königsberg.
98. Wisniewski, Ludwig, 7.6.79 Seymborze, Krs. Hohensalza, poln. Krim.-
Kom., RSHA IV E 5, Stapoleit Berlin.
99. de Wit, C. W., zuletzt: London, RSHA IV E 4, Stapoleit Stuttgart.
100. De Witte, Euten, 9.10.82 Karlsbad, Walmer/Kent, Garth Sidney
Road, RSHA IV A 1.
101. Wittkower, Erich, Dr., 1899 geb., Emigrant, Privatdozent, London,
Maudsley Hospital, RSHA III A 1.
102. Wittkower, Rudolf, Dr., 1901 geb., Emigrant, Dozent, zuletzt: Köln.
London. Warburg-Institut, RSHA III A 1.
103. Wlzumeler, vza, Mej. C. B., zuletzt: Holland, vermutl. England.
RSHA IV E 4.
104. Wnorowski, Mieczyslaw, Dr., 18.10.08 Warschau, Presseattaché b. d.
poln. Botachaft Berlin, RSHA IV E 5.
105. Wohlfahrt, Albert, 24.2.15 Altersberg b. Geilsdorf, Dienstpflichtiger.
Ashton-Wilts, the Cotswold (Bruderhaus), RSHA V D 2 f.
106. Wohlwill, Max, Dr., Mitarbeiter d. Merton, London, RSHA III D.
107. Wojcas, Leon, Polit. Grenzbeamter, RSHA IV E 5, Stapo Allenstein.
108. Wolf, M., Dr., Schriftleiter beim Manchester Guardian, London
W. C. 1. Nr. 17 St. Jour Street of Theobalds Street, RSHA IV B 4.
109. de Wolff, Pierre, Direktor der Swiss-Bank-Corp., London E. C. 2.
Gresham Street 99 (Täterkreis: Ignatz Petachek), RSHA III D 4.
110. Wolff, Leon, 21.4.96 Culmsee, Krs. Thorn, Getreidekaufmann.
RSHA IV E 5.
111. Wolsey, William, Verleger der Zeitschrift "Kameradschaft", London
S. E. 3, 2 Paragon, Blackheath. RSHA IV B 1.
112. Wondrak, Heinrich, 16.5.94 Meffersdorf, Manchester, Scholzrows
Wittington, RSHA IV A 1 b.
113. Woodhouse, Josef A., 14.1.93 Birmingham, ehem. brit. Polizeibeamter,
vermutl. England, RSHA IV E 4, Stapo Köln.
114. Woodman, Dorothy, Sekretärin d. Union d. demokratischen Kontrolle, RSHA VI G 1.
115. Woolf, Leonhard, 1880 geb., Schriftsteller, RSHA VI G 1.
116. Woolf, Virginia, Schriftstellerin, RSHA VI G 1.
117. Worcester, J., holländ. Polizeibeamter a. D., zuletzt: Ameland, vermutl. England (Täterkreis: August de Fremery), RSHA IV E 4.
117a Wright, William Wood, 17.6.89 Liverpool, zuletzt: Kopenhagen,
vermutl. England, RSHA IV E 4.
118. Wulstrup, Jan, zuletzt: Rotterdam, vermutl. England (Täterkreis:
Waldomar Potsch), RSHA IV E 4.
119. Wunderlich, Berta, 1.6.06 Schönbach, vermutl. England, RSHA
IV A 1 b.
120. Wunderlich, Emil, 4.12.97 Neuberg, vermutl. England, RSHA
IV A 1 b.
121. Wustra, Jan, zuletzt: Holland, vermutl. England (Täterkreis: Waldemar Potsch), RSHA IV E 4, Stapo Bremen.
122. Wuttke, Franz, Deckname: Georg Paul Rudolf, 26.11.90 Jos[...],
Krs. Rosenberg, Grubenarbeiter, RSHA IV A 1.

123. Wrzezynsky, Siegfried, 40.11.98 Gnesen, Kaufmann, London W. 1, 8 Grosvenor Street, Deckadresse: London W. 1, Alfordhouse 10 Parklane, Tel.: Fernsprechamt Primrose, Nr. 6155, RSHA IV E 4, Stapo Kiel.
124. Wright, John Lilleora, 12.6.86, Kaufmann, zuletzt: Riga, vermutl. England, RSHA IV C 6.
125. Wright, W. Charles, Direktor, London E. C. 3, 22. St. Helens Court, Shell Transport u. Trading Co., RSHA IV E 2.
126. Wynne, T. R., Direktor, London E. C. 2, Britannic, House, Anglo-Iranian-Oil-Co., RSHA IV E 2.
127. Wynyard, J. G. (Ivy), 4.7.98 Auckland, vermutl. England, RSHA IV E 4.

1. Yakobson, Sergei, Dr., 1901, London, Emigrant, Universität, RSHA III A 1.
2. Yankel, David, Inhaber d. „British International Jewish Agency", London West 1, Southampton Street, Tilsroy Square, RSHA IV A 1, IV A 5 a.
3. Young, E. P., Rundfunkantor, Oberstleutnant, RSHA VI G 1.
4. Young, G. Gordon, Warschauer Vertreter v. Reuter, RSHA IV B 4.
4a. Youngs, Edward Hueserud, 8.9.98 London, brit. N.-Agent, früh. Kopenhagen, vermutl. England, RSHA IV E 4.
5. Young, etwa 45—50 Jahre alt, Techniker, brit. N.-Agent, zuletzt: Holland, vermutl. England (Täterkreis: Wilhelm Willemse), RSHA IV E 4, Stapoleit Düsseldorf.

1. Zagorski, Waleman, 2.2.07 Kosmin, Poln. N.-Agent, RSHA IV E 5.
2. Zaka, Julia, brit. N.-Agent, richtig: Julius Gock (Täterkreis: Sudakoff), RSHA IV E 4.
3. Zaleska, Zofia, Mitgl. d. poln. Reg. RSHA IV D 2.
4. Zaleski, August, Außenmin., Mitgl. d. poln. Reg. RSHA IV D 2.
5. Zapf, Franz, 22.2.96 Wintergrün, London, RSHA IV A 1 b.
6. Zapf, Robert, 16.12.90 Dogissgrün, Krs. Ellbogen, Sheffield, 147 Rustlings Road, RSHA IV A 1.
7. Zassenhaus, Herbert Kurt, Dr., geb. 1910, Dozent, London, Emigrant, RSHA III A 1.
8. Zeisner, Arthur, fr. Abraham, 16.10.77 Podwoloziska, Kptm., poln. N.-Agent, RSHA IV E 5, Stapoleit München.
9. Zeitler, Hans, 8.9.19 Hamburg, Wehrpflichtiger, zuletzt: Südafrika, vermutl. England RSHA V D 2.
10. Zeligowski, Lucjan, General, Mitgl. d. poln. Nat.-Rat, RSHA IV D 2.
11. Zernatto, Guido, 21.7.03 Treffen, Schriftsteller, England, RSHA IV A 3.
12. Zernick, Rudin Rudolf, 7.2.01 Nicolai, poln. O. S., Kaufmann, poln. N.-Agent, RSHA IV E 5.
13. Zernike, J., Dr., zuletzt: Holland, vermutl. England, RSHA IV E 4.
14. Zeuner, Friedrich, Dr., 1905, Privatdozent, Emigrant, Universität, London, RSHA III A 1.
15. Zeylmans, J. W., zuletzt: Zaandam/Holl., vermutl. England (Täterkreis: Breijnen), RSHA IV E 4.
16. Ziaja, Anton, 7.6.04 Beuthen/O. S., Kellner, poln. N.-Agent, RSHA IV E 5, Stapo Oppeln.
17. Ziaja, Gerhardt, 4.9.13 Antonienhütte, Musiker, RSHA IV E 5, Stapo Oppeln.
18. Zibrid, Anton, 9.7.96 Graselits, Margate-Kent, Northdown Road, RSHA IV A 1 b.
19. Ziehm, Alfred, 10.2.96 Dresden, Gewerkschafter, RSHA IV A 1 b.
20. von Ziffhout, J., zuletzt: Holland, vermutl. England, RSHA IV E 4, Stapo Bremen.
21. Zimmern, Alfred, 1879, Professor, RSHA VI G 1.
22. Zingler, Alfred, 6.6.85 Sprottau, Redakteur, vermutl. England, RSHA IV A 1.
23. Zinner, Josef, 27.2.94 Janessen, England, RSHA IV A 1 b.
24. Zowanski, Generalkonsul, RSHA IV D 2.
25. Zucker, Arthur, 21.7.94 Berlin, Redakteur, London, RSHA IV A 1.
26. Zuckermayer, Karl, 27.12.96 Nockenheim, London, Schriftsteller, Emigrant, RSHA VI G 1, II B 5.
27. van Zuiden, Ph., zuletzt: Baarn/Holl., vermutl. England (Täterkreis: Breijnen), RSHA IV E 4.
28. Zunis, Leonie, Dr., geb. 1908, Emigrantin, Oxford (Universität), RSHA III A 1.
29. Zwart, Adrianus Johannes Josephus, 13.11.96 Loos op Zand, brit. N.-Agent, richtig: Vriesten, zuletzt: Rotterdam, vermutl. England (Täterkreis: Stevens/Best), RSHA IV E 4.
30. Zweig, Konrad, Dr., 1904, Assistent, Emigrant, London, RSHA III A 1.
31. Zweig, Stefan, Dr., 28.11.81 Wien (Jude), Schriftsteller, Emigrant, London W. 1, 49 Hallam Street, RSHA II B 2, II B 5, VI G 1.
32. Zychon, Jan Henryk, 1.1.96 Krakau, Kaptän, RSHA IV E 5.

Firmen

1. Francis Aldor, London, Herausgeber d. Buches „Dachau, die Nazi-hölle", RSHA IV B 4.
2. Allen und Unwin Ltd., marx. Verlag, London, Herausgeber der Bücher „South of Hitler" und „Six Years of Hitler", The Jews Under the Nazi Regime, RSHA IV B 4, III A 5.
3. Amazon Telegraph Co. Ltd., London E. C., Moorgate, RSHA IV E 4.
4. Andew u. Co., Reederei, London, RSHA IV E 4.
5. Anglo Amerika Telegraph u. Co. Ltd., London E. C. 2, RSHA IV E 4.
6. Anglo-Continental Security Services Ltd., London E. C. 2, Moorgate 26—31, Tel.: Metropolitan 3568, RSHA IV E 4.
7. Anglo Foreign Securitie Corp., London, RSHA IV E 4.
8. Anglo German-Agency, London S. W. 1, 53 Haymarket, RSHA IV E 4.
9. Anglo German Fellowship, London, RSHA IV E 4.
10. Anglo-Iranian (Ajoc), London, RSHA IV E. 4 u. III D.
11. Anglo Saxon Petroleum Co. Ltd., London, RSHA III D.
12. Associated Newspaper Ltd., London E. C. 4, Northcliffe-House, RSHA IV E 4.
13. Atlas Steel u. Iron Werke, Inh. Brown John u. Co., Sheffield, RSHA IV E 4.
14. Baird Televios Ltd., Inh. Major Archibald George Church, London S. W. 1, 66 Haymarket, RSHA IV E 4.
15. Baltic Publishing Comp., London E. C. 4, 53 King Williams Str., RSHA IV E 4.
16. Barclays Bank Ltd., London, RSHA IV E 4.
17. Barrass, Stefan, Godfrey, London W., New Quobecstreet 21, RSHA IV E 4.
18. Arthur Barker Ltd., London, 31 Garrick Street, Verlag, Herausgeber des Buches „Truffle Eater", RSHA IV B 4.
19. Bartlet u. Dixon Ltd., London W 1, 180 New Bond Str., RSHA IV E 4.
20. Bessie u. Kitchen Ltd., London E. C. 4, Queen Victoria Street, Teilhaber des d. Unilever-Konzerns, RSHA III D.
21. van den Bergh u. Jürgens, London E. C. 4, Blackfriars, Unilever-Haus, holländ. Tochtergesellschaft d. Unilever-Konzerns, RSHA III D.
22. William Blackwood u. Sons, Verlag, Edinburgh, London, Herausgeber d. Buches „Tales from Tyrol", RSHA IV B 4.
23. Bodley Head Ltd., John Lane, London, Verlag, London, RSHA III A 5.
24. Bonser u. Co. Ltd., London E. C. 4, 92 Fleet Street, Herausgeber d. Broschüre „Das wahre Deutschland", RSHA IV A 1 b, IV B 4, VI G 1.
25. British Aluminium Comp., London City, RSHA IV E 4.
26. British Dyestuffs Corp., Manchester, RSHA IV E 4.
27. British and Foreign News Service Cliffords Inn, London E. C., Fleet Street, RSHA IV E 4.
28. British Improved Timber Comp., London E. C., Billiterstreet 6, RSHA IV E 4.
29. British Insulated Cables Ltd., London W. C. 2, Surrey House Embankment, u. Prescot, Tel.: 47 936, RSHA IV E 4.
30. British Metal Co., London E. C. 2, 93 Greshham Street, Princes House, RSHA IV E 4.
31. Brit. Metallcorporation, Inh. Kpt. Oliver Lyttelton (Leiter), London, RSHA III D 5.

---

32. Die British Non-Secretarian Anti-Nazi Council to Champion Human Rights, London, Verlag, zet Herausgeber der Broschüre: „We are Nazi Hars", RSHA IV B 4.
33. British Securities and Estates Ltd., Inh. Sir Oliver Duncan, London E. C. 2, 36-38 New Broad-Street, Bulbaro House, RSHA III D 4.
34. Brown Ltd., London W. C. 2, Long Acre, RSHA IV E 4.
35. Builders u. Plumbers-Merchants-Association, London E. C. 38-39 Queen Street u. 212 Upper Thames, Tel.: Central 7656, RSHA IV E 4.
36. John u. Edwards Bumpus Ltd., marxist. Verlag, London W. 1. 350 Oxford Street, RSHA III A 5.
37. Cable Makers Association (C. M. A.), London W. C. 2, Sardina u. Sardina House, Tel. Holborn 4976, RSHA IV E 4.
38. P. Q. Cable Co., London E. C. 3, 24 Royal Exchange, RSHA IV E 4.
39. General Cable Works Ltd., Southampton, Tel. 2141, RSHA IV E 4.
40. Jonathan Cape Ltd., 30, Verlag, London, Bedfordsquare, Herausgeber d. Buches: „Insanty Fair", RSHA IV E 4.
41. Centrale Agence Ltd., Glasgow, RSHA IV E 4.
42. Chadburn's (Ship) Telegraph Co. Ltd., London C. 16, 93 Victoria Dock Road, RSHA IV E 4.
43. Chemical Solutions Co. Ltd., London E. 3, RSHA IV E 4.
44. I. P. Coats, Ltd., Baumwollstrick- u. Handarbeitsgarn-Konzern, Glasgow, RSHA III D.
45. Commercial Cable Comp., London E. C. 2, Wormwood Street, Murkay House, RSHA IV E 4.
46. Commissioner of Inland Revenue, London W. C. 2, Victory House, RSHA IV E 4.
47. Constable u. Co. Ltd., marxist. Verlag, London W. C. 2, 10-11 Orange Street, RSHA III A 5.
48. Thomas Cook u. Sohn (Reisebüro), London S. W. 1, Berkeley Street, RSHA IV E 4.
49. Dacre Engineering Co. Ltd., London S. W. 1, 66 Victoria Str., Westminster, RSHA IV E 4.
50. I. S. Darwen u. Co. Ltd., London E. C. 1, 38/40 Teaterstone Street, RSHA IV E 4.
51. J. M. Dents u. Sons Ltd., Verlag, London, Herausgeber des Buches „Hitler over Europe", RSHA IV B 4.
52. Departement of Overseas Trade (DOT), Leiter: Arthur Steel-Maitland, London, Zentr. d. gesamten Handelsnachrichtendienstes, RSHA III D 5.
53. Samuel Deycos u. Co. Ltd., London E. C. 3, 6. St. Mary Axe, RSHA IV E 4.
54. Dorien Leigh Ltd., London E. C. 4, Fleet Street, Ludgate House 107 bis 111, RSHA IV E 4.
55. English Electric Co. Ltd., London W. C. 2, Kingsway 28, Queen's House, RSHA IV E 4.
56. Embroidery Manufacturing Co. Ltd., London E. C. 1, 15 Aldersgate, St. Champion House, RSHA IV E 4.
57. Enfield Cable Works Ltd., London W. C. 1, 296—302 High Holborn Lincoln House u. Brimsdown, Tel.: 0591, RSHA IV E 4.
58. Engineering Co. Ltd., Inh. Rudolf R. Arnold Esven, London S. W. 1, RSHA IV E 4.

---

59. Engineers Inspection tests and consulation Physical and chemical laboratories, Inh. Robert W. Hunt Comp., London E. C. 4, 43-40 Ludgate Hill, RSHA IV E 4.
60. Ericsson Theiephones Ltd., London, RSHA IV E 4.
61. Esqu. Trebartta Cordford Cliffs, Inh. B. H. Rodd, Bournemouth/Braderest Avenue, RSHA IV E 4.
62. Edward Evans u. Co., Ing. u. Patentbüro, London, 27 Chansery Lane, RSHA IV E 4.
63. Exchange Telegraph Co., Ltd., London E. C. 2, 64 Cannon Street, RSHA IV E 4.
64. Farlow C. u. Co. Ltd., London S. W. 1, Panton Street, Haymarket, RSHA IV E 4.
65. Page Wate Farrer, London, RSHA IV E 4.
66. Federation of British Industry, London, RSHA IV E 4.
67. Fifteen Moorgate Unit Trusts Ltd., London, 15. Moorgate E. C. 2, RSHA IV E 4.
68. General Trading u. Shipping u. Co., London, RSHA IV E 4.
69. Victor Gollancz Ltd., Verlag, London, 14 Henrietta Str., Herausgeber d. Buches: „What are we to lose", RSHA IV B 4, VI G 1.
70. Great Northern Telegraph Co. Ltd. of Denmark 5—7, London E. C., St. Olsen's Place, RSHA IV E 4.
71. Grindlay u. Co. Ltd., London S. W. 1, 54 Parliament Street, RSHA IV E 4.
72. Lee Growder u. Co., Birmingham, 18 Newhall Street, RSHA IV E 4.
73. Guild Hall Civil Contractes, London, RSHA IV E 4.
74. Hanish Hamilton, marxist. Verlag, London, Herausgeber des Buches d. Buches, RSHA IV B 4, III A 5.
75. Henry Hardner u. Co., London E. C. 3, 2. Metall Exchange Buildings, Whitehall Avenue, RSHA IV E 4.
76. Harley u. Co., G. m. b. H., London E. C. 3, Leaden House, 101 Leadenhall St., RSHA VI G 1.
77. Harries-Scarfe Limited, London, 4 Lloyd's Avenue Fenchurch Street, RSHA IV E 3.
78. Haseltine, Lake u. Co., London W. C. 2, Chansery Lane 28 Southampton Buildings, RSHA IV E 4.
79. Manuel u. Schmitt, London S. W. 1, 43 Victoria Street, RSHA IV E 4.
80. William Heinemann Ltd., Verlag, London, Herausgeber des Buches „Return to Bavaria", RSHA IV B 4.
81. His Majesty's Stationery Office, London W. C. 2, York House, Kings Way, RSHA III B Holl.
82. Hubros Company, London E. C. 4, 81 Knightriderstreet, RSHA IV E 4.
83. Hutschinson u. Co., Verlag, London, Herausgeber der Bücher „Dollfuß and his Times" und „Germany and her Soies", A Story of the intrigues of the Nazis, RSHA IV B 4, VI G 1.
84. Imperial Chemical Industries Ltd., London, RSHA IV E 4.
85. Imperial Chemical House Technical, Section, Leiter: John Paterson, London S. W. 1, Buckinghamgate, RSHA III D 5.
86. Imperial u. International Communications Ltd., London E., Moorgate Electra-House, RSHA IV E 4.
87. Inclosed-Sewage Treatment Co. Ltd., früher: The Griffin Engineering Comp. Ltd., London E. C. 4, 52 Queen Victoria Street, RSHA IV E 4.
88. Industrial Mining Development Ltd., London E. C. 2, London Wall 450, Salusbury House, II St. (Täterkreis: Julius Petschek), RSHA III D 4.

---

89. International-Association for Promotion and Protection of Trade Ltd., London E. C. 4, 129 Cannon Street, RSHA IV E 4.
90. International-Bath-Association Ltd., London E. C. 4, 10/14 St. Pauls Churchyard Condor-House, RSHA IV E 4.
91. International Broadcasting Corp., London, Dir. Leonhard stand mit Gerta Luise v. Einem in Verbindung, RSHA IV E 4.
92. International Chemical Industries", Inhaber: Runcorn, London, Kampfgashersteller, RSHA IV E 4.
93. Internationale Combustion Ltd., Apparatebau, London, RSHA IV E 4.
94. International Publishing Comp.", London W. 1, 12. Greetcastle Str., RSHA VI G 1.
95. International Tramping-Tours, Ltd. Leeds", London, 6 Balchings Road, RSHA IV E 4.
96. Jarrold Publishers", marxistischer Verlag, London, 4 Paternoster Row, E. C., RSHA III A 5.
97. A. S. Kennford u. Co. Ltd", Deckadresse für eine Anzahl deutscher Kommunisten in London, London E. C. 3, Mineing Lane House, 26 Eastcheap, RSHA IV A 1 a.
98. Kingsway Trading Co. Ltd.", London C. W. 2, Africa House, RSHA IV E 4.
99. Kosmos Press Bureau Ltd.", Cliffords Inn, London E. C. 4, Fleet Street, RSHA IV E 4.
100. Martin Lawrence", marxistischer Verlag, London, RSHA III A 5.
101. Lecture Ltd., Agence Ltd.", London W. C., The Outer Temple Strand, Tel.: Zentral 3938, RSHA IV E 4.
102. Mac Lean u. Aenderson, Makler Firma, London, RSHA IV E 4.
103. Liadility, Ltd. Co., Reuters LTD, London 9, Carmelite Street, RSHA IV E 4.
104. J. Limon, London W. C. 1, Vernon Place, Victoria House, RSHA IV E 4.
105. James F. Lincoln Arc Welding Foundation, Cleveland, P. O. Box 5728, RSHA IV E 4.
106. Liverpool Electric Cable Co. Ltd., Liverpool, Linacre Lane Bootle, Tel.: Bootle 1040, RSHA IV E 4.
107. Long Acre Press LTD., Verlag „The People", London, 93 Long Acre, RSHA IV B 4.
108. Lloyd, Vorsitzender: S. J. Aubrey, London E. C. 3, Leadenhall Street, Lloydhouse, RSHA III D 4.
109. Loewy Engineering Company Ltd., Hydraulic Presses Rolling Mills, London W. C. 2, Kingsway Ingersoll House, RSHA IV E 4.
110. Lusmoore-Ball Esq., London W. 3, 23 Oxford Road, RSHA IV E 4.
111. Macfarlane, Walker, London E. C. 4, 12-13 St. Pauls Churchyard, Condor House, Tel.: Waterloo 6421, RSHA IV E 4.
112. Mac-Millan u. Comp., Verlag, London, RSHA IV B 4.
113. Malik Publishing Company, Verlag, London W. C. 1, 9 Gaters Lane, Bury Street, RSHA IV E 4.
114. Manufacturers Agent Wholesale and Retail Distributor, London, K. Dunn, Broadstreet u. Co., 455 High Street, RSHA IV E 4.
115. Marconi's Wireless Telegraph Co. Ltd., London W. C. 2, Strand Embankment Electra House, RSHA IV E 4.
116. Massie Publishing Co., London W. C. 2, 59 Chancery Lane, RSHA IV E 4.

117. **Methuen & Co. Ltd.,** Verlag, Herausgeber des Buches: „The House that Hitler built", London W. C. 2, Essex Street, RSHA IV B 4.
118. **Midland-Bank,** London (Täterkreis: Julius Petschek), RSHA III D 4.
119. **Monotype Corporation Ltd.,** London, RSHA IV E 4.
120. **National Federation of Associated Paint, Colour and Varnish Manufactures of the United Kingdom,** London W. C. 1, Tavistock Square, Tavistock House, RSHA IV E 4.
121. **Nightwatch Services Ltd.,** London, 7 Park Lane, RSHA IV E 4.
122. **Novello Edition,** jüdischer Musikverlag, London, RSHA III A 5.
123. **Österreichisches Amt,** London, Eaton Place 9, RSHA IV A 3 a.
124. **Ovesen Office,** London E. C. 4, 63 King-Williams-Street, RSHA IV E 4.
125. **Overseas Publicity and Service Agency Ltd.,** London W. C. 2, 33 Chancery Lane, RSHA IV E 4.
126. **Oxford University Press,** Verlag, Inhaber: Sir Humphrey Milford, London E. C. 4, Amen House, Warwick Square, RSHA IV B 4.
127. **Pallas Publishing Co. Ltd.,** London, Verlag, Herausgeber des Buches „Europe into the Abyss", RSHA IV B 4.
128. **Peace Book Co. Ltd.,** London W. C. 2, St. Martin's Lane, 5 Goodwin's Court, RSHA III B Holl.
129. **Penguin-Verlag,** Herausgeber des Buches „Germany what next?" Middlegex, RSHA IV B 4.
130. **P. R. Pohland und Sohn, Ltd.,** London L. C. 4, 19/20 Garlick Hill Minster House, RSHA IV E 4.
131. **Press Topixs,** Presseartikel, Lichtbilder, London W. C. 1, First Avenue House, RSHA IV E 4.
132. **Publishers, Printers and advertisement agents Ltd.,** Inhaber Burrow t. t. J. und Co., London W. C. 2, 130 Strand, Wellington-House, RSHA IV E 4.
133. **Publishing Co. Ltd.,** Inhaber Mc. Graw-Hill, London W. C. 2, Aldwych-House, RSHA IV E 4.
134. **Quasi Arc Company Ltd.,** London E. C. 4, 3 Laurence Poudbury, RSHA IV E 4.
135. **Reckmeier Trust Ltd.,** London E. C. 4, 10 The Temple Sergeants Inn, RSHA IV E 4.
136. **Reuters Ltd.,** London, Fleet-Street, RSHA II D 5.
137. **Rich und Cowan Ltd.,** Verlag, Herausgeber des Buches Germany, The Truth, London, RSHA IV B 4.
138. **George Routhledge und Sons,** Verlag, Herausgeber d. Buches Hitler-London, RSHA IV B 4.
139. **Rover und Co., Ltd.,** Birmingham, Acocks Green, RSHA IV E 4.
140. **Russia-Today-Society Ltd.,** London, RSHA VI G 1.
141. **Sargod, Son und Ewen,** London E. C. 1, 10/11 Bunhill Row, RSHA IV E 4.
142. **Sassoon und Co.,** London, RSHA IV E 4.
143. **Sattler-Metals Ltd.,** London W. 1, 16 Langhamstreet, RSHA IV E 4.
144. **Selwyn und Blount,** Verlag, Herausgeber des Buches „I saw for ...", London, RSHA IV B 4.
145. **Sidgwick and Jackson,** Verlag, London W. 6, 44 Museum-Street, RSHA VI G 1.
146. **Ernst Simon — Metallgesellschaft,** London E. C. 4, King William Street 73/76, RSHA IV E 4.
147. **Shapiro, Vallentine u. Co.,** jüdischer Verlag London, RSHA III A 5.
148. **Shell Transport and Trading Company,** RSHA III D.

149. **Sheppard und Co.,** London, A. E. Englische Schiffs- und Ver... rungsmakler, London E. C 3, 6 Lloyds Avenue, RSHA IV E 4.
150. **Stahlwerk,** Werkington, RSHA IV E 4.
151. **Standard Motor, Com. u. Co., Ltd.,** Coventry, England, RSHA I
152. **Standard Telephones and Cables Co.,** London W. C 2, Aldwych London E. 16 North Woolwich, Tel.: Albert Dock 1401, RSHA IV E 4.
153. **State Electricity Commission of Victoria,** Melbourne C. 1, 22/3 Flane Street, RSHA IV E 4.
154. **Stone und Cox Ltd.,** London W. C. 2, 188/180, Strand, RSHA IV E 4.
155. **Stubbs, Mercantile Offices,** Post Box 83, London E. C. 2, 42 Gress Street, Tel.: Metropolc 7731, RSHA IV E 4.
156. **Studd und Millington Ltd.** Sporting and Military Tailors, London W. C. 1, Conduits Street, RSHA IV E 4.
157. **Telegraph Construction und Maintenance So Ltd. (Telcon),** London E. C. 2, 38 Old Road-Street und Greenwich, Tel.: Greenwich 5050 und London Wall 3111, RSHA IV E 4.
158. **Telegraph Works Co. Ltd.,** London, Inhaber W. T. Henleys, London E. C. 1, Holborn Viaduct, RSHA IV E 4.
159. **Unilever — House Konzern,** London E. C. 4, Blackfriars, RSHA III D 2.
160. **Utilities Supply Co.,** London N. 15, 47 Blennheim Gardens, RSHA IV E 4.
161. **S. S. A. Waffenfabrik,** Birmingham England, RSHA IV E 4.
162. **Walker Grossweller Co.,** London, RSHA IV E 4.
163. **Warsop Petrol Drill und Tools Ltd.,** London, RSHA IV E 4.
164. **Watch Company Ltd.,** Inhaber A. Rotos, London W. C. 1, High Holborn House, RSHA IV E 4.
165. **Weekbed,** marxistischer Verlag, London, RSHA IV E 4.
166. **Western Union Telegraph Co.,** London E. C. 2, Grat Wichester str. RSHA IV E 4.
167. **Wheat leyand Mackencie,** London W. C. 2, 40 Chancery, RSHA IV E 4.
168. **Lincoln Williams,** Verlag Herausgeber des Buches Nazi Shadows, London, RSHA IV B 4.
169. **Wolseley, Flugmotoren Gesellschaft,** Inh. Lord Noffield, England. RSHA IV E 4.
170. **World Presse and Advertising Guld,** London, RSHA IV E 4.
171. **York Street Flax Spinning Co. Ltd.,** Belfast, RSHA IV E 4.

ACKNOWLEDGEMENTS

IT is impossible to thank adequately all the people who contributed to this book, nor is it entirely fair to say that this person or this institution was more helpful than that one. Some people who appeared to give no help because they had nothing to say or refused to say anything, nevertheless told me something I needed to know. I have omitted the names of a few of the people who gave me information in accordance with their wishes. Also there are certain facts in this book which have been checked but which, usually for obvious reasons, have not been attributed to specific sources. What follows is more or less an alphabetical list of people and organizations I approached.

Captain E. G. Archer, a member of the Eastern Command Ammunition Inspectorate, answered the questions I directed to Major George Styles, the Command's Senior Ammunition Technical Officer, about caches of Resistance explosives in Britain, and he also provided me with a full inventory of the explosives and sabotage equipment turned in by Mr Sennitt.

Mr Peter Atkinson, of the Boy Scouts Association, gave me a lot—but not all—of the information that I have recorded about the Boy Scouts and the Gestapo.

Lord Avon wrote to me that as far as he knew there were never any plans made for the evacuation of the Government to Canada, nor did he ever discuss such plans or hear them discussed. 'That,' he wrote, 'was not the mood of the time, either in the Government, or in the army at any level, nor among the British people.' He also pointed out that he had no private plans to get out himself or to get his family out. As Secretary of State for War he was too busy to think of such things.

Brigadier G. H. B. Beyts and his wife told me much about the early days at Coleshill, and through them I was able to begin to see how the Resistance activity that was planned for Britain was to effect other clandestine activity in other areas of the war.

Lord Boothby gave me the information attributed to him and also assured me that he personally never made any plans to get out of the country in the event of occupation, although he guessed at the time—correctly—that if the Nazis had prepared any sort of black list, his name would certainly be on it.

Mr Lambert Carmichael told me a lot about the Resistance in Northumberland and about certain things in which he was involved as far away from home as Balmoral and the Isle of Wight.

In meeting the Reverend P. B. 'Tubby' Clayton, of Toc H, I was able to shake the hand of one who had shaken the hand of one of the Welsh women who repelled the last actual invasion of Britain, in Fishguard in 1797. He also reminded me of some of the fictional literature concerning possible occupations of Britain.

The librarians in the reference department of the Colchester Public Library were ever courteous and helpful.

Commander Richard Colville explained to me the position about getting information about the Royal Family from official sources.

Miss Rose E. B. Coombs and her staff in the library of the Imperial War Museum not only gave me access to all sorts of published and unpublished material but also suggested a number of lines of research that I was too woolly to think of myself. No one writing anything about modern warfare can possibly avoid turning to Miss Coombs, Mr Rigby and the rest of the staff in this overworked library for help.

Mr Del Cooper, of Westward Television, made several important enquiries for me in Devon and Cornwall.

Mr G. J. Costello, of the Bank of England, confirmed that the *Reader's Digest* account of the exporting of Britain's gold was 'reasonably accurate'.

Mr Noel Coward, through his London representative, confirmed what I had guessed, that he had made no plans to flee Britain in the event of German occupation. I am sure that this is so, but I doubt that he himself 'does not know'—or at least suspect—why the Gestapo thought that he was a British spy.

Colonel Andrew Croft racked his brains for information for me and also suggested other people whom I should see.

Mr R. F. H. Darwall Smith was able to tell me about Resistance activity in several parts of the country.

Miss Duie, the librarian of the Fawcett Library, helped me to find out about the role of civilian women in the defence of Britain against invasion.

Colonel Frank Douglas was modest about his own role in the Resistance, but he answered a lot of my questions and very kindly gave me the names of several people who could answer those questions which he could not.

Mr J. W. Stuart Edmundson told me a great deal about the early days of the British Resistance, especially in the West Country.

Mr A. G. Fiddes-Watt told me about the Resistance organization he helped to create and run in the Outer Hebrides.

Lieutenant Colonel Norman Field took me on the second wildest ride of my life—in order to show me some of the hideouts in the woods that he had inherited from Peter Fleming or had created himself. Colonel Field also took the trouble to prepare for me a map of the entire network of Resistance bases in Kent. He introduced me to some of the patrol and group leaders who served under him, and he took me on an interesting tour of what would have been the Resistance's front-line areas.

Mrs James Fisher very patiently translated some of the Gestapo documents for me.

Colonel Peter Fleming suggested several people I should speak to about the British Resistance, gave me his own opinion of its chances, told me about his own experiences in trying to get information from the Germans when he was writing his excellent *Invasion 1940*, and was altogether too modest about his own role in Kent in the Resistance's earliest days.

Mrs C. S. Forester spoke to her late husband for me very shortly before his death and was able to confirm my guess, that his fictional account of a Nazi occupation of Britain, which appeared as a serial in the *Daily Mail*, was not based on any inside information.

Sir Frank Francis and one of his assistants, Mr G. B. Morris, gave me a lot of the information about the British Museum, and of course the Museum's Reading Room and its Newspaper Library at Colindale also yielded information.

The staff of the General Register Office, Somerset House, very promptly answered a number of questions.

The late Sir Victor Gollancz gave me several interesting facts.

Major-General Sir Colin Gubbins not only started me on the trail of the most important facts in this book but also answered a number of my questions and suggested people who proved to be very helpful.

Major Bill Harston recalled not only his own role in the Resistance but also the part played by many other officers, and he was also able to tell me a great deal about Coleshill which others had forgotten.

The Home Office helped me—although in a negative manner.

The Hoover Institution of War, Revolution and Peace, Stanford University, California, made available to me microfilms of certain of the Gestapo documents which are not readily available in Britain.

Dr Otto John found time to visit the Imperial War Museum with me in order to discuss a number of very interesting documents in the library.

The Reverend E. F. Johnson, of Seaford College, confirmed my guess that Walter zu Christian's name does not appear on the college's records.

Mr R. M. A. Jones was not only able to tell me about his own part in running the Resistance radio network but was also able to explain in simple language how the radio system worked.

Dr L. Kahn, of the Imperial War Museum's Foreign Documents Centre, made several useful suggestions about sources of information.

Lieutenant-Colonel Desmond Kirkness told me a lot about the espionage and communications sections of the Resistance and about the organization as a whole during its later days.

Mr Terence Le Goubin took many pictures for me.

Mr H. B. Light, of the Rover Car Company, dug out a lot of information for me on the war preparations made by his company, and public relations officers of the Ford Motor Company, the Rootes Group, Standard-Triumph and Vauxhall also looked into their companies' war histories for me—but all drew blanks.

The late Walter Leschander, of California, an acknowledged authority on espionage, suggested several interesting lines of research to me.

Captain Sir Basil Liddell Hart not only was kind enough to discuss my subject with me in general terms but also allowed me to read his interesting memoranda on the Home Guard. He also told me what some of the German generals had told him they thought their occupation of Britain would have been like, and he gave me his own opinion as well.

The staff of the Lincoln Public Library showed me cuttings on the 'Cromwell' alert and told me of their own personal experiences.

Mr Cecil Lines not only sent out one of his employees—a former Resistance patrol member—to show me the remains of one of their best hideouts but also told me a lot about Resistance activity in the Dover and Folkestone areas and about the situation in Kent generally.

Colonel Roderick MacLeod told me about the Ironside committee.

Brigadier C. R. Major was my most important single source of information about the British Resistance. He took the trouble to translate a number of his coded diaries and notes for me in order to provide extremely detailed information about the state of the Resistance during the time that he was in command. He also suggested other people I should see, patiently answered a shoal of questions, some of them several times, and even managed to find for me a unique group photograph of the military officers of the Resistance. To him I am especially indebted.

Major Eustace Maxwell not only told me a great deal about the Resistance organization in Scotland but was also able to recall many things that he saw in other parts of Britain during the first years of organized resistance.

Mr Brian Melland gave me some very straightforward advice as well as information.

Mr Adrian Monck-Mason told me about his clandestine radio station and showed me the 'aerial trees'.

Lord Montgomery of Alamein confirmed several anecdotes about himself and also gave me his own personal assessment of the British Resistance organization: 'I do not think the units you mention would have played an "important" military role; but they would have been a nuisance to the Germans and would have helped to raise morale in the area in which they worked—a very important factor in war.'

Mr J. F. Montgomery told me a great deal about Resistance groups east of Canterbury and about the training he and his men received at Coleshill. He was also able to recall—as the military leaders of the Resistance were not—the numbers of the Home Guard battalions to which the men in the individual patrols believed that they belonged.

Mr Howard Moorepark, my literary agent in New York, was as usual most helpful generally, and he also found information that I might otherwise have overlooked.

Mr David Niven confirmed my guess that the suggestion made to me that he was in the Resistance was incorrect but that he had been involved in other MI(R) activity.

Miss Eleanor Norman-Butler told me about her experiences running various radio control stations for the Resistance.

Dr Robert O'Neill suggested a number of possible German sources of information, archives as well as individuals, and allowed me to read his excellent book, *The German Army and the Nazi Party, 1933–1939*, before it had been published.

Mr Philip Oakes gave me a useful lead in Kent.

Mr R. J. Osborn, of Lloyd's of London, placed at my disposal a great deal of information about his company's wartime activities.

Mr Kenneth Parker, of Cassell, suggested a number of possible sources of information and wrote many letters of introduction.

Mr E. L. E. Pawley, Chief Engineer, BBC External Services, found for me a paper which explained how, if the Germans had occupied a part of Britain, it might have been possible for the BBC to continue broadcasting from unoccupied territory.

Mr George Perry told me a lot about the sources to which he went for the *Sunday Times Magazine*'s series on the year 1940.

Mr R. G. Potts described his own experiences both as a Resistance patrol leader and organizer and as a radio out-station operator, and he suggested several other people I should see.

Mr Perrott Philips provided an out-of-print book that it was important that I should consult.

Mr Donald Patterson, of the *Baltimore Sun,* explained his paper's arrangement with the *Manchester Guardian* in the event of Britain's occupation.

Commander Kyrle Pope recalled the days of the Much Marcle Watchers.

A Public Record Office spokesman told me what that department would have done if Britain had been occupied, and he also checked into his records to see what might be there of interest to me.

Mr Anthony Quayle told me about his experiences as a Resistance organizer in Northumberland and also how that series of experiences was later to be useful to him when he was with SOE in Albania.

Dr Jürggen Rohwer, the German military archivist, checked several facts for me.

Mrs Herta Ryder suggested several German sources to me.

Mr Reginald Sennitt told me of the activities of the Resistance in general and about his own role in particular.

The late Lieutenant-Colonel R. H. Stevens, although in bad health at the time, very patiently went through some of my microfilms with me at the Brighton Public Library so that we could discuss the things in them that concerned him.

Mr John Snagge gave me some good advice about the BBC.

Mr Norman Steed took me around the Isle of Thanet, showing me where his patrols operated.

Mrs M. A. Stranks told me about Coleshill and Hannington.

Mr Bickham Sweet-Escott amplified for me a number of points in his extremely interesting memoir, *Baker Street Irregular*, and suggested several lines of research which I subsequently followed.

Miss Beatrice Temple recalled for me her experiences as senior ATS officer in the British Resistance.

Lieutenant-General Sir Andrew Thorne himself gave me most of the anecdotes in this book which concern him, and he also discussed with me a number of aspects of the subject of the book.

The Times leader in Chapter 13 is quoted with the publisher's permission.

A member of the Information Division of the Treasury provided several bits of general information and also worked out for me what the currency exchange rate between the mark and the pound would have been in 1940—had such exchange been possible.

Mr John Ward allowed me to inspect his house so that I would be able to describe what Britain's first front-line Resistance headquarters had looked like.

Mr Roger Weeley told me about Resistance in Essex and about his own activities in particular.

Mr Dennis Wheatley provided me with hospitality and the anecdotes about himself.

Mr Ronald Wheatley gave me a lot of very sound general advice and also allowed me to quote certain Gestapo orders which are available only in his book, *Operation Sea Lion,* the most comprehensive work in English on the subject.

The Wiener Library allowed me to delve into their file of Nürnberg trial transcripts and also provided certain other material, some of it translated for me by a member of their staff.

Major Ray Woodyear, Senior Ammunition Technical Officer, Northern Command, told me about some of the caches of Resistance explosives which he has encountered.

In addition to the above I am indebted to the many people in Denmark who some years ago gave me the material which I incorporated into my book *The Savage Canary*, a study of the Danish Resistance. This enabled me to understand more clearly the significance of a lot of the material that has gone into this book.

John Bowra and Alex Hunter, both personal friends, indirectly helped me with this book, although not actually providing any of the material in it. And most of all I owe more thanks than I can give to my wife for helping at every stage with the research, with the sifting of the facts and, long after the material ceased to be fresh to her, helping patiently to edit the final manuscript.

INDEX

[211]